The Quest for an African Economic Community

European University Studies

Europäische Hochschulschriften

Publications Universitaires Européennes

Series XXXI

Political Science

Reihe XXXI Série XXXI

Politikwissenschaft

Sciences politiques

Vol./Bd. 591

PETER LANG

Frankfurt am Main · Berlin · Bern · Bruxelles · New York · Oxford · Wien

Wolff-Christian Peters

The Quest for an African Economic Community

Regional Integration and its Role in Achieving African Unity – The Case of SADC

PETER LANG
Internationaler Verlag der Wissenschaften

Bibliographic Information published by the Deutsche Nationalbibliothek
The Deutsche Nationalbibliothek lists this publication in the Deutsche Nationalbibliografie; detailed bibliographic data is available in the internet at http://dnb.d-nb.de.

Zugl.: Hamburg, Univ., Diss., 2010

Cover illustration:
Current chairperson (2020/11) of SADC,
Hifikepunye Pohamba,
and the SADC Executive Secretary,
Dr. Tomas Salomao.
Printed with kind permission of Stefan Fischer
(Windhoek, Namibia).

D 18
ISSN 0721-3654
ISBN 978-3-631-61032-9

www.peterlang.de

For my wife Genet

and

In memoriam of my mother Gertrud Peters (1927-2001)

Table of Contents

Part C: Regional Integration in Southern Africa: SADC

Part D: Annex

List of Text Boxes

List of Tables

List of Maps

Abbreviations

AEC	ASEAN Economic Community
AEC	African Economic Community
AEF	Afrique Equitorial Francaise
AfDB	African Development Bank
AFTA	ASEAN Free Trade Zone
AGOA	African Growth and Opportunities Act (USA)
AMU	Arab Maghreb Union
ANC	African National Congress (South Africa)
AOF	Afrique Occidentale Francaise
APRM	African Peer Review Mechanism
ARF	ASEAN Regional Forum
ARV	Antiretroviral Drugs
ASCCI	Association of SADC Chambers of Commerce and Industry
ASEAN	Association of South-East Asian Nations
AU	African Union
BLNS states	Botswana, Lesotho, Namibia and Swaziland
BTI	Bertelsmann Transformationsindex
CAF	Central African Federation
CCBG	Committee of Central Bank Governors
CEN-SAD	Community of Sahel-Saharan States
CEPT	Common Effective Preferential Tariff
CEMAC	Economic and Monetary Community of Central Africa
CET	Common External Tariff
CMC	Council of the Common Market
COMESA	Community of Eastern and Southern African States
CONSAS	Constellation of Southern African States
CPI	Corruption Perception Index
CU	Customs Union
EAC	East African Community
EC	European Communities
ECA	Economic Commission for Africa
ECCAS	Economic Community of Central African States (CEEAC)
ECOWAS	Economic Community of Western African States
ECSC	European Coal and Steel Community
EEC	European Economic Community
EIB	European Investment Bank
EISA	Electoral Institute of Southern Africa

EPA	Economic Partnership Agreements
ESA	Eastern and Southern African Region (under EPA)
EU	European Union
Euratom	European Atomic Energy Community
FDI	Foreign Direct Investment
FLS	Frontline States
FTAA	Free Trade Area of the Americas
FTA/Z	Free Trade Area/Zone
GDP	Gross Domestic Product
GTZ	Gesellschaft für Technische Zusammenarbeit (German Technical Cooperation)
HDI	Human Development Index
HPIC	Highly Indebted Poor Countries
ICM	Integrated Council of Ministers
IGAD	Intergovernmental Authority on Development
IGADD	Intergovernmental Authority on Drought and Development
IMF	International Monetary Fund
IPCC	International Panel on Climate Change
ISDSC	Inter-State Defence and Security Committee
KAS	Konrad Adenauer Stiftung
Mercosur	Mercado Comun des Sur
MDC	Movement for Democratic Change (Zimbabwe)
MDG	Millennium Development Goals
MISA	Media Institute of Southern Africa
NAFTA	North-Atlantic Free Trade Area
NEPAD	New Partnership for African Development
NTB	Non-tariff trade barriers
OAU	Organisation of African Unity
OECD	Organisation for Economic Cooperation and Development
PAC	Pan-African Congress (South Africa)
PPP	Purchasing Power Parity
PPP	Public Private Partnerships
PRSP	Poverty Reduction Strategy Paper

PTA	Preferential Trade Area
RETOSA	Regional Tourism Organisation of Southern Africa
RI	Regional Integration
RISDP	Regional Indicative Strategic Development Plan
RTFP	Regional Trade Facilitation Programme
SAB	South African Breweries
SACU	Southern African Customs Union
SADC	Southern African Development Community
SADCC	Southern African Development Coordination Conference
SAFTA	SADC Free Trade Area
SAP	Structural Adjustment Program
SDI	Spatial Development Initiative
SEATOC	South East African Tourism Committee
SIPO	Strategic Indicative Plan for the Organ
TDCA	Trade, Development and Cooperation Agreement between South Africa and the EU
TIFA	Trade and Investment Network Agreement
TNF	Trade Negotiation Forum
UNCTAD	United Nations Conference on Trade and Development
UNDP	United Nations Development Program
UZAREDI	Upper Zambezi Region Development Initiative
WATRA	West African Telecommunication Regulatory Association
WHO	World Health Organisation
WTO	World Trade Organisation
ZANU-PF	Zimbabwe African National Union - Patriotic Front
ZCCM	Zambia Consolidated Copper Mines
ZESA	Zimbabwe Electricity Supply Authority

Regional Economic and Political Cooperation in Southern Africa – SADC as Work in Progress

The phenomenon of regional integration is widely discussed within academic circles as well as in practical institutions of development policy. Regional integration attempts to improve the living conditions of less developed countries by politically agreed upon multilateral cooperation. Some scholars believe that the "new regionalism" which we can observe in many regions of the world today, is an unavoidable consequence of the challenging process of globalisation. The globalized world is characterized by reciprocal political, economic and social interdependence, common interests and to a certain extent, common values. As a consequence, there has been a growing tendency of cooperation and collaboration among states situated in the same region, in order to defend regional interests against a superior global player from outside. They all hope to increase the wealth and well-being of their people and strengthening their international competitiveness. This idea was also one of the motive powers of Pan-Africanism since the days of Kwame Nkrumah, Ghana's first president, whose bold policy of continental integration resulted in the founding of the Organisation of African Unity in 1963.

The most successful and promising attempt in Africa to achieve regional integration so far has been SADC – the Southern African Development Community, which is in the focus of Christian Peters' analysis. Peters has got first-hand knowledge about the political and economic developments in Southern Africa where he has worked in different functions as an expert in development for more than twenty years. In his dissertation he describes the history, structure, institutions and instruments of this regional organisation which acts under the hegemonic leadership of the Republic of South Africa since 1992.

According to the principles and objectives of the founding treaty of this regional organisation, SADC and its member states shall act in accordance with five major principles: 1. sovereign equality of all Member States; 2. solidarity, peace and security; 3. human rights, democracy, and the rule of law; 4. equity, balance and mutual benefit; and lastly 5. peaceful settlement of disputes. Therefore, SADC has committed herself to creating institutions to promote productive employment and utilization of resources of the region. It also feels the need to launch some effective developing policies aimed at the progressive elimination of obstacles to the free movement of capital and labour, goods and services among member states.

These are ambitious objectives and therefore Peters' main concern in his book relates to the evaluation of these programmatic aims. His meritorious research contains 46 tables with valuable statistics of all aspects of regional integration between the fifteen states of Southern Africa. Peters does not only analyse the various efforts achieving regional cooperation in Southern Africa, but also other political initiatives in West and East Africa (ECOWAS, EAC, COMESA) aiming at the same objective. He can demonstrate the many difficulties the African governments are facing when necessity arises to give up some area of their national sovereignty in order to build up regional common markets and institutions. One of their main sources of revenue (besides foreign aid) is the imposed taxes on imports and exports, - revenues which would be minimized in the case of a successful regional market development in line with the much admired example of the European Community.

Another aspect of this outstanding analysis of the regional integration project deals with the common assumption that South Africa as Africa's economic superpower would dominate SADC and would probably even misuse her advanced economy to hamper the development of her fellow countries. Peters comes to the conclusion that SADC has the potential of becoming a real building bloc for the African Economic Community, in spite of all the current delays and deviations the SADC integration process has had to deal with so far: he also contends that success will only be possible if non-state actors are allowed to play a stronger role in future.

One of the highlights of Peters' book is the analysis of the Zimbabwe crisis and its impact on the speed and predictability of SADC policies. From a Western view the failure of SADC to provide useful assistance to solve the Zimbabwe crisis, caused by the horrifying dictatorship of Robert Mugabe, fosters doubts on the successful implementation capacity of an effective and reliable regional governance architecture in the meaning of the promised "African Renaissance".

Academic scholars and development workers who are interested in the future development of Southern Africa will find in Christian Peters' most informative description of the economic history of Southern Africa many valuable facts and well-reflected insights. His comparative approach which encompasses regional cooperation attempts in Europe and Africa makes it possible to gain a realistic sober picture of one of Africa's great projects to escape the poverty trap. Peters concludes with a not too optimistic outlook on the future development of SADC; at the same time he reminds us of the truth that development is never linear and it often takes a step backwards before it moves forward again.

Rainer Tetzlaff, Jacobs University Bremen, August 2010

Introduction

Regional integration appealed as a concept to many economists, politicians and businesspeople for one simple reason: it promised to increase the wealth and well-being not just of one but a number of countries at a rate greater than the sums of the separate development of the economies of the participating countries. Historic evidence, however, seems to indicate that such hopes often led to disappointment. So far, only the European approach to integration, culminating currently in the existence of the European Union, and with considerable lesser degrees of success *Mercosur* in Latin America and ASEAN in Southeast Asia, has fulfilled these expectations. Conspicuously absent from the short list of success stories is the African continent despite the fact that the African Union (AU) relies on regional integration as an essential stepping stone for achieving African unity.

Only over the last decade, some promising regional integration bodies emerged in Africa. Amongst them are the revived East African Community (EAC), the Economic Community of Western African States (ECOWAS) and last but not least, the Southern African Development Community (SADC). Of these, SADC has probably made the most substantial steps towards sustainable and deeper regional integration. Previous attempts, some of which date back to colonial times ([1]), were more often than not mere proclamations without substantiated content, existing on paper but hardly in reality. This might be one explanation for the plethora of regional integration attempts on the African continent and the contrasting dismal rate of achievement.

Another reason for the low success rate of – especially economic – regional integration in Africa was the scant support the idea received for a long time from the organisation promoting African unity. The Organisation of African Unity (OAU), founded in 1963 in Addis Ababa (Ethiopia), understood African unity predominantly as a political and not so much as an economic objective. Following *Kwame Nkrumah's* famous words – *"Seek ye first the political kingdom and all else will follow"* – the OAU pursued political goals (eradication of colonialism; safeguarding territorial integrity of the new states; facilitating peace) and included the economic development and integration of the continent

1 In 1910, the predecessor to the Southern African Customs Union (SACU) was formed between different British colonies and territories including South Africa. Other attempts in East and Central Africa followed. In Western Africa, the French colonies cooperated in a system, which was to some extent functionally integrated into the French economy.

only as a late afterthought heavily influenced by ideas of *south-south-cooperation* and *collective self-reliance* ([2]). The "*Lagos Plan of Action*", adopted by the OAU in 1980, was the first notable document ([3]) dealing with economic integration of the African continent as a necessary component for political unity. However, it remained vague as far as implementation was concerned and its timeframe was from the onset too ambitious to be achievable. In 1991, after the fall of the *Berlin Wall* and the collapse of the Soviet Empire, a "fresh wind" of democracy and accountability started to blow also through Africa, which compelled the OAU to finally adopt the concept of forming the "African Economic Community" (AEC) through the "*Abuja Treaty*" - a framework still providing the parameters for African integration until now.

Despite the lack of conceptual and political support form the OAU but strongly driven by the immediate need to overcome the limiting economic fragmentation following independence several regional integration schemes sprung up during the 1960s and 70s. The collapse of the East African Community (EAC) in 1977 heralded the end of these often conceptually and politically naïve and thus ultimately futile attempts. It took another decade and major global changes (end of the Cold War; beginning of globalisation) before regional integration experienced a renaissance in Africa.

Facilitative external conditions were needed to allow internal – African – factors to resuscitate the idea of regional integration on a more realistic ground than before. The externally (IMF, World Bank) enforced liberalisation of economic regimes in many African countries during the "lost decade" of the 1980s turned out to be "blessing in disguise" as it did away with some of the obstacles to regional economic integration such as protected and overvalued national currencies, trade barriers and arbitrary state intervention. Economic liberalisation also swept a new and more capable managerial elite into the driving seats of many African economies whose macroeconomic understanding had been coined during their studies in the USA and Europe. With the conceptual support of the UN Economic Commission for Africa (UNECA) and the African Development Bank (AfDB) existing but stagnating regional integration schemes such as the Southern African Development Coordination Conference (SADCC), the Economic Community of Western African States (ECOWAS) or the Preferential Trade Area (PTA) of Southern and Eastern

---

2 See Hofmeier, Rolf (2004), Regionale Kooperation und Integration. In Ferdowsi, Mir A (ed.), Afrika – ein verlorener Kontinent? München. pp189-224.

3 It was based on an OAU declaration on „Cooperation, Development and Economic Independence" from 1973 and "Monrovia Strategy for Economic Development of Africa" from 1979; see Arnold, Guy (2005): Africa. A Modern History. London:608f

Africa were revitalised during the 1990s; even the previously abandoned EAC was revived in 1999.

When the AU succeeded the OAU in 2001/2, the idea of the AEC received a new and now crucial status on the roadmap of achieving African unity. Whereas the OAU had been predominantly concerned with political issues, the new AU from the very beginning has put strong emphasis on economic factors. This is based on the new conviction that African countries are after all themselves responsible for their well-being. The idea of an "*African Renaissance*", and based on that the concept of a "New Economic Partnership for African Development" (NEPAD), reinforced the belief amongst African leaders that the economic integration of Africa is a crucial condition for overcoming economic stagnation and achieving political unity. Consequently, the establishment of the AEC until 2034 is regarded as a crucial milestone towards achieving this objective. In the strategy officially adopted by the AU for attaining economic integration on the continent the various Regional Economic Communities (RECs), as regional integration schemes are now referred to, constitute the "building blocs" on which the continental economic community is to be founded ([4]).

The public often has a tendency to equate regional integration with economic integration; less attention is paid to the political side of regional integration. This may be derived from the fact that most regional integration schemes have an economic reference in their names such as 'free trade area', 'customs union', 'common market' or 'monetary union' and thus follow an economic logic. It also has to do with the fact that regional integration has so far mostly been based on economic mechanisms. However, political factors have always played a significant role with regard to the success or failure of regional integration as African countries had to experience to their own detriment. Despite the OAU's predominantly political outlook on RI, its fundamental political problems, which were also affecting negatively integration efforts, have hardly ever been addressed appropriately if at all. The controversial questions of national sovereignty vs. regional governance, the democratic legitimacy of several Governments, accountability as well as the defence of human rights were conveniently overlooked, ignored or put aside by the African rulers convening at OAU meetings. The overwhelming majority of these leaders had (and still have) suspect credentials in this respect. The OAU made it to one of its principles not to question the (colonially drawn) borders of its member states and - emanating

4 See: AU (2008), Assessment of Progress on Regional Integration in Africa. First Joint Annual Meetings of the AU Conference of Ministers of Economy and Finance and ECA Conference of African Ministers of Finance, Planning and Economic Development.Addis Ababa, Ethiopia. 29 February 2008.

from this principle - to follow a strict policy of non-interference into the domestic problems of member states. This contributed to a string of coup d'états, several civil wars and even genocides

Given the hardly encouraging past economic performances of regional integration blocs in Africa, the still existing problem of state consolidation (e.g. in the DRC, Somalia, Sudan, Liberia, Central African Republic, Chad or Sierra Leone), the continued existence of weak political systems in which arbitrary neo-patrimonial rulers continue to dominate and the marginal role of African economies (with the exception of the South African) in the globalised world - can it reasonably be assumed that economic integration as envisaged by the AU is achievable? Are the eight RECs officially recognised by the AU and other affiliated smaller regional integration bodies able to first become tangible and sustainable integration schemes on their own and eventually merge into the AEC?

SADC has been labelled by some experts as the currently most successful and promising attempt of regional integration in Africa ([5]). While smaller RECs such as the EAC, or the *Union Economique et Monetaire Ouest-Africaine* (UEMOA) may have achieved a formally higher degree of regional integration than SADC, their attempts lack real potential for substantive economic integration due to the still low complementarity and physical integration of their national economies ([6]). Nevertheless, although SADC is sometimes also criticised for its slow integration speed ([7]), insufficient political will to integrate further ([8]) and in particular for its failure to arrest the crisis in Zimbabwe when it was still time to prevent serious damage to the speed and direction of regional integration, it still sticks out as the regional integration effort in Africa with some tangible results. In other words, while SADC shows some encouraging signs of integrating regionally it also depicts a host of problems which make a successful attainment of its objectives not a foregone conclusion.

---

5 See for e.g. ECA (2008a), Assessing Regional Integration in Africa III; Mair, Stefan/Peters-Berries, Christian (2001), Regionale Kooperation und Integration in Afrika; Brandt, H., Gsänger, H. et al (2000), Ansatzpunkte zur Förderung der Regionalintegration in der Southern African Development Community (SADC). Bonn:167

6 The economically most deeply integrated regional body in Africa, the Southern African Customs Union (SACU), is a special case for historic, geographic and political reasons. SACU can, thus, only to a limited extent be compared to other RECs.

7 See for e.g. Chingono, M. and Nakana, S. (2009), The challenges of regional integration in Southern Africa. In: African Journal of Political Science and International Relations. Vol. 3 (10):396-408, October 2009.

8 See for e.g. Meyns, Peter (2000), Konflikt und Entwicklung im südlichen Afrika. Opladen

Examining SADC under these aspects – being the most promising of the African attempts to achieve RI and being faced with problems also typical of other regional bodies – may thus offer a chance to assess if the plans to create the AEC are realistic or just a pipe-dream. The thesis attempts under these premises to determine the chances for success with regard to SADC and by comparing SADC with the main RI efforts in other parts of Africa – namely, COMESA, EAC, and ECOWAS – make a prediction on the ultimate chances of the AU to realize its African integration dream within the stipulated timeframe and conceptual objectives.

This thesis cannot claim to be a review of the total body of literature produced on RI in general and RI in Southern Africa in particular as the available information and comments on RI have multiplied several times over the last few years thanks to the internet and new means of communication and documentation. Instead it tries to put together the main themes and strands of discussion based on major publications in order to provide a readable overview on RI with particular reference to Southern Africa. It follows a concept, which wants to provide the reader with important conceptual, factual, historic and current information, which gives orientation through fact-based evaluation and offers special information in separate text boxes, a glossary and numerous tables.

The thesis attempts as far as SADC is concerned to summarize the broader lines and trends of RI, interpret current developments and put into perspective the achievements and problems of SADC vis-à-vis other regional integration efforts in Africa. This required a mixed approach of analysis including not only an intensive scrutiny of a large number of official documents and reports of SADC itself but also the compilation and evaluation of statistical data regarding various economic and political aspects of RI. Furthermore, it necessitated apart from the analysis of the few academic books and articles on SADC also that of several African newspapers and news services in order to follow the latest events. Consequently, what may appear to be a description of events and developments contains already a substantial amount of interpretation and analysis.

In contrast to the amount of internal reports, newspaper articles or internet blogs, the actual number of published monographs, articles, papers and presentations on SADC is lower as one might expect given the general interest in the topic of RI in Africa. A discussion of crucial political junctures and economic options of SADC has taken place only to a limited extent ([9]). Especially the latest

9 The most comprehensive papers and reports on SADC have been produced by Peters-Berries, C./Marx, T. (1997), Regionale Kooperation und Integration im südlichen Afrika. In: KAS Auslandsinformationen 11/97:64-100; Peters-Berries, C./Marx, T.

developments in and around SADC have only been discussed in a rather cursory way. Politically, the impact of the economic meltdown in Zimbabwe coupled with constant and flagrant violations of human rights on the region and on RI in particular has so far been neglected by academic writing as has been the aspect of security integration and democratic convergence. The same is true on the economic side for the impact of the SADC Free Trade Area (FTA) on RI or the physical preconditions for integration such as transport networks and/or energy production and distribution. Neither has there recently been a comprehensive analysis of SADC in particular and the African integration process in general.

The few contributions dealing exclusively with SADC struggle with the interpretations of events in the region because they are often either coming from an exclusively economic or political angle and thus fail to apply a holistic approach to analysis ([10]). Others are concentrating on sectoral aspects of RI only

---

(2000), Peters-Berries, Christian and Marx, Michael T (2000), Monitoring the Process of Regional Integration in SADC, Harare; Meyns, P. (2000); Brandt, H., Gsänger, H. et al (2000; Mair, S./Peters-Berries, C. (2001),), Regionale Integration und Kooperation in Afrika südlich der Sahara. EAC, ECOWAS und SADC im Vergleich. München, Bonn, London; Gibb, R. (2001), The State of Regional Integration: The Intra- and Inter–regional Dimensions. In: South African Institute of International Affairs (SAIIA) (2001), Regional Integration Southern Africa: Comparative International Perspectives. Johannesburg:71-85. Oosthuizen, Gabriel H. 2006: The Southern African Development Community. The Organization, its Policies and Prospects, Midrand. Vogt, Jörgen 2007: Die regionale Integration des südlichen Afrikas unter besonderer Betrachtung der Southern African Development Community (SADC), Baden-Baden.

10 Some examples for the dominant economic focus are the three efforts of the ECA to assess regional integration in Africa (ARIA I, II, III), which also refer to SADC but leave out most of the political framework conditions for RI (see: ECA 2004; 2006; 2008[a]) or Kalaba, M., Wilcox, O., Fundira, T., Wiliams, B. (2006), Deepening Integration in SADC. South Africa – SADC's Economic Engine.
Examples for a political approach are much scarcer: on the impact of the Zimbabwe Crisis on SADC see: Peters-Berries, C. (2002), The Zimbabwe crisis and SADC: how to deal with a deviant member state? In: Hansohm et al (eds): Monitoring Regional Integration in Southern Africa. Yearbook, Vol. 2. 2002. Windhoek: 185-201; on democratic convergence in SADC see: Peters-Berries, C./Naidu, R. (2003), Macro-Political Developments in the SADC Region April 2002 – March 2003. in: Hansohm, Dirk; Breytenbach, Willie; Hartzenberg, Trudi (eds.) (2003): Monitoring Regional Integration in Southern Africa. Yearbook, Vol. 3- 2003. Windhoek:110-127; on security issues in the region see: Breytenbach, W. (2000), Security in the SADC Region: What a Performance Index of the Organ tells about Co-operation and Integration. In: Peters-Berries, Christian and Marx, Michael T (2000), Monitoring the Process of Regional Integration in SADC, Harare 2000:93-104; Hammerstad, (2003), A long road to SADC security integration: Is the OPDS heading in the right direction? In: Hansohm, Dirk; Breytenbach, Willie; Hartzenberg, Trudi (eds.) (2003): Monitoring

without relating their results to the broader framework of the integration process ([11]). The integration area of SADC, which attracted most of journalistic and academic interest, is trade and particularly to what extent trade integration is showing an impact. More recently, macroeconomic convergence in SADC also became a focus of intensified interest ([12])

So far the only attempt to provide a regular overview of regional integration in Southern Africa with special reference to SADC is the "Monitoring Regional Integration in Southern Africa Yearbook", which has been started *inter alia* by the author of this thesis in 2000 on behalf of the *Konrad Adenauer Stiftung* (KAS). It was afterwards organised and published jointly by KAS and – at first – the "*Namibia Economic and Policy Research Unit* " (NEPRU) and later by the "*Trade Law Centre for Southern Africa*" (TRALAC). 2008, the eighth yearbook was published; the ninth is in preparation.

However, the decision to produce a "Monitoring Yearbook" was actually a compromise. The original idea in 1999 had been to produce a regional integration index for SADC but had to be abandoned because of the poor quality of available economical and political data. For almost all SADC countries, the data available in 1999 had been more than three years old and sometimes not obtainable at all. Over the last decade, however, this has improved dramatically and made it thus possible to utilise statistical data for several aspects of measuring the depth and sustainability of RI particularly in SADC. Not only have most countries enhanced and standardised their domestic data collection and statistical departments but also several indices have either been improved or newly established such as the Corruption Perception Index (CPI) of Transparency International (TI) ([13]), the Bertelsmann Transformations Index

---

Regional Integration in Southern Africa. Yearbook, Vol. 3- 2003. Windhoek: 140-153; Meyns, Peter (2002): The Ongoing Search for a Security Structure in the SADC Region: The Re-establisment of the SADC Organ on Politics, Defence and Security (OPDS). In: Hansohm et al (eds.) (2002), Monitoring Regional Integration in Southern Africa. Yearbook, Vol. 2. 2002. Windhoek:141-168.

11 See for example regarding transport: Mutambara, Tsitsi (2008): Regional transport challenges within SADC and their implications for economic integration and development. In: Bösl et al (eds) (2008): Monitoring Regional Integration in Southern Africa Yearbook, Vol. 8. Stellenbosch:34-54.

12 See for example: Weeks, John (2008), Macroeconomic Convergence in East, Central and Southern Africa, 1980-2007. Paper presented at the Workshop on Macroeconomic Policy Convergence in Southern Africa. Pretoria, 23-26.09.2008; Roussouw, J. (2006), South Africa's role in macroeconomic convergence in SADC, mimeo. Peters-Berries, C. (2005), Is there Convergence in SADC? Essay for the SADC-Barometer. mimeo

13 www.transparencyinternational.org

(BTI) ([14]) or the Ibrahim Index of the *Mo Ibrahim Foundation*([15]). Despite the progress on the data front, one *caveat* has to be raised: for some countries such as Angola, the DR Congo (DRC) and more recently Zimbabwe the statistics offered by official handbooks and country reports remain to some extent doubtful and not always comprehensive.

I would like to thank my colleagues Detlev Tenzer (particularly for the great maps he designed) and Kristin Fedeler who helped me with editing and formatting. My brother Ralph-Michael Peters helped me with some of the research and provided encouraging and constructive comments throughout the process of writing the thesis. My special appreciation goes to my wife Genet for she had not only unlimited patience with me spending long hours – particular over weekends and during holidays – at my desk but also assisted me with my research. However, without the constant encouragement of my father Günter Peters I would most probably never have found the determination to write this thesis. Last but not least I have to thank Prof. Rainer Tetzlaff for his ongoing support and his willingness to accept me as a PhD student 25 years after I graduated with a Diploma in Political Science at his faculty at the University of Hamburg.

14 www.bertelsmann-stiftung.org
15 www.moibrahimfoundation.org

PART A: CONCEPTS AND THEORIES OF REGIONAL INTEGRATION

1. Regional Integration and Development – The Conceptual Rationale for Regional Integration

Regional Integration (RI) can be defined in a three-dimensional manner ([16]):

1. Spatial or geographic scope: which countries belong to the regional integration scheme?

2. Content or substantive coverage: which sectors and activities are covered by the regional integration agreement?

3. Depth of integration: which degree of national sovereignty is a country prepared to surrender to a regional body?

As a concept to improve the economic well being of a group of countries RI has an obvious link to developmental policies. As a stage on which to develop a 'culture of cooperation' which allows for the building of mutual trust amongst often volatile political leaders and systems and the development of peaceful mechanisms of conflict resolution, RI may also play an important role in democratisation processes in countries lacking a democratic political culture and in regional peace-building efforts. On the African continent, with most of the countries being having a pronounced authoritarian history, RI can provide some of the impetus to promote democracy beyond a shallow and superficial form of application. At the same time RI may also help to defuse conflict situations or ongoing conflicts between states.

What are the arguments for RI in detail?

---

16 I am following in this classification Kritzinger-van Niekerk, L. (2005), Regional Integration: Concepts, Advantages, Disadvantages and Lessons of Experience. World Bank:4

1.1. The Rationale for Regional Integration in Africa

Most economic textbooks describe RI as a suitable concept for developed economies but are rather silent on developing countries. Despite the scarcity of explicit reference to the developing world, the idea has always been appealing to development strategists, economists and politicians especially in Africa. Economic arguments for RI are often seen as more important as compared to political points of view supporting the idea. This is to some extent caused by the long standing tradition of economic theory dealing with RI, and to some extent, by the empirical evidence that sees RI in most cases emanating from an economic rationale and through an economic mechanism rather from a political angle.

The major theoretical arguments for RI can be differentiated into four economic and three political lines of thinking.

1.1.1. The Economic Rationale for Regional Integration

The economic arguments focus on the creation of bigger markets, improved welfare of citizens, attractiveness for development funding and the requirements of globalization.

(i) The 'market-size argument'

RI has always been viewed as the most promising approach to overcome the ***→economic balkanisation*** ([17]) of many parts of the African continent. Colonial borders especially in West and Central Africa but to some extent also in Southern Africa had divided once connected economic spaces and networks and eventually created a patchwork of small and often economically unviable new states ([18]). Even today 38 out of the 53 African states have populations of less

17 The first Ghanaian President *Kwame Nkrumah*, regarded the division of Africa into several small states, which he referred to as (political) "Balkanisation", as an instrument of neo-colonialism to keep Africa weak and exploitable; see McCarthy, C. (2007): Is African Integration in need of a paradigm change? Thinking out of the box of African integration. In: Bösl, Breytenbach, Hartzenberg, McCarthy & Schade (eds). Monitoring the Process of Regional Integration in southern Africa in 2007: 9

18 Like the south-east European Balkan area, where not only now but already after the end of the first World War (1914-1918) several economically unviable and politically disintegrated small states had been carved out of the collapsed Austrian and Turkish Empires. Some African scholars argue that instead of 20 states it would have been

than 15 million people and one third of all African countries have even less than 3 million inhabitants ([19]). For many of these small states, it seemed in the words of *Green/Seidman* (1968) a question of "unity or poverty" – regional integration or continuing misery. Their argument was that Africa was 'balkanized', i.e. split into too many, too small economic entities that were unable to overcome the narrowness and limitations of their markets by themselves. The prescribed remedy was to form integrated regional bodies consisting of the economies of several of these small states, which combined, would provide a larger population and thus demand base allowing industries to grow bigger and increasingly realize →'***economies of scale***' when producing goods and services ([20]).

Further advantages attributed to the creation of bigger markets through regional integration in this line of theoretical thinking are:

- The promotion of a more effective allocation of production factors, i.e. labour and capital. This means the concentration of investments – for which capital and labour is needed – in those countries which have the most conducive conditions such as political and social stability; minerals and/or productive farmland; good infrastructure, ports and airports. Investments would naturally tend to flock to countries that have the best framework conditions and labour would follow. Skilled workers would migrate to those countries within the regional framework where working conditions (availability of jobs; wage levels) as well as living conditions (price levels; housing; education and infrastructure in general) would be best thus creating centres of skilled manpower and through that, improving quality and efficiency of production. By the concentration of investments (capital) and labour (workers) in those countries with the best conditions, production in general would become more efficient and thus less expensive; the competitiveness of production would be increased. In short, RI would facilitate the restructuring of *"...the regional economy in a way that benefits the production base of the region."* ([21])

---

advisable to form only four states out of French West and Equatorial Africa, Belgian Congo and British East Africa; see: Nzongola-Ntalaja, G (2002), Good Governance and Conflict Management – Will the African Union make a Difference? Paper presented at the Evening Forum, Norwegian Peacebuilding Empowerment Programme, Oslo, 4th September 2002

19 See UNECA/AU, Assessing Regional Integration in Africa III (2008):23

20 See Kritzinger-van Niekerk, L. (2005):2

21 Gibb, R. (2001), The State of Regional Integration: The Intra- and Inter –regional Dimensions. In: South African Institute of International Affairs (SAIIA) (2001),

- If production becomes more competitive and internal markets are big enough, the supporters of this line of thinking argue, the rate of investment from both internal and international sources would increase ([22]). With additional investments, the number of jobs and level of income would increase.
- With the allocation and thus concentration of production in the most suitable locations, the argument goes further, the ***→economic transaction costs*** could be lowered and production could become even more effective. Economic transaction costs, such as transportation expenses, banking fees, duties etc. could decrease if production is more geographically concentrated (or clustered), banking and financial systems are less fragmented between various states and if duties are lowered or abolished as a result of regional integration.
- Sometimes the argument is extended even further and an improved ***→technology transfer*** from outside the integration area is seen as an additional possible benefit if the economic balkanization of a region is overcome. If more opportunities for profitable investments open up, more external investors are attracted which would lead them to import better technologies. The labour force within the regional integration area would thus be exposed to new technologies and skills which in turn would then also benefit local, smaller industries.

This logic still provides the most compelling justification for RI. It allows integrating developmental thinking into an otherwise very neo-classical economic concept.

(ii) The 'welfare argument'

RI is also supported from a different line of thinking, which has its origins in the neo-classical theory of economics (see below) and which comes to similar conclusions as the first argument. The proponents of this school of thought attribute improved ***economic and social welfare*** of the citizens of the participating countries to regional integration. The neo-classical integration theory is based on the work of the American economist *Viner* (1950) who combined the – in itself contradictory – concepts of free trade and protectionism. He showed in model calculations that if a regional economic zone is created with high external tariffs (duties) against the rest of the world (=protectionism)

Regional Integration Southern Africa: Comparative International Perspectives. Johannesburg:71.

22 ibid.

but all duties are abolished inside the regional bloc (=free trade), all countries within the regional bloc would realise improved national economic and social welfare. The latter refers to more jobs, higher incomes and, as such, better living conditions.
The 'welfare argument' goes as follows:

- If 'free trade areas' (FTA) or at an advanced level a 'custom union' (CU) are established, this will lead to ***→trade creation*** inside the integration area ([23]).
- Higher volumes of trade inside the integration area will be followed by higher rates of investment – even if it only facilitates increased trade volumes (such as investments in traffic and communication infrastructure and hardware; warehouses and/or petrol stations, hotels etc.).
- More trade and investments lead to higher employment rates.
- Higher employment levels lead to higher national/regional income levels, increased demand for other goods and services and thus to more economic growth.
- Regional integration can under these conditions easily result in higher economic growth rates, more employment and thus to a marked increase in national/regional general welfare.

(iii) The 'development funding argument'
While the first two economic arguments for regional integration are following the 'traditional' line of economic thinking based on the neo-classical concepts as developed by *Viner* there are two additional 'modern' arguments supporting regional integration. The first one argues from a developmental point of view that RI can also attract ***additional development funding***. This is particularly relevant for RI in developing countries or regions and has been put forward as a pragmatic view and as a result of practical experiences (Peters 1987).

From this angle, RI has a particular attractiveness for funders of big development projects such as development banks, multi-lateral donor agencies (e.g. EU) and specialised (often private) donors (such as the *Bill and Melissa Gates Foundation*; the *Clinton Foundation* etc.) as it allows the realisation of

---

23 The different forms and models of economic regional integration will be explained in detail in chapter 2.1. (see below); but also see: McCarthy, C. (2007): Is African economic integration in need of a paradigm change? Thinking out of the box on African integration. In: Bösl, T., Breytenbach, W., Hartzenberg, T., McCarthy, C., Schade, K (eds), Monitoring Regional Integration in Southern Africa Yearbook, Vol. 7 (2007), Stellenbosch (2007):15ff

- Cross-border projects such as railway lines, roads, electrical grids, dams and even environmental conservation areas, which make economic and environmental sense but cannot be realised at national levels.
- Capacity building projects of a regional nature, such as specialised universities, training funds and/or research stations which for lack of capacity or demand, have not been established at a national level.
- Regional policy support for health sector initiatives (HIV/AIDS; malaria, polio etc.); crime prevention efforts (drug trafficking; human trafficking etc.); investment promotions (e.g. in tourism) and even for practical projects such as the regional unification of driving licences, often makes more sense in a regional than a national context.
- Establishment of regional institutions or bodies such as meteorological services (of increasing importance in the context of adaptation to the impact of climate change); electrical power pools and/or police services which form part of the crucial infrastructure for Africa's sustained socio-economic development and attainment of the ***→Millennium Development Goals.*** This requires a regional orientation to be effective.

(iv) The 'globalisation argument'

The second 'modern' argument for RI is related to globalisation. At many international conferences, it has been pointed out that RI is regarded as a particular necessary step for African countries to become ***fit for globalisation***. Globalisation does not only refer to more intensive and liberalised trade and investment regimes, intensified currency and stock market speculation and increasing numbers of mobile experts and a chance of realising fast economic growth and wealth. For Africa, globalisation may also mean to be permanently excluded from the chance to ever reach the level of sustainable socio-economic development. There is the imminent threat that Africa could be reduced to the position of a mere supplier of raw materials, genetic variance, tourist attractions and entertainment talent (music, sports etc.)

Major global players such as the USA, EU (and its member states), China, Russia, India and increasingly also the Arab World and Brazil, are bargaining over the structure and rules to shape the future world at international institutions and within international organisations, while African countries (perhaps with the exception of South Africa) and organisations, appear to sit on the fence as mere spectators rather than parties defending their own interests. The major actors base their negotiation strategies on well-prepared and thought-out concepts, backed by extensive research and reliance on skilful negotiators. African countries usually neither have clearly defined national policies on issues such as climate change, trade liberalisation, energy security and/or intellectual and other property rights nor the information and negotiators to influence critical international negotiations.

The ongoing preparations for a post-*Kyoto* framework for climate change are a case in point. With the exception of South Africa, no other African country has so far developed its own climate change policy. The African Union (AU) has just very recently started to realise the importance of the issue. In the past, Africa has mostly sided with the G77 plus China and as a result, supported China's interests (a major emitter of greenhouse gases) rather than its own (a major victim of the negative impact of climate change) ([24]). In 2009, however, African Heads of State – undoubtedly attracted by the prospect of accessing substantial compensation and adaptation funds – for the first time in AU history agreed on a joint policy stance, the *Common Policy on Climate Change* at the AU-Summit in *Syrte* (Libya). The AU Summit also nominated with the Ethiopian Prime Minister *Meles Zenawi* a single spokesperson for international negotiations (COPP 15 in *Copenhagen* in December 2009). *Meles Zenawi* announced during a meeting of the *African Partnership Forum* (APF) in *Addis Ababa* in September 2009 that from no on Africa would speak with one voice and demands to be taken serious in their positions or would leave the negotiation table ([25]). Unfortunately, the progress made regarding climate change negotiations is not matched in other crucial fields of international dialogue such as trade and investment.

Development experts argue that African countries need to formulate, publicise and defend their often-similar interests regarding global developments. This can be easier achieved if African countries would no longer speak as individual countries but as regional blocs until the AU becomes more efficient. RI bodies would have;

- more weight in international bodies (WTO, UNDP, UNCTAD, IPCC, WHO etc.) and would be able to make their positions heard and interests count;
- a stronger position in investment negotiations (e.g. in the negotiations with the EU over the proposed ***Economic Partnership Agreements*** [EPA]);

---

24 See for example the African Appeal on Climate Change "Africa speaks up on Climate Change". www.africanclimateappeal.org

25 See Peters-Berries, C. (2009), Partnerschaft oder Auftakt zur Konfrontation? Das Treffen des „*African Partnership Forum*" zum Klimawandel. Interner Bericht, Heinrich Böll Stiftung, Sept. 2009; mimeo.

- a better position in enforcing their social, environmental, economic and legal standards in negotiations with multi-national corporations than dealing with such powerful global players individually.

1.1.2. The Political Rationale for Regional Integration

The political arguments for promoting RI are predominantly pragmatic and stem from empirical insights rather than principled political theory. They focus on security issues, international negotiation power, convergence pressure towards democracy and the creation of 'natural' socio-cultural and political entities.

(i) The 'security argument'
In politically unstable and volatile regions such as Africa, RI can – according to political scientists ([26]), – improve the national and regional ***security situation***.

They contend that;

- in areas of the world where states are not (yet) fully integrated and consolidated or where 'failed' states ([27]) exist, the probability of armed conflicts is high. The potential for conflict can be greatly reduced through RI schemes, which incorporate 'soft' or even 'failed' states. Functioning RI bodies can de-escalate civil wars and internal strife ([28]) through a catalogue of responses starting with sanctions and ending with military intervention. They may also calm down regional disputes and conflicts by enforcing regional standards of conflict resolution;
- regional bodies offer additional protection against external aggression as the potential aggressor might not want to engage with an entire region;
- functioning RI bodies can also be safeguards against coup d'états and armed rebellions if the regional body has established principles of not recognising governments formed by rebellious soldiers or even intervening militarily in such countries ([29]);

---

26 For example Meyns (2000); Peters-Berries/Naidu (2003); Hammerstad (2003).

27 Examples of 'failed' states are currently Somalia, the DRC and Afghanistan; examples from the past decade are Liberia, Sierra Leone and Iraq.

28 On the African continent, the cases of SADC and Mozambique (1992), Angola (1991 and again in 2002) but also ECOWAS in West Africa (Liberia 1995/6 and 2003) demonstrate the constructive role RI bodies can play in the de-escalation of civil wars.

29 The combined South African and Botswana intervention in Lesotho in 1998 to protect the legally elected Government of Prime Minister *Mosisili* against an alleged putsch of the army (Meyns 2000:190f) but also the immediate sanction imposed against the putchist Government of Mauritania and Guinea in 2008 and 209 respectively by

- RI bodies can improve regional security by coordinating their efforts in the fight against terrorism and international crime (drug trafficking; money laundering) through joint intelligence and policing strategies;
- RI can contribute to political stability through the professionalization of security forces, (which in many weaker states constitute a permanent factor of political insecurity), by organizing joint exercises and capacity-building exercises ([30]).

(ii) The 'democratic convergence argument'

RI has the potential to increase the ***→democratic convergence*** of a region. The EU, for example, has demonstrated this in the cases of Bulgaria and Romania. ([31]). The urgent wish of countries to join a prosperous and economically lucrative RI body can facilitate within a short time the adoption of democratic principles and standards even in countries with undemocratic pasts and traditions if the regional body demands that as a precondition for joining. The philosophy behind the application of the same democratic standards for all countries in a regional body is simple:

- Without adhering to the same legal standards and principles, a regional community would have no common legal basis and thus security of law, which in turn would undermine investor confidence.
- Only in regional communities where human and democratic rights are fully acknowledged and observed, will the citizens of the member states also support the idea of RI. If a regional body has member states where the governments are not accountable of how taxes are spend, the legitimacy of RI will suffer and thus the coherence of the regional community.
- The violation of basic human rights in even one member state will damage the international reputation of a regional community.

ECOWAS can be regarded as examples for the pro-democracy role of RI bodies. The same applies to SADC's swift suspension of Madagascar after the unconstitutional change of power in February 2009.

30 Such as the regular joint exercises of South African, Zimbabwean and Mozambican army units since 1996.

31 Even Turkey, which has been held off from joining the EU for several years, has democratised its legal system, improved its human rights record and modernised its institutions predominantly because it still has the hope of joining the EU in the near future. To achieve this, it will have to comply with the democratic standards of the EU. A recent study by the *German Development Institute* (DIE) concluded that the only instrument of democracy promotion which has worked so far is the membership promise of the EU; see DIE, 1/2009: Demokratieförderung: Kein Ende der Geschichte. Analysen und Stellungnahmen. Bonn 2009

If a regional community consists – as is often the case in the developing part of the world – of countries with different democratic records, the setting of democratic convergence standards can help to force even unwilling and undemocratic states to implement democratic reforms (such as free and fair elections, an independent judiciary and/or an improvement of the human rights record) in order for them to remain member states. However, this requires that the respective RI body is also willing to take the necessary steps to enforce this. In the case of SADC this has with regard to Zimbabwe not always been the case ([32]).

(iii) The 'putting-together-what-belongs-together' argument
Particularly, in the African context, where boundaries have in many cases been rather arbitrarily drawn by previous colonial masters, current states do often not reflect historic settlement and economic exchange patterns, RI can thus be a facilitation instrument to '***put together what belongs together***' ([33]). It has been claimed that RI can;

- soften the negative impact of the artificial colonial borders which are defining most states in Africa today; ECOWAS and SADC are examples for such a motivation ([34]).
- create transnational identities, which in turn can help minimize conflicts;
- facilitate the often-impeded free movement of people at least a regional level.

1.1.3. Summary

The economic and political models predict that regional integration if implemented successfully is capable of not only improving the economic well-being of the participating countries at the macro level but also that of their citizens at the micro level. It enhances the chances of member countries of becoming more democratic and secure. Moreover, and increasingly important, this line of thinking predicts that especially in Africa, countries will have a better chance of pursuing their interests in a rapidly globalising world when they

32 See Chapter 11

33 The former Chancellor of Germany, *Willy Brandt*, used these – now legendary – words to describe the German re-unification in 1989/90.

34 Clapham, C. (2001): The Changing World of Regional Integration in Africa. In: South African Institute of International Affairs (SAIIA) (2001), Regional Integration Southern Africa: Comparative International Perspectives. Johannesburg: 59f

overcome their political and economic fragmentation and speak with a more unified voice.

One could also argue that RI can be a useful instrument to fulfil some fundamental human needs for economic development, i.e. a better life, democracy and the rule of law, peace and justice. However, it should not be forgotten that socio-economic and political differences have always been important factors for progress and development and that people are by nature competitive and thus prone to be involved in conflicts. RI is therefore not a *panacea* for the problems the world and the African continent in particular are faced with. RI can, at its best and under favourable conditions become a tool for improving untenable socio-economic and political situations. Summarising the potential impact of RI, it can be stated that RI

- can be a strong facilitating factor for economic growth and the improvement of the socio-economic living conditions of people.
- has the potential to accelerate economic development and ensure economic efficiency through improved competition.
- may provide a better than fair chance for the socio-economic development of poor, less developed and internationally underprivileged countries.
- can become a catalyst for democracy and the rule of law even in countries with historically autocratic societies and political cultures.
- may facilitate the de-escalation of violent conflicts and discourage coup d'états and undemocratic means of accessing power.

RI can play an important role to bring about economic and democratic development.

2. Regional Integration in the Global Context

Before we focus on the various models of RI, it may help to understand the variety and complexity of regional integration models if we take a brief look at some major examples for successful RI in other parts of the world.

2.1. The European Integration Process After Six Decades

Probably the most successful, most influential and most often copied model for RI is the European one. It started as the grand idea of two politicians still shocked by the devastation of the Second World War – France's Minister of Foreign Affairs *Robert Schumann* and West Germany's first Chancellor *Konrad Adenauer* – in 1951, but from very modest beginnings of a functional cooperation between six countries in Western Europe ([35]) in the area of mining. The architects of the post-war RI in Western Europe had political motives: the prevention of a future war between 'arch enemies' France and Germany and the formation of a counter weight to the perceived threat from the Soviet-controlled Eastern Europe. They combined these cleverly with a particular economic interest, the supply of sufficient raw materials for the production of energy and steel in order to provide the desperately needed ingredients for economic revival in the participating countries to start the European integration process

The European integration process started with limited functional cooperation in the Coal and Steel Community, progressed to a Free Trade Area (FTA) and Customs Union (CU) before approaching the status of a Common Market and lastly that of a Political Union with a single currency, diversified political institutions and developing a common legal system.

The EU is based on four Treaties:

- The Treaty establishing the *European Coal and Steel Community* (ECSC) from 1951, which expired in 2002.
- The Treaty establishing *European Economic Community* (EEC) which entered into force on 1.1.1958 ("Treaty of Rome").

---

35 These were France, West Germany, Italy, Belgium, the Netherlands and Luxemburg.

- The Treaty which established the *European Atomic Energy Community* (Euratom), which was signed alongside the EEC Treaty.
- The Treaty on *European Union*, which was signed in Maastricht on 7.2.1992 and came into force on 1.11.1993 ("*Maastricht Treaty*").

TEXT BOX 2.1: Milestones in European Integration

- 1951: Belgium, Germany, France, Italy, Holland and Luxembourg sign the Treaty establishing the European Coal and Steel Community
- 1958: Establishment of the ***European Economic Community*** (EEC)
- 1967: Formation of the ***European Communities*** (EC)
- 1973: Expansion of the EC to include also the UK, Ireland and Denmark
- 1975: The Lome I Convention between the EEC and 46 ACP states
- 1979: First direct elections to the European Parliament
- 1981-1995: Further expansion to include Greece, Spain, Portugal, Austria, Sweden & Finland
- 1990: Treaty of *Schengen*, which led to the abolishment of internal border controls between the Netherlands, Belgium, Luxemburg, France and Germany
- 1990: German Re-unification
- 1992: Treaty of Maastricht, marking the establishment of the ***European Union*** (EU)
- 1993: Introduction of the Common Market
- 1999: The EURO is adopted by 11 member states and launched on the financial markets
- 2002: Introduction of the EURO as single currency in 12 of the 15 member states of the EU
- 2004: Further enlargement of the EU by ten countries from the former Warsaw-Pact-Area and Southern Europe: Lithuania, Estonia, Latvia, Poland, Czech Republic, Slovakia, Slovenia, Hungary, Malta and (Greek) Cyprus
- 2005: Proposed European Constitution rejected in national referenda in France & Holland.
- 2007: Further expansion of the EU to 27 member states, which now also incorporates Bulgaria and Romania

Source: Fontaine (2006)

The three early European Communities (ECSC; EEC and Euratom) merged in 1967 into a single Commission and a single Council of Ministers. At Maastricht the member states of the EU agreed to include also foreign and security policies as well justice and home affairs to the areas of cooperation.

In terms of major institutions, the EU has established the following bodies (see text box):

TEXT BOX 2.2: Major European Institutions

- The ***European Parliament***, which is elected every four years directly by the citizens of each member state;
- The ***Council of the European Union***, which consists of the heads of state of the member states and forms the Government of the EU;
- The ***European Commission***, which resides in Brussels, is the executive body of the Council;
- The ***European Court of Justice***, which is the last instance for all citizens, companies and organisations registered in EU member states in issues linked to European integration;
- The ***European Central Bank***, which has replaced the national central banks of all those member states which have introduced the EURO;
- The ***European Court of Auditors***, which checks whether the EU funds are used properly; based in Luxembourg; consists of one auditor from each member state.
- The ***European Ombudsman***, responsible for receiving and following up on citizens' complaints;
- The ***European Investment Bank*** (EIB), founded already in 1958, based in Luxembourg, promotes European investments outside the EU.

The three main decision-making bodies (the so called "institutional triangle") are:

- The European Parliament, which is elected directly every five years.
- The Council of the European Union representing the individual member states.
- The European Commission, which represents the interests of the EU as a whole.

The EU has two major ways of making decisions. It can issue a 'directive', which establishes a common aim for all member states but leaves it to the national authorities to decide on the form and method of implementing it. And it can issue a 'regulation' which is immediately applicable throughout the EU ([36]).

The European integration process has led to a number of remarkable achievements; they can be summarized as follows:

36 See: European Commission (2007): How the European Union Works. Your guide to the EU institutions. Brussels.

- Through the establishment of a Customs Union free trading within the EU;
- Free movement of people in 15 core countries; citizens can decide where they want to live, work, invest and/or travel to without restrictions and border controls;
- A European citizenship, which is expressed by the introduction of European passport;
- The introduction of a single currency – the EURO (€) – in the majority of the member states since 2002;
- The harmonization of laws and regulations regarding, economic, environmental, health, social and transportation issues;
- The transfers of parts of ***→national sovereignty*** to supra-national EU institutions.

Despite of all the successes, the regional integration process has slowed down in the last years because of an increasing hesitance in some member states to relinquish more of their national sovereignty to Brussels. The crucial project of developing and passing a European Constitution, which started in 2001 has been blocked on a number of occasions at member state level by referendums. Some of the newer members such as Poland, the Czech Republic as well as the still predominantly Euro-critical UK have repeatedly tried to use their veto power ([37]) to obtain special concessions from the other members.

However, despite the evident problems, the EU is still by far the most advanced RI project in the world. Although its members are mostly developed countries, which belong to the richest nations in the world, some of the lessons from the European integration process have universal relevance and should not be overlooked in other parts of the world:

1. Economic interests alone are not a sufficient base for RI; it requires an expressed political will to be successful.
2. The interests of smaller and/or weaker states must be respected and safeguarded in the process of RI so that the project is not dominated by the economic and politically most powerful countries.
3. Successful RI requires institutionalised mechanisms to ensure a 'just' distribution of costs and benefits from the integration process.

---

37 One of the pillars of the regional integration process in Europe has been the application of a consensual voting principal, which ensured that bigger countries and stronger economies did not disregard the interests of the smaller members. However, with the rapid expansion to now 27 member states, this principle has increasingly become an obstacle to further and deeper integration. It is planned to change the consensus principal to a qualified majority model.

4. A common political history and similar political cultures and values help to develop a common regional identity.
5. Adherence to similar democratic and legal standards is crucial for the functioning and acceptance of the integration process in member states.

2.2. Regional integration in Asia: ASEAN

The major RI project in Asia is *the* ***Association of South East Asian Nations*** (ASEAN), the successor of the Association of Southeast Asia founded 1961. ASEAN, with its headquarters in *Jakarta*/Indonesia, was established in 1967 in *Bangkok* by Indonesia, Malaysia, the Philippines, Thailand and Singapore against the backdrop of three closely interrelated developments of the 1960s:

- The foreign intervention in the region (Vietnam War 1964-75),
- the fear of further communist encroachments, and
- the competition for influence in the region between China and India.

Thus, ASEAN right from the start had a clear anticommunist outlook, pursued an approach of strengthening national sovereignty and of consolidating the independence of its member states through bloc building. In contrast to the European Union the foundation of ASEAN was not to ultimately prepare for gradually surrendering national rights to a regional institution but to serve nationalist interests. As a result of the strong emphasis placed on national sovereignty the principle of non-interference into internal affairs of the member states was introduced. Together with other distinct features as informality, a decision making process based on consensus and minimal institutionalization this constituted what became known as the 'ASEAN Way'. While fighting off potential aspirations and interference by the regional powers India and China ASEAN's creation was also connected to Indonesia's interest to establish itself as one of the regional power houses. Thus, the country's former president, Suharto, has been the main driving force behind ASEAN in the 1960 and 1970s.

The membership remained almost stable until the mid 1990s ([38]), mainly due to the political instability in the region. In 1995, Vietnam joined the organisation, Laos and Myanmar followed in 1997 and Cambodia became the tenth and latest member in 1999, bringing the total population in the ASEAN region up to 560 million people and the external trade volume to over 1,400 billion $.

---

38 In 1984, newly independent Brunei became the sixth member

After few real steps towards integration the process started to accelerate from the early 1990s onwards culminating in the signing in 2007 of the ASEAN Charter and ASEAN Economic Community Blueprint. In 1992, the ASEAN Free Trade Zone (AFTA) was agreed upon in order to improve the region's international competitiveness by eliminating tariffs and non-tariff barriers internally. The Common Effective Preferential Tariff (CEPT) accord/scheme, a phased programme of tariff reductions, was initially scheduled to pave the way for AFTA and to become effective in 2008. This was, however, brought forward and AFTA was already achieved by 2003. Later on it was supplemented by a range of AFTA-plus programmes (including the elimination of non-tariff barriers and the harmonization of customs). However, some of the relatively new members were given a longer time frame to meet the tariff reduction criteria. The ultimate goal – for the first time spelt out in the *Bali* Concord II in 2003 - is to establish the ASEAN Economic Community (AEC) by 2015. Further concrete and decisive steps were taken through the launch of the ASEAN Charter and the AEC blueprint, signed at the 13th ASEAN Summit in Singapore in November 2007 and officially established at the 14th Summit in *Jakarta* in December 2008. Through the Charter, ASEAN finally moved away from its more informal character and transformed itself into a legal entity. With the AEC blueprint the process for implementing the first of the three pillars made significant process, while the other two pillars, Political Security Community and the Socio Cultural Community, have not yet left the planning stage.

The highest organ is the ASEAN Summit that – if the four informal meetings ([39]) are taken into consideration – has been held on an annual basis unofficially since 1995 and officially since 2001. The most important single institution is the ASEAN Secretariat, based in Jakarta/Indonesia. By the end of 2008, altogether 19 ministerial consultation processes have been established. There are 29 committees and 122 working groups that support the organisation's efforts. Civil society organisations are represented in the working groups, but due to structural constraints their influence remains limited.

Politically, ASEAN subscribed to an agenda of promoting peace and stability. In December 1995 the *Southeast Asian Nuclear-Weapon-Free Zone Treaty* was signed. It, however, did not become effective until June 2001, when the Philippines as the last member state finally ratified the treaty, thereby confirming the current status according to which none of the member states possesses nuclear weapons. The Bali Concord II in 2003 firmly anchored democracy as a means to promote regional peace and stability in the region. By

---

39 They took place in 1996, 1997, 1999 and 2000. In 2001 it was officially decided to stage a summit every year.

signing off the concord even the non-democratic members of the organisation (Myanmar, Brunei, Malaysia, Singapore and Vietnam) accepted the establishment of a democratic form of government as the ultimate political goal. Partly in conceding to demands from Western countries but also as a result of persistent pursuit by the democratic governments of Indonesia, Philippines and Thailand the protection of human rights became an integral part of the ASEAN Charter. However, clinging to the principle of non-interference threatens to render the planned ASEAN Human Rights Commission toothless. This became evident when the organisation remained soft on the violent military suppression of the peaceful protests in Myanmar in 2007. ASEAN rejected any economic sanctions and any consideration of suspending the membership of the country. The formulation of two of the three pillars (Security Community and Socio Cultural Community) is still ongoing.

The ASEAN Regional Forum (ARF) was established in 1994 as a formal official dialogue forum to reach out to non-members in order to have a broader clout in promoting confidence building and preventive diplomacy in the region. By 2008 the ARF consists of 27 participants, including China and therefore excluding Taiwan.

After initial resistance by the US had evaporated in the wake of the 1997 East Asian financial crisis, the Malaysian initiative to foster closer links of the organisation with the economic heavy weights of the region, China, Japan and South Korea, was agreed upon to establish the ASEAN plus three.

2.3. Regional Integration in Latin America: Mercosur

Until the 1990s, Latin America had a number of mostly failed RI projects to look back to. In 1991 Argentina, Brazil, Paraguay and Uruguay established the *Mercado Comun del Sur* (MERCOSUR), which has made some remarkable progress and can be regarded as the most successful attempt of RI in Latin America ([40]).

The protocol of the MERCOSUR-treaty of 1994, signed in *Ouro Preto*, established the organisation as an international legal entity and set up its internal structure with six organs. A Summit takes place twice a year as a meeting of the

40 Most of the information regarding MERCOSUR was derived from: Council on Foreign Relations: Backgrounder – MERCOSUR: South America's Fractious Trade Bloc: www.cfr.org/publication/12762/mercosur.html

heads of state, usually at the same time with the meeting of the Council of the Common Market (CMC), the organisation's supreme controlling organ.

The main goals of MERCOSUR are laid down in the preamble of the founding treaty from 1991, usually referred to as the Asuncion Treaty:

- Enlargement of the national markets of the member states as a precondition of accelerated economic growth with particular emphasis on social justice, the protection of the environment, and the improvement of the member states' infrastructure.
- Adequate integration into the international structure of the big economic blocs.
- Strengthening of the scientific and technical cooperation of the member states.
- Moving towards a broader union of peoples.

The initial goal of establishing a common market by the end of 1994 proved far too ambitious and has still not been realized by the end of 2008. After years of stagnation, however, important progress was made when in 2004 at the 25th summit in Montevideo the Commission of Permanent Representatives with its President, the former Argentinean head of state *Eduardo Duhalde*, was officially launched. Considerable leverage was vested in the commission (assisting the CMC, negotiations with non-members, present own initiatives to promote the integration). The so far rather "toothless" secretariat was reformed from a subordinate administrative entity into a full technical secretariat. In the same period the Court of Appeal as a permanent organ was set up, thus further boosting the process of institutionalisation. This was followed in May 2007 by the inauguration of the organisation's 90-member parliament in Montevideo in Uruguay (each member state nominates 18 members).

Further progress in the integration process has been hampered mainly by the impact of traditional rivalries between Brazil and Argentina, aggravated by the implications of Brazil's size and economic power. A major conflict centred around the inconclusive search for a strategy towards the more US-dominated Free Trade Area of the Americas (FTAA): While members of MERCOSUR cannot individually enter into free trade agreements with a third country, the signing of the Trade and Investment Network Agreement (TIFA) by Uruguay with the United States caused rifts within MERCOSUR, particularly as both FTAA and MERCOSUR are competing for supremacy, but also as an exemption from common tariff regulations is considered for the potential new MERCOSUR member Bolivia.

With the view of establishing eventually a regional integration body for the whole of Latin American and building on the momentum after the establishment of the Commission the members of MERCOSUR and the Andean Community (Bolivia, Chile, Colombia, Ecuador and Peru) granted each other the status of Associated Members. Bolivia is under consideration for full membership. Bolivia's tariffs, however, are lower than those of MERCOSUR and it would need an exemption, which Brazil in order to gain access to Bolivia's gas resources would be willing to grant, very much to the detriment of Uruguay.

In 1998, the member states expressed their full commitment to democracy as the best form of government. By the end of 2008 all member states were ruled by left wing governments. This, however, did not pre-empt political frictions: Though Venezuela has been accepted as a new member in 2006, the membership has by the end of 2008 not become effective, as the ratification process had not been concluded by Paraguay and Brazil, particularly due to concerns about infringements into press freedom in Venezuela. The entry of Venezuela with its President *Hugo Chavez* as a new member, possibly later followed by Bolivia under *Evo Morales*, has also caused concern about potential attempts to shift focus, away from economic issues towards a more political agenda in pursuing a more left wing cause. However, the organisation's power houses, Brazil and Argentina, appear committed to a strengthening of the economic aspects of the integration process.

By 2006, MERCOSUR had a combined population of more than 260 million people and covered about 72% of the area of South- and 56% of the area of Latin America. The Gross Domestic Product of the member states reached USD 1 billion and equalled 75% of the total GDP of Latin America, making it the fourth largest regional trading bloc after the EU, NAFTA and ASEAN.

3. The Neo-Classical Model of Regional Integration

Neo-classical theory starting with *Viner* (see above) and further refined first by *Meade* ([41]) and later by *Balassa* ([42]), developed a five-stage model of economic RI. Each step is regarded as a precondition for reaching the next as it provides the required achievements for further regional integration. The underlying principle is that of market integration; it prescribes the increasing liberalisation of goods, services, labour and capital as the path to a fully integrated region.

3.1. Stage 1: The Free Trade Area (FTA)

The FTA ([43]) may be preceded by a Preferential Trade Area (PTA) but in the classical approach, it can also be established on its own. A FTA is characterised by internal trade liberalisation, i.e. by the abolition of customs tariffs and so called ***→non-tariff trade barriers*** (NTTB) between countries, which have chosen to form the FTA. While tariffs are abandoned internally, each member state may determine individual external custom regimes and tariffs.

The positive effects to be expected from abolishing internal trade barriers within the FTA are:

- Increased intra-regional trade (within the region) as the volume of goods and services demanded will grow when their prices decrease ([44]): more people (customers) are able to afford goods and services generated or available in the other member states of the FTA.
- Increased intra-regional investments (inside the FTA) from within and from outside the FTA. The creation of an FTA increases the market volume in terms of potential customers and makes it thus attractive for businesses to invest. This makes particular sense if the member countries of the FTA follow an import-substituting industrialisation strategy.

---

41 Meade, James (1955), The Theory of Customs Union. Amsterdam

42 Balassa, Bela (1961), The Theory of Economic Integration. London

43 I will use the term Free Trade Area (FTA) as it appears to be the one most commonly used.

44 Many African countries have extremely high custom duty rates, as these not only protect strategic infant national industries but also constitute an easy way of revenue generation. Due to this, imports are more expensive for the consumer then they need to be.

Moreover, the bigger market also calls for additional investments to link the various parts of the FTA through roads, railways, communication links etc.

However, the establishment of a FTA may also have unwelcome side effects such as:

- Pressure to lower the remaining external custom tariffs (towards third countries) in order to attract additional investment: for example if the external tariffs of country A are 100% for machines and semi-processed materials but only 50% and 25% in other member states of the FTA, companies (from both within and outside the FTA) will most probably opt for country C as an investment destination. As the absence of internal tariffs and NTTB's allows free trade within the FTA, the country with the lowest external tariffs attracts most investments. As a result, there will be competition between the members of an FTA to lower external tariffs in order to attract such investments, which might have negative effects on both government revenue and being able to determine the direction of development.
- Loss of revenue for countries A and B that have higher external tariffs as most of the imports, which attract duties, will enter the FTA through country C.
- The existence of protected national industries is being threatened: most African countries are at the beginning of their industrialization and thus need to protect their infant industries (often in the textile and food processing sectors) through high external tariffs from the competition of bigger (and cheaper) international companies. In a FTA, such protection of 'infant industries' is undermined if other members have lower tariffs and open the 'backdoor' to the importation of cheaper goods.
- More bureaucracy is required to counter such unwelcome side effects as the threat to national industries through the application of ***→rules-of-origin*** procedures or compensationary duties. Such measures are increasing the costs of doing business and offsetting to a certain degree, the gains through trade creation ([45]).

Because of these negative side effects, the creation of an FTA is often only regarded as a necessary, but if possible, brief transition period on the way to the establishment of a customs union (CU). Examples of FTA's are the 'North American Free Trade Area' (NAFTA) or the early stage of the European integration process. Under normal circumstances, it takes some years before the

45 See Balassa (1961):71ff

all the internal tariffs are abolished and all the precautionary measures against unwelcome side effects have been implemented. The establishment of a full-fledged FTA is the result of intensive negotiations between the participating countries.

3.2. Stage 2: The Customs Union (CU)

If a FTA has achieved its objectives (abrogation of internal tariffs), its member states may feel it is time to progress to the stage of a CU. In contrast to an FTA, a CU has not only liberalised its internal trade, but also unified the external customs tariffs of its members. In other words, within a CU there is protected liberalized internal trade.

The positive effects to be expected from the establishment of a customs union can be summarized as follows ([46]):

- Efficient allocation of ***production factors*** in the most suitable country within the union. If all countries have the same external custom tariffs and there are no tariffs inside the regional grouping new investments will naturally take place in the country where the best conditions (infrastructure, vicinity to harbours, political stability, skilled labour force, natural resources etc.) can be found. As a result, the production factors are being allocated where production can be realised in the most efficient way.
- ***Trade creation*** effects as a result of the efficient allocation of production. Trade creation takes place when the external tariffs of the CU and the free internal trade regime displace the thus far duty-protected production of a good in country A by the production of the same good in a more efficient and cheaper way in country B of the CU. As a result, country A must now import the good from country B which is according to the neo-classical theory (→ ***comparative cost advantages***) beneficial to the customers in country A. They can get this good at no cheaper price from anywhere else. The resulting additional trade is being regarded as increasing the welfare of the citizens of the CU.

---

46 This follows the arguments of Bechler, E. (1976) International Arbeitsteilung und Dritte Welt – Handelsbeziehungen auf Kosten oder im Dienste der Entwicklungsländer? Köln and Wegener, A (1979): Integration als entwicklunspolitisches Konzept. Bochum

- Additional '***economies of scale***' effects are possible in a CU when production of a good is becoming more concentrated and thus higher volumes of the same good can be produced. This lowers the unit price and thus makes the production of that good more competitive.
- Facilitation of ***supra-national development planning*** especially if developing countries engage in a CU. To establish a CU amongst developing countries requires the joint planning of e.g. infrastructure projects (road links, railway lines, communication links, energy supply generation, interconnections etc.) – otherwise the economic potential of the CU might not be fully realized as such infrastructural links do not always exist. This in turn encourages planning approaches, which go beyond national interests and boundaries and can foster deeper regional integration.

However, CU's are far from being the ultimate and most efficient stage of regional integration. They also have potential inherent problems that express themselves most often in the form of

- An increase of the joint external tariffs, which enhances the immediate danger of → ***trade diversion***. To compensate for the loss of state revenue because of the abolition of internal tariffs and to protect industrial production within the CU, members states tend to raise the external tariff levels. If that happens, the member states of the CU, which have in the past imported goods from outside the union at cheaper prices, can no longer do so but must obtain this good from another member of the CU at higher prices. In such a case, the neo-classical theory talks of trade diversion, which is regarded as a sub-optimal allocation of production factors and thus not beneficial to the economic welfare of the state and its citizens.
- ***Unequal distribution of customs revenue*** causes friction between member states. The revenue from tariffs on imports from countries outside the CU is obtained at the port of entry into the CU. This will often be the most efficient port or the biggest airport from where the goods are then shipped to the member state of the CU, which has ordered them. In a perfect world, the duty levied on these goods would be transferred immediately from the authorities of the country where the point of entry is to the treasury of the importing country – in reality, there are numerous (technical) problems attached in trying to do so. One, might be the delayed transfer of duties to the recipient government, second, exchange rate fluctuations and third, unclear destinations. A technically less complicated but politically even more controversial approach is to agree on a fixed ratio of how to distribute the revenue

from custom duties ([47]) – but this requires a large degree of political good will.

From the neo-classical point of view, a CU makes only economic sense if ([48])

- The effect of trade creation outweighs that of trade diversion, which can only be expected if the founding states have already joined the CU on a rather high level of external tariffs. In that case, the effect of trade diversion remains relatively small as imports from outside the CU have already attracted high duties and had never been very cheap;
- The regional market created by the CU is big enough to allow for intra-regional division of labour and thus the specialisation of production according to the most effective allocation of production factors. This would increase the potential for trade creation substantially.

While the CU offers a much wider range of advantages than the FTA, it is still far from being the optimal state of affairs according to the neo-classical theory. The still existing imperfections pertain, for example, to the high probability of trade diversion and concrete problems of determining politically acceptable formulas for sharing the customs revenue amongst member states. In other words, for a CU to function, intensive and often permanent political negotiations are required which would have to address not only an economic interest but the need for a basic political will for integration.

3.3. Stages 3 & 4: The Common Market/The Economic Union

The next stage of RI is according to the neo-classical theory the formation of a common market followed by an economic union. A common market has the features of a CU coupled with the full liberalisation of the movement of people and capital within the integration area. If a common currency – like in the EU – is adopted, the next and rather similar stage of an economic union is reached. Both stages are similar in their aims and thus often mentioned together.

---

47 This is e.g. the approach of SACU. However, it is very much a remnant of the past when *apartheid* South Africa agreed to a distribution of customs revenue favourable to the other members in an attempt to buy political allegiance from black African states and at the same time make, them even more financially dependent on South Africa (see also chapter 5.1.).

48 See: Wegener, A (1979)

A common market is characterised by;

- A highly efficient allocation of production factors as there is total freedom of movement of capital and persons within the integration area. This allows investments to take place anywhere within the region, for people from any country of the integrated area to invest anywhere inside the common market and for people (labour) to move and settle anywhere within the region. According to the neo-classical theory, this will lead to investments taking place where they can utilise the best combination of production factors.
- An increased attractiveness for investments from both within and without the integration area. If the rates of return on invested capital are high due to the optimal allocation of production factors and the integrated internal market is large enough to support meaningful 'economies of scale', additional investments will be attracted.
- An improved competitiveness in a globalised economy as a result of the optimal allocation of production factors. If the production of goods and services is organised in an efficient manner and at a large enough scale inside the common market area, it will make these goods and products also increasingly competitive on the world markets. Several small to medium-sized companies from Northern Italy especially in the textile sector but also in mechanical engineering, have utilised the protection of the European Common Market in the 1980s to develop into companies which were eventually also able to compete worldwide with their products.

The closely related next stage of an ***Economic Union*** is further characterized by the introduction of a common currency. That has successfully been achieved so far in the European Union with the introduction of the Euro in 2002. However, apart from that, an economic union also calls for further harmonization of policies as this become increasingly necessary to create a regional even economic playing ground. If for example labour laws or environmental regulations keep on differing between the member states of an economic union, there will be distortions in the allocation of production factors and thus less economic and social welfare gains.

The disadvantages emanating from the creation of common markets or economic unions are less pronounced than in previous stages of regional economic integration but some still exist:

- High pressure for smaller/less-efficient countries to 'adapt or die'. Smaller economies have hardly a choice: they must specialise economically or face decline. For example, in the EU small countries like Holland, Luxemburg or Denmark did this successfully ([49]) for the price of having to import a large number of its consumer items such as electronic goods, vehicles, machines, textiles, furniture etc. The larger economies of the EU such as Germany, France, UK and Italy are the providers of many of these products. In the neo-classical theory, this is called 'realizing the comparative cost advantages'.

- Tensions between national interests and regional necessities may also arise in common markets and economic unions as national states are often unwilling to give up or transfer parts of their sovereignty such as for instance monetary authority to the regional authority. In the EU, there are due to this reason, still long-standing member states such as the UK that have not joined the EURO-zone despite a heavy economic price ([50]).

However, on the whole the benefits of creating or joining common markets and economic unions are usually much higher than the costs. Member states of regional integration schemes at these stages are much better placed to assert themselves in the globalizing international economy and are gaining in terms of employment creation, raising income levels and general wealth.

3.4. Stage 5:The Political or Supranational Union

The last stage of regional integration according to the neo-classical theory is that of the *Supranational Union.* This stage has so far been proven to be rather illusive and has never been reached. The European Union has probably come closest but in the last few years, many policy initiatives meant to facilitate the establishment of such a supranational union were thwarted at national levels. In a number of referendums the Dutch, Danish, French and most recently, Irish voters, for example, have rejected the idea of a European Constitution.

Even without a constitution, the EU has already adopted several of the features of a supranational union without reaching it fully yet. The EU has all the

49 Holland specialised to become a major producer of vegetables, flowers and dairy products within the EU; Luxemburg became one of the EU's financial centres and Denmark flourished because of it concentration on dairy products and tourism.

50 The British Pound was appreciating against the EURO for a number of years that made British products increasingly expensive in the rest of Europe and dented the British trade balance.

characteristics of an economic union coupled with some of the political superstructures of a supranational union such as regional institutions, the European Parliament and parts of a regional government (Commission) and administration. However, the last and most important step towards the formation of a supranational Union has not yet been taken: member states renouncing their national sovereignty in favour of a regional (federal) state. The adoption of a European constitution would have been a decisive move towards it but has for the time being been put to rest.

A supranational union or regional state would – according to the neo-classical approach – not only encompass all the economic advantages outlined above but also combine them with the formal power of a politically unified entity. In the case of the EU – and without reaching this stage yet – the advantages of a supranational union are already becoming apparent:

- Vastly enhanced position in international negotiations on trade, climate change, development aid, justice and various crisis interventions;
- adoption of standard-setting internal technical and political norms such as regarding emissions of cars, power stations etc as well as human rights, labour standards and development;
- sufficient financial 'muscle' to stimulate the economic development of disadvantaged regions (as done in the EU), influence world global financial transactions etc.; and
- assume an increasingly important (but not always well coordinated yet) role in international conflict prevention and crisis regulation.

3.5. Summary: The Limitations of the Neo-Classical Concept of Regional Integration

While the history of RI worldwide has a number of FTA's, CU's , a few Common Markets and one functioning Economic Union (the EU) to show for, few of these RI bodies have been following the prescribed model by the letter. In fact, in most cases, either major modifications have been made in order to achieve results or the label attached to the RI approach did not accurately describe the content as has often been the case with RI attempts in the developing world ([51]).

51 Examples for this kind of mis-labelling are COMESA and to some extent also ECOWAS; see chapter 7

This is but one indication that theory and practice often differ when it comes to implementation. In the case of RI, the discrepancies between the neo-classical theoretical approach and reality have been particularly big when applied to RI amongst developing countries. The major criticism of using a neo-classical approach to RI in the developing part of the world focuses on the following points:

- The neo-classical approach regarding regional integration usually does not take sufficiently into account the differences in the resource endowment, political power and economic opportunities between the member states of a regional integration scheme. The neo-classical approach does not make allowances for differences but develops its argument always *"under ideal conditions"* which in reality hardly ever exist ([52]).
- The neo-classical approach does not foresee any mechanisms to ensure an equitable distribution of costs and benefits, losses and gains through regional integration ([53]). On the contrary, it assumes that the market forces will ensure an optimal allocation of production factors irrespective of potential disadvantages and costs to individual member states of a RI body. Political interests are not foreseen in this approach. Any 'polarization', which will have a negative effect on the willingness between the members to further integrate regionally, because of the divergences in accrued costs and benefits are not considered at all.
- Pure neo-classical approaches tend to overlook developmental requirements of regional integration outside the industrialised North as the concept was not developed for developing countries.
- The neo-classical approach to RI does not offer any real strategy for regionally integrated developing countries to react to the steep gradient in power relations in the world economy and the challenges of globalisation ([54]). Under the assumptions and dogma of the neo-classical approach, the intensified utilisation of cheap production factors by multi-national enterprises are to be regarded as beneficial while the reality of multinational enterprises engaging in developing countries has a far from beneficial record.

What are the alternatives? A younger, less market-faithful and more interventionist school of thought stresses the developmental role of RI. In this view RI should promote ([55]):

---

52 See: Gibb (2000):73f

53 Ibid.

54 See Gibb (2000):74

55 This follows the argumentation of R.Davies as summarized by Gibb (2000):74

- the co-ordination of regional industrial development;
- the creation of regional development funds or banks to support the least developed member states;
- the preferential access of less developed member states to the regional market;
- the co-ordination of macro-economic policies already at an early stage of integration.

This approach became never as prominent as the trade-centered neo-classical concept but elements of it have become part and parcel of the practical application of RI in some of the most successful cases such as the EU or ASEAN ([56]). While the EU is very much based on the trade integration approach, it also pursues intensively redistribution policies in favor of disadvantaged regions and subsidizes farms otherwise unable to survive under free market conditions. Even ASEAN, often regarded as the model for trade-led RI, allows a variety of non-tariff trade barriers to protect domestic markets and industries from external competition.

---

56 See Gibb (2000):74f

PART B: THE HISTORICAL DIMESNION OF REGIONAL INTEGRATION IN AFRICA

4. Regional Integration Attempts in Africa – An Overview

The African continent has seen numerous attempts of RI of which most must be categorized as failures ([57]). The list of RI projects dates as far back as to the end of the 19th century when the British colonial administrations realised that some of their colonies would be better off if they joined together into a regional economic scheme. In French West and Central Africa, regional cooperation started after World War I. The different styles of colonial administration (British "*indirect rule*" vs. French "*incorporation*") influenced to some extent the concrete form of regional cooperation and integration in the respective territories; the dominance of settler-colonialism in parts of the "*British Colonial Empire*" favoured the establishment of economic customs unions rather than political federations ([58]) as could be found in the French part of Africa.

In West Africa, the British colonial administration introduced a common currency for their for colonies (Nigeria, Ghana, Sierra Leone and Gambia) and at some time established an airways company for them: the *West African Airways Company*. However, no formal economic or political integration scheme emerged. In East Africa, the colonial power established in 1917 a customs union initially for Kenya and Uganda which was extended to Tanzania (then called "*Tanganyika*") in 1927. At a later stage it became the East African Community (EAC) ([59]). In Southern Africa, the origins of regional cooperation date back to 1889. The Southern African Customs Union (SACU) was

---

57 See for example ECA (2002) or Clapham (2000), who is even more pronounced in his criticism.

58 The exception – at least in a formal sense – was the *Central African Federation* (CAF) between Southern and Northern Rhodesia and Nyasaland, which existed in the last decade of colonial rule from 1953-1963. It was clearly created to serve the interests of the settler-regime in Southern Rhodesia (now Zimbabwe); its political form (Federation) was to some extent camouflage of the economic interests of the Rhodesian settlers and to some extent an instrument to ensure that these interests were politically legitimized. See also chapter 5.2.

59 See Chapter 7.1.1.

established between the Protectorates of *Bechuanaland* and Swaziland, the colony of Lesotho and the South African Union by the British colonial administration and continued by South African after it became independent in 1910 (*'dominion-status'*) ([60]).
In the French administered part of Africa the emphasis was more on political cooperation. The French colonial administration grouped their 13 "territories" into two federations: French West Africa (*Afrique Occidentale Francaise*, AOF) and the French Equatorial African Federation (*Afrique Equitorial Francaise*, AEF). Each federation even had its own currency. But both federations were abolished in 1956 when it became apparent that independence for the colonies was inevitable. The French Government wanted to ensure that the new states were weak enough to need a close relationship with their former colonial masters in order to survive; instead of two big political entities, 14 new states were formed ([61]).

RI continued to remain fashionable and in fact gained popularity in sub-Saharan Africa after independence - although there was a short pause in which the newly created African states had to re-orient and re-group themselves – because it befitted the prevailing economic and political conditions African states had to function in. African leaders understood that their economies were too small to prosper and their countries to weak and un-important to have much influence in a globalizing world if they would remain singular and isolated. Pan-Africanism with its strong sense of continental solidarity provided the political ideology, neo-classical approach the economic concept and the EU the shining but also misleading (because it developed under totally different framework economic and political conditions) example for the numerous emerging regional integration schemes ([62]). So far, more than 20 major attempts have been undertaken to form RI schemes in Africa (see Text Box 4.1).

In order to assess if SADC can serve as a model for further RI in Africa and can contribute to the formation of the AEC it is important to look first at the concrete historical experience in the region (Southern Africa) with RI and its influence on SADC and then at the general conceptual development and practical experience of RI in Africa. This allows not only to put SADC's achievements and problems into the political and theoretical framework of pan-

---

60 See Chapter 5.1.

61 See: Adedeji, A. (2002), History and Prospects for Regional Integration in Africa. Paper presented at the Third Meeting of the African Development Forum, Addis Abeba,5.3.2002.
http://www.uneca.org/eca_resources/Speeches/2002_speeches/030502adebayo.htm

62 See: Clapham, C. (2000): 59f

African integration but also to provide the reference for comparison and eventual assessment of the guiding question of this analysis

TEXTBOX 4.1.: Major Attempts of Regional Integration in Africa

Name	Full Name	Duration	Member states/HQ	Goal
AMU	Arabic Maghreb Union	Since 1989	Algeria, Libya, Morocco, Mauretania and Tunisia	Full Economic Union
CAF	Central African Federation	1953-1963	between Southern Rhodesia (now Zimbabwe), Northern Rhodesia (now Zambia) and Nyassaland (now Malawi)	Political Union
CEAO	Communaute de l'Afrique de l'Ouest	1974-1994	transformed into → ***UEMOA*** in 1994	
CECAS	Conference of East and Central African States	1986-	No further information	
CEEAC/ ECCAS	Communaute Economique des Etats de l'Afrique Centrale,	1983	Chad, Sao Tome and Principe, Gabon, in Libreville (Gabon)	Full Economic Union
CEMAC	Economic and Monetary Community of Central Africa	Since 1991	succeeding →***UDEAC*** in 1999	Full Economic Union
CEN-SAD	Community of Sahel-Saharan States	Since 1998	Benin, Burkina Faso, CAR, Chad, Comoros, Cote d'Ivoire, Djibouti, Egypt, Eritrea, Gambia, Ghana, Guinea, Guinea-Bissau, Kenya, Libya, Liberia, Mali, Mauritania, Morocco, Niger, Nigeria, Sao Tome & Principe, Senegal, Sierra Leone, Somalia, Sudan, Togo and Tunisia.	FTA

CEPGL	Communaute Economique des Pays des Grand Lacs	1976, standstill since 1994	Rwanda, Burundi, DR Congo based in Rwanda	Full Economic Union
COMESA	Common Market for Eastern and Southern Africa; followed→ PTA	Since 1993	Burundi, Comoros, Djibouti, Egypt, Eritrea, Ethiopia, Kenya, Libya, Madagascar, Malawi, Mauritius, Rwanda, Seychelles, Somalia, Sudan, Swaziland, Uganda, Zambia, Zimbabwe based in Lusaka (Zambia)	Common Market
EAC	East African Community	1967-1977, new in 1999	Kenya, Tanzania and Uganda, joined in 2007 by Rwanda and Burundi	Full Economic Union
FLS	Frontline States;	1974-1991	Angola, Mozambique, Tanzania, Zambia and (from 1980) Zimbabwe.	Informal co-operation
IGAD	Intergovernmental Agency for Development (successor to the Intergovernmental Authority on Drought and Development [IGADD] 1986-1996)	Since 1996	Ethiopia, Somalia, Djibouti, Sudan, Kenya, Uganda; Eritrea joined in 1993 and suspended its membership in 2007 based in Djibouti	Full Economic Union
MRU	Mano River Union	Since 1973	Sierra Leone, Liberia and Guinea: membership promise of the Cote d'Ivoire 2008)	Multi-sectoral integration
NBI	Nile Basin Initiative	Since 1999	Egypt, Sudan, Ethiopia, Uganda, Kenya, Tanzania, Burundi, Rwanda, the Democratic Republic of Congo and Eritrea.	Sectoral cooperation
PTA	Preferential Trade Area of Southern and Eastern Africa	1981-1993	transformed in 1993 into → ***COMESA***, based in Lusaka; consisting of 18 members.	Trade integration
SACU	Southern African	Since	Botswana, Lesotho,	Customs

	Customs Union founded in 1910	1889 and 1910	Namibia, Swaziland and South Africa	Union
SADCC	Southern African Development Coordination Conference established in 1980	1980-1992	transformed into → ***SADC*** in 1992; consisting of Angola, Botswana, Lesotho, Malawi, Mozambique, (from 1990) Namibia, Swaziland, Tanzania, Zambia and Zimbabwe. based in Gaborone	Multi-sectoral cooperation
SADC	Southern African Development Community established 1994	Since 1992	Angola, Botswana, DR Congo (since 1997), Lesotho, Madagascar (since 2005), Malawi, Mauritius (since 1995), Mozambique, Namibia, South Africa (since 1995); Swaziland, Seychelles (1997-2005); Tanzania, Zambia and Zimbabwe. based in Gaborone	Full Economic Union
UDEAC	Union Douaniere et Economique de'l Afrique Centrale → superceded by CEMAC in 1999	1964	Cameroon, Central African Republic, Chad, Congo, Equatorial Guinea, Gabon. based in Brazzaville	Customs and Economic Union
UEMOA	Union Economique et Monetaire Ouest-Africaine	Since 1994	Benin, Burkina Faso, Guinea-Bissau, Ivory Coast, Mali, Niger, Senegal and Togo	Full economic union

Source: ECA (2004), own compilation

The following chapter looks first at RI under colonial rule with particular emphasis on Southern Africa before switching to the pan-African concept of RI and subsequent attempts of integrating Africa. In a third step, post-colonial development of RI in Africa is reflected upon.

5. Regional Integration in Colonial Times

Of the colonial RI schemes two had a decisive impact on later approaches in Southern Africa. We will thus look at SACU and CAF in some detail in order to determine their impact on current attempts of RI in the region.

5.1. Southern African Customs Union (SACU)

The first attempts towards RI in Africa were made by British colonial administrations in Southern Africa in 1889 which was further formalised by the newly formed Government of the South African Union in 1910 with the establishment of the ***Southern African Customs Union*** (SACU) ([63]). SACU originally consisted of the newly independent South African Union (later 'Republic of South Africa') and the three British territories *Basutoland* (Lesotho; colony), *Bechuanaland* (Botswana, protectorate) and Swaziland (protectorate). South Africa tried several times until the 1960s to incorporate the three territories until these attempts were stopped when they became independent in 1966 (Botswana and Lesotho) and 1968 (Swaziland).

During the colonial era, the small economies of the three British colonies became highly dependent on and structurally deformed by the much bigger South African economy. In terms of transportation, communication but especially industrial development, investment and employment opportunities the three smaller members of SACU were, in the 1960s, mere extensions of the South African economy rather than independent entities. The independence of these three colonies – often referred to as the → ***BLS-states*** – caused the character of RI in SACU to change.

In 1969, when all of the three former colonies and protectorates had become independent, the SACU treaty was renegotiated. The interest of South Africa was to bind the newly independent BLS-states closely to the *apartheid* regime. In order to achieve this, South Africa offered a distribution formula for the income from the customs union (from duties on imports) ([64]) which were

63 Meyn, Mareike (2007), Regional Integration and EPA configurations in southern and eastern Africa – what are the feasible alternatives? In: Bösl, Breytenbach, Hartzenberg, McCarthy & Schade (eds). Monitoring the Process of Regional Integration in southern Africa in 2006: 142

64 See: Chapter 3.2.

favourable to the BLS-states. As none of the BLS-states had at that stage a strong revenue base, the income from the customs union soon constituted a major and thus welcome source of state revenue ([65]). The price, which especially Lesotho and Swaziland had to pay, was that of political compliance with the *apartheid* state in its fight against the growing tide of liberation movements in the region. In the view of the *apartheid* strategists in Pretoria, the BLS-states formed the first ring of protection around South Africa, they were to become its *cordon sanitaire* ([66]). When the newly independent Namibia joined SACU in 1990, it also benefitted from the favourable formula for the distribution of SACU-revenue. In other words, after 1969 SACU became an instrument for *apartheid* South Africa to buy some political compliance from its neighbouring states.

To attach the economies of the BLS-states further to South Africa, the *apartheid* state compelled the smaller countries to join the → ***Rand Monetary Union*** (RMU), which pegged the national currencies of the BLS-states to the South African Rand. Botswana left the RMU in 1976 when its economy – based on diamond and beef exports – had become strong enough to stand on its own feet ([67]).

In 1994 ([68]), after a majority Government under Nelson Mandela took power in South Africa, the willingness of South Africa to continue with the established and costly revenue distribution formula declined rapidly. It engaged the governments of the other member states of SACU in negotiations to adjust the revenue-sharing formula. However, due to the still high degree of dependency of at least three of the four members on SACU-revenue with respect to their budgets, their willingness to accept a less favourable deal was rather low. Only in 2002, a new SACU-treaty was agreed upon and signed; it entered into force on 15 July 2004 ([69]).

---

65 Even in the comparatively well off Botswana, the income from the SACU Revenue Pool constituted in 1979/80 approximately 37% of all state revenue: Peters (1987:67).

66 See Meyns (2000): 44ff;

67 See: Peters, C. (1987):67ff

68 I will portray the history and development of SACU in one chapter (unlike that of the EAC, ECOWAS and SADCC) because it has not been interrupted (such as EAC) or re-invented itself conceptually as has been the case with ECOWAS and SADC(C).

69 See: WTO (2009), Trade Policy Review: Southern African Customs Union (SACU). Document WT/TPR/S/222:14. http://www.wto.org/english/tratop_e/tpr_e/tp322_e.htm

Map 5.1. The member states of the Southern African Customs Union (SACU)

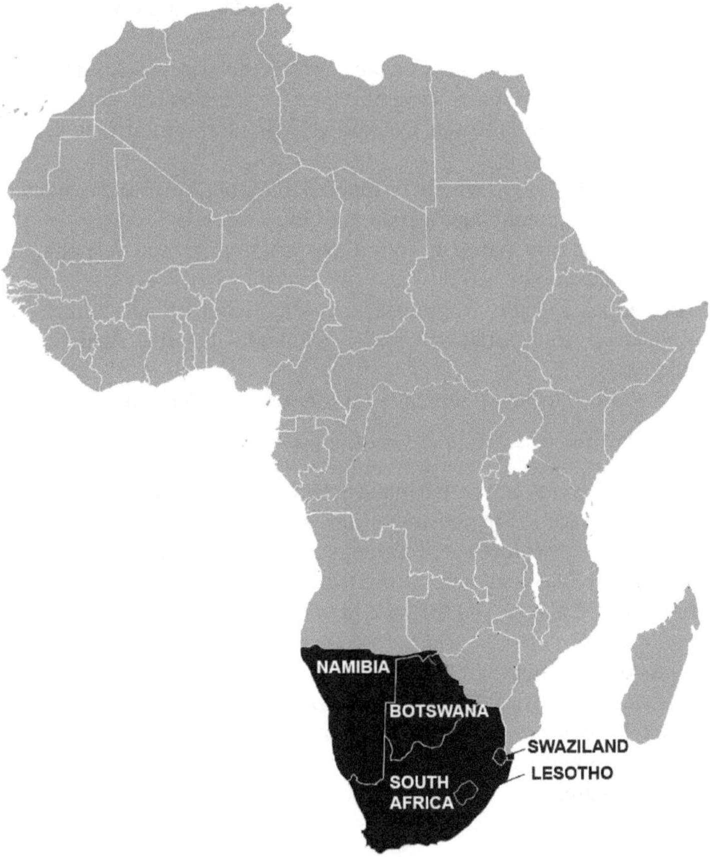

Source: D.Tenzer (2010)

While the trade policy instruments did not change much, SACU became, in total, more democratic after 2002. For example, the power to set tariffs was removed from the South African Board of Tariffs and Trade to the newly established SACU Tariff Board ([70]). South Africa was supposed to manage the

---

70 In late 2009, however, Botswana's minister for Finance and Development Planning, alleged that the high external tariffs of SACU were still set by South Africa alone; see

revenue pool only for the initial two years but continued to do so until now ([71]). Another innovation was the establishment of six new SACU institutions. In the past, all institutional support for SACU was provided by South Africa and no separate SACU institutions existed. The new SACU Treaty established the ([72]):

- The Council of Ministers as the supreme decision-making body.
- The Tariff Board consisting of experts from member states which makes recommendations to the Council of Ministers on tariff levels and other trade related issues.
- The Commission, which is responsible for the implementation of the SACU Agreement and decisions of the Council.
- The Secretariat based in Windhoek (Namibia) and responsible for the administration of SACU.
- Technical Liaison Committees in the fields of agriculture, trade and industry, transportation and technical matters, which assist the Commission.
- An ad hoc Tribunal, which is tasked with settling any arising disputes in SACU.

A new formula of revenue distribution based on the original agreement was agreed upon as well for the new agreement. Instead of sharing a fixed percentage of all duties collected amongst the four smaller economies, the new formula takes into account their socio-economic performance and developmental needs ([73]). The formula now contains ([74])

- A customs component, whose income benefits the BNLS states despite the fact that most of the customs income is generated by South Africa.
- An excise component, whose income goes to 79% to South Africa; and
- A development component, which is based on the per capita income in the member states.

Tralac:www.tralac.org/cgi-bin/giga.cgi?cmd=cause_dir_news_items&news_id=79543&cause_id=1694 (accessed 02.01.2010)

71 See: WTO (2009):17f

72 WTO (2009):16f

73 See: Hartzenberg, Trudy (2003): The new SADC agreement: Implications for regional integration in Southern Africa. In: Hansohm et al. (eds), Monitoring Regional Integration in Southern Africa Vol 3; Windhoek 2003:180ff. The formula can be found below.

74 See: WTO (2009):18f

Table 5.1.: Intra SACU- Trade 2002-2007

Country		2002	2003	2004	2005	2006	2007
Botswana	**Exports** USD mill.	**251.2**	**289.5**	**332.0**	**402.5**	**301.5**	**526.3**
	% to SA	99.0	98.5	98.4	96.8	95.6	98.2
	Imports USD mill.	**2,711.8**	**3,375.2**	**2,705.4**	**2,674.4**	**2,640.4**	**3,354.9**
	% from SA	99.4	99.6	99.5	99.4	99.2	99.3
Lesotho	**Exports** USD mill.	**151.6**	**92.9**	**173.9**	**161.2**	**118.3**	**239.4**
	% to SA	100.0	99.9	98.0	100.0	100.0	100.0
	Imports USD mill.	**617.3**	**915.5**	**1,094.4**	**794.7**	**804.4**	**927.7**
	% from SA	99.9	100.0	100.0	99.9	100.0	99.9
Namibia	**Exports** USD mill.	**332.2**	**420.7**	**642.0**	**776.1**	**845.9**	**1,198.5**
	% to SA	98.2	97.6	98.0	98.4	98.0	97.8
	Imports USD mill.	**1,015.3**	**1,151.1**	**2,072.7**	**2,101.2**	**2,317.9**	**3,161.3**
	% from SA	99.8	99.8	99.4	99.6	99.4	99.4
South Africa	**Imports** USD mill.	**0.5**	**4.7**	**0.7**	**430.9**	**791.4***	**350.7**
	% from Botswana	6.1	86.4	48.2	70.2	33.5	62.3
	% from Lesotho	37.0	12.2	27.9	29.7	16.9	37.6
	% from Namibia	35.4	0.5	23.3	0.1	0.0	0.0
	% from Swaziland	21.5	0.9	0.6	0.0	0.0	0.1
Swaziland	**Exports** USD mill.	**659.3**	**1,183.4**	**1,584.4**	**1,175.2**	**619.4**	**833.3**
	% to SA	100.0	100.0	100.0	99.7	91.6	58.8
	Imports USD mill.	**769.7**	**1,245.9**	**1,634.0**	**1,460.6**	**1,013.4**	**1,129.4**
	% from SA	100.0	100.0	100.0	100.0	98.3	95.7

Source: WTO (2009):47f

* = according to the information provided by the WTO 49.2% of South Africa's imports from SACU were attributed to South Africa itself. No further explanation for that contradiction was provided.

SA = South Africa

The impact of the world economic crisis in 2008 and 2009 caused a decline in revenue from SACU for the smaller member states due to the reduced volume of trade and prompted the Botswana Government to request for an increase in the share of customs union revenue from South Africa ([75]).

Intra-regional trade in SACU is high due to South Africa which provides the bulk of consumer goods, some capital goods as well as food to the other member states. Botswana imported 85% (2005) of all its good and services from South Africa, Lesotho 82% (2003), Namibia 80% (2003) and Swaziland 95% (2004) ([76]). With regard to intra-regional trade the dominance of South Africa is even more pronounced. Both in terms of intra-regional exports and imports is South Africa the main destination rsp. source. Nearly all of intra-SACU exports are destined for South Africa and nearly all intra-regional imports of the other SACU member states are originated in South Africa (see table 5.1.).

Parallel to SACU, South Africa, Lesotho, Namibia and Swaziland also form the *Common Monetary Area* (CMA) with the South African *Rand* as lead currency with which the other currencies are on parity. This is meant to reduce transaction and information costs ([77]).

However, a number of problems have not yet been solved. First is the impact of the *Trade, Development and Cooperation Agreement* (TDCA) of 2000 between South Africa and the EU on the revenue base of the other SACU member states. After a 12 years transition period all imports from the EU into South Africa will have to be duty-free. Since the distribution formula of the revenue obtained from import duties in SACU is still beneficial to the BNLS-states a reduction in South African revenue from import duties will reduce the overall amount due to the smaller states ([78]). In 2006, South Africa imported goods and services for Rand 160.8 billion from the EU (=34.6% of total imports), which attracted ca. Rand 12.2 billion in duties, which –according to the calculations of *Tralac* ([79]) – were approximately Rand 2 billion less than without the application of TDCA reductions; for 2007 the estimated losses in customs duties from EU imports

---

75 See:www.tralac.org/cgi-bin/giga.cgi?cmd=cause_dir_news_items&news_id=79543&cause_id=1694 (accessed 02.01.2010)

76 See: Sandrey, R. (2007): Living in the shadow of the mountain. In: Bösl et al (eds.) (2007):

77 See; Meyn (2006):144

78 See: Sandrey, R. (2007):253ff, who also reports that tariffs under the TDCA in selected sensitive areas for the BNLS states will be readjusted and renegotiated.

79 *Tralac* is the *Trade Law Centre for Southern Africa* based in Stellenbosch (South Africa). It undertakes detailed and in-depth research into trade relations in Southern Africa.

were ca. Rand 5.7 billion ([80]). Currently (2006 figures), Namibia receives ca. 41% of its total revenue from SACU; the shares for Lesotho and Swaziland are even higher with 53% and 56% respectively; even Botswana's government revenue depends to about 20% on the SACU revenue pool (see table 5.2.).

Due to the complicated revenue distribution formula (see TEXT BOX 6.1.) the actual amount due to the SACU member states remains often unclear. With respect to the impact of the application of the TDCA on EU imports to South Africa it is not apparent how much lower than the optimal income the actual revenue in the BNLS states has been because. While the overall revenue from the SACU revenue pool has not decreased in the last years due to the rise in overall imports to South Africa and the region until 2008, it can be expected that the economic crisis since September 2008 has sharply reduced this source of government income for the BNLS-states. None of the BNLS-states has many if any options to replace the revenue from the SACU pool; growing budget deficits for 2009 and the following years can be expected.

Although the new SACU treaty resolved that all member states have to consent if an individual member state intends to negotiate or enter new trade agreements with third parties or change existing trade agreements ([81]), Botswana, Lesotho, Namibia and Swaziland entered into an interim EPA with the EU in 2007 without the consent of South Africa, which thus demanded renegotiations of the EPA in order to protect its national interests ([82]).

Table 5.2.: The Importance of the SADC Revenue Pool for SACU Members in 2006

Country	Total Revenue from SACU Pool (Mill. Rand)	SACU Pool Revenue as % of GDP	SACU Pool Revenue as % of total Revenue
Botswana	5,634	9	20
Lesotho	2,836	28	53
Namibia	5,403	12	41
Swaziland	3,708	24	57
South Africa	17,625	1	4

Source:Tips/AusAid (2007), Intra-SADC Trade Performance Review. http://www.sadctrade.org/files/TPR-2007.pdf

80 See: Sandrey, R. (2007):254

81 See: WTO (2009):14

82 See: Vines, A. (2008),Regional Integration in Southern Africa: Challenges and Opportunities. Speech delivered to the *Instituto Superior de Relacoes Internacionais (ISRI),* Maputo, 26.03.2008. www.chathamhouse.org.uk. See also chapter 10.2.2

TEXT BOX 5.1.: The 2002 SACU Revenue-Sharing Formula

The revenue sharing formula of the 2002 SACU Agreement, for a given financial year, is:

$$Ri = C\ (Ai/A) + (0.85)\ E\ (GDPi/GDP) + 20*(0.15)\ E\ (1-((Yi/Y)-1)/10)$$

where:

Ri = revenue share of SACU country i;
i = Botswana, Lesotho, Namibia, South Africa or Swaziland;
C = all customs duties actually collected on goods imported into SACU, less the cost of financing the Secretariat, the Tariff Board, and the Tribunal, less the customs duties rebated or refunded;
Ai = c.i.f. value (at the border) of imports of SACU country i from all other SACU members, less re-exports;
A = total c.i.f. value (at the border) of intra-SACU imports, less re-exports;
E = all excise duties actually collected on goods produced in the SACU area, less the cost of financing the Secretariat, the Tariff Board, and the Tribunal, less the excise duties rebated or refunded;
GDPi = gross domestic product of SACU country i;
GDP = total gross domestic product of SACU members;
Yi = gross domestic product per capita of SACU country i; and
Y = average gross domestic product per capita of all SACU members

After some algebraic manipulations, Ri becomes:

$$Ri = C\ (Ai/A) + (0.85)\ E\ (GDPi/GDP) + (0.3)\ E\ (11-Yi/Y)$$

The customs component: C (Ai/A)

The pooled customs revenue will be distributed according to intra-SACU imports. On the basis of 1998/99 trade, South Africa would have contributed about 80% to the customs component, and its share of this component would have been 20.5% (in 1998/99 South Africa's intra-SACU imports were R 7,520 million, while total intra-SACU imports amounted to R 36,706 million). On the same basis, the BLNS would have contributed around 20% to the customs component, and their shares of the customs pool would have been: Botswana (26.6%), Lesotho (13.4%), Namibia (24.9%), and Swaziland (14.6%). These shares are expected to remain stable over time, though the size of the customs pool (C) will depend upon the value of imports and changes to the SACU tariff regime.

The excise component: (0.85) E (GDPi/GDP)

The size of the excise component has been set initially at 85% of the excise pool, and will be distributed on the basis of the GDP of each of the SACU countries. In 1998, South Africa's GDP represented 92.8% of SACU's total GDP, and its share of this component would have been 78.9% (92.8 times 0.85). The remainder of the 85% of the excise component would have been distributed as follows: Botswana (3.0%), Lesotho (0.5%), Namibia (1.8%), and Swaziland (0.8%).

The development component: (0.3) E (11- Yi/Y)

The development component has been set initially at 15% of the excise pool, and will be distributed inversely to each country's GDP per capita: the smaller the GDP per capita, the greater the share of the development pool. In 1998, GDP per capita in the SACU area was: Botswana (R 17,968), Lesotho (R 2,395), Namibia (R 9,615), South Africa (R 17,578), and Swaziland (R 7,024); this leads to an average GDP per capita of R

10,916. On this basis, the 15% share of the development component would have been distributed as follows: Botswana (2.80%), Lesotho (3.23%), Namibia (3.04%), South Africa (2.82%), and Swaziland (3.11%).

The composition of SACU payment by component:

On the basis of the previous figures, the BLNS countries would largely derive their SACU revenue from the customs component: Namibia (83.7%), Botswana (82.1%), Swaziland (78.9%), and Lesotho (78.2%); while South Africa would receive 20.1% from this component. South Africa would get the majority of its SACU revenue from the excise component (77.2%), followed by Botswana (9.3%), Namibia (6.1%), Swaziland (4.3%), and Lesotho (2.9%). The development component is relatively more important for Lesotho and Swaziland (18.9% and 16.8%, respectively, of their total SACU revenues), followed by Namibia (10.2%), Botswana (8.6%), and South Africa (2.7%).

Source: WTO (2009):18f

Another problem is that of competing membership particular with regard to COMESA. While there is no problem between SACU and SADC membership as all members of SACU also belong to SADC and SADC has made great strides towards becoming a customs union itself ([83]), Lesotho and Namibia terminated their COMESA membership mainly because of conflicting regulations between SACU and COMESA ([84]). However, Swaziland remained a member of COMESA. The small kingdom is also part of another controversy: as a COMESA member it is not part of the *Eastern and Southern African Economic Partnership Agreement* (ESA EPA) region to which most COMESA members belong and has been pressurised to leave the SADC EPA framework, to which all other SACU members (South Africa as an observer) belong. With the signing of an *Interim EPA* with some countries of the ESA negotiation group ([85]) in August 2009 more pressure on Swaziland to join in has been exerted. However, if Swaziland would leave the SADC EPA and join the ESA EPA this would cause major problems for its membership in SACU as it would open the SACU market not only to European goods and services but would make it more difficult for the SADC EPA countries to negotiate an (*Interim*) EPA on its own and to its conditions.

The ultimate aim of SACU – to establish a Common Market – may thus be a rather ambitious one especially if the smaller member states still feel they do not receive their fair share of benefits and if reforms of crucial RI arrangements

83 See: Chapter 10.2.2
84 See: Hofmeier (2004):214; Meyn 2006:145
85 The Interim EPA was signed between the EU and Mauritius, Seychelles, Zimbabwe and Madagascar; Zambia and the Comoros indicated they would sign later; see: The Sub-Saharan Reporter, 4..09.2009

already agreed in 2002 are still not fully implemented. The unresolved issue of the EPAs pose another uncertainty for the future development of SACU.

Although being the oldest still existing African RI body and oldest continuously operating customs union worldwide, SACU has often been overlooked when RI is discussed in the African context. While this may be understandable to some extent with regard to its tainted history as a product of colonial rule and a "pet" of *apartheid* South Africa, SACU's development after 1994 merit more attention. It is after all one of the very few if not the only functioning customs union on the African continent. The new treaty of 2002 contains elements which can give guidance to other RI bodies and especially to SADC of how to develop solutions for the crucial areas of cost-benefit sharing and setting of tariffs as well as monetary integration. The latest developments are also a showcase of the problems arising of the WTO-inspired global free trade arrangements for small countries existing "*in the shadow of a mountain*" ([86]).

5.2. The Central African Federation (CAF)

While SACU has its roots in colonial times but continues to exist and function till today, the other major colonial attempt to establish a regional integration scheme in Southern Africa – the ***Central African Federation*** (CAF) – did not survive the end of colonialism. It existed between 1953 and 1963 between the then three British colonies of Southern and Northern Rhodesia (later Zimbabwe and Zambia), Nyasaland (later Malawi).

In contrast to other RI bodies that were formed in Africa at later stages, the CAF was in character a federal body with a number of institutions and regulations. CAF was to some extent an early and rather artificial attempt to establish a supranational body. However, as it was a construction forced on the majority of the people by a colonial regime in the interest of a ruling settler minority, it had never a real chance to flourish and last. In fact, the political character of the Federation was only meant to hide the economic motivations behind its formation.

But being a political body with a federal assembly (in which the Southern Rhodesian settlers dominated) its mere existence stirred the anti-colonial resistance especially in Northern Rhodesia and Nyasaland. CAF became a rallying point for the liberation movements in those colonies, as they perceived

86 This is the title of a paper by Sandrey, R. (2007) on SACU.

the federation as an instrument to benefit the white settler colony in Southern Rhodesia ([87]). Costs and benefits of the federation were unequally distributed between the three members, benefitting predominantly Southern Rhodesia. While Nyasaland was treated as a reserve for cheap labour ([88]), the considerable income from the booming copper mines of Northern Rhodesia were to a large extent utilised for the further development of the Southern Rhodesian infrastructure and industry ([89]).

The dominance of Southern Rhodesian settler interests in the federal Parliament and thus administration, assured that the revenue from the customs union and Northern Rhodesian mines went to a great extent, into the development of the settler colony at the expense of the other members. This was symbolised strongly by the building of the Kariba dam at the Zambezi River, which was financed mainly by the income from the Northern Rhodesian copper mines. The competing Kafue dam project close to the Northern Rhodesian capital Lusaka was, however, rejected although it would have fitted Northern Rhodesia's interests much better ([90])

With the coming of independence to Northern Rhodesia and Nyasaland in 1964, CAF ceased to have a political and economic basis and was quietly put to rest. Partly due to the negative memories connected with CAF, RI was regarded with some suspicion by Malawi and Zambia. In fact, neither country joined another RI body or attempted to establish one until 1979 when the Southern African Development Coordination Conference (SADCC) was founded.

5.3. Conclusion

In Southern Africa, RI had its roots already in colonial times and has thus always been a concept, economic planners and politicians alike were aware of. Both major attempts – SACU and CAF – however, also tainted the idea of RI due to their instrumentalization for preserving and/or serving the interests of (racist) minority regimes. This can be regarded as one of the reasons why it took

87 See, Ki Zerbo, Joseph (1981)

88 A substantial percentage of adults were forced through heavy tax burdens ('hut tax') to look for work in the mines of Northern Rhodesia and farms and households of Southern Rhodesia.

89 According to Green/Seidman (1969), Southern Rhodesia accounted for 56% of all investments during the federation period and even for 75% of all investments into the manufacturing industry.

90 See Hazlewood 1967:217

so long after independence for RI to take root in the region again. A related reason was the domination of SACU through *apartheid* South Africa, which delegitimized RI in the eyes of the liberation movements. However, when RI was finally accepted as a means to improve chances for economic development and to lower dependence from South Africa ([91]), it took into consideration some of the lessons learned from the colonial attempts of RI:

- to avoid domination by one member state,
- to create a common physical infrastructural foundation for integration; and
- to base RI on a political rationale superseding a mere economic justification.

---

91 See: Chapter 7.1.3.

6. Pan-Africanist Integration Attempts

Many of the first leaders of independent African states such as *Kwame Nkrumah* (Ghana), *Sekou Toure* (Guinea) or *Julius Nyerere* (Tanzania) were influenced by pan-Africanist ideas ([92]). For them, the liberation from colonial rule was thus not just a 'national' task, but a continental one. Nkrumah's slogan "*Africa must unite*" was never forgotten and was recalled in a timely fashion by former South African President Thabo Mbeki in 2002 during his speech at the inauguration of the African Union (AU). Pan-Africanism despite its illusiveness in practical politics remains to the current day an important part of the identity of the African elites and an engine for continuous attempts to unite Africa. It was the main ideological concept behind the formation of the Organisation of African Unity (OAU) in 1963 and it is still influencing the policies of its successor, the AU.

6.1. Pan-African (Pipe-)Dream of Integration: The Organisation of African Unity (OAU)

The Organisation of African Unity (OAU) was established in 1963 – at the height of decolonisation – in *Addis Abeba*, Ethiopia. Eventually all but one (Morocco) of the 53 independent states of Africa became OAU members. In 2002, the OAU was transformed into the African Union (AU).

The OAU was predominantly a political body, formed after lengthy negotiations in 1963 by 30 Heads of State as a compromise between a 'radical' socialist group of countries, which advocated for immediate African unity (so called *Casablanca Group*) and a more conservative alliance (so called *Monrovia Group*), which was in favour of a gradual integration process through smaller blocs ([93]). Instead of a supranational body (*United States of Africa*), the OAU ended up as a lose-knit organisation whose main aims were (according to the *OAU-Charta*):

1. Unity and Solidarity amongst African States
2. Coordination of intra-African and international cooperation

---

92 See: e.g. Green and Seidman (1968); McCarthy (2007)

93 See: Ngwenya, S. (2008): Regional Integration in COMESA. Paper prepared for the 13th COMESA Summit of Heads of States and Government in Victoria Falls (Zimbabwe), on 7-8 December 2008. mimeo

3. Protection and defence of the sovereignty, territorial integrity and independence of its member states (but not being a defence treaty)
4. Overcoming all forms of colonialism
5. Promotion of international cooperation on the basis of the UN-Charta and the Declaration on Human Rights

The long-dominating issue of liberation from colonial rule came to an end in 1994 when South Africa for the first time elected a democratic Government. That together with guaranteeing the established (colonial) borders and the non-interference in the internal affairs of its member states ([94]) can be regarded as the most important principles of the OAU. Apart from these two issues, the OAU activities exhausted themselves mostly in the adoption of (non-binding) declarations. The impotence of the OAU due to its 'non-interference principle' became painstakingly visible during the Rwandan genocide, when an African intervention to protect the *Tutsi* (and moderate *Hutu*) could not be organised.

For most of its existence, the OAU has been pre-occupied with pan-African ideas of African unity heavily influenced by some of its dominant founding fathers such as *Nkrumah* and *Toure*. Their dream of a United States of Africa never really died despite the sobering realities on the ground (disintegrating states, genocides and an increasing number of internal and inter-state conflicts and wars). It has been resurrected by Libya's *Muammar a-Ghaddafi* in 1999 and was intensively discussed in recent years as one of the strategic objectives of the African Union (AU) ([95]).

Concerned mainly with political issues, the OAU left the economic field to a UN-institution: the ***Economic Commission for Africa*** (ECA). The ECA started advocating for RI on the African continent already in the 1960s. ECA was also the main author of the *Lagos Plan of Action* (1980), which became the first pan-African concept for integrating Africa economically via the establishment of RI

---

94 It may be argued though that this contributed to the political strife encompassing the continent. The colonial borders not only divided political entities and ethnic groups but also confined historical adversaries to the same state thus contributing to the long series of bloody civil wars, liberation wars, failing states and even genocides. *Nzongola-Ntalaja* (2002:3) even goes as far as saying: "*Governments were free to massacre their citizens without interference from OAU member states ...*". However, without the border guarantee Africa might have disintegrated politically especially in the turbulent years immediate after gaining independence.

95 See Sturman, K. (2007), New growth on deep roots. Prospects for an African Unity Government. ISS Paper No. 146, Pretoria; see also Chapter 6.2.

bodies. It envisaged three regional arrangements in the three main African sub-regions ([96]):

- In West Africa, the already existing ECOWAS would take care of RI.
- For Southern and Eastern Africa, the Lagos Plan of Action foresaw the establishment of the Preferential Trade Area (PTA), which was established in 1981.
- Central Africa was to be catered for by the Economic Community of Central African States (ECCAS), which treaty was approved in 1983 but never fully ratified.

The Lagos Plan of Action also wanted to include the Arab Maghreb Union (AMU) to round up the geographical arrangements for the formation of a common African market until 2000.

It is interesting to note that the OAU and the ECA were rather pragmatic when it came to other RI bodies, which had emerged outside the framework of the Lagos Plan of Action. ECOWAS, SACU and SADC(C) for example have always been treated as additional to the proposed regional architecture and not as adversaries. There was, however, substantial unease regarding the efforts of ECA to promote African economic unity on the side especially of SADC(C). It regarded first the PTA and later its successor COMESA as competitors and issued a political directive that member states could not be a member of both organisations ([97]). As a consequence, Lesotho, Mozambique, Namibia and Tanzania withdrew from COMESA, while the Seychelles left SADC for a while (2005-8) ([98]).

Much of the initial conceptual ideas regarding economic integration of Africa as proposed by ECA were developed on the basis of the neo-classical model of RI and tried to copy the EU. As *Clapham* ([99]) notes, this was "*a completely misconceived analogy*" as hardly any of the preconditions (complementary production structures; functioning regional transport and banking systems; export-oriented industrialisation; sufficiently large national and regional markets

---

96 See Mathews, A. (2003) Regional Integration and Food Security in Developing Countries. Prepared for theAgricultural Policy Support Service Policy Assistance Division. Training Materials For Agricultural Planning 45. FAO, Rome. http://www.fao.org/docrep/004/Y4793E/y4793e0a.htm

97 At the 1995 Summit, SADC leaders reaffirmed their position taken 1994 that "*...the region covered by the geographical area of COMESA should be split into PTA North and PTA South; the latter comprising the current SADC member States.*" This motion was raised and defeated at a COMESA meeting in April 1996 in Lusaka; see: http://www.sardc.net/editorial/Dev/dev1/SadcIntegration.html

98 See: Meyn (2006):146

99 Clapham (2001):59

etc.) which made RI so successful in Europe existed in the African context. It was thus not surprising that none of the early endeavours of RI in Africa (with the exception of SACU) produced the desired results.

When it became apparent that the Lagos Plan of Action and its objectives were by no means achievable, the OAU, again with the support of ECA and now also the ***African Development Bank*** (AfDB), drafted the text of the *Abuja Treaty* in 1991 which foresees the establishment of an ***African Economic Community*** (AEC) until 2025 ([100]). It entered into force in 1994 after two thirds of the OAU member states had ratified the Treaty. The Abuja Treaty envisages a six-stage process towards the creation of a continent wide economic union strongly rooted in the neo-classical approach towards RI. The model is still based on the EU but incorporates developmental and political elements.

TEXT BOX 6.1.: The Phases of Achieving the AEC

Phase	Objective	Timeframe
1	Creation of regional blocs in regions where such do not yet exist	Until 1999
2	Strengthening of intra-REC integration and inter-REC harmonization.	Until 2007
3	Establishing of a Free Trade Area and Customs Union in each regional bloc.	Until 2017
4	Establishing a continent-wide Customs Union and thus also a Free Trade Area	Until 2019
5	Establishing of a continent-wide African Common Market or ACM	Until 2023
6	Establishing of a continent-wide economic and monetary union (and thus also a currency union) and pan-African Parliament	Until 2028
7	End of all transition periods	Latest by 2034

Source: ECA (2008a):29

But even with this renewed commitment the economic and political integration of the African continent faced several, often massive, obstacles as even ECA

100 Later adjusted to 2034 as the final date of all transitions to the AEC

had to admit. The major structural impediments to RI before the African Union (AU) was established have been summarized as follows ([101]):

- The prevalence of North-South instead of South-South relationships of many African countries involved in RI attempts: high dependence from former colonial masters in the context of the *francophonie*, the *Commonwealth* and the *Lomé Conventions*. Most African countries are incorporated "*as sources of primary products and markets for manufactured goods and services, within a global structure of north-south trade dominated by their colonial metropoles*" ([102]).
- The insufficient participation of the private sector and the general public in the promotion of RI; instead all regional organisations are driven by Governments or public sector organisations. This has led to a preponderance of bureaucracies in RI and is stifling popular ownership.
- A tendency amongst Governments while showing only limited commitment to the actual objectives of RI (expressed by their unwillingness to relinquish even tiny bits of national sovereignty to a supra-national institution and to honour their financial obligations) to utilise regional bodies as instruments of political patronage (political appointments) and political showmanship (during summits). As a consequence, many regional integration efforts remained at the planning stage rather than progressing to actual implementation.
- The existence of several weak (or "soft") states in Africa, which are afraid to share power with regional bodies and thus weaken these institutions. "*Politically, arrangements for regional integration fell foul of the intense concern of the rulers of newly independent African states for the maintenance of their own sovereignty, and indeed for the preservation of their own power within their states*" ([103]). As a result, instead of creating supra-national institutions RI in Africa has led often to mere "intergovernmental" structures barely above the level of cooperation but substantively short of integration.

Another, often underestimated factor that made RI a difficult endeavour in the African context has been the import-substitution model of industrialisation, which was favoured by many African states for the first two decades of independence. It fostered despite all integration rhetoric at regional summits an inward looking, protectionistic and interventionist approach towards economic policies and regional cooperation. Only with the collapse of this paradigm amidst mounting debts, high inflation and burgeoning fiscal deficits in the early

---

101 See Mathews, A. (2003): chapter 6
102 Clapham (2001):60
103 Clapham (2001):60

1980s and the subsequent enforced application of IMF-sponsored structural adjustment programs (SAP) became many African economies sufficiently liberalised to concur with the minimum requirements of a trade-led integration model. However, some economies were liberalised so intensively that they were eventually more integrated into the global economy (through free trade) than into regional RI bodies. The radical liberalisation of the Zambian economy for example after *Fredrick Chiluba* ([104]) in October 1991 took over from *Kenneth Kaunda* - one of the stalwarts of interventionist economic policies in Africa - destroyed within a few years nearly all of Zambia's infant manufacturing industry ([105]). The interest of the Zambian Government and business sector in regional economic integration has since always been conspicuously muted: regional economic integration did not offer much in terms of tangible advantages; in fact, a free trade arrangement in the region or a customs union inevitably leads to costly ***→trade diversion***.

In 2001, at a summit of the Heads of State in Lusaka (Zambia) the majority of African states agreed to transform the OAU into the AU. This can be seen both as a reaction to the OAU's embarrassing role during the Rwanda genocide and the recognised need to intensify the efforts aimed at economic integration of the continent.

6.2. The African Union (AU): A Genuinely New Approach?

The African Union was officially established in 2002 at a summit in Durban (South Africa).

The major difference between OAU and AU lies in its mandate regarding the continental security architecture. Whereas the OAU had insisted on total sovereignty of African states and persevered on a non-intervention approach, the

104 Chiluba was a former Secretary General of the Zambian Congress of Trade Unions (ZCTU) and as such not automatically suspected of being a supporter of economic liberalisation. However, driven both by the strong faction of 'businessmen' (often with relations to drug traffickers) in his Government and the donors which provided a large 'democracy bonus' against economic reforms, the Chiluba Government abolished more or less all duties for the imports of not only raw materials but also finished products. One result was that in 1993 20 out of 22 textile producers in the southern city of Livingstone had to close down; see Peters-Berries, C. (1995): Sambia – Von Demokraten, Drogenschiebern und Wendehälsen. Unpublished manuscript. mimeo

105 Which had been protected by high duties and heavy Government subsidies and was far from capable to compete in a liberalized market.

AU – in the light of the genocide in Ruanda and the collapse of states in Liberia, Sierra Leone and, most pronounced, Somalia – agreed on the principle of "*Responsibility to Protect*". This can even mean the right of the AU to actively restore peace and stability if legitimate order is seriously threatened or overthrown ([106]).

However, there has also been a noticeable change with regard to economic integration facilitated by the realization that for Africa to unite, the previous attempts of economic integration were insufficient and based on illusionary ideas and objectives. The original integration concepts of the OAU which had been heavily influenced by import substitution and protectionism and which found their expression in the Lagos Plan of Action had been gradually replaced by more liberalized and pragmatic ideas. The Abuja Treaty of 1991 was the first expression of this new thinking; it was further reinforced by the Sirte Declaration of 1999 ([107]) and the Constitutive Act establishing the African Union ([108]).The ideas of the Abuja Treaty have been reaffirmed as the prevailing concept for economic integration in Africa.

> *"The Abuja Treaty Establishing the African Economic Community (AEC) in 1994 [...] laid a new framework and foundation for Africa's integration, with regional economic communities (RECs) as the building blocs."* ([109])

A change at the helm of the ECA in the first half of the 1990s, which had been and continued to be the conceptual mastermind behind the attempts of regional economic integration in Africa, helped to alter the conceptual outlook further. In 2004, the ECA published its first of - so far - three *Assessments of Regional Integration in Africa* (ARIA) ([110]). This followed up on an earlier attempt (1993) by the African Development Bank (AfDB) to provide an overview of the state of RI in Southern Africa but has been more comprehensive and topic centred than the regional AfDB report ([111]). In 2006, the African Heads of State at the Summit of the AU in *Banjul* (The Gambia), mandated ECA to continue to play a vital role in assisting and facilitating the work of the RECs in advancing the development agenda on the continent.

---

106 See Fandrych 2008:2

107 OAU (1999) Sirte Declaration, Fourth Extraordinary Session of the Assembly of Heads of State and Government, Sirte, Libya 8.-9.9.1999

108 AU (2002) Constitutive Act of the African Union. http://www.au2002.gov.za/docs/key_oau/au_act.htm

109 ECA (2008): ix

110 While planned as an annual assessment, so far only three reports have been produced by ECA; the first in May 2004, the second in May 2006 and the latest was in November 2008. See www.uneca.org

111 AfDB (1993), Economic Integration in Southern Africa. Abidjan.

The AU considers eight of the more than 20 existing regional integration schemes in Africa, which are covering five sub-continental regions, as the building blocs for the African Economic Community (AEC) ([112]). These are:

- CEN-SAD in the northern part of Africa
- COMESA in the southern and eastern parts of Africa
- EAC in East Africa
- ECCAS/CEEAC in Central Africa (including CEMAC)
- ECOWAS in Western Africa (including UEMOA)
- IGAD in Eastern Africa (Horn of Africa)
- SADC in Southern Africa (including SACU)
- AMU/UMA in Northern Africa

Table 6.1. Recognised REC's, their Objectives and Status

Community	Specified Objective	Status	Comments
CEN-SAD	Free trade area and integration in some sectors	Free trade area stalled	Not yet achieved
COMESA	Common Market	Customs union proposed for 2008	Progress exists to a large extent only on paper
EAC	Full economic union	Customs union in force	Progress but unclear how much is really implemented
ECCAS/CEEAC	Full economic union	Free trade area proposed for 2007; customs union proposed for 2011	Not yet achieved
ECOWAS	Full economic union	Customs union proposed for 2008	Not yet achieved
IGAD	Full economic union	Stalled	Internal blockage
SADC	Full economic union	Free trade area achieved 2008; customs union proposed for 2010	Slow but steady progress
AMU/UMA	Full economic union	stalled	Not yet achieved

Source: www.AU.int; own compilation

112 See: ECA (2008): 28ff

Table 6.2.:The Eight RECs of the AEC in Comparison (2004)

REC	Area (km²)	Population	GDP (PPP) ($US)		Member states
			in millions	per capita	
AEC	**29,910,442**	**853,520,010**	**2,053,706**	**2,406**	**53**
ECOWAS	5,112,903	251,646,263	342,519	1,361	15
ECCAS	6,667,421	121,245,958	175,928	1,451	11
SADC	9,882,959	233,944,179	737,335	3,152	15
EAC	1,817,945	124,858,568	104,239	1,065	5
COMESA	12,873,957	406,102,471	735,599	1,811	20
IGAD	5,233,604	187,969,775	225,049	1,197	7
Other African blocs					
CEMAC *	3,020,142	34,970,529	85,136	2,435	6
SACU *	2,693,418	51,055,878	541,433	10,605	5
UEMOA *	3,505,375	80,865,222	101,640	1,257	8
UMA **	5,782,140	84,185,073	491,276	5,836	5

Source: CIA World Factbook 2005, IMF WEO Database
Explanations:
* = Economic bloc inside a pillar REC
**= Proposed for pillar REC, but objecting participation

According to the Abuja Treaty, (see text box 6.1.) they shall merge by 2019 to a continent-wide customs union. This will be the decisive step to reach after some nine more years to the stage of an African economic and monetary union. Even its main promoter, the ECA, however, understands that this will not be a smooth development but one which has to clear substantial obstacles:

- The issue of overlapping membership in two or more regional blocs has to be sorted out. According to the roadmap of the Abuja Treaty, this was to be accomplished by 2007. However by the end of 2008, the process of harmonization had just started. Some countries such as Egypt, Eritrea and Djibouti are members of at least three regional blocs (CEN-SAD, IGAD, COMESA), while others such as Swaziland belong to SACU, SADC and COMESA at the same time. Many other countries are members of at least two major regional blocs ([113]). If one country belongs to two RI bodies which have reached different levels of integration, it can act like a *Trojan Horse* in the more advanced RI body. Tanzania is a member of SADC, which reached the level of a FTA in 2008, and of the EAC, which became a customs union in 2005. According to this arrangement it is possible for SADC members to export via Tanzania (with which they have an open trade regime) to the

113 See Meyn (2006):144ff

EAC, which has adopted a common external customs tariff against imports from outside the region. Tanzania with its double membership may have opened a door into the EAC (and Kenya, its most advanced economy) for South African products. This also applies *vice versa* but since products from the EAC are less competitive than those from South Africa the potential damage could take place in the EAC.

- The membership issue has been further complicated by the negotiations between the EU and African countries to restructure trade relations under the *Cotonou-Agreement* in a manner compatible with World Trade Organisation (WTO) rules. The mechanism proposed by the EU to achieve this are the so called "*Economic Partnership Agreements*" (EPA), which intend to transform the old non-reciprocal trade preference granted by the EU to the ACP countries into economic integration agreements ([114]). However, disregarding the regional integration architecture as defined by the AU, the EU demarcated its own "African regions" for the EPA negotiations. While west and central African EPA regions correspond more or less with ECOWAS and CEMAC, countries of East and Southern Africa have been grouped in two EPA regions ([115]) cutting across the existing RI bodies SADC, EAC and COMESA. As the EU constitutes for most African countries the biggest market for both in terms of im- and exports, a trade agreement with the EU is for them often more important than intra-African regional integration. Although so far only interim EPAs have been signed with some of the eastern and southern African states, the unresolved membership question has disturbed the regional integration process within SADC, EAC and COMESA on the one hand ([116]) and has on the other hand probably accelerated the unification process amongst the existing RI bodies. In 2008, the leaders of SADC, EAC and COMESA agreed to join forces

114 See Mathews, A. (2003):chapter 6

115 Namely, the "Eastern and Southern African Region" (ESA) and the SADC region. The SADC EPA comprises of the SACU members minus South Africa, Angola, Mozambique and Tanzania. The other SADC members DR Congo, Madagascar, Malawi, Mauritius, Zambia and Zimbabwe, as well as the EAC members minus Tanzania and the remaining COMESA members except Egypt and Libya opted for the ESA EPA. South Africa, which entered into a Free Trade Agreement with the EU in 2000, was given the status as an observer; see Meyn: 147.

116 Tanzania e.g. left COMESA in 2000 but is a member of both SADC and the EAC. In terms of EPA alignment it chose to join the SADC EPA in order to intensify its relations to South Africa. This, however, upset the customs union arrangements within the EAC. The case of the DR Congo – a member of SADC since 1997 - is even more interruptive for RI in Southern Africa as it opted to join the CEMAC EPA without even being a member of CEMAC; see Meyn 2006:147ff.

and establish a Free Trade Area by 2012 ([117]) in an obvious response to overcome the divisions created by the EPA negotiation process and the problems emanating from that for RI in Southern and Eastern Africa.

- Actual trade-based regional integration is making very slow, if any progress at all ([118]) as the percentage of intra-African trade is remaining at a very low level. This is attributed to the lack of "*a strong industrial capacity to produce diversified manufactured goods for trade within regional markets*" ([119]). If there are no goods to trade, how can countries engage in successful regional economic integration?
- Doing business in Africa is still rather expensive "*due in part to infrastructure gaps, duplicative border procedures and cumbersome paper requirements*" ([120]). This means that even those goods being traded within African FTA's or Customs Unions are traded at considerable higher costs than they have to, making such trade less lucrative and attractive.
- With a few exceptions, African currencies are not convertible to each other forcing many countries to use US-$ or € as the currency for even intra-regional trade.

The latest assessment report on RI in Africa by ECA (2008) comes thus to the conclusion that "*outcomes of decades of experimentation with integration in Africa have on balance remained modest*" ([121]). However, it must be conceded as well that as compared to the previous decades under the OAU, the AU has attached a new emphasis to economic regional integration and gave new impetus to the old (and nearly forgotten?) objectives of the Abuja Treaty regarding the establishment of an African Economic Community. Although probably externally induced, the October 2008 principle agreement of the leaders of COMESA, EAC and SADC countries to create a unified free trade zone can be regarded as a first success on the rocky way of establishing the AEC. As far as economic integration in Africa is concerned, the AU has not just relabelled the

---

117 See: The Daily Monitor (Addis Abeba), 29.10.2008; also: Disenyana, Tsidiso (2009), Towards an EAC, COMESA and SADC Free Trade Area. Issues and challenges. AfDB Working Paper, October 2009. http://www.afdb.org/fileadmin/uploads/afdb/Documents/Knowledge/2009%20AEC-%20Towards%20an%20EAC%20COMESA%20and%20SADC%20Free%20Trade%20Area%20Issues%20and%20Challenges.pdf

118 See: AFREXIMBANK (2008; 2009) African Trade Reports 2007, 2008. Cairo

119 ECA (2008): 29. The missing trade potential of African RI attempts had already been noticed by Oyejide, Ademola T. (2000): Policies for Regional Integration in Africa. Economic Research Papers No. 62, AfDB, Abidjan: 11

120 ECA (2008): 29

121 ECA (2000):29

old concepts but has facilitated, with the assistance of an equally changed ECA, some progress .

6.3. The Latest Attempt: The New Partnership for African Development (NEPAD)

One feature that has given RI, under the auspices of the AU, a new dynamic and legitimation is the → ***New Partnership for African Development*** (NEPAD). Launched on the initiative of former South African President *Thabo Mbeki* together with former Nigerian President *Olusegun Obasanjo* and Senegalese President *Wade*, NEPAD was still adopted by the OAU and immediately awarded the status of an AU organ at the inaugural meeting of the AU in Durban in 2002. It can be described not as a new regional integration program, but rather a mechanism to make better use of existing ones ([122]).

As an organ of the AU, NEPAD has its own secretariat which was at the beginning conspicuously South African (location in Midrand; South African Director-General) but started to emancipate itself after some years. In 2005, a Mozambican chief executive (*Firmino Mucavele*) was appointed. He resigned in 2008 and was succeeded in 2009 by the former Niger Prime Minister *Ibrahim Hassane Mayaki* ([123])

NEPAD has conceptual roots both in Pan-Africanism and the concept of "***African Renaissance***" as developed ([124]) by Thabo Mbeki. It can be regarded as the amalgamation of various ideas and concepts discussed in the second half of the 1990s of how to give Africa's development a new impetus ([125]). They all

---

122 Breytenbach, Willie (2002), The African Renaissance, NEPAD and the African Union: The Prospects for Co-operation and Integration in Africa. In: Hansohm, Peters-Berries, Breytenbach, Hartzenberg, Maier, Meyns, Monitoring Regional Integration in Southern Africa, Volume 2 – 2002. Windhoek 2002: 171

123 See: http://www.nepad.org/2005/news/wmview.php?ArtID=95

124 Some scholars such as Nzongola-Ntalaja (2002) might argue that Mbeki merely rediscovered or revived an idea already put forward by Marcus Garvey, one of the early champions of Pan-Africanism, during the 1920s; see: Nzongola-Ntalaja, G (2002), Good Governance and Conflict Management – Will the African Union make a Difference? Paper presented at the Evening Forum, Norwegian Peacebuilding Empowerment Programme, Oslo, 4th September 2002.

125 Obasanjo had developed the concept of a Conference on Security, Stability, Development and Co-operation' in the late 1990s, while Wade had come forward with an 'Omega' Plan for Africa's revival.

center on the need to provide Africa with an enabling modern infrastructure (transportation, communication, energy, education, health etc.) which should be financed by western donors (G8) in order to achieve an annual growth rate of 7%. According to the NEPAD secretariat, this would cost USD 64 billion annually ([126]). The deal proposed by the AU and NEAPAD was to offer the assurance of Good Governance and promotion of democracy against the funding of the proposed projects. However, it remained unclear which institution – NEPAD secretariat, UN-ECA or the African Development Bank – would devise and handle the infrastructural projects. As a result, donors remained reluctant to commit themselves ([127]), and so far, little has been realized in terms of these grand plans.

Despite the rather unimpressive performance of NEPAD with regard to raising funds for infrastructural projects, one of its features has raised hopes that Africa really means business with regard to development and democracy: the → ***African Peer Review Mechanism*** (APRM). The APRM is the attempt of African governments to institutionalize (although participation is voluntary) a regular, independent and constructive assessment of their political and socio-economic development. Once governments have signed the APRM, they are obliged to conduct a first round self-assessment before a team of eminent African experts (peers) undertakes the actual review by consulting representatives from all major stakeholder groups in society including civil society. By 2009, seven countries have undertaken the full peer review: Ghana, Ruanda, Kenya, Uganda, Algeria, South Africa and Nigeria. The reports need to be officially adopted at AU-Summits before they can be accessed through the internet ([128]). By mid 2008, 29 countries had formerly joined the Memorandum of Understanding of the APR.

The assessment results and recommendations of the so far available reviews point out weaknesses in the respective national development processes. For example, in Ghana, the low representation of women in politics was highlighted, while in Kenya the widespread corruption was criticized. It is interesting to not that in many instances the recommendations of the APRM are quite similar to those proposed by the World Bank in the 'Poverty Reduction Strategy Papers' (PRSP). However, the recommendations emanating from the APRM process are far more acceptable to the respective governments as they are the result of a national and voluntary and not of an externally enforced assessment. It has thus

126 See Breytenbach (2002): 176

127 The donors quickly declared that the handling of the unfolding Zimbabwe Crisis after 2002 would be the 'lackmus test' for NEPAD and used the AU's and NEPAD's unwillingness to intervene as an excuse to remain uncommitted towards NEPAD.

128 www.uneca.org/aprm/ and http://www.nepad.org/2005/files/aprm.php

been argued that the recommendations of the APRM's are much more likely to be implemented than those of the PRSP's ([129]).

With the existence of NEPAD and its APRM the AU has an instrument to promote crucial political standards for integration. Without the establishment and adherence to minimum standards of good governance regional and continental integration is not possible. NEPAD's APRM process is currently the most promising attempt to introduce such minimum standards.

129 The responsible expert for the APRM process at the ECA, Dr Busia, concluded this during a discussion on the APRM organised by the Heinrich Böll Stiftung in Addis Abeba in June 2007. mimeo

7. Post-Colonial Attempts of Regional Integration in Africa

In contrast to the pan-African view ([130]) which classifies the RI process in Africa with regard to its affinity to the OAU/AU devised integration plans (Lagos Plan of Action and Abuja Treaty) a second standpoint is more structural and considers the historic perspective as well as the preferred mechanism of RI ([131]). While the pan-African view considers RI as a means of achieving African unity and as one process, the structuralist approach differentiates historically between two 'post-colonial waves' of RI attempts and two different integrative models in Africa.

The first phase or "*first generation of regionalism*" ([132]) started in the 1960s and petered out towards the late 1980s. During this phase, the underlying idea was that by overcoming Africa's economic → ***balkanisation*** the project of political unity of the continent could be achieved. Nearly all RI attempts in this phase were based on the (neo-)classical model of economic integration and employed concepts of import-substituting industrialization. The rationale behind RI in this period is neatly summarized by McCarthy: "*... a perceived need to catch up with the developed world and to do so by using market integration as the solution to the problem of small markets and scarcity of resources of balkanized countries brought about by the artificial borders of imperial design"([133]).*

Although propelled forward by a sense of pan-African solidarity hardly any member state was willing to give up national sovereignty in favour of a regional super structure . *Nkrumah's* famous words "*Seek ye first the political kingdom and all else will follow*" described the political logic in many African states: political state consolidation was the parole of the day and economic considerations especially if they were related to RI were of secondary nature.

130 This is summarised by the Mathews, A. (2003): chapter 6

131 See: McCarthy, C. (2007): Is African economic integration in need of a paradigm change? Thinking out of the box on African integration. In: Bösl, T., Breytenbach, W., Hartzenberg, T., McCarthy, C., Schade, K (eds), Monitoring Regional Integration in Southern Africa Yearbook, Vol. 7 (2007), Stellenbosch (2007):10f

132 See: Awoumou, C. D. G. (2008): ECCAS or CEMAC? Which regional economic community for Central Africa? In: Ayangafac, C. (ed), Political economy of regionalisation in Central Africa. Tshwane (2008): 109. He links the first generation of regionalism to the Lagos Plan of Action and the second generation of RI bodies to the Abuja Treaty.

133 McCarthy, C. (2007):15

This phase coincided with the period of "Cold War" as well as with several political crises, coup d'états and civil wars.

The second phase or "*second generation of regionalism*" more or less started around the same time as the fall of the Berlin Wall and the sub-sequent second wave of democratization in Africa in the early 1990s and lasts until now; the dominant integration concept in the second phase is still the neo-classical, trade-based one but it has incorporated increasingly also political (security aspects) and developmental issues and is less static then previous attempts.

The pan-African agenda provides still the ideological cement for attempts to integrate sub-regional and regional markets. But since at least two of the most dynamic and successful RI attempts (EAC and SADC) have started outside the framework of the Lagos Plan of Action and on a pointedly regional rationale the driving force behind the current RI efforts is a more clearly perceived self-interest than in the past. Globalisation, problems with new qualities (HIV/AIDS; Climate Change) and rapidly improving communication possibilities have convinced several African leaders that their only hope of asserting themselves is to cooperate and pool resources.

7.1. The First 'Wave' of Regional Integration in Post-Colonial Africa

The first 'wave' or phase of RI in Africa had its roots in the already described pan-African dreams of African Unity, which found its expression in the formation of the OAU and produced only at a very late stage as its major document on the economic front, the Lagos Plan of Action in 1980. In the first years after independence, most African governments showed at first little or no interest in RI. The consolidation of their fragile new states had absolute priority and the painful memories of forced RI under colonial rule were still too fresh. Only in the 1970s some African leaders started to realise the potential of RI for the economic well being and political stability of their countries.

The few examples of RI to mention from this phase include

- the East African Community (EAC), which existed from 1967-1977, which had colonial origins;

- the Economic Community of West African States (ECOWAS) founded in 1975 and the Southern African Development Coordination Conference (SADCC) which existed from 1980-1992 which were established out of political necessities.

As Textbox 4.1. (see above) shows only one (UDEAC) new RI body was established during the 1960s apart from the EAC. And also the 1970s the saw relatively few new RI schemes emerge in sub-Saharan Africa. With the exception of ECOWAS and SADCC, which will be looked at with some detail later on ([134]), only the CEAO in West Africa ([135]), the CEPGL in the Great Lakes Region and the Frontline States (although with only political and no economic objectives) as the precursor of SADCC were established in this decade. That was despite the fact that the ECA actively advocated the establishment of RI bodies throughout Africa during the 1970s in line with its idea to have one big RI body for each of the four sub-regions of Africa ([136]). The difficulties in establishing new RI organisations in Africa during the second half of the 1970s when the idea was catching some renewed interests again had to do with the severe economic crisis Africa ([137]) was facing in this period. However, while UDEAC, CEAO and CEPGL carried on, albeit without much tangible success, the EAC was the only RI body which was officially dissolved: due to insurmountable differences between the member states it collapsed in 1977.

7.1.1. The East African Community (EAC) 1967-1977

The original EAC consisted of Kenya, Uganda and Tanzania. It had its roots in the colonial period (Customs Union in 1917; East African High Commission in 1948), which also continued after independence and formed the basis for the official establishment of the EAC in 1967. The EAC had a number of features,

134 See: Chapters 7.1.2. and7.1.3.

135 The CEAO was transformed into UEMOA in 1994; it was restricted to the French-speaking countries of West Africa and to some extent a result of the existence of the Franc-Zone.

136 Adedeji (2002):4f narrates the story of how ECA managed to facilitate the establishment first of ECOWAS in 1975, then of PTA in 1981 and lastly of ECCAS in 1983, which he regards as achievements under the Lagos Plan of Action.

137 Starting with the first oil-crisis in 1974, many African countries fell into the debt-trap and had by the early 1980s entered into IMF-orchestrated Structural Adjustment Programs, which had on balance disastrous socio-economic effects and led to a de-industrialization of African countries.

which made it one of the most promising attempts of neo-classically inspired RI in Africa:

- Regional identity formation through two common languages. While English was the generally accepted official language, the regional language ties were even further enhanced by the wide acceptance of Swahili as the region's colloquial language.
- The existence of joint regional service providers in banking (East African Development Bank), air traffic, railways, post & telecommunication, and harbour services.
- Regional political institutions in form of the East African Legislative Assembly and the East African Council of Ministers.
- Close infrastructural ties with a road and railway network that interconnected the region (Uganda and Kenya in particular).

That the EAC despite all the favourable conditions did not last longer than ten years was mainly due to ([138]):

- The Kenyan economic domination predominantly based on the large investments into the manufacturing industry during colonial times, which led to large deficits the intra-regional trade for Uganda and Tanzania.
- The gradually deepening perception in Uganda and Tanzania of an unequal distribution of costs and benefits of integration in the absence of any mechanisms to balance them.
- Divergent ideological convictions between Kenya (firmly pro-capitalist and western oriented) and Tanzania (socialist '*ujamaa*' orientation and leadership role in the Non-Aligned Movement).
- National economic policies of import-substitution which run contrary to the requirements of a customs union and led to the introduction of trade-preventing NTTBs.
- The political animosities, after *Idi Amin* took power in Uganda in a coup d'état in 1971, especially between the Tanzanian President *Julius Nyerere* and the Ugandan dictator.

Especially, the Kenyan dominance and the political divisions resulted in the paralysation of the regional administration and its various service providers. In 1977, after the border between Kenya and Tanzania was closed, the EAC was officially dissolved. With the EAC, one of the main attempts of RI based purely

138 See Mair/Peters-Berries (2001):88f

on neo-classical ideas and rooted in a common colonial history failed. This had repercussions for future attempts of RI especially in Southern Africa.

7.1.2. The Economic Community of Western African States (ECOWAS)

ECOWAS was established in 1975 and consisted then of 15 Anglophone, Francophone and Lusophone states; it was revamped in 1993 after a long period of inactivity and insignificance ([139]).

The initiative for the formation of ECOWAS came from Nigeria and Togo and was motivated mainly by political reasons:

- Competing hegemonial interests in the region not only pitted Nigeria against the francophone Cote d'Ivoire but also Cote d'Ivoire against Senegal. Nigeria hoped with the support of francophone Togo to ascertain a dominant role.
- Togo needed political support from Nigeria in simmering conflicts with Ghana, Benin and Burkina Faso.

Furthermore, the hope of the francophone countries to participate in the sudden Nigerian oil-based wealth of the mid-70s smoothened the way for the formation of ECOWAS. In the beginning, ECOWAS aimed mainly at RI through economic means. Another facilitative factor was the prevailing interest of the region's leaders to intensify South-South Cooperation.

ECOWAS never lived up to its promises in the first phase of its existence predominantly due to the:

- Divergences between Anglophone and francophone member states in terms of culture, language, institutional set up and political orientation.
- Increasing political instability of the region with several coups and civil wars ([140]).
- Economic decline of Nigeria in the late 1970s, which prevented it to play the much needed economic engine for RI

---

139 ibid: 185ff

140 West Africa is Africa's most volatile region as far as coup d'états and violent regime changes are concerned. It has, at least in Africa, the highest number of such unconstitutional regime changes for the last 40 years.

- Insufficient economic diversity ([141]) and immense divergences in terms of wealth between the member states.

Despite these significant impediments to deeper RI, ECOWAS was going through a stage of revitalisation in the early 1990s, which culminated in 1993 into a revised treaty, which adopted the principle of ***→variable geometry***, increased the importance of peace, stability, human rights and democracy as well as decisions made by the ECOWAS summits (see also chapter 7.2.3.).

7.1.3. The Southern African Development and Coordination Conference (SADCC)

SADCC was formed by nine Anglophone and Lusophone states in 1980 immediately after the independence of Zimbabwe. In 1990, Namibia became the tenth member of SADCC. In 1992, it was transformed into SADC.

SADCC was established on the initiative of the **→ *Frontline States*** (FLS) ([142]) with the view of breaking the economic dependency *apartheid* South Africa held over many of its neighbours in Southern Africa and in order to strengthen the ongoing liberation struggle in South Africa itself. The leaders of the FLS and prospective SADCC countries had realized three important issues:

1. The political struggle for liberalization needed an economic foundation to be successful. The mineral-rich landlocked countries of Botswana, Zambia and Zimbabwe had to route their external trade mainly through railway lines connected to South African harbours. In order to reduce this economic vulnerability ([143]), SADCC aimed at renovating and modernizing the railway lines to Mozambique and Angola as well as their harbours (Maputo, Beira, Nacala in Mozambique and Luanda and Lobito

---

141 The major source of economic income is the exploitation of either mineral or agricultural raw materials, which are not processed in the producing countries, but exported in a stage of low value.

142 Founded in 1974 after the collapse of the Portuguese colonial empire in Africa and consisting of Botswana, Tanzania, Mozambique, Zambia and Angola and Zimbabwe in 1980, the FLS dispersed when both Namibia and South Africa were liberated in the 1990s.

143 South Africa reduced fuel exports to Zimbabwe in December 1982, for example, to underscore its demands for Zimbabwe to stop supporting the African National Congress (ANC). Martin, David & Johnson, Phyllis (1986):71 in Johnson/Martin (eds.), Destructive Engagement. Southern Africa at war. Harare 1986

in Angola). The South African sponsored rebel movements in Mozambique and Angola, however, were able to destroy the link to Angola and interrupt the rail links to Maputo and Nacala; only the so called Beira-Corridor was kept open with massive support of the Zimbabwean army ([144]).

2. In order to integrate economically, a basic physical foundation in form of intra-regional infrastructure and institutions was necessary. Thus, SADCC's strong focus on transportation links (inclusive harbours), intra-regional energy and water supply as well as building up a regional strategic food reserve.
3. RI in Southern Africa with its strong emphasis on costly infrastructure programs did not have a realistic chance without getting the donor community involved. Consequently, the SADCC leaders lobbied for donor support for their various projects from the very beginning. Particularly, the Scandinavian countries, the EU, but also the Netherlands, UK, the USA and Germany provided substantial funds during the 12 years of SADCC's existence ([145]).

SADCC chose a – careful – cooperative approach to integration very much in line with neo-functionalist thinking and avoided the typical pitfalls of other African RI attempts: to aim at achieving too much too fast without the required resources and commitments. The probably most surprising thing about SADCC was that despite of the sometime fundamental political differences ([146]) and deep-rooted personal animosities of the leaders ([147]), the overarching consensus amongst all Governments was that without reducing the economic vulnerability from South Africa, no effective support to the liberation struggle both in South Africa and Namibia was possible. Moreover, even such conservative regimes

---

144 See Hanlon (1986), Peters (1987), Meyns (2001).

145 Until early 1997 – four years after SADC took over from SADCC – the regional body had received ca. 3.9 bill. USD from donors for regional projects; see Peters-Berries/Marx (1998):68

146 As for example between the ‚socialist' oriented allies of the Soviet Union such as Mozambique and Angola and the pro-western capitalist countries like Botswana, Malawi and Swaziland.

147 Zimbabwe's Robert Mugabe and Zambia's Kenneth Kaunda for example had clashed during the Zimbabwean liberation struggle, when Kaunda had openly supported and favoured Mugabe's rival Joshua Nkomo. This burdened the relationship between these leaders for nearly the whole time of SADCC's existence until Kaunda lost power in elections in October 1991. Likewise the relationship between several regional Heads of State and Malawi's Hastings Kamuzu Banda was strained due to the latter's support for the Mozambican rebels of RENAMO, assassinations and kidnapping of Malawian opposition politicians in/from Zambia and his rather friendly relationship with South Africa.

like that of *Hastings Kamuzu Banda* in Malawi could not afford to be seen as being against the liberation struggle.

However, SADCC never fully realized its potential due to the→ ***destabilisation policy*** (see Text Box 7.1.) of *apartheid* South Africa and a host of practical and conceptual problems:

- The request for donor support for the funding of the infrastructural projects was certainly a pragmatic necessity when SADCC started but it developed into a donor dependency, which in the end hampered if not paralysed the efforts of member states to mobilize and provide their own resources for strengthening regional cooperation and integration. In fact, in some cases, the most important reasons for SADCC membership seemed to have been the possible access to additional donor funding and no longer the idea of liberalisation and regional integration.
- SADCC countries had very similar production structures and thus trade structures. With the exception of Zimbabwe, no other SADCC member state had a manufacturing industry worth talking about. The production and export of unprocessed raw materials dominated in most other countries the structure of the economy (see also below tables 10.2 and 10.3.). The potential for intra-regional trade was thus weak. Expanding the transport sector to reduce the dependency from South Africa was thus cementing the unequal incorporation of the SADCC countries into the world market with the potential to deepen the already existing dependency patterns.
- Most SADCC countries had problems to ensure the functional and even territorial integrity of their states ([148]). As a consequence, the primacy of national sovereignty prevailed over the interests of regional cooperation. For example, the SADCC Food Security Unit, which was based in Harare (Zimbabwe), was never able to establish the intended regional food security reserve. The other member states preferred to keep or sell their agricultural surpluses rather than making it available for the region.

After Namibia had gained independence and joined SADCC in 1990, it become increasingly evident that the days of the *apartheid* regime in South Africa were numbered and a majority-ruled Government was only a question of time. In that case, the *raison d'être* for SADCC – the reduction of dependency from South Africa – would cease to exist but it would also open new opportunities for

148 That was particularly true for the countries ravaged by civil war such as Angola and Mozambique but to some extent also for countries such as Malawi (which hosted large numbers of Mozambican refugees as well as armed bands of the Mozambican rebels of *Renamo*) or Zambia, where the state was losing control over the sparsely populated peripheral areas.

regional integration. In anticipation of South Africa's 'liberation', the leaders of SADCC decided at a summit in Windhoek in 1992 to transform SADCC into SADC, to change from a regional functional co-operation concept to a trade-based regional integration model.

TEXT BOX 7.1.: South Africa's Destabilisation Policy towards SADCC

The *apartheid* Government of South Africa under *Pieter Willem Botha* (South African Prime Minister from 1978-1989) pursued an aggressive policy against its neighbors in order to defend their minority regime and prevent the neighboring states from providing assistance to the South African liberation movements ANC and PAC.

The Botha administration developed the '*total national strategy*' in order to ward off the *'total onslaught'* on *apartheid* both from internal and external forces. It was the attempt to modernize *apartheid* in order to enable it to survive in an increasingly antagonistic regional and international context. The new strategy conceded that this was not possible only with military oppression but that it also required the use of diplomatic, economic and socio-psychological means. The *total national strategy* was centered on the security apparatus of the *apartheid* regime.

The *total national strategy* had its regional expression in the concept of the *'Constellation of Southern African States'* (CONSAS). When it was announced in 1979, it was meant to counter the already discernable attempts of the FLS to create SADCC and divide the region. CONSAS was supposed to include, apart from South Africa, also the so called '*Bantustans'* (the pseudo-independent 'homelands' of South Africa) as well as the BLS-states and Malawi. Even Zambia and Zimbabwe were earmarked as potential members. The intensive economic dependency of the BLS-states and Malawi coupled with the economic 'blackmailing' potential concerning the landlocked countries, Zambia and from 1980 onwards Zimbabwe, were meant to serve as integrating mechanisms. The objective of CONSAS was to replace the previous buffer-zone of white-ruled regimes and colonies (Angola, Mozambique and Rhodesia) with a belt of dependent African states which would prevent the liberation movements to launch attacks against South Africa. The idea, however, did not find any support even amongst the conservative African regimes in Malawi and Swaziland, and CONSAS remained a stillborn concept.

After the failure of CONSAS, the establishment of SADCC was regarded as a potentially deadly challenge by *apartheid* South Africa. South Africa's new approach was to prevent SADCC from establishing new transportation routes which would allow its landlocked member states to avoid South Africa harbors. To achieve this, South Africa fuelled already simmering rebellions to develop into full-fledged civil wars in Mozambique and Angola by giving military, logistical and training assistance to rebel movements in these countries (RENAMO and UNITA) and later to some extent, 'dissidents' in Zimbabwe (the so called 'Super-ZAPU'). The aim was to force these countries to enter into special relationships with South Africa.

In the case of Mozambique, this led to the signing of the *Nkomati-Accord* in 1984, which compelled both Governments to stop all attacks from their respective territories against the neighbor and also not to support attacks from a third country against their countries. In essence, the *Nkomati Accord* was a document of surrender from Mozambique, where the Government had lost control over most of its territory, faced a deep humanitarian crisis and hardly had any resources to keep on fighting the South African backed rebellion in its hinterland. However, despite the promises made in the treaty, South Africa kept on supporting the RENAMO rebels which now operated from bases in Malawi so that the Mozambican Government was unable to recover. The RENAMO operations disabled Mozambique's economy, which had always been based on service provision (railway lines, roads, oil-pipeline and harbors) and the production of electricity from the huge *Cabora Bassa* dam, by cutting or disrupting major railway links, isolating harbors and destroying the electricity grid. In 1990, international pressure and a new more pragmatic Mozambican Government led to peace negotiations in Rome, which allowed for democratic elections – in which RENAMO participated – to take place in 1994. They ended with a victory for the ruling MPLA but left RENAMO in a strong opposition role.

In Angola, the South African backed rebels of UNITA were unable to destabilize the MPLA Government because of the massive Cuban backing for the Angolan Government. However, UNITA managed to destroy the railway link to the Zambian Copperbelt and the Katanga-Province of (then) Zaire and hold on to large tracts of territory in the eastern part of the countries, where they controlled the diamond mines. In contrast to Mozambique, South African troops intervened several times directly in Angola but had to realize in 1988, after the battle for *Cuito Cuanavale,* that their military power was insufficient to break the Angolan/Cuban defenses. This – together with the changing international climate (Gorbatschov's *perestroika)* – and the increasing economic problems of South Africa, paved the way for negotiations resulting in the independence of Namibia and the removal of Cuban troops from Angola in 1990.

Other SADCC countries also became victims of the South African destabilization policy both in military and economic terms. Lesotho and Botswana suffered from commando raids against alleged ANC offices, Zimbabwe from the destruction of most of its air force and new military equipment through South African sabotage as well as from assassinations of ANC representatives and bombs, and Zambia from bombings in Lusaka directed at the ANC headquarters. Economically, South Africa harmed its neighbors by interrupting oil supplies and other imports, export shipments and/or labor migration. It also used maize supplies as a 'food weapon' and last but not least increased the trading costs for the landlocked countries Botswana, Lesotho, Malawi, Swaziland, Zambia and Zimbabwe tremendously through the interruption of the railway links. Most countries had to increase their defense spending and were hampered in their economic growth perspectives. Green/Thompson (1986) put the cost of South Africa's destabilization in 1986 at more than USD 10 billion. However, in the end, South Africa's destabilization policies delayed but could not prevent the inevitable: the arrival of majority rule and the end of the inhuman *apartheid* system in South Africa.

Sources: Hanlon (1986); Kühne (1985);Martin/Johnson (1986);Green/Thompson (1986); Peters (1987), Meyns (2000)

7.1.4. Conclusion

The examples of the first 'wave' of RI in Africa at first demonstrated little awareness of the practical problems of integration such as cost-benefit balancing, the question of national sovereignty and the missing tradable goods and services. Only the last of the major RI schemes of the first phase – SADCC – showed a greater understanding of the practical problems which can afflict RI. SADCC started deliberately not as an integration endeavor but as a less demanding cooperation scheme. What made SADCC stand out further was its pronounced political motivation and attempt to utilize regional cooperation/integration for developmental purposes. The awareness for the need of a political rationale for regional integration arose also in ECOWAS but only at a later stage and became then the engine for the reforms, which put ECOWAS back on track for RI.

The earliest of the attempts reviewed in this chapter, the EAC, was still too rooted in colonial structures and its leaders were too unwilling to agree on compensation schemes to succeed although the physical and institutional pre-conditions were the most favorable for RI. It seems however, as if the Tanzanian leadership under *Julius Nyerere* learned its lesson and was able to transfer its insights from the failure of the EAC to the process of establishing SADCC.

It became also apparent from the three examples of RI until the beginning of the 1990s that;

- the expectations of the participating countries were too high both in terms of the speed and depth of integration and thus out of touch with the practical realities;
- the economic basis for RI was in most cases insufficient as the production and trading structures were too similar and few tradable goods and services were available for intra-regional trade;
- national political interests regarding state consolidation and preservation of political power by far outweighed the willingness to give up even tiny pieces of national sovereignty;
- the prevailing industrialization strategy (import substitution) fostered inward-looking protectionist policies which would have required effectively harmonized regional investment planning, trade and financial policies in order to promote RI. Such endeavors were in the first two decades of independence with its consolidations crises' and frantic state-building efforts hardly realistic – the emphasis was as in the economic policies on national rather than regional efforts.

7.2. The Second 'Wave' of Regional Integration in Post-Colonial Africa

Towards the end of the 1980s most of the existing RI bodies in Africa were either performing rather disappointingly or were being blocked in their development (SADCC). The consternation over the many unfulfilled promises, however, did not last long and by 1989/90 a new surge for regional integration set in. This was predominantly facilitated by new international and regional framework conditions:

- The end of east-west conflict symbolized by the fall of the Berlin Wall in November 1989 not only ended the many proxy wars in which African countries were supported by either the USA (and some other western countries) or the Soviet Union (and some of their allies) but also undermined a number of authoritarian regimes in Africa, making them 'vulnerable' to democratic demands.
- The resulting second wave of worldwide democratisation reached in 1989 (Namibia) and 1990 (Benin and Zambia) ([149]). The new 'democracies' were more open to regional cooperation (in order to solidify democracy) and less concerned with inward-looking state consolidation efforts than their one-party, authoritarian predecessors.
- The IMF-enforced liberalisation of most African economies during the 1980s did not only lead to the collapse of many inefficient parastatal or state-subsidised companies but allowed also for greater economic convergence between previously divergent regimes. Socialist, state-controlled economies survived only in few countries; the overwhelming majority adopted a free-market-approach, which made it easier to enter into regional integration efforts. The liberal market approach superseded the import-substitution paradigm of economic development.
- Despite the rapid 're-democratization', the number of violent conflicts (both internal and inter-state) increased as well. The need for new approaches towards peace building became apparent and influenced leaders especially in Western Africa to reform the existent but mostly in-effective RI bodies such as ECOWAS.

The new phase of RI efforts was from the beginning more political than the previous ones as they recognised the importance of political will and interest nto

149 According to Bratton/van der Walle (1997), between 1989 and 1994 elections in 40 of the 53 African states took place; in 15 cases new Governments replaced incumbent regimes through elections.

integrate, underscored the importance of the adherence to democracy, good governance and the rule of law, and also pursued to some extent political goals as explicit objectives of RI. After 1990, RI schemes are moreover characterised by an increasing involvement of non-state actors in the integration process such as civil society organisations, trade unions, employers associations etc.

The most relevant examples of the second wave of RI in Africa are:

- The Common Market for Eastern and Southern Africa (COMESA):
- The new East African Community (EAC):
- The rejuvenated Economic Community Of West African States (ECOWAS):
- The new Southern African Development Community (SADC):

Although the AU in its grand scheme for the establishment of the AEC recognises eight regional economic communities (RECs) as building blocs the remaining four are far from being effective and thus only briefly introduced:

- The *Economic Community of Central African States* (ECCAS), established in 1983 with strong support and encouragement of the ECA ([150]) and operational in 1985, consists of eleven member states (see Text Box 5.1.) and has its headquarters in *Libreville* (Gabon). However, ECCAS never really took off due to a host of problems among them intensive armed conflicts in seven of the eleven member states, failing states structures, changing membership composition and low commitment by member states because of financial problems ([151]). Only after the end of the war in the DR Congo and the stabilisation of Government authority in Congo, Rwanda and Burundi after 2002/3 a slow revival of ECCA began. Due to the (second) withdrawal of Rwanda in 2007 and ongoing disputes over the settlement of payment arrears, ECCAS is, however, still far from stabilised and functioning. The FTA, which ECCAS wanted to have created by 2007 ([152]), is still not in place. With CEMAC a second and overlapping RI body exists in the region. Both AU and ECA are concerned that ECCAS and CEMAC could duplicate efforts and block progress and are thus urging both organisations to start harmonizing their operations ([153]).

150 See: Adedeji, A. (2002): 4f
151 See: Awoumou, C.D.G. (2008):128f
152 See: www.ceeac-eccas.org
153 See: See: AU/ECA (2008): Assessment of Progress on Regional Integration in Africa. Presented at the First Joint Annual Meetings of the AU Conference of Ministers of

- The *Community of Sahel-Saharan States* (CEN-SAD) which was established in 1998 consists of 25 states ([154]) stretching from Djibouti at the Horn of Africa to Senegal in the West. Its headquarters is located in *Tripoli*, Libya. CEN-SAD ([155]) was acknowledged as a REC in 2000 at an AU Summit held in Togo. It aims at establishing an Economic Union. It has the normal organisational setup with a Conference of Leaders and Heads of State, an Executive Council and a General Secretariat but also two special features (an Investment and Trade Bank; an Economic, Social and Cultural Council). CEN-SAD overlaps in membership with ECOWAS, AMU, EAC, ECCAS and COMESA. This and the dominant role of Libya have rendered CEN-SAD so far rather ineffective.
- The *Intergovernmental Agency for Development* (IGAD), which was established in 1996 as successor to the Intergovernmental Authority on Drought and Development (IGADD), consists of seven member states and has its headquarters in Djibouti. IGAD aims at increased cooperation in the fields of food security, environmental protection, promotion and maintenance of peace and security as well as economic cooperation and integration. It subscribes to the objectives of COMESA, to which most member states belong. IGAD has a number of institutions (Assembly of Heads of State and Government; Council of Ministers; Committee of Ambassadors; Secretariat led by an Executive Secretary) ([156]) but they have been unable to actively promote its objectives due to the hostility between Ethiopia and Eritrea and the collapsing state of Somalia. Eritrea, which had left IGAD in 2007, has recently been condemned first by IGAD, then by the AU and eventually also by the UN Security Council for its attempts to topple the Government in Somalia and its hostile actions against Djibouti ([157]).
- The *Arab Maghreb Union* (AMU) was established in 1989 and consists of five member states; its headquarters is located in *Rabat* (Morocco). Although established for security reasons (solidarity and protection against external aggression [[158]]) its aims also include a customs union,

---

Economy and Finance and ECA Conference of African Ministers of Finance, Planning and Economic Development. Addis Abeba, 28.02.2008:10

154 It is interesting to note that the information about the number of member states seem to vary according to source. The CEN-SAD website (www.cen-sad.org) states it as 23, while the ECA puts it at 25.

155 See: www.cen-sad.org

156 See: www.igad.org

157 See: http://afri-russ-archiv.blog.de/2010/01/02/eritrea-von-uno-sanktioniert-wegen-unterstuetzung-somalischer-islamisten-l-erythree-sanctionne-par-l-onu-pour-son-aide-aux-islamistes-somaliens-7677321/

158 That was particularly in the interest of Libya, which felt threatened by the US after the Lockerbie incident.

regional enterprises and utilities as well as free movement of people. Several regional institutions (regional court, Summit, consultative council etc.) have been formed ([159]) but are dependent in their performance on the mood of the bilateral relations between member states (tensions between Algeria and Morocco over West Sahara, between Morocco and Libya), the state of internal stability especially in Algeria and Mauretania and the whims of the Libyan leader *Muammar al-Gaddafi*. A Summit was not held for 15 years until 2009 until the Presidency of *Gaddafi* made it possible. Due to such delays and personal agendas AMU has not been able to achieve its objectives ([160]).

None of these four RECs seems capable of becoming a functional building bloc for the AEC in the near future. As long as the state-building process, inter- and intra-state conflicts and overlapping membership issues are not sorted out and the political commitment for integration not increased there is hardly a chance that any of the four RECs can start to create functioning FTAs or even customs unions. To announce such trade regimes at conferences and sign agreements is mere symbolism than real politics.

7.2.1. The Common Market for Eastern and Southern Africa (COMESA)

COMESA is probably the most conventional amongst the new RI bodies that sprung up in the 1990s. It is the successor to the mainly ineffective Preferential Trade Area for Eastern and Southern Africa (PTA), which was established in 1981 with strong support and guidance of the UN Economic Commission for Africa (ECA), which also played a leading role in PTA's transformation into COMESA in 1993 ([161]). COMESA as already before the PTA is a regional integration scheme established in line with the ideas of the Lagos Plan of Action. One might argue ([162]) that the drive to establish the original PTA was a direct consequence of the failure of the first EAC in 1977.

---

159 See: www.maghrebarabe.org

160 See: Haunit, T. (2005), AMU in: Gieler, W. (Hg.), International Wirtschafts-organisationen. Entstehung – Struktur – Perspektiven. Münster 2005: 11-20

161 See: Adedeji (2002):4f. The transformation of the PTA into COMESA was in line with the provisions of the PTA Treatry, which foresaw the formation of a common market after ten years.

162 See: Ngwenya, S. (2008)

Table 7.1.: Basic Economic Indicators for COMESA (2007)

Member state	Total Area (km²)	Population (mill.)	GDP (current prices; USD mill.)	Intra-COMESA exports (% of total exports)	Intra-COMESA imports (% of total imports)
Burundi	27,830	8	974	21.6	29.0
Comoros	1,861	1	449	0	3.5
DR Congo	2,344,860	62	8,955	7.1	17.7
Djibouti	23,200	1	830	18.1	5.7
Egypt	1,001,450	75	128,095	3.1	1.2
Eritrea	117,600	5	1,201	8.3	2.0
Ethiopia	1,104,300	79	19,395	9.8	3.7
Kenya	580,370	38	29,509	26.4	4.1
Libya	1,759,540	6	58,333	0.2	1.6
Madagascar	587,040	20	7,326	4.3	5.2
Malawi	118,480	14	3,552	21.2	10.4
Mauritius	2.040	1	6,363	7.7	3.2
Rwanda	26,340	10	3,320	34.8	38.5
Seychelles	460	>1	728	0.3	3.6
Sudan	2,505,810	39	47,632	5.0	5.2
Swaziland	17,360	1	2,942	15.2	2.1
Uganda	241,040	31	11,214	37.2	15.7
Zambia	752,610	12	11,363	14.2	10.3
Zimbabwe	390,760	13	n/a	9.9	9.2
TOTAL	**11,602,951**	**416**	**342,182**	**4.2**	**4.7**

Source: www.comesa.int and own calculations

COMESA's biggest problem is its artificial character as a regional body. It combines 21 countries from the far north (Egypt) and far South (Swaziland) of Africa who have little if anything in common. The region covered by COMESA houses three other major regional bodies, i.e. SADC, EAC and IGAD, whose member states are not always also members of COMESA. This makes it very difficult for COMESA to be accepted as a kind of regional superstructure. Especially with regard to SADC, the problems arising from an overlapping membership has led five countries (Angola in 1996, Mozambique and Lesotho in 1997, Tanzania in 2000, Namibia in 2004) to leave COMESA. South Africa never showed any interest in joining which undermined COMESA and gave SADC an additional push.

Despite these practical problems COMESA's vision is ambitious ([163]):

163 See: Ngwenya, S. (2008)

- a borderless region,
- with a single currency,
- free mobility of people and factors of production,
- a single market for investments, goods and services.

If the willingness of member states to pay their membership fees and contributions is an indicator for the seriousness of an RI approach, COMESA is one of the less promising attempts. According to the second assessment report on regional integration in Africa by the ECA and AU the rate of collected membership contributions in COMESA in the latter half of the 1990s was rather low ([164]).

Integration progress

1. Trade integration:

The commitment level in COMESA is still rather low, as the benefits of the membership remain hypothetical for many countries. In the beginning, only the most industrially advanced member states such as Kenya and (until 2000) Zimbabwe were able to realize some of the opportunities of the free trade arrangements in COMESA. Intra-regional trade in 2000/1 stood below 6% of the overall trade of the member states. By 2005, intra-regional exports in COMESA had increased to 8.7% and the intra-regional imports to 11.1% ([165]). This was close to the average of intra-regional trade of all African RI schemes but still small and cannot be regarded as a basis for accelerated and deeper RI. However, in 2007 these shares had declined again to 4.2% and 4.7% respectively (see table 8.1.), which was probably due to the surge in commodity prices. Libya, which accounted in 2007 for about 60% of the value of total exports of COMESA is exporting predominantly oil to countries outside COMESA. Egypt, Libya and Sudan as the biggest importers of COMESA (together nearly 55% of total value of imports in 2007), are also the member states with rather low shares of intra-regional imports (see table 8.1.). Some of the smaller member states – such as Burundi, Rwanda and Uganda but also as far as intra-regional exports are concerned the DR Congo, Kenya and Malawi – appear to be rather well integrated as far as intra-regional trade is concerned. It is, however, conspicuous that with the exception of Malawi these countries are neighbouring each other, are engaged in another REC (EAC) (except the DR Congo) and have been embroiled in a regional war which saw regular troops from Rwanda and Uganda invade parts of the DR Congo.

---

164 See ECA/AU (2004): 44f

165 See: ECA/AU (2008):35

Map 7.1. The Member States of COMESA ([166])

Source: D. Tenzer (2010)

In 2000, COMESA officially created a Free Trade Area, but only nine of its member states were able and willing to participate. The originally envisaged introduction of a customs union for 2004 was postponed to 2008 and eventually launched on 07.06.2009. The negotiations to establish the COMESA customs union had been slowed down by the political turmoil in Zimbabwe and the details of agreeing to a *Common External Tariff* (CET) ([167]). Currently it appears

166 Namibia left COMESA in 2004

167 See: INSAT, Issue 17, October 2009:2. The agreed CET foresees a four-band tariff structure differentiating between raw materials (0% tariff), intermediate and semi-

as if member states are reluctant to apply the CET, for which they have been given a five years transition period. As four members of COMESA are also members of the EAC, which has its own customs union and CET, eight member states are part of SADC, which plans to establish its own customs union in 2010 (again with its own CET) and one member (Swaziland) is part of SACU this makes it virtually impossible for the COMESA customs union and its CET to be accepted by the member states. Furthermore, the WTO rules are prohibiting that a country belongs to two customs unions at the same time, which requires considerable adjustment if adhered to. The EAC announced that its members will not implement the COMESA CET ([168]). Fearing to give up national authority to collect duties few member states have want to see a regional body established which could coordinate the regional trade policy, monitor the implementation of the CET and collect and distribute the duties.

The impact of the customs union on the development of intra-regional trade needs to be assessed in the next years when sufficient data is collected. But it is possible that the customs union and the agreed CET attract very few member states and that the COMESA customs union might in the end remain just a paper tiger. However, the fact that several SADC states have joined the COMESA EPA instead of the ESA EPA and that EAC, SADC and COMESA are negotiating over the establishment of a combined free trade area are indications that COMESA is after all a regional factor to reckon with.

2. Free Movement of people:

The free movement of people is envisaged but not yet even close to being achieved. The only case where the free movement of people is allowed is based on bilateral agreements.

3. Transportation:

The most relevant progress made by COMESA in terms of transportation arrangements was the introduction of the 'Yellow Card' for car/truck insurances, which has cut down on the red tape and waiting time when crossing from one country into another ([169]). Under the auspices of COMESA, also two one-stop-

---

processed goods (10% tariff) and finished and processed goods (25% tariff); an additional tariff band for 'sensitive' goods is under discussion.

168 ibid:3

169 However, as the author experienced it itself, the process is much less smooth than promised on paper. When travelling in May 2006 by private car from Malawi (COMESA member state) via Tanzania (non member) and Kenya (member) to Ethiopia (member) it was impossible to obtain one single travel document in Malawi, that would allow the transit through Kenya into Ethiopia.

border-posts ([170]) have been set up: one between Kenya and Uganda at Mataba and one between Zimbabwe and Zambia at Chirundu. Integration in the transportation sector has still not been achieved as there are no road links between many of the northern member states of COMESA and railway links exist only in the southern part of COMESA ([171]).

4. Energy:
In the energy field, COMESA is limping behind. While it has facilitated the establishment of the East African Power Pool (EAPP) in the context of the EAC, ([172]) South Africa and other SADC countries have shut COMESA out as far as the Southern African Power Pool (SAPP) is concerned. Especially in the energy sector, it becomes apparent that COMESA is on the one hand, a latecomer regarding RI and on the other hand, does not represent a cohesive region as such.

5. Monetary integration:
The harmonisation of macro-economic and monetary policies throughout the region is one of the objectives of COMESA but is far from being achieved. The failed experiment with a clearinghouse under COMESA's predecessor PTA is continued also by COMESA ([173]). The PTA clearinghouse was established to facilitate intra-regional trade by allowing participating states to balance their trade bills at the end of a year in hard currency instead of financing each and every deal with hard currency. The clearing arrangement worked for a few years but was mostly utilised by Zimbabwe and Kenya, the countries with the biggest manufacturing industries in PTA. The clearinghouse run into trouble when debtor countries fell behind schedule in settling their balances but was taken on as an instrument by COMESA. The Regional Payment and Settlement System as envisaged by COMESA is still not yet operational ([174]).

---

170 The concept of a one-stop-border-post in Africa was first developed in the context of SADC. Instead of lengthy procedures with one exit and entry at each border, checks will only be made at entry points. However, representatives of the exit country are also present at the entry point.

171 For example, the only road link between Kenya and Ethiopia is so bad and insecure that fewer than 10 cars per day are passing the border at Moyale. Between Ethiopia and Sudan, between Kenya and Sudan and between the DRC and most of its neighbours, no or very bad road links exist. The intra-regional railway network in the central and northern part of COMESA is in bad repair and often only link two countries (such as Uganda and Kenya).

172 See: ECA /ECA 2008:48

173 A COMESA Clearing House based in Harare, Zimbabwe, exists but has like its PTA predecessor been mostly ineffective and under-utilized; see: www.comesa.int

174 See: AU/ECA (2008): Assessment of Progress on Regional Integration in Africa. Presented at the First Joint Annual Meetings of the AU Conference of Ministers of

Additionally, COMESA also set up a Regional Development Fund to provide funding especially for infrastructure projects in the region. However, not all COMESA members have ratified the fund agreement yet ([175]). COMESA contemplated the establishment of the COMESA Monetary Institute with the mandate to prepare the creation of a monetary union ([176]).

6. Other sectors:
In other sectors crucial for regional integration such as water, health or telecommunication, COMESA has not made much progress. The only remarkable development was the establishment of the 'Association of Regulators for Information and Communication for Eastern and Southern African States' (ARICEA); but since most of the other RI bodies in the area have established such regulatory bodies much earlier, the COMESA one has not yet had much impact.

In conclusion, COMESA suffers from an artificial design, is too diverse and far apart for members to be able to realize benefits of regional integration in practical terms, and an overlapping and competing membership with other more dynamic RI bodies such as SADC and EAC. Being a project of and supported by the ECA, COMESA will be kept alive but will only have a further and sustainable impact in promoting RI if the project of a joint FTA with the EAC and SADC materializes.

7.2.2. The New East African Community (EAC)

When the EAC was closed down in 1977, few people believed that it could be revived ever. Nevertheless, once the *Museveni* Government brought political stability and economic development to Uganda and the successors of President *Nyerere* in Tanzania abandoned '*ujamaa*' and embarked on a market-friendly economic approach the obvious benefits of RI in the region became irresistible. Starting in 1993 negotiations were concluded in 1999 when the three countries signed a new Treaty for the creation of the EAC which entered into force in July 2000 ([177]). In 2006/7 it was expanded to include also Rwanda and Burundi. At

---

Economy and Finance and ECA Conference of African Ministers of Finance, Planning and Economic Development. Addis Ababa, 28.02.2008:7

175 ibid:6

176 ibid:7

177 See: Mothae Maruping (2005), Challenges for Regional Integration in Sub-Saharan Africa: Macroeconomic Convergence and Monetary Coordination. In: Teunissen, J.J.

the first of January 2005 EAC officially established a customs union. This is to be followed according to the EAC integration roadmap by a Common Market (end of 2009) and a Monetary Union (until 2012) and ultimately a Political Federation of East African States.

The apparent progress in RI has attracted the interest of other countries from the region to join the EAC: the DR Congo, Ethiopia, Eritrea, Somalia and the southern Sudan ([178]). While the inclusion of Rwanda and Burundi made a lot of geo-political and economic sense, a further expansion of the EAC would not only stretch the already thin consensus amongst the member states about the costs and benefits of RI to a breaking point. It would hardly be rational from neither a political nor economic point of view to even consider including failed states like Somalia, failing states such as DR Congo and Eritrea or potentially unviable new states as Southern Sudan ([179]) into the Community.

The only candidate, which could economically (energy) benefit the existing EAC, is Ethiopia. However, to date the only transport connection between Ethiopia and the rest of the region is via air. The road link to Kenya is on the Kenyan side in a very shape and does not allow for much trading. Although there are plans to link the Ethiopian electricity grid with the Kenyan and as such with the East African Power Pool (EAPP), the physical pre-conditions for RI will take years to be completed. Apart from that, Ethiopia is a much more autocratic state than any of the other member states of the EAC and has a highly regulated economy, which is to a large extent in the hands of the state (parastatals), the ruling party, and a half Saudi, half Ethiopian business tycoon ([180]). These factors do not qualify Ethiopia as an ideal candidate to join the EAC.

---

and Akkerman, A. (editors), Africa in the World Economy - The National, Regional and International Challenges. The Hague, December 2005, www.fondad.org

178 See: The Standard online (Nairobi), 23.11.2009 http://www.standardmedia.co.ke/print.php?id=1144028817&cid=4

179 In 2011, a referendum will decide if the southern part of Sudan will remain part of the original state or will become a new sovereign entity.

180 The *Sheik al-Ahmoudi* is one of the 100 richest people in the world according to *Forbes Magazine*. In Ethiopia he owns thanks to his close relations with the ruling party of Prime Minister *Meles Zenawi*, banks, hotels (*inter alia* the Sheraton), breweries and soft drink producers, gold mines, construction companies and large tracts of agricultural valuable land; see Peters-Berries, C. (2009a): Country Report Ethiopia. Bertelsmann Transformation Index 2010. www.bertelsmann-stiftung.de

Map 7.2. The Members States of the East African Community (EAC)

Source: D. Tenzer (2010)

Integration Progress

1. Trade Integration:

In the first five years of its renewed existence, EAC members exported on average 12.6% of their total exports of goods and services to other EAC members and received 18.7% of their total imports from other EAC states ([181]). While this was higher than the average of intra-regional trade in African RI schemes, it was still not substantial enough to facilitate deep and intensive trade-led regional integration. It indicates that the tradable goods and services in Eastern Africa were limited which was also underscored by observations from ECA/AU (2004), which states:

> *"Industrial cooperation in regional economic communities has hardly boosted production, productivity, or value added. The main reasons are weak intersectoral links and a limited range of products across countries...Overall intra-community trade in manufactures has remained low (2-7%) and in some cases has declined as a share of total trade." ([182])*

That changed to the better when the Heads of State of the original three EAC member states signed an agreement setting up a customs union in 2005 – which became effective in 2006 – and when Rwanda and Burundi joined the club in 2006; intra-regional trade increased ([183]). It is envisaged under the customs union agreement ([184]) that by the end of 2009 all countries have introduced the agreed CET – which has three tariffs bands of 0, 10 and 25 percent for different categories of goods – will have been implemented by all member states. Due to his relative stronger industrial base and to avoid another dispute over uneven costs and benefits, Kenya removed all tariffs on Ugandan and Tanzanian imports from the start ([185]): However, it agreed to a 25% duty charge on its exports to Tanzania and 10% to Uganda which were to be reduced by 5% and 2% respectively on an annual basis during the five year transitional period. With the end of the transition period, approaching (31.12.2009) Tanzania and Uganda are said to have pushed for an extension of some duties on Kenyan goods because they fear the competition of Kenya's much more productive and advanced industry ([186]).

Estimates put the → ***trade creation*** effect of the customs union at 47% of intra-regional trade from 2005 to 2008 ([187]). However, national figures are not available and it is unclear if Uganda and Tanzania contributed to the increased trade volume as much as Kenya.

---

181 See ECA/AU (2008):35

182 ECA/AU (2004): 57/58

183 See: Interview with Prof. Dr. R. Hofmeier in November 2009 in Addis Abeba.

184 For a detailed discussion of the stipulations of the EAC customs union see: ECAPAPA electronic newsletter February 11, 2005 – Vol. 8, No.2: Implications and Benefits of the EAC Customs Union.

185 See: http://go.worldbank.org/LNA7K97L30

186 See: The Standard online (Kenya). 23.11.2009

187. See: ibid. In absolute figures, the increase is estimated to amount to USD 0.87 bn.

2. Free movement of people:
From the very beginning of EAC, the free movement of people was an important issue on the agenda. An East African passport was officially launched on 1 April 1999, several months before even the Treaty was signed. Citizens of the EAC countries can thus move without visas from one member state to another. This is already a better situation than in COMESA and in SADC and in January 2008 negotiations for a new protocol for the free movement of labour and goods commenced, which propelled the EAC into the stage of a Common Market ([188]) by the end of November 2009. However, a number of unresolved issues regarding the free movement of people accompany the establishment of a Common Market in East Africa.

One problem refers to the clause that a five-year residence period qualifies citizens of EAC member states for the nationality of another member state. Especially Tanzania's Government is concerned that too many 'foreigners' will be seeking citizenship; it even indicated that it may review its EAC membership in case that it is overwhelmed by too many new citizens from other EAC countries ([189]).

Another issue not yet sufficiently solved is that of land ownership. The free movement and settlement of people has an integrative impact only if it is also accompanied by the right to acquire land at any place within the confines of the Common Market. That would imply in the case of the EAC that e.g. a Kenyan investor has the right to buy land in Tanzania, settle down and establish a business on his/her premises. While private land ownership is a legal option in Kenya, it is not allowed at all in Tanzania where the state (and communities) holds all the land and distributes it to peasant farmers without title deeds ([190]).

3. Transportation:
The transportation network in East Africa is not only underdeveloped but the existing links are often also in a state of bad repair. That applies to both the road and railway networks. Uganda's external trade fully depends on the Kenyan transportation system as the country has no links to Tanzania's harbour. The same applies for Burundi and Rwanda. The entire interior of Tanzania lacks functioning links with the coastal regions although efforts are underway to build roads to link Dodoma with Dar es Salam and the South to the North. The road

---

188 See: Business Daily (Kenya) January 24, 2008.

189 See: The Standard online (Nairobi), 23.11.2009.

190 See: Olenasha, W. (without year), Reforming Land Tenure in Tanzania: for whose benefits? http://www.hakiardhi.or.tz/HA-Docs/WILLIAM%20FINAL%20SUBMISSION.pdf

network in Kenya is probably the most appalling in the EAC due to decades of negligence and corruption.

The only intra-regional railway line exists between Uganda and Kenya. Since it has been handed over to a private concessionary to operate it, there have been some improvements.

4. Energy:
The major sources of electricity production in the EAC countries are hydro-power (79%), thermal (16%) and geo-thermal (4%) ([191]). The by far biggest portion of energy is still being provided by biomass (see table 8.2.); electricity although crucial for industrial development accounts only for a fraction of biomass.

Table 7.2.: Energy Sources and Capacity in the EAC

Country	Installed Capacity (MW)	Hydro (%)	Thermal (%)	Geo-Thermal (%)	Biomass (%)	Electricity (%)	Fuel (%)
Burundi (1)	49	n/a	n/a	n/a	**86**	**3**	**11**
Kenya (2)	1,177	57	32	11	**68**	**9**	**22**
Rwanda (3)	41	65	35	0	**93.1**	**0.9**	**6**
Tanzania (4)	1,081	52	48	0	**90**	**1.2**	**8**
Uganda (3)	380	99.3	0.7	0	**93**	**1**	**6**

Source: Karekezi et al (2009):56ff
(1)=2004; (2)=2006; (3)=2007; (4)=2008

Kenya and Tanzania have an energy deficit which is regularly aggravated by droughts. Kenya intends to cover this by importing electricity from neighbouring countries with a (potential) surplus such as Ethiopia or even countries as far away as Zambia. The formation of the East African Power Pool (EAPP) in February 2007 will mainly assist Kenya to balance its structural deficit by facilitating the importation of electricity. So far, only the Owen Dam hydro-electrical plant in Uganda is feeding into the EAPP and provides electricity to Kenya and Tanzania ([192]).

191 See: Karekezi, S. et al (2009): Large Hydropower, Renewable Energy and Adaptation to Climate Change. Climate Change and Energy Security in East and Horn of Africa. Nairobi. AFREPREN/FWD Occasional Paper No.33:8

192 ECA/AU (2004): 46

East Africa relies on the sustained and increasing availability of electricity for further industrial development and thus for RI. However, currently energy supplies are not secured due a high dependency on hydropower and the occurrence of regular droughts. In the last decade, most EAC member states suffered from droughts on average every second year. Consequently, expensive emergency power generation facilities (mostly diesel-fired generators) had to be installed which in some cases could not prevent the loss of economic growth due to electrical load shedding ([193]).

The insufficient electricity generation and the high dependency on hydropower is thus a critical problem for the EAC which has to be addressed if further RI is to happen. As the region has only limited conventional potential for generating electricity, the solution might lie with investments into renewable energies. Kenya has just commissioned the construction of a large-scale 300 MW wind farm at the shores of *Lake Turkana* in the north of the country ([194]).

<u>5. Monetary Integration:</u>
Based on the already existing free convertibility of the currencies of Kenya, Tanzania and Uganda, there are concrete plans to introduce a single regional currency. A study to that extent had been conducted in 2006 but no further concrete action has taken place since.

<u>6. Other sectors:</u>
EAC has in one other area, made remarkable advances towards RI. Since September 2006 EAC has an integrated regional cell phone network (operated by the private company CelTel), which allows calls throughout the region without extra roaming costs ([195]).

In conclusion, it can be stated that EAC has made some remarkable progress on the path to deeper RI, which has been helped to some extent by the previous regional ties. Nevertheless, the new EAC is still a long way from achieving a similar intensive integration level as between 1967 and 1977. The memories and legacies of that failed attempt are still too fresh and contribute to a more careful, costs and benefits assessing approach to RI. The issue of overlapping membership regarding Tanzania (also in SADC) and Burundi, Kenya, Rwanda

193 GDP growth dropped in Uganda in 2005/6 from 6.2% to 5.3% because of the its hydro capacity was halved by the 2m drop of water levels of Lake Victoria. Kenya lost about 1% growth in 2000 due to drought and reduced hydropower generation capacity; see: Karekezi et al (2009):28f. The impact of the current (2009) drought in Kenya on electricity production and GDP growth can not yet be estimated.

194 See: www.laketurkanawindpower.com

195 ECA/AU (2004):: 53

and Uganda with regard to COMESA ([196]) will have to be addressed in order to clear the way for the Common Market to become a reality and not just remain a 'paper tiger'. The negotiations with COMESA and SADC about a joint FTA could address - if successful - the issue of overlapping memberships.
The inclusion of Burundi and Rwanda has added another business language (French) to the proceedings of the EAC but has also acknowledged the close ties of these two countries to the three original member states.

7.2.3. The Renewed Economic Community of West African States (ECOWAS)

While ECOWAS was not closed down like the EAC in 1977, it nearly went the same way before it was rejuvenated in 1993 by the redrafting of its Treaty. The reforms were brought about by the change in the international (end of cold war, onset of globalisation, the re-democratization wave reaching West Africa) and regional (gradual withdrawal of France from its former colonies; end of military rule in Nigeria, and increasing number of civil wars threatening to spill over into other countries) framework conditions ([197]).

The member states have reaffirmed their view of ECOWAS as a building bloc for the African Economic Community and as the only relevant RI body in Western Africa. ECOWAS became probably best known for its (often internationally harshly criticised) military and political interventions into the civil wars in Liberia (1990-98; 2003), Sierra Leone (1997-2000); Guinea-Bissau (1998/9) and Ivory Coast (2002/3). In 2008, ECOWAS suspended temporarily, the membership of Mauretania – where a coup d'état had overthrown the rightfully elected Government – and then Guinea in an attempt to force the country politically back to a democratic order.

The re-drafting of the Treaty also led to the organisational reform of ECOWAS. However, instead of strengthening decision-making powers and implementation capacities, the still prevailing mistrust between Anglophone and Francophone member states necessitated several compromises. In the end, this led to an ineffective, slow and weak management structure. The only organ with real power was the "Authority", consisting of the Heads of State of the member countries, which meets once a year and requires the full consent of all members

196 As well as the membership of Kenya and Uganda in IGAD, which is however, less relevant as it has become rather inactive.

197 Mair/Peters-Berries (2001):190f

to make a decision binding. Other organs such as the Council of Ministers, the Secretariat, the Community Parliament or the Technical Commissions did not wield much power and were sidelined in many cases ([198]). In 2007, however, the Executive Secretariat of ECOWAS was transformed into a Commission ([199]) in order to speed up integration processes.

Map 7.3. The Member States of ECOWAS

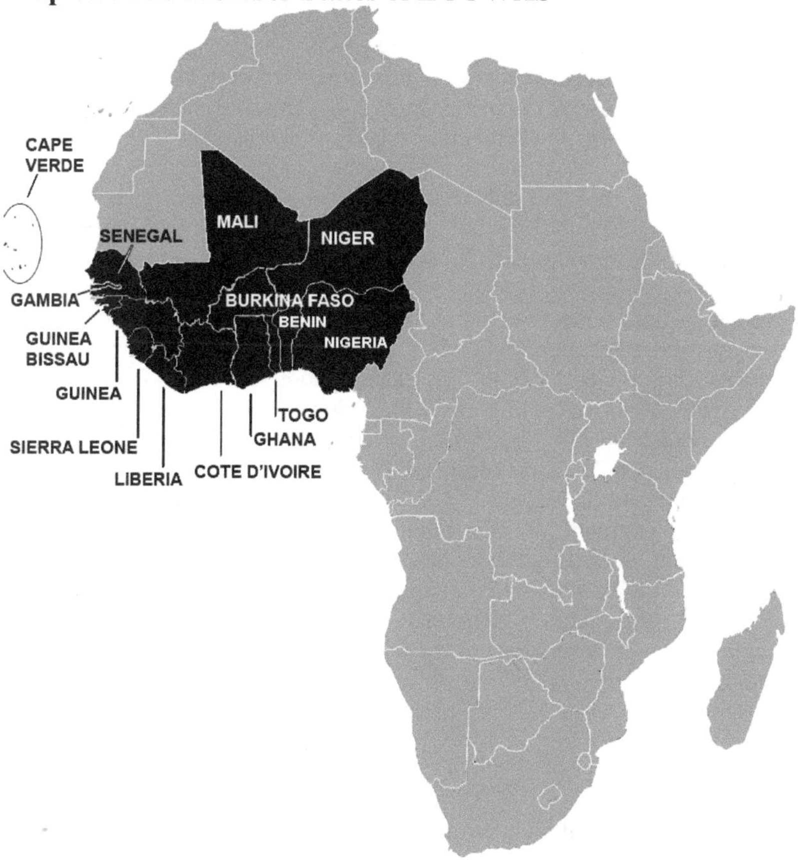

Source: D. Tenzer (2010)

198 ibid: 197ff.

199 See: ECA/AU (2008):8. This leads Cernicky, J. (2007): Was nützt ECOWAS? In: KAS Auslandsinformationen 8/2007:87ff, to argue that the 'real' power brokers in ECOWAS are sectoral experts and -since its inception - the Commission.

Similar to the EAC and SADC, the major integration mechanism are protocols and conventions. Until 2006, ECOWAS member states signed 52 protocols and conventions, of which 35 had been fully ratified and another eleven at least provisionally. The average time span between signing and ratifying of a protocol has been 42 months, but some took between five and ten years ([200]).

The progress of RI in ECOWAS is somewhat checked by a number of inconsistencies:

- The clear commitment to democracy of the Treaty is put into question by several members who even today are far from being democratic (Ivory Coast, Guinea, Guinea-Bissau, Togo, and Burkina Faso).
- Another major regional integration body was established (UEMOA in 1994) amongst the francophone member states despite the claim of ECOWAS to be the only RI body for West Africa. This led to considerable irritation, but has seemingly been resolved by the decision of ECOWAS to adopt the UEMOA tariff structure by the end of 2008 ([201]).
- The long time unresolved struggle for regional hegemony between the Anglo- and francophone members of ECOWAS, which pitted Nigeria against Ivory Coast. With the disintegration of Ivory Coast in the aftermath of the elections in 2002, Senegal took over as the leading francophone country. The sudden wealth from the windfall of increasing oil prices since 2005, however, put Nigeria firmly back into the driving seat of the regional leader.
- The low payment morale amongst the member states regarding membership fees and other dues. While this has recently somewhat improved, until 2000 annual membership fees never reached more than 50% of the agreed amounts putting the administration and implementation structures of ECOWAS under considerable financial strain.

Integration Progress

In terms of sectoral regional integration, ECOWAS shows a mixed performance.

1. Trade Integration:

The intra-regional export and import figures are with 13.9% for exports and 15.8% for imports slightly above the African average but not significant enough

200 See: Cernicky (2007):93

201 See: ECA/AU (2008): 32

to support trade related RI ([202]). However, most of the intra-regional trade is accounted for by five countries: Nigeria, Ghana, Senegal, Cote d'Ivoire and Togo ([203]). ECOWAS had established a FTA as early as 1981 for certified goods but it was only partially realised due to the apprehension of member states to apply intra-regional tariff reductions and the political turmoil in some member states. The aim to establish a customs union by 2004 failed due to the fear of member states to loose part of their government revenue. When the integration efforts of the eight French-speaking countries of UEMOA started to bear fruit, ECOWAS decided to adopt UEMOA's external tariff and tested this from 2006 to 2008 ([204]) although it remained unclear at the time of writing whether this was fully implemented or was lagging behind schedule.

Trade integration is also hampered by the application of NTTBs notably by Nigeria, which imposed blanket restrictions on the importation on certain goods.

As compared to COMESA and EAC, trade integration in ECOWAS lags to some extent behind as it appears that the strength of ECOWAS lies more in the political field than in trade integration.

2. Free movement of people:

One of ECOWAS' objectives is the creation of an ECOWAS citizenship. Towards that end, visas were abolished and the ECOWAS passport is being promoted. So far, however, only Senegal and Benin have realigned their national passports to the agreed ECOWAS format ([205]). It needs to be seen if Anglophone countries, especially Nigeria and Ghana are willing and capable of adopting the regional passport as well. If Nigeria will do so, this might do the project a disfavor as it will probably undermine its credibility given the wide-spread passport frauds involving Nigerians. Furthermore, some of the ECOWAS member states are politically fragile and in economic crisis, as they are either recovering from long years of civil war (Liberia, Sierra Leone and Cote d'Ivoire) or teetering on the brink of internal conflict (Guinea and Mauretania), which usually is a strong push factor for people to leave their home countries and seek refuge in more stable and prosperous countries. Potential targets for intra-regional migration such as Ghana, Nigeria or Senegal are hardly willing to

---

202 ibid:32ff

203 See: Cernicky, J. (2007):81

204 ibid: 34ff; see also: Cernicky, J. (2007):81ff and Anadi, S.K.McDonald (2005), Regional Integration in Africa. The case of ECOWAS. Phd Thesis presented to the Faculty of Arts of the University of Zurich:98ff

205 See: ECA/AU (2008):37

play host to scores of refugees as their economies are not robust enough to absorb them.

3. Transportation:

The physical integration of West Africa is by far less developed than, for example, in the Southern African region. Due to separate colonial and post-colonial developments in the Franco- and Anglophone parts of the region and later long periods of civil war in Liberia, Sierra Leone, Cote d'Ivoire and Guinea-Bissau, neither road nor rail systems effectively link the various countries. As far as the road sector is concerned, there are efforts underway to complete the West African Highway network, to rehabilitate the national road systems in countries coming out of civil war and establish a modern and effective border post infrastructure. Starting in 1980, two major trans-regional highways were designed and implemented:

- the trans-coastal high way linking *Lagos* (Nigeria) with *Nouakchott* (Mauritania), which is 4,676km long and was in 2005 to some 83% completed; and
- the trans-Sahelian highway linking *Dakar* (Senegal) with *N'Djamena* (Chad) covering a distance of 4,633km and which was to 87% completed in 2005 ([206]).

Independent of these two trans-regional highways, by 2000, a system of seven mostly older intra-regional highways already existed in ECOWAS. But while the physical features for intra-regional transport might have been in place, the practical movement of people and goods was severely restrained. According to information of the ECOWAS secretariat all these highways were interrupted by several checkpoints (up to seven per hundred kilometers on the *Lagos – Abidjan* highway) which made travelling slow, cumbersome and expensive (see table 7.3.).

206 See: Anadi, S K McD (2005):101

Table 7.3.: Official Checkpoints on Selected Routes of West African Highways, December 2000

Highway	Distance (km)	No of Checkpoints	No of Checkpoints per 100km
Lagos, Nigeria—Abidjan, Côte d'Ivoire	992	69	7
Lomé, Togo—Ouagadougou, Burkina Faso	989	34	4
Niamey, Niger—Ouagadougou, Burkina Faso	529	20	4
Abidjan, Côte d'Ivoire—Ouagadougou, Burkina Faso	1,122	37	3
Cotonou, Benin—Niamey, Niger	1,036	34	3
Accra, Ghana—Ouagadougou, Burkina Faso	972	15	2

Source: ECA (2004: 87).

ECOWAS and UEMOA are sharing the responsibility of developing different transportation corridors, with UEMOA having the more detailed and advanced transportation sector development program ([207]). ECOWAS is also supporting the extension of the Nigerian railway system into Niger.

However, the major structural challenge – the connection of landlocked and often resource-rich member states and some of the remote areas of coastal countries with the existing harbors – has not yet been sufficiently addressed. An important part of the physical infrastructure – the transportation system – is not sufficiently developed to support and facilitate intra-regional trade.

4. Energy:

Like in many other African regions, hydroelectric power is also in ECOWAS, the main source of electricity despite Nigeria's (and in the future Ghana's) wealth in oil. ECOWAS has been promoting the establishment of joint power stations ([208]) and has established in 2000 the West African Power Pool (WAPP). Through WAPP, Ghana is able to supply electricity from its *Akosombo* dam to Benin, Togo and Ivory Coast.

207 See: ECA/AU (2008):41f

208 So far, there are two such power stations: the *Nangbeto* hydro-electrical station (65 MW) between Benin and Togo and the *Manantali* hydro-electrical power station (200 MW) between Mali, Mauretania and Senegal. An additional such power station is under construction between Benin and Togo at *Adjarala* (96 MW); ECA/AU (2008): 46

In order to make use of the rich gas fields in the region, a gas pipeline connecting the Nigerian gas fields with Ghana, Togo and Benin was inaugurated in late 2006 ([209]).

5. Monetary Integration:
Africa's main experience with monetary integration took place in West Africa among the francophone countries in the form of the *"Communaute Financiere Africain"* (CFA) more commonly known as the CFA-Franc Zone. Formalised in 1973, a joint currency was adopted – the *CFA-Franc* – which received its stability from its fixed parity with the *French Franc*. In 1994, the CFA had to be devaluated against the *French Franc* to keep the exports of the CFA countries competitive in their overseas markets. Since 1999, the CFA-Franc is pegged to the EURO. Overall, the CFA zone experienced a slightly better economic performance (in terms of rate of inflation and economic growth) and stability but also intensified externalisation of profits and capital flight than the anglophone countries in West Africa. Despite being linked to the EURO, the French Ministry of Finance is the guarantor of the CFA-franc's stability.

For ECOWAS, the existence of the CFA-Franc zone within its confines has thus far not been a problem; indeed, it might prove to be an asset once ECOWAS moves ahead with plans to introduce a regional currency. A regional bank, ECOBANK, was established to facilitate intra-regional trade and investment.

6. Other sectors:
ECOWAS was one of the first RFI bodies in Africa with a telecommunication regulatory body (WATRA) and which established direct microwave links between the region's capitals. For 2007, a regional GSM roaming system was supposed to have been set up ([210]). Furthermore, ECOWAS established a regional court of justice dealing with regional issues ([211]).

The commitment for democracy and human rights is comparatively strong in ECOWAS. Not only intervened ECOWAS with own (mostly Nigerian) troops in the civil wars of Liberia and Sierra Leone ([212]) but it also took immediate action whenever a member state had flawed elections or an unconstitutional regime change. Mauretania after the coup d'état in 2008 was suspended from ECOWAS as were Guinea (after the coup d'état in 2009) and Niger because of flawed elections ([213]).

209 ibid.:46ff
210 ibid.: 51f
211 See: Cernicky (2007):83
212 See: Mair and Peters-Berries (2001):243ff
213 See: Daily Monitor (Addis Abeba), 22.10.2009

In conclusion, it appears that ECOWAS receives considerable strengths from shared political ideas and values focusing on democracy and the prevention of violent conflicts. The economic and physical features of RI are improving in West Africa but still remain patchy (only linking some countries) or weak. The division of the region into Franco- and Anglophone states emanating from colonial times has still not been overcome and may in the future be one of the major obstacles on the way to achieve deeper RI.

7.2.4. Conclusion

The second wave put RI in Africa into a more realistic framework, recognized the many existing obstacles and stimulated a new Pan-African approach towards integration which culminated in the formation of the AU in 2002. The examples of three major regional integration attempts show that in some of the RI bodies the stated objectives are still very much declarations of intention rather than realistic goals or even policies because major integration mechanisms – intra-regional trade and physical infrastructure – are still not sufficiently developed to provide an integrating stimulus. At least in the case of the EAC RI appears to make considerable progress facilitated both by the historic roots of RI and the small number of countries attempting to integrate. However, even in the case of the EAC the timetable for integration is probably too ambitious – declaring the establishment of a Common Market before the CET of the customs union is fully implemented by the member states – to be kept, which eventually might slow down the overall speed of further integration.

The examples as well as the concept of NEPAD indicate that African leaders have understood the important role of physical integration at a functional level. Without the technical infrastructure in the form of roads, bridges, railways, electrical grids, communications systems, educational and research institutions as well as financial services, the potential for intra-regional trade can be neither realized nor developed further. The potential for intra-regional trade depends on the production structures: as long as African countries mainly produce minerals and agricultural raw materials, the basis for intra-regional trade will remain severely limited.

Thus still hardly discussed at the many conference tables across the continent is the question which strategy is best for accelerated industrialization and who can be the drivers of such strategies. For a host of reasons African entrepreneurs are in most countries incapable of becoming such a strategic group. They are too weak as organized stakeholders, hardly production-oriented and often strongly dependent on the protection of the ruling elites with whom they are on top of that frequently personally intertwined. Stifling bureaucracies, rampant corruption and lacking supportive infrastructure are other reasons why so few African entrepreneurs are successful beyond their local markets. As such – with few exceptions (South Africa, Nigeria, Kenya) – indigenous entrepreneurs are not (yet?) strong enough to become the much needed vehicle for productive investments in Africa. Their place is taken by foreign companies which are becoming increasingly interested not only in the exploitation of raw materials but also in cheap production locations on the continent. The question is whether foreign investors are sufficiently interested in not just serving the world market but also in developing local markets and thus can become the engine for RI?

The plans of the AU to establish an African Economic and Monetary Union within the next 20 years look thus very optimistic. But even if they are not fully realized, they provide direction and stimulation for the existing RI bodies to deepen their integration efforts.

PART C: REGIONAL INTEGRATION IN SOUTHERN AFRICA: SADC

8. The Southern African Development Community (SADC) – History and Organisational Setup

The assessment of RI in Africa, since 1990, has left out the Southern African Development Community (SADC) as we will look at this endeavour more closely. SADC is often referred to as the most successful and promising attempt regarding RI in Africa. The next two chapters will evaluate if this claim is true.

Map 8.1. The SADC Region

Source: D.Tenzer (2010)

8.1. Origins, Objectives and Organisational Development

Established in 1992 at a summit of its predecessor SADCC, the new SADC was formed in anticipation of the political changes in the region and the resulting economic opportunities. SADC became possible because the white minority regime in South Africa could no longer sustain the *apartheid* system; as a result the paralyzing economic and political destabilization of key countries in the region (Mozambique, Angola and Zimbabwe) through South Africa stopped. At the SADCC summit in *Windhoek* (Namibia) in August 1992 the ten Heads of State and Government adopted SADC.

The establishing document – the 'Windhoek Treaty' (see Text Box 8.1.) – agrees on five (mainly political) principles for RI which in turn provide the framework for a long list of mostly economic and development oriented RI objectives.

TEXT BOX 8.1.: The Principles and Objectives of SADC (Excerpts from the TREATY)

ARTICLE 4: PRINCIPLES

SADC and its Member States shall act in accordance with the following principles:

a) sovereign equality of all Member States;
b) solidarity, peace and security;
c) human rights, democracy, and the rule of law;
d) equity, balance and mutual benefit;
e) peaceful settlement of disputes.

ARTICLE 5: OBJECTIVES

1. The objectives of SADC shall be to:

a) achieve development and economic growth, alleviate poverty, enhance the standard and quality of life of the people of Southern Africa and support the socially disadvantaged through regional integration;
b) evolve common political values, systems and institutions;
c) promote and defend peace and security;
d) promote self-sustaining development on the basis of collective self-reliance, and the Interdependence of Member States;
e) achieve complementarity between national and regional strategies and programs;

f)	promote and maximize productive employment and utilization of resources of the Region;
g)	achieve sustainable utilization of natural resources and effective protection of the environment;
h)	strengthen and consolidate the long standing historical, social and cultural affinities and links among the people of the Region.
2. In order to achieve the objectives set out in paragraph 1 of this Article, SADC shall:	
a)	harmonize political and socio-economic policies and plans of Member States;
b)	encourage the people of the Region and their institutions to take initiatives to develop economic, social and cultural ties across the Region, and to participate fully in the implementation of the programs and projects of SADC;
c)	create appropriate institutions and mechanisms for the mobilization of requisite resources for the implementation of programs and operations of SADC and its Institutions;
d)	develop policies aimed at the progressive elimination of obstacles to the free movement of capital and labor, goods and services, and of the people of the Region generally, among Member States;
e)	promote the development of human resources;
f)	promote the development, transfer and mastery of technology;
g)	improve economic management and performance through regional co-operation;
h)	promote the coordination and harmonization of the international relations of Member States;
i)	secure international understanding, co-operation and support, and mobilize the inflow of public and private resources into the Region;
j)	develop such other activities as Member States may decide in furtherance of the objectives of this Treaty.

Source: www.sadc.int

SADC started in 1992 with ten members (the original members of the former SADCC) ([214]) but quickly included South Africa and Mauritius in 1994. Three years later, the Democratic Republic of Congo (DRC) and the Seychelles joined SADC. When the Seychelles left SADC again in 2005, Madagascar joined to keep the membership at 14. The Seychelles applied for re-joining SADC in 2007, which was approved in 2008,

SADC took over from its' predecessor a decentralized, sectoral organizational structure and the Secretariat, which was housed in Gaborone (Botswana). In some aspects the new SADC continued like its predecessor: the Summit stayed the main decision-making body; the Council of Ministers kept on advising the

214 These were Angola, Botswana, Lesotho, Malawi, Mozambique, Namibia, Swaziland, Tanzania, Zambia and Zimbabwe.

Summit; sectoral responsibilities were still country-based; and SADC and donors met every year at special conferences to discuss project funding ([215]). New elements introduced to facilitate the process of RI were:

- Sector Protocols ([216]), which became the main mechanism to concretize the strategy of integration for specific policy fields and integration sectors.
- Several new fields of cooperation for integration were established and often formalized through protocols, e.g. Gender, Trade, Finance and Investment and Combating Illicit Drugs.
- Various charters and memoranda of understanding which specified policies and set agendas for cross-cutting issues.
- The Organ for Politics, Defense and Security (OPDS), which was supposed to cover the security aspect of RI in a broad sense ([217]).
- Instead of self-reliance and inward-looking national industrialization policies SADC embraced economic liberalization and globalization.

While keeping several elements of its predecessor, SADC no longer was a cooperation scheme trying to create the physical fundaments for RI but based its strategy on trade integration. This also required at least gradually a change in the approach to RI from a government induced and managed cooperation to a market-driven quasi automatic process of integration which would have to be managed by a supra-national body. However, most SADC leaders were not prepared to let go of the political controls and did not want to give up national sovereignty. As a result SADC's integration process was slower than anticipated by some of its architects and was time and again struggling to overcome political motivated obstacles.

This was realized rather soon and in 1996 a study was launched to assess the options for a reform of the organizational structure and integrative mechanisms of SADC. Two options were proposed: one arguing for the rationalization of the status quo and a second one advocating for the concentration of activities and the formation of integration clusters ([218]). It took some time before internal resistance against the idea of reforms was overcome and an option chosen. But then SADC aimed for the more fundamental choice of reforming the SADC structure and strategic orientation. It was agreed that the Secretariat was to be considerably strengthened in organizational terms, the overall program of RI to

---

215 See: Peters, W.-C. (1987):36ff for SADCC and Peters-Berries, C./Marx, M. (1997):73ff for the early SADC.

216 See: Chapter 8.3.4.

217 See: Chapter 8.2.2.

218 See: Peters-Berries, C./Marx M. (1997):92ff

become more focused, a comprehensive new strategy to be adopted, and a new leadership principle to be introduced. The reforms, which were adopted at an extraordinary summit in March 2001 in Windhoek, included ([219]):

- The streamlining of the institutional and management structure, which resulted in the concentration of program implementation in five directorates housed in the Secretariat instead of 21 sectoral decentralized Coordination Units.
- The adoption of a regional ***Common Agenda*** with a 15 year ***Regional Indicative Strategic Development Plan*** (RISDP) which is supposed to be implemented in five phases.
- The adoption of the ***TROIKA*** approach (see Textbox 5.4.) in the leadership of the major SADC institutions (chairmanship of the Summit, chairmanship of the Council of Ministers, chairmanship of the OPDS).
- The adoption of a new financing system for member states starting in April 2003.
- The introduction of new institutions such as the Integrated Committee of Ministers, the SADC National Committees and the SADC Tribunal (2005).

SADC has since become more centralized as a result of the reforms and has for the most part, abandoned its former decentralized country-based approach of cooperation. The new structure and approach has taken cognizance of the fact that the new SADC aims at a trade-based integration approach. If the payment morale of member states is an indicator for ownership, then the ownership level is high: for 2008/9 all members paid their contributions to the SADC Secretariat ([220]).

Table 8.1.: The SADC Integration Timetable

Objective	Deadline	Remark
Free Trade Area	2008	Officially achieved in August 2008
Customs Union	2010	Delays probable
Common Market	2015	Delays probable
Monetary Union	2016	Delays probable
Regional Currency	2018	Delays probable

Source: www.sadc.int.

219 See: SADC (2001c), Report on the Review of Operations of SADC institutions. Gaborone

220 See: Dlamini-Zuma, Nkosazana (2009), Talking Notes for post council media briefing by Dlamini Zuma, Chairperson of the SADC Council of Ministers. Cape Town, 27.2.2009. www.sadc.int

Despite the improved payment morale, the SADC member states are struggling to comply with the rather ambitious "roadmap" for further integration as agreed upon in the RISDP. While the establishment of the SADC Free Trade Area (SAFTA) was achieved just in time in August 2008 and not without problems the establishment of the SADC Customs Union – earmarked for 2010 – will be delayed ([221]). The majority of member states are not meeting the macroeconomic convergence criteria due to the impact of the world economic crisis ([222]). If the customs union deadline cannot be met in time or if the conditions for joining the customs union are compromised the further timetable might become obsolete.

8.2. The Organisational Structure

The new structure of SADC consists of four hierarchical levels and four horizontally integrated bodies and institutions (see Text Box 8.2.).

8.2.1. The Main SADC Institutions

The four main institutions of SADC follow a pattern known from other RI bodies.

The highest body of SADC is the ***Summit*** of the Heads of State and Government, which meets at least once a year but can be summoned in urgent cases also more frequently. The Summit is the highest decision-making body of SADC and

- Adopts decisions regarding SADC.
- Determines the organizational structure of SADC and any changes thereof.
- Elects the annually rotating SADC Chairperson.
- Appoints the Executive Secretary of SADC.

The Summit follows the consensus principle, which has made it sometimes difficult to reach mutual decisions. Furthermore, the Summit applies the

221 See: SADC countries fail to meet customs union, currency targets. PANA 09.04.2009. http://www.afriquejet.com/news/africa-news/sadc-countries-fail-to-meet-customs-union-currency-targets-2009090434424.html

222 See: Chapter 9.5

TROIKA-principle to its leadership: the predecessor and successor always support the current chairperson. This principle was adopted in the reforms of 2001 because of disputes over the leadership of SADC and the Organ for Politics, Defence and Security (OPDS) in the late 1990s. It is supposed to ensure that leadership in SADC is collective and not individualized in order to prevent personality clashes as between *Nelson Mandela* and *Robert Mugabe* over the OPDS ([223]). With the 2001 reforms, the annual rotation of the SADC leadership (and other major SADC bodies) was also formally introduced ([224]). Since 2001, the member

TEXT BOX 8.2.: SADC Institutional Framework

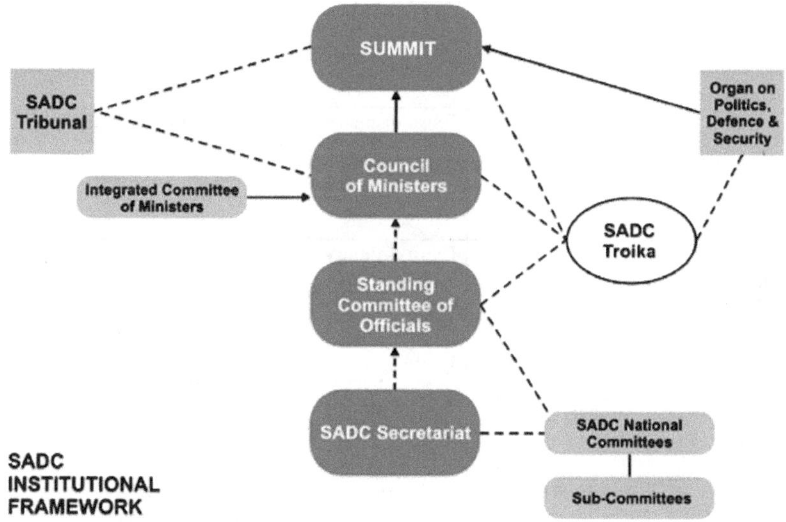

Source: SADC(2008)

223 See: Chapter 8.2.2. for the details

224 Before that the chairmanship of SADC was first held by the Batswana President (until 1996) as his country hosts the SADC Secretariat, and then by the South African President *Nelson Mandela* (until 1999); see Peters-Berries, C./Marx, M. (1999):56. After Mandela's retirement in 1999, the Mozambican President *Joaquim Chissano* was elected SADC chairperson.

state providing the SADC Chairperson also organizes the regular SADC Summit. At first this was regarded by some countries as an additional and unnecessary financial burden ([225]) but was then quickly recognised as an opportunity to present the country's President as a regional leader and to attract international interest in the country itself.

TEXT BOX 8.3.: SADC Summits

Venue	Date	Type of Summit	Decisions
Windhoek, Namibia	August 1992	Ordinary	Adoption of SADC Treaty
Mbabane, Swaziland	September, 1993	Ordinary	
Gaborone, Botswana	August, 1994	Ordinary	
Johannesburg, South Africa	August, 1995	Ordinary	
Pretoria, South Africa	December, 1995	Extra-ordinary	Special Summit on Nigeria
Probably Gaborone, Botswana	May, 1996	Extra-ordinary	Endorsement of SADC ministers recommendations on OPDS
Gaborone, Botswana	June, 1996	Extra-ordinary	Launching of OPDS
Maseru, Lesotho	August, 1996	Ordinary	
Blantyre, Malawi	September, 1997	Ordinary	Suspension of OPDS
Grand Baie, Mauritius	September, 1998	Ordinary	Lesotho Election investigation
Pretoria, South Africa	August, 1998	Extra-ordinary	Emergency Summit on recognition of DRC Government
Maputo, Mozambique	August, 1999	Ordinary	Creation of SADC Parliamentary Forum
Maputo, Mozambique	March, 2000	Extra-ordinary	Special Summit on impact of Cyclone 'Eline'
Mbanane, Swaziland	May, 2000	Ordinary	Protocol on OPDS initiated
Windhoek, Namibia	August, 2000	Ordinary	Protocol on Tribunal signed
Windhoek, Namibia	March, 2001	Extra-ordinary	Adoption of SADC reform
Blantyre, Malawi	August, 2001	Ordinary	Adoption of OPDS Protocol

225 Before the 2001 Summit in *Blantyre* (Malawi), the opposition but also some members of the ruling party criticized the expenditure for the meeting; personal scrutiny of Malawian newspapers at the time.

Harare, Zimbabwe	September, 2001	Extra-ordinary	Summit on Task Force on Development in Zimbabwe
Blantyre, Malawi	January, 2002	Extra-ordinary	Special summit on the conflicts in the Congo Basin
Luanda, Angola	October, 2002	Ordinary	HIV/AIDS
Dar es Salam, Tanzania	September, 2003	Ordinary	Adoption of the RISDP Solidarity with Zimbabwe
Dar es Salam, Tanzania	May, 2004	Extra-ordinary	Special Summit on Agriculture & Food Security
Grand Baie, Mauritius	August, 2004	Ordinary	
Gaborone, Botswana	August,2005	Ordinary	Madagascar joins New Executive Secretary
Maseru, Lesotho	August, 2006	Ordinary	
Johannesburg, South Africa	October, 2006	Extra-ordinary	Review of SAFTA
Dar es Salam, Tanzania	March, 2007	Extra-Ordinary	SADC mandates Mbeki to mediate in Zimbabwe Crisis
Lusaka, Zambia	August, 2007	Ordinary	
Johannesburg, South Africa	August, 2008	Ordinary	Zimbabwe elections
Johannesburg	November 2008	Extra-ordinary	Meeting on Zimbabwe
Pretoria, South Africa	January 2009	Extra-ordinary	Emergency meeting on Zimbabwe
Mbabane (Swaziland)	March 2009	Extra-ordinary	Emergency meeting on Zimbabwe and Madagascar
Johannesburg, South Africa	June 2009	Extra-ordinary	Emergency meeting on Madagascar
Kinshasa, DRC	October 2009	Ordinary	
Maputo, Mozambique	January 2010	Extra-ordinary	Double Troika Summit

Source: own compilation from www.sadc.int and various newspaper articles

The ***Council of Ministers*** is the second highest level of authority and the highest functional level in SADC. It consists of one national minister (usually those responsible for foreign affairs or finance/development planning) of each member state. The Council of Ministers advises the Summit and always meets before the Summit takes place. As for the Summit, it meets at least once a year but can also be convened on more occasions.

The council elects a chairperson on an annual basis, who serves assisted by predecessor and successor (TROIKA principle). The major function of the council apart from advising the Summit is to oversee the work of the five directorates. Furthermore, it has to approve the annual budget for the SADC institutions including the Secretariat. For 2007/8, the budget stood at USD 45.3 million which is 12% higher than the 2006/07 budget ([226]).

The Council of Ministers has been advised itself by the ***Integrated Committee of Ministers*** (ICM). The ICM was created after the Sectoral Committees were abolished in the first round of reforms in 1992 provided policy guidance and coordination on cross-sectoral activities and as such, had an oversight (quality assurance) function on the core areas of RI in SADC. It consisted of at least two Ministers per member state.

TEXT BOX 8.4.: The TROIKA PRINCIPLE

SADC is one of the few international organizations which use TROIKA as a leadership principle. This basically means that the leadership of SADC is performed in a collective manner. The SADC leadership Troika consists of the current, past and future SADC Chairperson.

The Troika principle has been applied in SADC from 1999 onwards. Before that, the chairpersons of SADC had been the President of Botswana (until 1996) and Nelson Mandela (1996-1999). The first chairperson under the Troika principle was President Chissano of Mozambique.

In SADC, the Chairperson serves for one year, meaning that the Summit do not elect the current but always the Chairperson for the next year.

The Troika at a Summit level has the function of a Steering Committee for SADC; important decisions are not taken alone by the current Chairperson but always by the trio.

The Troika principle is also applied to the OPDS, the Council of Ministers and the Integrated Council of Ministers.

By applying the Troika principle to the SADC leadership, a higher degree of continuity is ensured (than for example in the EU, where the 'Presidency' changes every six months), the team spirit is enhanced and the potentially controversial rotation of leadership is regulated.

Source: Adopted from the Amended SADC Treaty (SADC 2001b)

In detail the ICM was to:

- Monitor and control the implementation of RISDP.
- Provide policy guidance to the Secretariat.
- Make decisions on matters pertaining to the directorates.
- Monitor and evaluate work of the directorates.
- Create ad-hoc committees where necessary.
- Report to the Council of Ministers.

226 See http://www.sardc.net/Editorial/Newsfeature/07190307.htm

The ICM had decision making powers to ensure the rapid implementation of programs. Like other SADC bodies, it meet at least once a year and followed the 'consensus principle'. However, in the course of ongoing reforms it was in 2007 replaced by six ministerial clusters ([227]).

The fourth SADC institution is the ***Secretariat***. It is housed in Gaborone as was its predecessor under SADCC. The Secretariat was originally established in 1981; it was restructured in 1992, and again in 2001. In order to strengthen the overall decision making and management structures, the Secretariat is undergoing since 2003 a continuous organisational development process, which involved various evaluations and assessments ([228]). The Secretariat has the function of a management unit and has increasingly become, since the reforms started in 2001 the implementing agency for SADC programs. Headed by an Executive Secretary (currently *Dr. Tomáz Augusto Salomão* of Mozambique), who is supported by initially one and since 2008 by two Deputy Executive Secretaries ([229]), the Secretariat consists of four ***Directorates*** and the ***Gender Unit***, which were overseen by a Chief Director until 2007 ([230]). The four Directorates are:

- The Directorate of Trade, Industry, Finance and Investment (TIFI) launched in August 2001; is composed of trade and industry, mining, and finance and investment intervention.
- The Food, Agriculture and Natural Resources Directorate (FANR) was launched in December 2001. Its focus areas include food security and crop development; livestock; agricultural research and training; wildlife; forestry; fisheries; and environment and land management.
- The Directorate of Social and Human Development and Special Programmes was launched in September 2002. It incorporates human resources development, education and training, culture and sports, information, health, employment and labour and control of illicit drugs.
- The Infrastructure and Services Directorate is made up of focus areas such as Energy, Transportation, Communications and Meteorology, Tourism and Water. It was officially launched on 12 December 2002 at the SADC Secretariat.

---

227 See: Giuffrida, L. and Müller-Glodde, H. (2008):Strengthening the SADC institutional structures – capacity development is the key to the SADC Secretariat's effectiveness. In: Bösl, T. et al (eds.) (2008), Monitoring Regional Integration in Southern Africa Yearbook. Volume 8. Stellenbosch:125

228 Ibid:120

229 One is responsible for regional integration and the other for Finance and Administration; ibid:134

230 Ibid:126; 133

The Gender Unit is located directly under the Executive Secretary of SADC and is responsible for both Gender programs as well as gender mainstreaming. The main objectives of the Gender Unit are:

- to facilitate, coordinate, monitor and evaluate the implementation of gender equality;
- to facilitate the equity objectives as formulated in the *SADC Declaration on Gender and Development* and the *Protocol on Gender and Development* of 2008; and
- to ensure observation of the regional and global gender equality and equity instruments that SADC Member States have signed up to.

Under the new organisational structure of the Secretariat (since 2008) a policy planning and resource mobilisation section was added ([231]).

According to the decision of a Council of Ministers meeting (*Arusha*) in 2004, the expansion of the staff of the Secretariat was initially incremental following the expansion of functions and responsibilities of the Secretariat. This approach coupled with a non-competitive remuneration policy and a country-based quota system ([232]) impacted negatively on the performance of the Secretariat and did not turn it into the anticipated engine for integration ([233]). On the basis of a job evaluation study the human development and recruitment policy was changed enabling the Secretariat to recruit nearly its full staff complement of 130 experts and support personnel by now ([234]).

The Secretariat has also the task to receive annual contributions of the member states and development partners and to manage the SADC budget, which is approved by the Summit. The budget consists mainly of the member states contributions and grants of the development partners. In 2008/9 the overall budget stood at USD 50.7 million of which USD 49.1 million (96.8%) was spend. The budget approved for 2009/10 amounts to USD 53.9 million of which development partners contribute 52.2% and member states 45.9%; 1.9% come from other sources. On the expenditure side the budget is utilized to pay for the implementation of the Secretariat's strategic plan, i.e. for the implementation of

231 ibid:134

232 This limited the number of staff which could be recruited from one member state.

233 See: Giuffrida, L. and Müller-Glodde, H. (2008):129f

234 In contrast, in August 2006, only 45 regional positions had been filled, candidates for 22 positions were interviewed and 11 were scheduled for interviews later in 2006; see SADC (2006a):6. The remaining positions were for support staff often recruited from Botswana.

activities of the OPDS, the four directorates of the Secretariat, the Gender Unit and the policy, planning and resource mobilization unit ([235]).

In 2005, the foundations for a new headquarters for the SADC Secretariat were laid in *Gaborone*. In August 2007, the Heads of State and Government of SADC (with the exception of *Robert Mugabe* of Zimbabwe) signed a MoU on the new headquarter during the Summit in Lusaka ([236]). It appointed the Government of Botswana as the underwriter of the project, which made Botswana effectively the guarantor. In the MoU the SADC leaders also agree to pay contributions towards the construction costs according to their annual contribution obligation to SADC. The building, which was constructed by a private company, was estimated to have cost USD 25 million. SADC expected it to be finished by June 2009 ([237]).

8.2.2. The Organ on Politics, Defense & Security (OPDS)

The probably best know organ of SADC is the Organ on Politics, Defense and Security (OPDS). It is in some way, the successor of the cooperation amongst the→***Frontline States*** ([238]). The OPDS was established in 1996 at a SADC Summit in *Gaborone*. The Summit derived the legitimacy to establish the OPDS on the one hand, from Article 4 of the SADC Treaty (see text box 8.1.) which spells out the main principles of SADC – amongst them "Peace and Security" and the "peaceful settlement of disputes" – and on the other hand, from the authority of the SADC Summit to establish such institutions it felt necessary.

The main objective of the OPDS is the promotion of peace and security in the SADC region. This in turn is broken down into a number of more specific goals which have as a common denominator, the concept of 'human security' instead of the traditional idea of 'military security'. The specific goals pertain to

---

235 See: Dlamini-Zuma (2009)

236 See: SADC (2007b), Memorandum of Understanding amongst the member states of SADC on the new headquarters of SADC. Gaborone. www.sadc.int

237 SADC Secretary General Dr Salomao predicted this at a press conference in August 2008; see: http://www.info.gov.za/speeches/2008/08081409451001.htm

238 See Meyns, Peter (2002): The Ongoing Search for a Security Structure in the SADC Region: The re-establishment of the SADC Organ on Politics, Defence and Security (OPDS). In: Hansohm et al (eds.) (2002):144. and also Breytenbach, Willie (2000): Security in the SADC Region: What a Performance Index of the Organ tells about Co-operation and Integration. In: Peters-Berries, Christian and Marx, Michael T (2000), Monitoring the Process of Regional Integration in SADC, Harare 2000:94f

- the formulation of a common foreign policy of SADC,
- the enforcement of peace when all other measures have failed,
- the evolution of common and democratic political values, practices and institutions,
- the observance of human rights, and
- the promotion of democratic institutions and practices ([239]).

The 1996 Summit also decided that the *"Interstate Defense and Security Committee"* (ISDSC) – a committee comprising of the Ministers of Defense and Security set up by the FLS – would become one of the institutions of the OPDS. This was confirmed by the 2002 Protocol on OPDS.
When the OPDS was first established in 1996, its organizational status remained somewhat vague. It remained unclear whether the OPDS, after all created by a SADC Summit and to be based upon a Protocol, was a part of SADC or independent of it.

The OPDS was, according to the founding communiqué of 1996 supposed to:

> *"operate at Summit level, and [...] function independently of other SADC structures. The organ shall also operate at Ministerial and technical levels. The chairmanship of the Organ shall rotate on an annual and on a Troika basis".* ([240])

The decision to operate the Organ with a high degree of autonomy but still as part of the SADC structures was challenged by Zimbabwean President *Robert Mugabe*, who was elected to be the first chairperson of the OPDS, as he had also been the last chairman of the FLS ([241]). He tried to establish the OPDS as a parallel structure to SADC, insisting on separate Summits and ministerial meetings (which was provided for by founding communiqué of 1996) but also on an equal status of the OPDS chairman as the SADC chairperson ([242]). Although *Mugabe* had apparently been prepared to relinquish his position as chairman of OPDS at the *Blantyre* (Malawi) Summit of SADC in September 1997, he was not removed for tactical reasons.

---

239 See SADC (2002). The Protocol on Politics, Defence and Security. Gaborone.

240 SADC (1996), Communiqué of the Summit, Gaborone, 28 June 1996

241 Another factor in his election as the first chairman of the Organ was probably that it was felt amongst the other Heads of State, that he 'deserved' an elevated position in view of his merits in the liberation struggle which would put him on a similar level as the newly elected SADC chairman *Nelson Mandela*; see Meyns (2000):258..

242 In August 1997 a draft Protocol on the OPDS, which had been developed under strong Zimbabwean guidance, was adopted at a meeting at a ministerial level in Harare. It formally established the OPDS at a Summit level parallel to SADC and thus went beyond the original idea.

The dispute over the status of the Organ can also be interpreted as a struggle between a group of SADC member countries with South Africa at the helm and others aligning themselves with Zimbabwe, in other words, as a struggle for supremacy in the region between the 'old FLS' and the new economic and political 'superpower' South Africa. On the surface of the dispute, was the question whether the OPDS fell under the authority of the SADC Summit, and thus, under the SADC chairman or was independent of it. At the core of the quarrel, however, was the issue of whether South Africa was to be accepted as the new regional leader. No consensual solution could be found at the Summit in *Blantyre* 1997 and consequently SADC suspended the Organ ([243]) but left *Mugabe* in its (suspended) chair.

It took two years before SADC was able to commence working on a new consensus of how to re-activate the Organ. In the meantime, Mugabe had (mis-)used his 'position' as chairperson of the suspended Organ to justify the military intervention of Zimbabwe, Angola and Namibia in the Congolese civil war in August 1998 as an SADC operation. This was strongly rejected by the SADC chairperson *Nelson Mandela*; and indeed no official SADC document endorsed the intervention. As long as *Mandela* was SADC Chairperson he tried to check *Mugabe* and his often reckless regional activities; however, this did not allow for any rapprochement over the OPDS issue. Only after *Mandela* had handed over the chairmanship of SADC to Mozambican President *Joaquim Chissano* and retired himself from active politics in April 1999, the path was open for a new attempt to make the Organ work.

The first step was to incorporate the restructuring of the OPDS into the planned overall review of SADC. At a meeting of the ISDSC in Swaziland in October 1999 it was agreed that the Organ should be a part of SADC structure and report to the SADC Summit. At an extraordinary SADC Summit in March 2001 in *Windhoek* (Namibia), it was finally decided that;

> *"the Organ will now be integrated into the SADC structures and will be coordinated at Summit level on a Troika basis reporting to the Chairperson of the Summit"* ([244])

This meant that the chairperson of the Organ was to be a Head of State, but that the Organ would have no separate Summit meeting and the chairperson of the OPDS would be elected by the SADC Summit to which he also would report. It was also decided that the chairperson of SADC could not at the same time head

---

243 The suspension was enforced with the threat of SADC chairman Mandela, that South Africa would resign as SADC chair if the Summit agreed to a separate OPDS Summit; see Meyns (2002):146

244 SADC (2001), Communiqué of the Extraordinary Summit, Windhoek, 9 March 2001

the Organ. Like in all major SADC institutions, the Organ was to be collectively governed by a Troika of leaders (see TEXT BOX 9.4.). The structure of the OPDS was also determined: three permanent committees and a roving secretariat provided for by the country which holds the chairmanship. Furthermore, the SADC Secretariat in *Gaborone* would provide additional services to the Organ ([245]).

Parallel to the negotiations about the status of the Organ, the Protocol on the OPDS had been adjusted as well. It was officially adopted and signed by 13 of the 14 SADC member countries at the *Blantyre* Summit in August 2001. By 2004, it had been ratified by the required two thirds of the signatories and entered into force. *Mugabe* was allowed to stay on as chairperson after the decision of the extraordinary SADC Summit in March 2001 in *Windhoek*, until a new chairperson was elected at the Summit in 2001 in *Blantyre* (President *Chissano* of Mozambique).

In line with SADC's overall approach to develop strategic plans for each major sector, the OPDS drafted a *"Strategic Indicative Plan for the Organ"* (SIPO). The SIPO, which was launched at the 2004 Summit in *Grand Baie* (Mauritius) sets on the one hand, the guidelines for the implementation of the Protocol on OPDS, and on the other hand, spells out the institutional framework for the work of the OPDS. According to SIPO, the work of the OPDS is divided into four sections:

- Politics
- Defense
- State Security
- Public Security

For each section, the OPDS has - through SIPO - set objectives and strategies of how to realize them.

Although the OPDS met on a regular basis, agreed on a strategic plan and organized its secretariat it remained inactive with regard to the major political crisis of the region: the political and socio-economic melt-down of Zimbabwe since 2000. This may be explained by the fact that Zimbabwe on the one hand still wielded substantial influence within the OPDS and that on the other hand the officially appointed SADC mediator, the then South African President *Thabo Mbeki*, did not appear to have pushed the issue at regional level. Only in 2009, the OPDS for the first time became actively involved in the Zimbabwe

245 See: SADC (2002a)

crisis when it leadership TROIKA met instead of an extraordinary full SADC Summit to discuss the temporary withdrawal of the MDC from the joint Government in Zimbabwe ([246]).

SADC managed to resolve the potential crisis emanating from the unclear status of the OPDS vis-à-vis SADC and the personality clash between South Africa's *Nelson Mandela* and Zimbabwe's *Robert Mugabe*. The OPDS is since 2001 integrated into the overall SADC structure with the function to organize human security in the region and facilitate solutions for political crisis. It has not been able to achieve in the latter field (Zimbabwe, Madagascar) but this might be owed to the fact that SADC itself has started to become active in political crisis mediation ([247]).

8.3. Integration Mechanisms

8.3.1. The SADC Treaty

The SADC Treaty establishes the framework for RI in Southern Africa. The Treaty was originally adopted in 1992 in *Windhoek* ([248]). While its principles are predominantly political and pertain to democracy, human rights, peace and national sovereignty, its objectives are mainly socio-economic and focus on developmental goals, poverty reduction and to some extent also collective self-reliance amongst others.

The Treaty was amended in 2001 at an Extraordinary Summit – again – in *Windhoek*. The amendments reflected previously agreed changes in the structure of SADC regarding new institutions (OPDS, Integrated Council of Ministers, and SADC National Committees) as well as the introduction of the Troika leadership principle. Moreover, they included the adoption of the "Common Agenda" and the "Regional Indicative Strategic Development Plan" (RISDP) ([249]).

By agreeing to the Treaty and its amendments, the SADC member states aim at facilitating the;

---

246 See: www.zimbabwejournalists.com/print.php?art_id=6166 and for further discussion on the issue Chapter 11.

247 See: Chapter 11

248 That is why the Treaty is also referred to as the ‚Windhoek Declaration'

249 See: Chapter 8.3.3.

- Harmonization of their developmental, security, foreign affairs and socio-economic policies.
- Creation of suitable institutions and mechanisms for the implementation of these policies and for the mobilization of resources.
- Development of strategies to overcome integration obstacles.
- Promotion of desperately required human capacity development.
- Promotion of the transfer of technologies both from outside the region and on an intra-regional basis.
- Soliciting additional development funds from donors.

The SADC Treaty allows for sanctions against states, which fail to implement the policies and decisions agreed by SADC, and also against states, which apply policies undermining the decisions taken by SADC. If sanctions are imposed, they are to be determined by a Summit and on a case-by-case basis ([250]).

The political agenda of SADC puts it in line with similar undertakings in other regional integration bodies in Africa. But by declaring to also foster the creation of common political values, systems and institutions, SADC attempts to deepen RI in an area which other regional bodies in Africa have so been less vocal about ([251]), but which is crucial for the ultimate success of RI.

8.3.2. The Common Agenda

The amended Treaty introduced the "Common Agenda" as one of the major results of the *Report on the Restructuring of SADC Institutions*. The Common Agenda is meant to enhance and concretize the Treaty and was approved at the extraordinary Summit in March 2001 in Windhoek.

It is based on the following principles:

- Development orientation;
- ***→ Subsidiarity***;

250 See SADC (1993)

251 The ECOWAS Treaty e.g. does not list any political issues in its aims and objectives. Only on a second tier level the Treaty advocates for the maintenance of peace and stability as well as for the adherence to human rights and the promotion and consolidation of a democratic system of governance. See: www.ecowas.org The Treaty of the EAC lists amongst the organisation's objectives the promotion of peace, security, and stability within, and good neighbourliness and advocates for democracy, good governance and human rights as leading principles; see: www.eac.org

- Market integration and development;
- Facilitation and promotion of trade and investment; and;
- → ***Variable Geometry***.

Its objectives are both developmental and political:

- The promotion of sustainable and equitable growth and socio-economic development that will ensure poverty alleviation/eradication,
- The promotion of common political values, systems and other shared values which are transmitted through institutions which are democratic, legitimate and effective.
- The consolidation and maintenance of democracy, peace and security in the region.

The Common Agenda reconfirmed, re-emphasized and modernized crucial political principles and objectives for RI in SADC. The use of the terms "*subsidiarity*" and "*Variable Geometry*" mark important innovations in the conceptual thinking of SADC. They express the understanding that RI has greater chances of succeeding if it allows for a flexible approach and has regard for the varying degrees of national willingness and ability to surrender national sovereignty. "*Subsidiarity*" in the context of RI means, that a central authority (i.e. SADC) should only perform those tasks which cannot be performed at a lower (more immediate) level; in other words, it may only act in form of making laws or regulations where the action of member states is insufficient. The EU had been the first regional body that has applied the principle of 'subsidiarity' in the "*Treaty of Maastricht*".

"*Variable Geometry*" refers to the speed of integration at country level. It is a concept that was developed and tried out first in the EU. It allows for a differentiated speed of regional integration according to the ability and willingness of member states to comply with a set of economic and political requirements. Some countries might be able and willing to implement these requirements faster than others but instead of waiting for the 'slower' countries to catch up, the concept of "variable geometry" allows the 'faster' countries to move ahead. By this, they are setting benchmarks and providing practical experiences for the 'slower' countries. The introduction of the EURO in the EU is an example for "variable geometry". Countries such as the UK and newcomers such as Poland, the Czech Republic, and Hungary etc. are either politically unwilling or economically not yet sufficiently prepared, have the chance to join the EURO-zone at a later stage.

By applying these concepts, the SADC leaders took cognizance of the fact that there is a considerable gradient in the socio-economic development status and also in regard to the political commitment to RI amongst the member states of SADC. The formulation and implementation of the Sector Protocols (see chapter 8.3.4.), which are defining necessary steps for RI, which had to be agreed upon regionally and which also have to be enforced regionally, can be regarded as an attempt to apply the principle of 'subsidiarity'. The principle of 'variable geometry' has been implicitly applied in SADC with countries such as Angola, the DRC and even Swaziland, which are lagging behind in the signing and ratification of Sector Protocols (see chapter 8.3.4.1.) and explicitly in the implementation of the Trade Protocol (see chapter 8.3.4.2), which allowed economically less developed countries to reduce tariffs at a slower pace.

Table 8.2: Comparing Guiding Principles of Regional Integration in Selected RECs

REC	Rule of Law	Demo-cracy Promo-tion	Human Rights	Vari-able Geome-try	Com-ple-men-tarity	Sub-si-dia-rity	Collec-tive self reliance	Deve-lopment Orienta-tion
COMESA	X	X	X				X	
EAC	X	X	X	X	X	X		X
ECOWAS		X	X	(X)			X	X
SADC	X	X	X	X		X	X	X

Source: Treaties. In: www.sadc.int; www.comesa.org; www.eac.org; www.ecowas.org; own compilation

As table 8.2. shows, all four functioning RECs specifically advocate basic political principles and values but only EAC and SADC apply also dynamic and innovative principles such as "variable geometry" and "subsidiarity". The more traditional RECs as COMESA and ECOWAS still derive some of their motivation for their integration efforts from the idea of "collective self-reliance". The fact that SADC also refers to it in its Treaty can be seen as a spill-over from the concepts of its predecessor SADCC. All but COMESA have a "development orientation". It can be speculated that the differences in guiding principles are due to the determining influence of the ECA in the formation and conceptualization of COMESA and ECOWAS on the one hand, and the exposure to European advice ([252]) in the case of EAC and SADC.

252 Both EAC and SADC are e.g. being advised by the German GTZ and other European donor agencies.

8.3.3. The Regional Indicative Strategic Development Plan (RISDP)

The RISDP was adopted by SADC leaders at the Dar es Salam Summit in 2003. It aims at providing SADC with a consistent and comprehensive program for long-term economic and social development by operationalizing SADC's Common Agenda over a 15 year period, sub-divided into 3 year sections. The plan was developed by the Secretariat which consulted for this not just Governments and experts of member states and international cooperating partners but also representatives from civil society and the private sector. The RISDP provided SADC for the first time with a comprehensive framework for regional integration and development.

The RISDP identifies framework conditions for successful RI, two so called *"key integration enablers"*:

- ***Peace, Security, Democracy and Political Governance***: based on § 5 of the amended SADC Treaty, SADC member states vouch to "*promote common political values, systems and other shared values which are transmitted through institutions that are democratic, legitimate and effective*". In the RISDP, SADC countries are going further and acknowledge that economic growth and development cannot take place under "*...conditions of political intolerance, the absence of the rule of law, corruption, civil strife and war*" ([253]).
- ***Economic and Corporate Governance:*** especially the further integration through trade first in form of the SADC FTA and later the SADC customs union is only possible if "good economic and corporate governance" is being complied with at regional and national levels. This includes according to SADC "*sound macro-economic management; transparent public financial management and accountability; transparent first-class banking supervision and financial regulation; and rigorous, best practice corporate governance*" ([254]).

Apart from the key integration enablers, the RISDP also lists other "*Integration and Development Enablers*", which are crucial to facilitate deeper RI ([255]):

---

253 Ramsamy, Prega (2004), the Regional Indicative Strategic Development Plan (RISDP) as a Strategic Framework for Deeper Economic Integration and Social Development in the SADC Region. In: SADC Review 2004. Gaborone

254 ibid.

255 See: SADC (2003), www.sadc.int/attachment/download/file/75

- Intensifying the fight against HIV and AIDS;
- Gender mainstreaming and the empowerment of women;
- Private sector development;
- Rapid adoption and internationalization of ICT;
- Diversification of regional economies;
- Trade liberalisation and development;
- Liberalization of factors of production;
- Research science and technology innovation, development and diffusion;
- Productivity and competitiveness improvements; and
- Enabling institutional environment.

Some of these 'enablers' are directly related to the deepening of RI, others such as 'fighting HIV/AIDS' or 'Gender mainstreaming' are more cross-cutting issues and not directly linked to RI.

The RISDP aligns itself closely to the → ***"Millennium Development Goals"*** (MDGs) and puts 'poverty eradication' as its overarching objective. The RISDP identifies a number of intervention areas for regional cooperation and integration based on the SADC objectives. They are differentiated into '*cross-sectional intervention areas*' and '*Sectoral cooperation and integration intervention areas*'.

The cross-sectional intervention areas are ([256]):

- Poverty eradication,
- Combating HIV/AIDS,
- Gender equality and development,
- Science & Technology,
- Information and communications technology,
- Environment and sustainable development,
- Private sector development and,
- Statistics.

The sectoral cooperation and integration intervention areas are:

- Trade/Economic Liberalization and Development,
- Infrastructure Support for Regional Integration and Poverty Eradication,
- Sustainable Food Security and,
- Human and Social Development.

---

256 ibid

SADC regarded it as crucial for the realization of the RISDP, to raise sufficient and sustainable funding. One way of improving the funding base - which has always predominantly been based on grants and to a lesser extent, contributions from member states - was to change the formula for membership contributions. Until 2002, member states had been making equal contributions to the SADC institutions. This had overstretched some of the smaller and poorer countries' resources and they had fallen behind in the payment of their contributions. As of April 2003, the formula for the membership contributions has changed and has since taken into account the relative size of the GDP of a member state. This has ensured not only improved payment morale but also an increase in revenue as bigger and more affluent economies such as South Africa, Mauritius, Botswana and more recently, also Angola have to shoulder a bigger part of the payments.

The RISDP comes with an elaborate "Coordination and Implementation Strategy", which is supposed to ensure that the plan really has an impact. Politically, the Council of Ministers initially through the Integrated Committee of Ministers then through the new ministerial clusters is responsible for policy direction, oversight to implementation and assessment of goal attainment. The Secretariat is in charge of the coordination and management of the plan; implementation itself needs to be coordinated between the Secretariat, Technical Advisory Committees and Subcommittees, Programme Steering Committees, participating Member States and SADC National Committees. With the support of donors, the implementation of some programmes is outsourced to companies and contractors.

Probably inspired by the extensive advisory support of several donors at the Secretariat, the RISDP has developed a result-based M&E system, which allows for a continuous checking of the progress and impact of the RISDP projects. The oversight of the M&E system is vested in the SADC Summit. The Secretariat is charged with the technical monitoring of the projects; at a national level, the SADC National Committees are responsible for the monitoring with regular feedback from the Secretariat.

However, after only three years the SADC Summit of 2006 (*Maseru*, Lesotho) realized the need for a "re-prioritization" of the broad and not sufficiently structured intervention areas and established a task force on regional economic integration consisting of the ministers responsible for finance, investment, economic development, trade and industry in order to "fast-track" RI. A 'job evaluation study' ([257]) to ensure that the positions at the Secretariat were aligned to the SADC priorities was also commissioned.

---

257 Conducted by KPMG

At an extraordinary Council of Ministers meeting in 2007 (*Lusaka*, Zambia), SADC approved on the basis of these studies a re-prioritized integration agenda, which now consists of the following four sectors ([258]):

- Peace and Security Cooperation as a pre-requisite for RI.
- Trade/economic liberalisation and development through progressive market integration (free movement of goods, services and factors of production; macro-economic convergence; financial market integration and monetary cooperation; intra-regional investment and FDI; productive competitiveness etc.).
- Regional infrastructure and services (transport, energy, water and ICT).
- Special programs of regional dimension (Education; Health, HIV/AIDS; food security; transboundary natural resources; gender equality; statistics; science and technology.

Another result of the meeting was the decision to replace the *Integrated Council of Ministers* with six ministerial clusters ([259]). The new ministerial clusters replacing the ICM followed the likewise newly set priorities ([260]):

- Cluster for trade, industry and finance.
- Cluster for infrastructure and services.
- Cluster for food and agriculture, natural resources and environment.
- Cluster for social, human development and special programs.
- Cluster of the OPDS.
- Cluster on cross-cutting issues related to science and technology and gender.

To some extent this re-organisation can be seen as a revival of old structures (sectoral ministerial committees) but more important is the clear strategic re-positioning, which puts economic factors and particular integration through trade and investment at the helm of RI process.

The Secretariat responded to the identified needs for organisational streamlining and concretizing by breaking up the implementation of the RISDP into manageable levels:

---

258 Giuffrida, L. and Müller-Glodde, H. (2008):131

259 ibid:123f, 132. The ICM had a last meeting in June 2008 before being replaced by the ministerial committees.

260 ibid:132

- The 15-year RISDP implementation framework with the above mentioned 'milestones' as the overall strategy.
- Five-year RISDP Strategic Plans (starting 2009/10-2013/14), which are directorate and/or unit based.
- Detailed Annual Business Plans with budgets, which are also directorate-/unit-based. ([261])

As a result of the re-organisation process, the Secretariat is increasingly becoming the driving force for RI in SADC. The enhanced capacity of the Secretariat is enabling it to prepare concepts, strategies and mechanisms for integration and to monitor them. This gives additional bureaucratic power (definition of policies; performance monitoring) to the Secretariat on whose facilities, competence and direction the policy makers at the Summit and the Council of Ministers rely. A certain parallel to the development of the EU where the Commission has assumed a not always appreciated leading role in the integration process cannot be denied.

However, the reform process was anything else but smooth and organized ([262]). It took several years and intensive lobbying to agree on the adoption of a medium-term development strategy for SADC, a streamlining and concentration of its decision-making process and an - at first - only gradual strengthening of the Secretariat. But even when this was agreed and the Treaty amended in 2001, it took another couple of years before the Common Agenda was concretized in form of the RISDP in 2003 and even more time to recruit the necessary staff for the Secretariat to start functioning properly. Only since 2007/8 has the organizational development process of SADC reached a stage allowing the Secretariat to steer regional integration in a systematic, planned and assessable manner.

8.3.4. The Sector Protocols

One major innovation of SADC as compared to the old SADCC was the introduction of sector protocols. A Protocol is a legal instrument of implementation under the SADC Treaty, which outlines a course of action

---

261 ibid:127

262 Some researchers even call the process an „administrative chaos"; see Adelmann, Martin (2008): Fundraising or common foreign policy? 30 Years of SADC Consultative Conference. In: Bösl, T. et al (eds.) (2008), Monitoring Regional Integration in Southern Africa Yearbook. Volume 8. Stellenbosch:356

aimed at achieving a specific goal of the institution. Based on the previously agreed cooperation areas under SADCC and complemented by crucial areas not yet covered by the functional cooperation, SADC developed a number of protocols which set sectoral objectives. Elaborate annexes are describing the implementation strategies and procedures of each protocol. The introduction of protocols marks the transformation from mere cooperation to regional integration. The protocols are major integration instruments as they not only define sectoral integration objectives, but also determine implementation strategies and timeframes and make their implementation obligatory. It requires the consensus of 75% of the member states present at a Summit to change or amend a Protocol.

Protocols (see table 8.3.) were until 2001 usually drafted by one member state and then presented to the Council of Ministers for approval before eventually submitted to the Summit for adoption; however, after its organizational upgrading the Secretariat has assumed a leading role in this respect. The first draft of a protocol produced by the Secretariat and then circulated and commented upon amongst the member states before it enters the actual SADC process of approval. It is discussed, amended and lastly approved first by senior officials, and then by the Council of Ministers before it is adopted by a Summit. Before the Draft Protocol reaches the Summit, it goes through various committees and sub-committees of experts and stakeholders (including the private sector and civil society) to allow for a wide range of concerns and interests to be noted. Protocols enter into force upon ratification by 2/3 of the signatory states. In most countries, ratification of a Protocol requires that it is passed by Parliament. However, in case of latecomers to SADC such as the DRC and Madagascar, it is also possible for them to join a protocol through "*Accession*".

Each protocol consists of a main body of text and the Annexes, which regulate and determine the process of integration. The integration concept of SADC rests on the 'Trade Protocol', which determines the establishment of the SADC Free Trade Area (SAFTA). The roadmap for further trade-led RI is outlined in the RISDP: it foresees the establishment of a customs union by 2010, a common market by 2015 and a monetary union by 2016.This integration strategy regards the Trade Protocol as the driving force behind RI which is complemented by Protocols on infrastructure (transport; energy), human resource development, and finance and investment. Of these protocols only the one on Finance and Investment has not yet been ratified.

Table 8.3.: SADC Sector Protocols and their Status

No	Protocol	Date of Signature	Date of Ratification	Comments
1	Treaty of the Southern African Development Community	17.8.92	30th September, 1993	Treaty has been ratified by all members
2	Immunities and Privileges	17.8.92	30th September, 1993	Treaty has been ratified by all members
3	Shared Watercourse Systems	28th August 1995	28th September, 1998	Not yet ratified by Angola and Mozambique; not acceded by DRC.
4	Energy	24th August 1996	17th April, 1998	Not yet acceded by DRC
5	Transport, Communications and Meteorology	24th August 1996	6th July, 1998	Not yet acceded to by DRC
6	Combating Illicit Drugs	24th August 1996	20th March, 1999	Not yet ratified by Angola and not acceded to by DRC
7	Trade	24th August 1996	25th January, 2000	Not yet acceded to by Angola and DRC
8	Education and Training	8th September,1997	31st July, 2000	Not yet ratified by Angola and DRC
9	Mining	8th September,1997	10th February, 2000	Not yet ratified by Angola and Swaziland. Not yet acceded to by DRC.
10	Development of Tourism	14th September 1998	26th November, 2002	Not yet acceded to by Angola and DRC ; not yet ratified by Malawi and Zambia
11	Health	18th August 1999	14 August 2004	Not yet acceded to by Angola, DRC, Swaziland and Zambia
12	Wildlife Conservation and Law Enforcement	18th August 1999	30th November, 2003	Not yet acceded to by Angola, DRC, Swaziland and Zimbabwe

13	Legal Affairs	7 August, 2000	Not yet	Not yet ratified by Angola, Mozambique, South Africa, Swaziland, Zambia and Zimbabwe; Not yet acceded to by DRC
14	Tribunal and the Rules of Procedure	7 August, 2000	14 August 2001.	The Protocol entered into force upon the adoption of the Agreement Amending the Treaty of SADC at Blantyre on the 14 August 2001.
15	Revised Protocol on Shared Watercourses	7 August, 2000	22nd September 2003	Not yet acceded to by Angola, DRC and Zimbabwe
16	Amendment Protocol on Trade	7 August, 2000	7th August, 2000	Not yet acceded to by Angola and DRC
17	Adoption Agreement Amending the Treaty of SADC	14 August, 2001	14 August, 2001	No ratification required
18	Politics, Defence and Security Cooperation	14 August, 2001	2nd March, 2004	Not yet acceded to by Angola, DRC, Swaziland and Zambia
19	Controls of Firearms, Ammunition and other related Materials in SADC	14 August, 2001	8th November, 2004	Not yet ratified by DRC, Swaziland and Zimbabwe. Not yet acceded to by Angola
20	Fisheries	14 August, 2001	8th August 2003.	Not yet acceded to by DRC, Swaziland and Zimbabwe
21	Culture, Information and Sports	14 August, 2001		Not yet ratified by Angola, DRC, Swaziland, Zambia and

				Zimbabwe
22	Protocol against Corruption	14 August, 2001		Not yet ratified by Angola, DRC, Mozambique, Namibia and Swaziland
23	Extradition	3 October, 2002		Not yet acceded to by Mozambique. Not yet ratified by Angola, Botswana, DRC, Malawi, Namibia, Swaziland, and Zimbabwe
24	Forestry	3 October, 2002		Not yet acceded to by Botswana, Mozambique and Namibia. Not yet ratified by Angola, DRC, Malawi, Swaziland, Zambia and Zimbabwe
25	Mutual Legal Assistance in Criminal Matters	3 October, 2002		Not yet acceded to by Mozambique. Not yet ratified by Angola, Botswana, DRC, Lesotho, Malawi, Namibia, Swaziland, Zambia and Zimbabwe
26	Agreement Amending the Protocol on Tribunal	8 August 2002	8 August 2002	No further ratification required
27	Facilitation of the Free Movement of People (Draft Protocol)	18 August 2005		Still in draft
28	Finance and Investment	18 August 2006		Signed by all member states
29	Gender and Development	18 August 2008		

Sources: www.SADC.int
http://ejn.org.za/component/option,com_docman/task,cat_view/gid,70/Itemid,129/
http://knowledge.uneca.org/member-states/observatory-on-regional-integration/sadc-treaty-and-protocols/sadc-treaty-and-protocols
http://www.tralac.org/cgi-bin/giga.cgi?cmd=cause_dir_news_item&news_id=45318&cause_id=1694

Apart from these Protocols and the Treaty, SADC has also agreed on other documents of a less binding nature:

- The SADC Charter of the Regional Tourism Organisation of Southern Africa (RETOSA), which was signed and entered into effect on 8, September 1997 (still not signed by the DRC).
- The Memorandum of Understanding on Cooperation in Taxation and related Matters, which was signed and entered into force on 8, August 2002 (required signatures of the DRC and Mozambique).
- The Memorandum of Understanding on Macroeconomic Convergence, which was signed and entered into force on 8, August 2002 (required signatures of the DRC and Zambia).
- The Southern African Development Community SADC Mutual Defence Pact, which was signed by most SADC members on 26, August 2003 but still needs to be signed by Angola and be ratified by Angola, DRC, Lesotho, Malawi, Mozambique, South Africa, Swaziland, Tanzania and Zambia.
- SADC Charter of Fundamental Social Rights, was signed and entered into force on 26, August 2003 (still needs to be signed by Angola and Botswana).
- The Declaration on Gender and Development was passed on 8, September 1997 and immediately entered into force. The declaration was amended on 14, September 1998 by an *Addendum* on the Prevention and Eradication of Violence against Women and Children. The declaration provided the basis for the Protocol on Gender and Development, signed by all SADC member states by August 2009.
- The Declaration on Productivity was passed on 18, August 1999 and did not require any further ratification.
- The Declaration on Information and Communications Technology (ICT), was passed in August 2001 and did not require any further ratification.
- The Declaration on HIV and AIDS, was passed on 4, July 2003 and did not require any further ratification.
- The Declaration on Agriculture and Food Security, was passed on 15, May 2004 and did not require any further ratification.

The four Directorates and the Gender Unit in the Secretariat are responsible for the implementation of the Protocols, Charters and Memorandum of Understandings. They each produce an annual status report, which is published and accessible online ([263]).

8.3.4.1. The Ratification Process

The accession and ratification of the Protocols provide some indications on the willingness, interest and capability of countries to engage in RI in SADC. The countries, which seem to be the least committed to RI, appear to be Angola and the DRC. By August 2004, the DRC had not yet acceded to 14 of the then 26 Treaties and Protocols and not ratified 21 of the 24 Protocols and Treaties, which required ratification. The respective figures for Angola were six documents not signed and 16 not ratified. The country with the third worst record is Swaziland with four documents not signed and 12 not ratified. The only countries at this stage (2006), which had both signed and ratified all protocols, were Mauritius, South Africa and Tanzania. The time span between signing and entry into force of a Protocol varied between 13 months (for the Protocol on Immunities and Privileges) to 60 months (for the Health Protocol).

In comparison to ECOWAS, SADC's record of accession to Protocols is slightly better and a bit faster. By the end of 2006, ECOWAS had 52 Protocols and conventions signed, of which 35 had been ratified and thus entered into force while 17 were still in the process of ratification. The time required to ratify a Protocol in ECOWAS varied between two and five years; the average time was 42 months ([264]).

Ratification requires usually ([265]) an act of Parliament in all SADC countries. While in most SADC countries, the Government used to have a solid majority or was even ruling unopposed (Angola, DRC, Swaziland and Zimbabwe [until 2000]); it should have been a simple act to pass these Protocols through Parliament. The fact that this hardly ever happened and especially not in some of the autocratic countries (Angola, DRC and Swaziland) seems to indicate that the law-making process in many SADC countries is quite poorly organized, that the

263 www.sadcreview.org

264 See: Cernicky, J. (2007):93

265 Exceptions are the latecomers such as the DRC or Madagascar in order to allow them to catch up faster with the integration process.

'translation' of regional decisions into national law is hampered by a lack of capacity and/or that RI issues have a rather low priority.

The experience with the implementation of Protocols has been mixed. Some Protocols that are central to the further integration process such as the ones for Trade, Energy or Transportation, Communications and Meteorology have been relatively well implemented. Technically well-developed Annexes prescribing the required procedures and practical implementation steps also support the actual execution of these Protocols. Other Protocols such as the ones for Health, Wildlife Conservation and Law Enforcement or Tourism took up to five years to be ratified and they are only slowly being enforced.

8.3.4.2. The Trade Protocol

The Trade Protocol is the most crucial of all Protocols for the further development of SADC as it deals with the main integration mechanism, but there are also other Protocols, which play an important role for the further integration in SADC. They are the:

- Protocol on Transport, Communications and Meteorology,
- Protocol on Energy,
- Protocol on the Facilitation of the Free Movement of People,
- Protocol on Politics, Defence and Security Cooperation,
- Protocol on Tribunal, and
- Protocol on Finance and Investment.

This is not to say that the Protocols not mentioned are unimportant, but they do not have the same catalytical function for the physical, economic and political integration of the region. The Protocol on OPDS was already discussed above (see chapter 8.2.2.); the one on the Tribunal will be assessed below (see chapter 8.3.6.) ([266]).

The Trade Protocol aimed at establishing a SADC FTA until 2008 (12 years after it had been signed and eight years after it had been ratified).

266 This section will not only discuss the Protocols on Transportation, Energy, Agriculture and Labour Movement as such, but will highlight the regional situation and problems in each of the sectors.

"The Protocol on Trade commits members to phase out existing tariffs, to harmonise trade procedures and documentation within SADC, to define SADC Rules of Origin and to reduce other barriers to trade".([267])

It had required substantial negotiations in the nearly four years between the signing of the Protocol and subsequent ratification before especially South Africa was willing to ratify the Protocol and thus pave the way for its implementation. Twelve of the 15 member states of SADC up to now have ratified the Protocol. Angola, the DRC and the Seychelles have yet to do so.

The major areas of concern for South Africa's strong private sector which played a central role in shaping the South African agenda for the trade protocol negotiations pertained to the car, textile and sugar industries ([268]). For these particular industries, there was the fear that near-to-completion-goods could be imported from abroad to one of the SADC countries where they would just be assembled (in the case of cars) or relabelled (in the case of textiles products) before being dumped on the lucrative South African market. The South African side thus insisted on clear parameters concerning ***→"rules of origin***", customs procedures, the tariff reduction schedule ([269]), a dispute settlement mechanism and transit trade (crucial for the five landlocked member states) being in place and enforced ([270]).

The fears of the smaller SADC countries regarding the full implementation of the FTA focussed on:

---

267 SADC (2008f):4

268 See Peters-Berries/Marx (2000): 36f, Stahl, H.-Michael (1999), The Southern African Development Community's (SADC) Regional Trade Integration Strategy – Overview and Assessment. Paper prepared for the Seminar on 'Benefiting from Regional Integration and Globalisation – Opportunities and Challenges for Malawi. 10-12.11.1999, *Lilongwe*, Malawi.

269 Agreeing on the tariff reduction schedule amongst the SADC countries proved to be a very arduous task as each country had between 5000 and 9000 individual tariff lines; see Stahl (1999):3

270 South Africa especially, as the biggest market in the SADC region had previously made some sobering experiences with 'backdoor' trade. South Africa had to halt Malawian textile exports in the mid 1990s in the context of a bilateral preferential trade agreement because the amount of (cheap) Malawian textiles entering South Africa exceeded by far the production capacity of the Malawian textile companies. Chinese traders had used the Malawian 'backdoor' to enter the otherwise heavily protected South African market. A similar row developed in 1995 between South Africa and Botswana in the confines of SACU over the assembly of (inexpensive) South Korean *Hyundai* cars in Botswana and their (duty free) export to South Africa: see Chauvin, Sophie & Gaulier, Guillaume (2002): Regional Trade Integration in Southern Africa. CEPII Working Paper 12/2002. Paris.

- The loss of revenue from duties, which for some countries amount to a substantial portion of their overall revenue ([271]).
- The sudden and stiff competition for their infant industries from more efficient producers from South Africa and Zimbabwe.
- The loss of control over national economic development policies when protection through tariffs fell away.

At a regularly organised 'Trade Negotiation Forum' (TNF), the various stakeholders bargained intensively over the details of the operationalisation of the Protocol, which were eventually laid down in five voluminous Annexes. In the end, the South African negotiation team, due to their better preparations, extensive resources and experienced negotiators, ensured that their interests were safeguarded. Smaller countries with much less bargaining power and expertise felt to some extent overwhelmed and outmanoeuvred ([272]).

In order to operationalize the Protocol, member states of SADC had to find pragmatic solutions to overcome the above outlined technical and political hurdles. They agreed during the TNF negotiations on:

- A phased reduction of tariffs over an eight to twelve year period. One group of goods ("list A products") was liberalized immediately when the FTA entered into force. The second group of goods ("list B products) were to be liberalized gradually and in asymmetric fashion over an eight-year period until 2008. Lastly, the third group contained goods ("list C products" = sensitive products), which would only be liberalized until 2012 due to their sensitive nature for the economic development of the members countries. Furthermore, South Africa and the SACU members agreed to liberalize most of their tariffs on intra-SADC imports immediately in 2000, while middle-income countries such as Mauritius (but also Zimbabwe) were given eight years to gradually reduce their tariffs and low-income countries such as Mozambique and

---

271 Customs Revenue as a percentage of total Government Revenue ranged in 1996 from 11.6% in the case of Zambia and 15.4% in the case of Botswana to 33.5% in the case of Mauritius, 45% in the case of Lesotho and 49.4% in the case of Swaziland; only South Africa with only 1.8% is not dependent on customs revenue. Most affected by the reduction in customs revenue are Mauritius (-5.7% in total government revenue) followed by Zimbabwe (-5.6%), Malawi (-5.3%) and Zambia (-3.3%); see Chauvier/Gaulier:16

272 Personal communication with one of the leading figures on the Zimbabwean trade protocol negotiation team, Eddie Cross, in 1998 and 1999.

Zambia had to reduce their tariffs only at the very end of the transition period in 2007/8 ([273]).

- A 'rules-of-origin' regime that safeguards the national and particularly the 'infant' industries in the SADC countries. According to the agreement, only those products which, have either a maximum of third country ingredients of not more than 60% of the import (→ ***cif***) value and/or at least 35% of their value added in a SADC member state have preferential access to the SADC market. The problem is the ability of SADC customs authorities to determine the exact amount of local value added and/or that of third country components ([274]).

Under the Trade Protocol, three main institutions were established:

- The Committee of Ministers responsible for Trade (CMT)
- The Committee of Senior Officials (Permanent Secretaries responsible for trade), which serves as an advisory body to the CMT; and
- The Trade Negotiation Forum (TNF) composed of all major stakeholders at which the actual fine-tuning of the implementation took place.

Despite the considerable technical problems in implementing the intra-SADC tariff reductions and delays on the way ([275]), by mid 2008 the target set in reducing and abolishing the tariffs had been reached. SADC was able to launch in August 2008 the SADC FTA and declare that by 2010, SADC would become a customs union. The Executive Secretary of SADC had already announced in 2006 that SADC will pursue its plans according to the timetable laid down in the RISDP to establish a Common Market in 2015, a Monetary Union by 2016 and to introduce a regional currency by 2018 ([276]). Also in 2006, a SADC Customs Union Task Force was established which met first in December 2006 in Maputo, Mozambique, and then in March 2007 in Maseru, Lesotho, to initiate studies preparing for the establishment of the SADC Customs Union. However, when

---

273 See SADC (2008b), SADC FTA. Growth, Development and Wealth Creation. Gaborone

274 See Stahl (1999):5f; The World Bank criticised the SADC rules-of-origin as overly complex and rather an obstacle to trade; see INSAT 2006/6:3

275 See the midterm review on the reduction of SADC tariffs, which the Secretariat published in 2004 and a second review which was conducted by The Services Group (2007). A report on the audit of the implementation of the SADC Protocol on Trade; see: Elago, P. and Kalenga, P. (2007); Wither the SADC Customs Union? In: Bösl et al (eds.), Monitoring Regional Integration in Southern Africa Yearbook 2007:118-136. Cape Town. They report that in 2007 Malawi, Tanzania and Zimbabwe were behind schedule in phasing down their tariff structure.

276 See SADC (2006a):7)

the SADC FTA was launched in August 2008, Angola and the DRC did not join as they had not yet signed the Protocol ([277]).

So far SADC did not conduct a comprehensive evaluation of the impact of the FTA on intra-regional trade although some data seem to suggest that the increase in imports to South Africa from other SADC states is probably a result of the early phasing out of intra-regional tariffs by the SACU members ([278]). Most of the increase in imports is in "traditional raw materials" such as copper, nickel, coffee, tea, tobacco, cotton, wood, sugar and semi-precious gemstones as well as some textiles ([279]).

It is doubtful that SADC can achieve the necessary macroeconomic convergence to establish a working customs union by 2010. More likely it will announce the establishment of a customs union but will give it a timeframe of up to five year to become operational (as it has been done in the case of the EAC). The introduction of a common external tariff (CET) will require a harmonization of the rationales for tariff policy. While the SACU members employ tariffs as an instrument of industrial policy protecting their industries from harsh global competition the other members of SADC such as Mauritius use low tariffs to achieve the opposite: a deeper integration into the global economy. The majority of SADC members regard tariffs as an easy to apply revenue-generating mechanism ([280]). Apart from the SACU member states ([281]) especially the governments of Madagascar (49%), the DRC (41%), Tanzania (38%), Zambia (29%) and Mauritius (22%) are dependent to quite a substantial degree on tariffs for revenue ([282]). It remains to be seen if SADC member states can agree on a CET which will for most of them lower revenues without an immediate compensation through e.g. higher taxes from industrial production or incomes. However, the timely establishment of the customs union is a crucial juncture for the trade-led regional integration concept of SADC.

277 See SADC (2008b):6
278 See: Elago and Kalenga (2007):122
279 ibid.
280 ibid:124f
281 See: table 5.1.
282 See: Elago and Kalenga (2007):127. Figures for 2003.

8.3.4.3. The Protocol on Transport, Communications and Meteorology

This protocol is concerned with transportation systems and infrastructure, telecommunications, postal services and meteorology. It acknowledges that transportation, communication and meteorology "*...are a prerequisite for the promotion of economic growth and development*" ([283]). Being an exporter of several bulky minerals (copper, cobalt, coal, iron, gold, platinum, soda ash, diamonds, bauxite etc) agricultural products (cotton, tobacco, tea, coffee, beef, sugar, horticultural products etc) and a large importer of fuel, machines, vehicles and consumer goods, the SADC region needs functioning, well maintained and integrated transportation and communication systems.
Regarding transport, the biggest challenge is not so much the physical expansion of the transportation systems but its harmonization and the establishment of a supportive technical and managerial infrastructure required to run a regionally integrated transportation network on road, rail, air and water.

This Protocol can be regarded, to some extent as a broadened extension of the cooperation under SADCC in this sector. SADCC had established a special *'Southern African Transport and Communication Commission'* (SATCC) as it attached great importance to transportation and communication to lower the politically crippling dependency from (*apartheid*) South Africa ([284]). Due to the required large amounts for investment, the transportation and communication sector received under SADCC the bulk of the donor support and investments. Between 1980 and 1996, SADCC and SADC received roughly USD 3.9 billion in terms of donor support for a total of 416 projects. Out of this, USD 2.9 billion went towards the finance of 174 transportation and communication projects ([285]) although this represented only 46% of the envisaged costs for these projects. Despite the destabilisation of South Africa during the 1980s, which destroyed substantial parts of the railway system in the region, the effect of these investments have made Southern Africa in terms of rail transport the most integrated region in Africa. In total, Southern Africa has an interconnected railway system of 33,000 km plus another 4,200 km of railways which are not connected with the rest or have a different gauge (Tanzania) ([286]).

---

283 SADC (1996b), The Protocol on Transport, Communication and Meteorology: 4
284 See: Text Box 7.1.
285 See: Peters-Berries/Marx (1997):76
286 See Peters-Berries/Marx (2000): 54f

There are railway connections from the major ports of Durban and Port Elizabeth (South Africa) up to Dar es Salam (Tanzania). The connections further extend from the major mineral producing areas in landlocked Zambia ("Copper Belt") and Zimbabwe to harbours not only in South Africa and Dar es Salam but also in Mozambique (Maputo, Beira, Nacala). Only the Angolan and the Congolese economies are not yet reconnected to the rest of SADC by rail due to the massive destruction caused by the Angolan civil war, which only came to an end in 2002. However, plans have been developed to rehabilitate the *Benguela* railway line and to modernise the Angolan harbour of *Lobito* ([287]). Construction is underway to link the Angolan railway system with Namibia and in a separate move also with Zambia ([288]). In the late 1990s, a private concession closed the last gap in the regional railway system between Beitbridge and Bulawayo in Zimbabwe effectively, linking the South African railway system directly to the Zambian Copperbelt ([289]). However, few of these railway systems have been operating in the past without problems due to the often, rather ineffective, management of state-owned railway companies.

Also part of the regional transport infrastructure are fuel storages and pipelines. The oldest oil pipeline in the region is the *Beira* (Mozambique) to *Mutare* (Zimbabwe) pipeline, which ensured during the Zimbabwean liberation war (1972-1979) and later during the destabilisation of Mozambique through the South Africa backed rebels of RENAMO (1982-1990) the independent supply of Zimbabwe. Currently, plans are underway to build a pipeline from the Mozambican port of *Nacala* and Malawi. In Namibia, the state-owned oil company *Namcor* has started to build a huge oil storage at the harbour of *Walvisbay* ([290]).

The inefficiencies in terms of both management and capacity of the regional railway system led to a parallel extension of the regional road network. By the year 2000, there were more than 100,000 km of primary roads in the SADC region, which in the cases of countries like Botswana, Swaziland, Mozambique, Zambia, Malawi and Tanzania are still expanding. It is now possible to drive from as far as Arusha (Tanzania) to Cape Town (South Africa) in a little more

287 See: Rochas (2008), Regional Infrastructure Gains Ground in SADC. http://www.rtfp.org/news.php?id=77

288 ibid.

289 Such a link also existed before via Botswana. However, it was time-consuming (additional borders to cross) and longer in terms of distance to use this railway line. Botswana was not happy about the opening of the Beitbridge Bulawayo Railway line.

290 See: Rochas (2008)

than week on perfectly tarred roads on different routes ([291]). The upcoming FIFA 2010 Soccer World Cup in South Africa has facilitated a massive facelift of roads particularly in South Africa. In the *Gauteng* Province alone investments in the road sector USD 1.2 billion are taking place ([292]).

In 1995, the total cross-border trade in the SADC region amounted to ca. 31.2 million tons of which 50.4% were transported by rail and the rest by road ([293]). Southern Africa has several big ports, which have the capacity to handle the considerable bulk of regional trade.

In order to streamline planning processes, SADC adopted – influenced by the South African Government – the concept of "*Transport and Development Corridors*" or "*Spatial Development Initiatives*" (SDI). It delineated the region into a number of such corridors of which some are already functioning and others are in the rehabilitation or planning stage:

- The *Maputo Corridor*, which was the first transport corridor linking the South African industrial heartland in *Gauteng* Province with its nearest harbour.
- The *Beira Corridor*, linking the harbour with landlocked Zimbabwe and Zambia.
- The *Walvis Bay Corridor*, providing an integrated link to the Namibian hinterland and connecting it to
- The *Trans-Kalahari Corridor*, which provides an alternative link for the South African *Gauteng* Province via Botswana.
- The ambitious *Durban-Lubumbashi Corridor*, which intends to connect the mineral-rich *Katanga* Province in the DRC with the biggest South African port and thus will provide a North-South transport axis for the SADC region; and
- the *Dar es Salaam Kapiri Mposhi Corridor*, which is in fact a new name for the Chinese-build *TaZaRa/TanZam* link between the Zambian *Copperbelt* and the Tanzanian harbour of *Dar es Salaam*.
- The *Lobito Corridor,* which when finalised will link the Angolan harbour via the *Benguala* Railway to the mineral rich areas in the *Katanga* Province of the DRC and the Zambian *Copperbelt.*

---

291 Commercial trucks and buses would obviously take longer due to lengthy border clearance processes. The author drove – on separate occasions – the route from Durban to Nairobi with a private car.

292 See: Rochas (2008)

293 ibid

- The *Nacala Corridor* and its extension the *Shire Zambezi Waterway Project*, which will link the northern Mozambican port of *Nacala* with landlocked Malawi.
- Other corridors in the planning stage or under development are: the *Central Development Corridor* in northern Tanzania; the *Mtwara Development Corridor* in southern Tanzania; the *Zambezi Valley SDI* along the course of *Zambezi* River in Mozambique, Zimbabwe and Zambia; the *Malange Corridor* in northern Angola; the *Namibe Corridor* in southern Angola; and the *Gariep SDI* along the *Orange River* including Namibia, South Africa and Botswana ([294])

However, agreeing on the technical details of harmonizing transportation and communication often proved much more difficult and cumbersome than assenting on the broader political objectives. Some of the difficulties to be overcome were:

- The conflicting regulations pertaining to road usage of roads by trucks. There were huge variations about the number of axles allowed, the maximum lengths or maximum load for trucks between SADC member states. Weighbridges had to be built and personnel for them be trained even after there had been agreement on axle-loads and maximum loads.
- Differentiations in road user fees amongst SADC countries make it cumbersome (in case direct fees are charged), expensive and arbitrary to engage in intra-regional trade.
- The required paperwork (insurances, import licences, transit bonds etc.) had not only to be harmonized but also simplified in order to facilitate smooth intra-regional trade relations.
- The lengthy and cumbersome controls and checks at the several intra-regional border posts such as *Beitbridge* (South Africa – Zimbabwe), *Chirundu* (Zimbabwe – Zambia), *Nyamapanda* (Zimbabwe – Mozambique/Malawi), *Tunduma* (Zambia – Tanzania), *Mwanza* (Mozambique – Malawi) or *Mutare* (Zimbabwe – Mozambique). It was estimated that in 1995 (at a time when intra-regional trade was just starting to pick up), unnecessary delays of 60 hours on average per truck at the *Beitbridge* Border Post alone caused costs of more than USD 75 million annually ([295]).

---

294 See: SADC (2007):20f

295 Mushauri, Joshua (1997): Opportunities and Problems of Regional Road Freight Transport. KAF Occasional Paper, Harare 1997. According to AU/ECA (2004):141 the border delays improved only marginally by 2000. The longest waiting periods were still recorded at the *Beitbridge* crossing (36 hours average), followed by *Victoria Falls* (between Zimbabwe and Zambia; 36 hours); *Mutare* (26 hours), *Chirundu,*

SADC has not been able to develop harmonised policies on these issues. For example, a decision of the Council of Ministers in 1995 to harmonize the road user charges in SADC was by 2007, still not implemented due to disagreement on the principles and insufficient implementation capacity.

> *"As a result, the region has different sources of road financing arrangements in place including road or bridge tolls (Mozambique, South Africa and Zimbabwe), fuel levies (all States), fixed charges per unit of distance (SADC States that are also members of COMESA) and other taxes. .... The differences continue to impact negatively on the smooth flow of traffic across borders within the region."* ([296])

The same is true for improving the speed of border control and clearance procedures. The lines of trucks forced to wait in *Beitbridge* have not decreased; in fact, the South African Government had to construct a huge parking facility in 2004 in order to unblock the road from hundreds of trucks waiting to clear the border. Despite the development of a model Customs Act, no country has yet adopted it ([297]).With support from a number of donor-financed programmes, including the Regional Trade Facilitation Programme (RTFP), plans for the establishment of "one-stop-border posts" are underway for the border crossings between Zimbabwe-Mozambique (*Forbes-Machipanda*), South Africa-Mozambique (*Lebombo-Ressano-Garcia*) and Zimbabwe-Zambia (*Chirundu*) ([298]). The latter was officially opened in December 2009 after it had been established under the auspices of COMESA ([299]).

Weighbridges have been introduced in many SADC countries after the ratification of the Protocol, but are not all operated regularly due to insufficient personnel and the sheer amount of road traffic passing through the SADC region. Furthermore, only in some countries are the weighing certificates parts of the required customs clearance documents.

The harmonisation of transportation regulations and procedures will gain even more significance when SADC moves towards the establishment of a customs union. Then intra-regional border controls must be abolished or at least reduced to those products, which will still be exempted from the customs union regime. Divergent road, rail and air transport regimes in terms of user fees, technical specifications and operation permits within the region, could then be regarded as NTTBs and undermine the credibility of the customs union.

Machipanda (Zimbabwe and Mozambique) and *Zobue* (Malawi and Mozambique) (24 hours each).

296 SADC (2008a). The SADC Review 2007/8

297 SADC (2008b):10f

298 SADC (2008b):11; Rochas (2008)

299 See: Sub-Saharan Informer (Addis Ababa), 4.12.2009

8.3.4.4. The Protocol on Energy

The Protocol on Energy was one of the first to be signed (1996) and ratified (1998). Its main objective is to harmonise the national and regional energy policies:

> *"to ensure the availability of sufficient, least-cost energy services that will assist in the attainment of economic efficiency and the eradication of poverty, whilst ensuring the environmentally sustainable use of energy resources."* ([300])

On the basis of the RISDP, a SADC Energy Activity Plan was developed which has energy trade, investment, information, training and organizational capacity building as components.

The energy sector (in particular as far as electricity is concerned) is, together with the transportation sector, the most regionally integrated sector. The *Southern African Power Pool* (SAPP), which was established in 1995, will eventually incorporate all 12 SADC countries on the African continent. SAPP is formed by 12 national power utilities, a private company operating the *Cabora Bassa* hydro-electrical power plant in Mozambique and a transmission company *Motraco*, which is linking *Cabora Bassa* via Swaziland to South Africa. Since 2006, SAPP is based in *Harare* (Zimbabwe) as an official SADC institution. The SAPP had in 2008, an installed capacity of 54,742 MW, out of which 46,391 MW was dependable capacity, i.e. permanently available ([301]).

However, not all SADC countries are yet physically linked to the SAPP power grid. Malawi found out the hard way in 2003, what it meant not to be connected to the electricity grid of any other country. After a massive technical fault at one of the four hydro-electrical plants at the *Shire River*, the country's electricity generation dropped by one third necessitating load-shedding in most of Malawi for several months. Only after that sobering experience were the authorities planning in earnest to construct inter-connectors, at least to the Mozambican

---

300 SADC (2008a), SADC Review 2007/8

301 See: SADC Today Volume 10 No.5, April 2008 documenting the official Communiqué of the SADC Energy Ministerial Task Force on Implementation of Power Sector Projects. *Gaborone,* Botswana, 21.02.2008

grid ([302]). In 2007, SADC at a special conference on infrastructure adopted a program to achieve full connectivity in the region by 2012 ([303]).

As electricity in Southern Africa is generated mainly through thermal (coal) and hydroelectric resources (with one nuclear facility in South Africa), the region is dependent on good and regular rainfalls to supply the dams. In periods of severe drought (as in 1991/2) the region easily falls short of its electricity generation requirements. However, drought is not the only challenge to a sufficient supply of electricity. Despite early warnings about a foreseeable shortage of electricity especially in South Africa due to a strongly growing demand for electricity and management problems at South Africa's sole power utility *Eskom*, which had led to stalled or postponed investments into new or maintenance of existing power plants, sufficient preparations were not made. In 2006 and 2007, and more severely in 2008, this caused a shortfall of electricity and massive economic problems in South Africa ([304]). The interconnection with the SAPP power grid was not sufficient to cover the supply gap in South Africa.

Zimbabwe is another example where the integration into SAPP has not solved the power supply problems. The country experienced power cuts for several years as the country's shortage of hard currency due to its prevailing economic crisis (see below chapter 12) prevented urgently needed maintenance and replacement of spare parts in the coal fired power stations in *Hwange* and *Harare* and the hydro-electric power station in *Kariba* ([305]). The shortage of foreign exchange also caused severe backlogs in payments for imported electricity with the effect that neither Zambia nor Mozambique were eventually willing to provide power to their neighbor.

One of the reasons why South Africa promoted the accession of the DRC to SADC in 1997 was probably the expectation to tap into its huge energy potential. The DRC has a potential hydroelectric capacity of 100,000 MW. The *Inga III* dam, on the *Congo River*, alone has a potential generation capacity of 39,000 MW ([306]), which could supply nearly all of Southern Africa's electricity

---

302 The author lived during that period in Malawi and experienced impact of the power shortages on Malawian businesses, administration and private life personally.

303 See SADC (2007), Action on Infrastructure. Strategic Intervention on Accelerating Provision of Priority Regional Infrastructure. Gaborone:11

304 South Africa's exports declined due to power rationing; see: WTO (2009), Trade Policy Review: Southern African Customs Union (SACU). Document WT/TPR/S/222:12 http://www.wto.org/english/tratop_e/tpr_e/tp322_e.htm

305 In 2003, Zimbabwe had to import about 35% of her electricity requirements from South Africa, Zambia, DRC and Mozambique. See http://www.eia.doe.gov

306 See: SAPP (no year), Westcor Power Inter-Connect, mimeo

needs. Of this, only a small portion has yet been developed ([307]) and it will take several more years before this untapped potential can eventually be made available to the industrial centers of the SADC region. SADC supported the conceptualization of the so called "*Westcor Project*", which was supposed to develop hydro-electrical plants at the Inga dam and build connecting power lines from the DRC via Angola, Namibia and Botswana to South Africa. Construction of a new phase on the Inga dam was supposed to have started in 2009 ([308]) but the project is on the verge of failure because the Government of the DRC decided in 2009 to develop *Inga III* alone ([309]). During the 2009 SADC Summit in *Kinshasa* the President of the DRC, *Joseph Kabila*, reconfirmed that *Inga III* is still a regional project, *Westcor*, however, is no longer regarded as the only option of implementation ([310]).

Currently, the region has the following major dams producing electricity:

- ***Angola***: the *Capanda* dam produces ca. 520 MW and is the main source of electricity for the country.
- ***DRC***: the *Inga* I, II and III power stations are either operating, under construction or being planned. They have the capacity of generating up to 40,000-45,000 MW once all are functional. The investment for Inga III will require, however, some USD 50 billion and is very unlikely to be realized soon. The plan to develop *Inga III* through a SADC-based consortium of utility companies (*Westcor*) has been more or less put aside as the DRC Government prefers to undertake the investment itself. Currently, the DRC exports some of its electricity; the internal consumption is to 100% generated with hydropower.
- ***Lesotho***: The *Highland Water Project* generates power and provides water mostly for South Africa. Its installed capacity is 110 MW at the moment; a further 166 MW are planned ([311]).
- ***Malawi***: the *Shire Hydropower* stations produce so far more than 80% of the 285 MW installed Malawian electricity output ([312]). But as the

---

307 The total installed generating capacity was in 2001 estimated at just short of 2,500 MW; of this no more than 650-750 MW were actually produced because most of the turbines were not functioning; ibid.

308 See: SADC Today Volume 11 No.3, December 2008

309 See: PANA 13.08.2009; http://www.afriquejet.com/news/africa-news/westcor-pulls-out-of-inga-iii-power-project-2009081333393.html

310 See: Real Economy: Electricity Generation. Published 25 Sep 2009. http://www.polity.org.za/article/westcor-chief-moves-from-despair-to-delight-as-ingas-regional-status-is-reportedly-confirmed-2009-09-15

311 See: www.lhwp.org.ls

312 See: www.mbendi.com/indy/powr/af/ma/p0005.htm

breakdown of one of it's turbines in 2003 demonstrated, Malawi has no backup in case problems arise as it is not connected to the SADC grid.

- ***Mozambique***: the *Cabora Bassa* hydropower station is the main producer of electricity in Mozambique with an installed capacity of 2,075 MW. Located ca. 1,200 kms north of the capital Maputo and even further from the South African, it is so far only delivering part of its potential output to the consumers. Up to 35% of the output of *Cabora Bassa* was sold to Zimbabwe until the country became unable to pay for the electricity.
- ***Namibia***: The *Ruacana* Hydroelectric station on the *Kunene* River with an installed capacity of 240 MW, generates the bulk of electricity in Namibia of which excess is exported to South Africa ([313]). Further projects are being planned, and amongst them, are the controversial power stations on the *Okavango* River, which Botswana fears will damage its unique *Okavango Swamps*.
- ***South Africa***: has only two hydropower stations: the *Vanderkloof Dam* (240 MW) ([314]) and the *Sterkfontein Dam* with an installed peak capacity of 250 MW. It imports electricity from hydropower sources from Mozambique and to a smaller extent, Zambia and Namibia.
- ***Tanzania***: has six hydro-power stations of different sizes which are supplying a maximum of 557MW ([315]) (=60% of national demand), which suffer from varying water levels and maintenance problems. In 2006, Tanzania had to severely ration power supplies because of extremely low water levels in the dams.
- ***Zambia***: has a number of hydro-power stations of which the biggest are the *Kariba Hydropower Station*, jointly owned with Zimbabwe with an installed capacity of 1,266 MW and the *Itezhi-Tezhi Dam* on the *Kafue* River. The latter's capacity will be raised by 120 MW through an investment of the Indian *Tata Group* ([316]). The country is nearly 100% dependent on electricity generated through hydropower and, as such, extremely vulnerable to droughts.
- ***Zimbabwe***: The country has only one hydropower station: the plant in *Kariba* which can produce up to 666 MW but has struggled to produce at this level. Power rationing has been the rule since the early 2000s, as the country's structural shortfall of supply could be imported no longer due to severe shortages in foreign exchange currency.

---

313 See: http://www.mbendi.com/indy/powr/af/na/p0005.htm
314 See: www.vanderkloofdam.co.za
315 See: http://en.wikipedia.org/wiki/Category:Hydroelectric_power_plants_in_Tanzania
316 See: http://allafrica.com/stories/200805130339.html

However, the majority of the people in the SADC region are not yet connected to the electricity grid as they live either in rural areas, which in most SADC countries have been neglected in terms of infrastructural development, or in undeveloped urban areas. Their major source of energy is fuel wood (wood, charcoal), which has contributed to deforestation and soil degradation throughout the region or paraffin if affordable. The promotion of renewable energies (solar, wind, biogas) would thus be not only a cost effective options for rural (off-grid) electrification programs but also a way to halt the rapid environmental destruction through the overuse of natural resources.

It should be noted that the promotion of agro fuels (sugar cane, *castor* and *yatropha* beans, palm oil etc) makes only limited sense in Southern Africa. Traditionally, sugar-cane producing countries such as Mauritius, Swaziland, South Africa, Zimbabwe, Zambia, Tanzania and Malawi may find it cost effective to utilize some of the molasses produced by sugar-cane plantations for electricity generation ([317]). But in general, no SADC member state has sufficient un- or under-utilized land to grow agro fuels ([318]). Given the often precarious food security situation in many SADC countries, none can afford to use farm land for the production of agro fuels.

The Energy Protocol also calls for the development of other forms of energies such as natural gas, oil and coal ([319]). In terms of carbon-based energy sources the SADC region has the following reserves that can be or are already exploited:

1. Six of the SADC member states have ***natural gas deposits***; only a small part of the potential is currently being utilized ([320]):

   - Angola has large deposits of natural gas that is up to now mostly flared during oil-production. But *Chevron* and *Sonangol* are currently constructing a liquefied natural gas facility, which will be able to produce five million tones per year once ready.

---

317 Mauritius has a 70MW co-generation facility using biomass refuse mostly from sugar cane processing; in 2001 about 40% of the islands electricity demand was met by co-generation; Swaziland also increasingly uses electricity from co-generation (41.4% of installed capacity); see: Karekezi et al (2009):37ff,. Tanzania and Malawi also have already installed small co-generation facilities. However, other big producers o f sugar cane such as South Africa, Zimbabwe and Zambia have not yet shown much interest in this form of energy generation.

318 See Watson, Helen (2009), External Impacts of European Union (EU) Biofuels Policies. Report prepared for the Institute of European Environmental Policy (IEEP), Belgium, January 2009

319 Nuclear Power is only used by South Africa.

320 See: www.OilGasArticles.com accessed on 04.12.2009

- Namibia has a large quantity of natural gas in the so called offshore *Kudu* field. The *Kudu* field is operated by a British company as major shareholder and will provide once ready a 800MW power station at *Oranjemund* which is currently being build by the Namibian utility *NamPower*.
- Tanzania has an offshore gas field (*Songo Songo*) which is partly developed and provides gas for industrial user in *Dar es Salaam*. Another gas field in *Mnazi Bay* is under development.
- Mozambique has a number of offshore natural gas fields, of which two are being exploited since 2005 by the South African energy company *Sasol*.
- Botswana has a substantial natural methane gas field, which is currently under exploration.
- South Africa has discovered a natural gas field offshore adjacent to Namibia's *Kudu* field and intends to pipe the gas to a big liquefied natural gas facility close to *Mossel Bay*.

2. ***Oil reserves*** have been found so far in seven of the SADC member states ([321]):
   - Angola has by far the biggest proven and already exploited oil reserves in the region. In 2007, Angola was producing 1.7 million barrels of oil a day ([322]) of which most is exported.
   - South Africa meets about 10% of its oil consumption from the production of some offshore fields. Current production stands at 23,000 barrel a day.
   - The DRC also has some offshore oil fields which are operated by the state oil company *Perenco*. The country produces about 20,000 barrel a day of which a part is exported.
   - Madagascar discovered oil and natural gas fields in exploration along its coasts. They are not yet producing.
   - Namibia is exploring offshore fields adjacent to the Angolan oil fields but does not produce any oil yet.
   - Tanzania is also still exploring potential oil reserves offshore.
   - Mozambique has awarded several international companies – amongst them the South African *Sasol* – offshore exploration rights.

Angola has not yet entered into any bilateral or regional supply agreements with other SADC member states but exports its oil predominantly to the US and to China. The oil refinery capacities are concentrated in South Africa

321 ibid.
322 See: http://www.eia.doe.gov/cabs/Angola/Oil.html

with some national refineries in Angola, Madagascar, Tanzania and Zambia. Botswana and Namibia are importing nearly all of their oil from South Africa.

South Africa is the major consumer of oil (ca. 68% in 2003) due to her large number of vehicles. The import bills for oil have sharply risen over the past two years (and only fallen towards the end of 2008 again) due to increasing international oil prices making it difficult to guarantee regular supplies to some SADC countries (Zimbabwe, Zambia, and Malawi).

The region has two oil pipelines supplying landlocked Zambia – from *Dar es Salaam* – and Zimbabwe – from *Beira* – with most of their requirements.

3. Probably the biggest source of hydro-carbon energy in the SADC region are the already know coal fields in five member states ([323]):
    - South Africa is the sixth biggest coal producer in the world with about 6% of the world's reserves. In the *Mpumalanga* Province alone 83% of South Africa's coal reserves are to be found. The biggest share of its electricity is produced by coal-fired power stations which are often close by the coal mines.
    - Mozambique is considered to be the largest unexplored coal area in the world, with an estimated 2.4 billion tons of reserves. In the past, coal was produced in *Moatize* in small quantities; new discoveries have led to plans to build a railway line from *Moatize* to the ports of *Nacala* and *Beira*.
    - Malawi has a small coal mine operating but at least two large fields yet totally unexploited.
    - Zimbabwe has a large coal field around *Hwange*, where also a colliery and a power station is located. Another coal field has been discovered at *Sengwa* but is not yet exploited.
    - Botswana has also proven coal reserves but has so far not started to exploit them.

Next to hydro-energy, coal is the most important energy source in the SADC region but also one of its most controversial. South Africa is the biggest consumer of the mineral on the continent. As such, the country is also the biggest emitter of the greenhouse gas CO^2 not only in SADC, but in Africa. Despite the negative impact of the use of coal on global warming and climate change, most SADC countries are either intensively exploring their coal deposits or are already producing, using and exporting coal. The increasing

323 See: www.OilGasArticles.com accessed on 04.12.2009

international pressure to reduce greenhouse gas emissions has led South Africa's Government to announce at eve of the *Copenhagen* Climate Summit in December 2009 that it will reduce its greenhouse gas emissions by 34% by 2020 ([324]) – an objective, which can only be realized if South Africa either reduces the output of its coal burning power stations or modernizes them.

The demand for electricity outstripped in 2007 for the first time the regionally available supply. The construction of additional power stations, better utilization and management of existing ones and the upgrading of the interconnecting lines (between SADC countries) are the main measures SADC wants to employ in order to avoid further power shortages. The slowing down of economic growth and thus a decrease in demand for electricity will contribute over the next couple of years to a more balanced supply and demand situation in the SADC region. As a reaction to the current energy supply constraints, the SADC energy ministers developed a program to spend about USD 7.9 billion from 2007-2010 to boost power supplies and a further USD 32 billion on longer-term electricity generation projects ([325]).

The prospects for the SADC region in terms of energy security over the medium- to long-run are quite good as the region has considerable – to some extent still unexploited - energy reserves, which should ensure sufficient and sustainable supply of especially electricity for its further industrial development. The development of the various energy options constitutes also a major investment potential in the region; companies from South Africa but also increasingly China ([326]) and India have begun to invest in the energy sector.

The SADC Protocol on Energy addresses some, but not all the issues which are pertinent to the energy sector. Environmental degradation and greenhouse gas emissions also need to be included into energy development plans.

8.3.4.5. The Protocol on the Facilitation of the Free Movement of Persons

The (draft) SADC Protocol on the Facilitation of the Free Movement of Persons is next to the Protocols on the OPDS and the Tribunal, one of the more controversial. While it has always been acknowledged by all concepts of RI that

---

324 See: Daily Monitor (Addis Ababa), 8.12.2009

325 See http://www.sardc.net/Editorial/Newsfeature/07260407.htm

326 See e.g. Alden, Chris (2007), China in Africa. London. New York. Cape Town

the free movement of people is one of the pre-requisites for a successful regional integration process, proposals for a Protocol in this respect were long blocked by political considerations at national level within the region.

The issue at the core of the Protocol, is the fear of the more affluent countries in the south of the SADC Region, i.e. South Africa, Botswana, Swaziland and Namibia to be overwhelmed by economic migrants from the poorer northern SADC states. Income levels and opportunities in the southern SADC states are substantially higher than in the poorer member states and a removal of travel, labor and residence restrictions would with high probability, increase the North-South migration. In low-income countries such as Malawi, Mozambique, DRC, Zambia, Zimbabwe and Tanzania, such an out-migration would exacerbate the already critical brain drain of professionals, skilled workers and well-educated youth and added to the economic woes.

Caught in the quagmire of interests standing against a regional liberalization of the movement of people, and at the same time understanding the integration necessity to allow exactly this, the SADC leaders developed a Protocol which can be regarded as a compromise. It sets out as the main objective:

> *"... to develop policies aimed at the progressive elimination of obstacles to the movement of persons of the Region generally into and within the territories of State Parties."* ([327])

Instead of passing a protocol on the free movement of people as in the EAC they only agreed on a protocol which would facilitate such as process.

The immediate objectives the Protocol are to facilitate for each citizen of SADC member states

- *"entry, for a lawful purpose and without a visa, into the territory of another State Party for a maximum period of ninety (90) days per year for bona fide visit and in accordance with the laws of the State Party concerned;*
- *permanent and temporary residence in the territory of another State party;*
- *establishment of oneself and working in the territory of another State Party."* ([328])

In order to operationalize the Protocol, all member states have to harmonize their national policies, laws and regulations regarding immigration, visas, labor permits and residence accordingly. Furthermore, they have to introduce computer readable passports, reliable population registers, abolish visa requirements where they still exist, establish separate SADC-desks at all border

327 SADC (2007), Draft Protocol on the Facilitation of the Movement of Persons
328 ibid

crossings and airports, and allow for the granting of residence permits and establishment of businesses. All these requirements practically ensure that the free movement of persons in the SADC region will not be possible in the foreseeable future.

The ongoing crisis in Zimbabwe has forced probably as many as four million Zimbabweans to leave their country; approximately three million have sought refuge in South Africa alone, others in Botswana, Zambia and Malawi. South Africa is trying to deport as many refugees back into Zimbabwe as it can and is thus, at least momentarily, not interested in making the Protocol work ([329]). The substantial amount of work and harmonization required before the Protocol will be effective is another obstacle towards its implementation. Member states which have problems with the Protocol but cannot openly say so can easily delay its coming into effect by e.g. simply not introducing computer readable passports.

8.3.4.6. The Protocol on Finance and Investment

The Protocol on Finance and Investment is one of the 'youngest' protocols; it was presented to the SADC Summit only in 2006 and signed by all member states by August 2007 ([330]) has since not yet been ratified by the required number of signatory countries. Despite this, the protocol is next to the Protocol on Trade probably the most important for the future development of SADC because it prescribes that "*State Parties shall converge on stability-orientated economic policies...*" ([331]) and defines the parameters for macroeconomic convergence. As such the Protocol on Finance and Investment is the crucial juncture on the way from a mere FTA to a Common Market in SADC.

The protocol sets out to "*...to foster harmonisation of the financial and investment policies of the State Parties in order to make them consistent with objectives of SADC and ensure that any changes to financial and investment policies in one State Party do not necessitate undesirable adjustments in other State Parties*" ([332]). This implies a substantial delegation of national sovereignty

329 See: Afrika Süd (5/2009:4) reports that South Africa was in 2009 close to another xenophobic outburst due to the high number of Zimbabwean (illegal) immigrants.

330 See: SADC (2008e), The SADC Macroeconomic Convergence Programme: Progress to Date. TIFI Directorate. Gaborone:4

331 SADC (2006): Protocol on Finance and Investment. Gaborone: 17. See: www.sadc.int

332 ibid:15

to the regional level. The Protocol, however, remains somewhat vague regarding define which supra-regional institution(s) will have to be established to ensure the implementation of the protocol. In some instances the Protocol advocates the establishment of coordinating bodies/committees consisting of senior officials and topical experts ([333]).

In case of disputes arising from the first objective – harmonisation of financial and investment policies – the Protocol appeals to the common sense and "*best endeavours*" of the member states to settle them. Only in the case of disputes related to the second objective of the protocol – a wide range of mechanisms geared towards achieving the first objective – "*... within three months from the time the disputes or differences arose, such dispute or difference shall be referred to the Tribunal for adjudication*" ([334]). These stipulations are compromises as most SADC Governments had serious reservations against further limitations to their national sovereignty.

The Protocol addresses eleven areas for cooperation, of which the first five can be deemed central ([335]):

- cooperation on Investment
- macroeconomic convergence
- cooperation in taxation and related matters
- cooperation and coordination of exchange control policies
- harmonisation of legal and operational frameworks
- cooperation on payment, clearing and settlement systems
- cooperation in the area of information and communications technology amongst Central Banks
- cooperation and coordination in the area of banking regulatory and supervisory matters
- cooperation in respect of development finance institutions
- cooperation on non-banking financial institutions and services
- cooperation in SADC stock exchanges

But the key issue of the Protocol is the acknowledgement that SADC requires economic stability and macroeconomic convergence if it is to attract regional

---

333 These are: Committee of Senior Treasury Officials responsible for implementation of macroeconomic convergence; SADC Exchange Control Committee, which reports to Committee of Senior Treasury Officials, and works towards full liberalisation of exchange controls; and the Committee of Insurance, Securities and Non-Banking financial Authorities of SADC (CISNA); see: SADC (2008): annexes

334 ibid:22

335 ibid: annexes

investments and integrate further. Macro-economic convergence in a regional integration scheme is also crucial for the introduction of a common currency and helpful in paving the way for the introduction of a customs union. The ECA authoritatively stated:

> *"The success of regional integration depends critically on member countries pursuing convergent macro-economic policies. Misalignments of tariffs, inflation rates, exchange rates, debt-to-GDP-ratios, rate of money growth and other vital macroeconomic variables between member countries would be disruptive to economic integration. ... It is therefore imperative that the process of strengthening regional integration should include guidelines for the convergence of the macro-economic and trade policies of the entire regional space so as to strengthen the overall regional integration agenda."* ([336])

The Protocol aims at ([337]):

> *"(a) restricting inflation to low and stable levels;*
> *(b) maintaining a prudent fiscal stance based on the avoidance of large budget deficits, monetisation of deficits and high or rising ratios of public and publicly guaranteed debt to GDP;*
> *(c) avoiding large financial imbalances in the economy of the State Party; and*
> *(d) minimising market distortions."*

The indicators to measure macroeconomic convergence in the SADC region are defined in general terms but are not quantified in the Protocol([338]):

> *"(a) the rate of inflation in a State Party;*
> *(b) the ratio of the budget deficit to GDP in a State Party;*
> *(c) the ratio of public and publicly guaranteed debt to GDP, taking account of the sustainability of such debt, in a State Party; and*
> *(d) the balance and structure of the current account in a State Party."*

The quantification of the indicators for macroeconomic convergence can be found in the special *Memorandum of Understanding (MoU) on Macroeconomic Convergence* that had become effective already in 2002 ([339]). The MoU not only determined the quantitative targets but provided also a timetable for achieving them (see table 8.4). A secondary set of quantitative indicators with a timetable were agreed upon in the RISDP (2003) (see table 8.5). The problems the SADC Secretariat was facing in the beginning were twofold:

---

336 ECA/AU (2008a):2

337 ibid:38f

338 ibid:39

339 See: ECA (2007), Macroeconomic Policy and Institutional Convergence in Member States of Southern African Development Community. Addis Abeba:4ff

- the scarcity and sometimes unreliability of comparable economic data from member states;
- insufficient capacity at the Secretariat to collect, analyse and aggregate country data to a regional convergence picture.

It took until 2007 before the TIFI directorate of SADC was able to produce the first annual report on macroeconomic convergence ([340]).

It is obvious that the indicators for macroeconomic convergence are following closely the so called → ***Maastricht Criteria*** of the EU ([341])), which shaped the European economic integration process over the last two decades. Only the indicator regarding interest rates ([342]) is not included. The additional economic indicators defined in the RISDP follow the same logic of urging the member states of SADC to adopt economic policies aimed at a structural stabilisation.

In November 2008, a workshop to review the macroeconomic convergence indicators made recommendations to change the architecture of the indicators as follows (see table 8.4.), which, however, still have to be accepted by the SADC institutions:

---

340 See: chapter 9.5

341 See: Fontaine, Pascal (2006): Europe in 12 lessons. Brussels:34f. The *Maastricht Criteria* served mainly as the preparation for the introduction of the EURO; member states interested in joining the EURO-zone had to achieve the macroeconomic convergence criteria.

342 "Long-term interest rates may not vary by more than two percentage points in relation to the average interest rates of the three member states with the lowest interest rates"; Fontaine, P. (2006).

Table 8.4.: SADC's Indicators for Macro-Economic Convergence

Indicator/Year	2008	2012	2018
Annual rate of Inflation	< 10%	< 5%	< 3%
Fiscal Deficit/GDP	< 5%	< 3%	< 3%
Public/GDP	< 60%	< 60%	< 60%
Current Account/GDP	< 9%	< 9%	< 3%

Source: SADC (2009a)

Table 8.5.: Other Macro-Economic Targets of SADC

Indicator/Year	2008	2012	2018
Economic growth rate (%)	7	7	7
External reserves (import cover, months)	3	6	6
Central bank credit to governments (%of revenue)	10	5	5
Domestic savings (% of GDP)	25	30	35
Domestic investment (% of GDP)	30	30	30

Source: SADC (2009a)

Table 8.6.: Proposed Architecture of Indicators for Macro-Economic Convergence

Year/Indicator	2008	2012	2018
Primary Indicator			
Annual Inflation Rate	<10%	< 5%	< 3%
Secondary Indicators			
Primary Fiscal Balance/GDP	Tba	Tba	Tba
Public Debt/GDP	< 60%	< 50%	< 40%
Current Account Balance/GDP	< 9%	< 7%	< 5%

Source: SADC (2009a):20

In how far the indicators have been achieved for 2008 will be discussed in chapter 9.5.

The fact that it took another four years before the Protocol was signed after the MoU on the macroeconomic convergence criteria has been ratified indicates that it was far more difficult to come to a regional agreement on the other issues addressed in the Protocol. Controversial were particularly the chapters regarding the coordination of investment policies, exchange rate policies, taxation and the legal frameworks for Central Banks. However, conveniently overlooked is the fact that macroeconomic convergence, which had so easily be accepted earlier, can only be sustainable if the underlying economic principles policies are harmonised; without such a policy convergence any achievements regarding macroeconomic convergence indicators may be accidental, due to external circumstances but hardly sustainable.

The Mozambican Government commissioned in 2004 an assessment of the impact of the Protocol on Finance and Investment on the Mozambican economy and in particular on the private sector ([343]). The assessment was conducted before the Protocol was officially accepted by the SADC Summit in 2006. Nevertheless, some of its findings hold true even now:

- *"The objectives expressed are extremely broad, but there is little or no indication of how these will be achieved.*
- *In general, the Protocol lacks clear targets, timing and decision making structures to define the detail it currently lacks. There are no enforcement mechanisms to ensure that unilateral behaviour at member state level is sanctioned.*
- *Where desirable aspirations are expressed, these are bound by the limits of existing national legislation. It is therefore unclear how the protocol will effect progress in establishing a favourable investment climate as it does not force any change outside of the status quo" ([344])*

It will probably take some more time before the sufficient number of member states will have ratified the Protocol and thus let it enter into force. If this is not done latest by 2010/1 when SADC will declare itself a customs union the integration process will face serious problems and might even derail.

Other Protocols are for themselves not of an equally high importance for the further deepening of RI in SADC although together they form the backbone for integration ([345]).

---

343 See: Nathan Associates Inc. (2004), Finance and Investment Protocol SADC. Assessment of Impact on Mozambique and Mozambican Private Sector. www.nathaninc.com

344 ibid:1

345 The texts of all adopted Protocols can be found on the SADC website: www.sadc.int

8.3.5. The Consultative Conference

The Consultative Conference has been a major annual event from 1979 to 1999 presenting SADC(C) to the world and maintaining a regular dialogue with the donor community. It is a unique feature amongst RI bodies in Africa.

During the first decade of regional cooperation and integration under the auspices of SADCC, the Consultative Conference – at first called 'donor conference' – was a major annual event and highly instrumental to raise funding for SADCC programs and projects. Due to the change of the international climate ("fall of the Berlin wall" in 1989) and the increasing problems of SADCC to implement especially some of the ambitious transport sector projects the interest in the annual meeting decreased ([346]) the Consultative Conference lost some of its relevance during the early 1990s ([347]). In the following years, the Consultative Conferences became less funding oriented and focused more on a dialogue with the international community ([348]). The frequency of the conferences changed to bi-annual after 2000, but has been held only thrice since (2002; 2006 and 2008).

The Consultative Conferences had two major functions until 2000:

1. The soliciting of funds for SADC projects and programs.
2. The establishment of a network of external relations for SADC mainly via the Secretariat ([349]).

The 2006 Consultative Conference in Namibia changed the character of the relationship as it agreed on a framework for a partnership agreement between SADC and donors ("*international cooperating partners*" [ICP]) in support of the implementation of SADC's RISDP. The "*Windhoek Declaration on a new SADC/ICP Partnership*" specified the roles of the key cooperating stakeholders

---

346 The author attended the 1988 Consultative Conference in Arusha (Tanzania), which did not raise substantial new funding for SADCC anymore; see: Peters, Christian (1988), Die SADCC-Konferenz in Arusha: *Development of Infrastructure and Enterprise*. in: Afrika Spectrum 23(1988)1:105-110

347 See: Adelmann (2008):360ff

348 According to Adelmann (2008):362ff, several international partners had become worried about the implementation capacity of SADC(C) and were reluctant to make further financial pledges. The new SADC reacted by changing the focus of the conference: more communication about the programs and less financial soliciting.

349 ibid:356

for the achievement of the SADC socio-economic development agenda ([350]) and developed a resource mobilisation strategy ([351]). It is linked to the Paris Declaration on Aid Effectiveness.

The "Windhoek Declaration on a new SADC/ICP partnership" was the culmination of a three-year long process of intensive dialogue between SADC and its main international partners. Already in 2003, a Joint SADC-ICP Task Force (JTF) was set up, whose aim was to improve coordination between SADC and the ICPs so that the latter could make a meaningful contribution to the implementation of the RISDP. The formulation of the "Windhoek Declaration" was the result of the close consultations ([352]). The EC Delegation in Botswana is the lead agent of the ICPs, acting in close liaison with the SADC Secretariat's Unit for Policy and Strategic Planning.

The JTF consists of two working levels:

- a so called "Wider Task Force" of ICPs and representatives of the SADC Secretariat with the possible participation of the SADC Troika. The "Wider Task Force" convenes twice a year;
- a technical Core Group for the day-to-day work and follow-up on recommendations of the "Wider Task Force", which consists of the ICPs represented in Gaborone (i.e. EC, Sweden, France, Germany, UK, UNDP, USAID) and representatives of the SADC Secretariat. It meets monthly co-chaired by the EC-Delegation and the SADC Secretariat ([353]).

The so far last Consultative Conference took place in April 2008 in Mauritius. Originally been planned as a separate conference on poverty and development it was 'relabelled' by SADC as the bi-annual Consultative Conference with the theme: "*Regional Economic Integration: A Strategy for Poverty Eradication towards Sustainable Development*". It was attended by the EU Commissioner *Louis Michel* and focussed against the intentions of the SADC organizers more on the Zimbabwe elections than on the mobilisation of the international community for the SADC integration process ([354]).

---

350 http://www.sadc.int/icp/windhoek_declaration/index.php

351 SADC (2006a): Talking notes for Pre-Summit Media Briefing by Executive Secretary T.A. Salomao. 8.8.2006. Gaborone.

352 The Windhoek Conference had originally been planned for November 2004 but had to be postponed twice; see: Adelmann (2008):368

353 see http://www.sadc.int/icp/

354 See: Adelmann (2008):368ff

During the times of SADCC and SADC's formation years in the 1990s, the consultative conferences were an important mechanism for the regional body to ensure international political and economic recognition and support. It was an event, at which member states had to demonstrate their commitment for RI and SADC to the outside world, thus indirectly strengthening also the internal cohesion of the regional body. It was also an event, which helped SADC to solicit urgently needed financial and technical support from the donors and thus proving to integration-sceptics that RI was indeed 'paying off'. With the maturing and visible progress of SADC, the annual 'justification', meeting vis-à-vis the donors, became redundant. Its place – and this also demonstrates the new self-confidence of SADC – took a consultation process on more equal terms concerning development issues.

8.3.6. The SADC Tribunal

SADC had early on realized that it would need at one stage, a mechanism to settle inevitable disputes arising from the RI process. With article 9 of the Treaty, SADC established a Tribunal already in 1992. However, it took until 2000 before a Protocol on the Tribunal was ready for signing. It entered into force upon the adoption of the Agreement Amending the Treaty of SADC at the *Blantyre* Summit on 14 August 2001, thus without going through the normal national ratification process. It took though, another four years before the Tribunal became operational. The members of the Tribunal were appointed by the 2005 Summit in August in *Gaborone* (Botswana) and sworn in on the 18th of November 2005 in *Windhoek* (Namibia) ([355]).

The Tribunal ([356]) is a permanent SADC institution based in *Windhoek* which has jurisdiction over SADC matters in accordance with the Treaty and the Protocols. This includes:

- The interpretation and application of the Treaty,
- The interpretation and application of the Protocols and all "subsidiary, instruments adopted within the framework of the Community, and acts of the institutions of the Community",

---

355 See: Ruppel, O.C. and Bangamwabo, F.X. (2008): The SADC Tribunal: a legal analysis of ist mandate and role in regional integration. In: Bösl et al (eds) (2008): Monitoring Regional Integration in Southern Africa Yearbook, Vol. 8. Stellenbosch:179

356 see: http://www.sadc.int/tribunal/

- Matters which member states of SADC recognise the jurisdiction of the Tribunal for,
- Disputes between member states, and between natural or legal persons and states and,
- Interpretations, applications and validity of provisions that are referred to by courts or tribunals of a member state ([357]).

The first major cases ([358]) brought to the Tribunal referred to the expropriation of white owned farms in Zimbabwe. At first a Zimbabwe registered company (*Mike Campbell [Pvt] Limited*) operating a commercial farm challenged in October 2007 at the Tribunal the right of the Zimbabwean Government to expropriate agricultural land belonging to the company ([359]). It sought first an interim measure to stop the Zimbabwean Government to evict the company from its land as long as the case was not finally decided at the Supreme Court of Zimbabwe and secondly challenged the expropriation on grounds that this was motivated by racism and thus illegal according to Article 6 of the SADC Treaty and the AU Charter. *Mike Campbell* was joined by group of 74 other Zimbabwean farmers with a similar case.

The Tribunal ruled December 2007 that *Campbell* should remain on his legally already expropriated farm until the second matter was finally decided by the Tribunal and that in the meantime the Zimbabwean authorities were by no means allowed to evict the farmer. This interim relief was also granted to the other farmers in March 2008. The Zimbabwean Supreme Court, however, ruled in January 2008, that the application of the farmers was illegal as the Zimbabwean Parliament had passed a law which did not allow for any challenge of the land acquisition in court. The Zimbabwean Government said it would proceed with the farm seizure despite the pending case at the Tribunal. Until the Tribunal sat again on the case in July 2008 *Campbell* and family members were attacked and severely beaten.

The Tribunal ruled on 18 July 2008 that the Zimbabwean Government was in contempt of the Tribunal's orders and that it would report the matter to the next SADC Summit. The final hearing on the *Campbell* case at the Tribunal took place on 28 November 2008 and ruled in favor of Mike Campbell and 77 other applicants. It stated that

357 ibid.

358 Before that the Tribunal had only dealt with a few cases regarding employments contracts; see: Ruppel/Bangawambo (2008):181ff

359 The description of the legal cases which Zimbabwean farmers brought to the Tribunal follows to a large extent the analysis of Ruppel/Bangawambo (2008):183ff

- it was illegal for the Zimbabwean Government to disallow for any legal appeals against eviction orders for farms;
- the farmers were discriminated against because of race and as such Article 6 (2) of the SADC Treaty was violated;
- all evictions to be cancelled and that those farmers who had already been evicted have to be fairly compensated appropriately until 30.6.2009 ([360]).

Rather predictably, the Zimbabwean Government and Supreme Court have been ignoring and outrightly rejecting the Tribunal's ruling ([361]), which is in direct contempt of the SADC Treaty and the Protocol on the Tribunal. They place the primary responsibility to enforce and execute the Tribunal's decisions and rulings in the hands of the respective member states. If they chose to ignore this responsibility there is little the Tribunal can do to enforce its decisions apart from taking the case to the SADC Summit. ? It did so in the case of the ruling on the Zimbabwean farmers but the August 2008 Summit chose not to react ([362]) – probably in order not to derail the precarious negotiations for the formation of a Unity Government.

No SADC member state has so far passed any law which would compel it to implement verdicts of the SADC Tribunal. In fact, most member states have a clause in their constitution that the national courts are independent and subject only to the national constitution ([363]). This contradiction – giving the responsibility to implement Tribunal decisions to the legal system of a member state which constitution is forbidding just this – puts SADC in awkward position. It is so far impotent to enforce the decision by one of its institutions if a member states refuses to comply. Although the first major case the Tribunal had to handle has been – admittedly – a politically highly sensitive one charged with emotions over racial injustice (one way or another) the final outcome (Zimbabwe ignoring the ruling) has been unsatisfactory and casts severe doubts on the effectiveness of the Tribunal as an instrument for the settlement of intra-SADC disputes. What will happen to the integration process if one country chooses to ignore a Tribunal ruling on a dispute over e.g. the distribution of revenue from the forthcoming customs union? Would that signal the end of the trade-led integration process, lead to the suspension of membership of that

360 See: Ruppel, Oliver (2009), Das SADC Tribunal – Eine Zwischenbilanz. In Allgemeine Windhoeker Zeitung vom 5.2.2009. www.az.com.na/afrika/das-sadc-tribunal-eine-juristische-zwischenbilanz.80234.php

361 see: http://www.talkzimbabwe.com/news/117/ARTICLE/3827/2008-12-01.html

362 See: Ruppel, O. (2009)

363 See: Ruppel/Bangawambo (2008):198 who explain the Namibian case.

member state or to a new consensus over the enforceability of the Tribunal rulings?

Until April 2009, altogether 18 cases have been brought to the Tribunal, of which none was concerned with disputes between member states. Two were labor disputes and the rest cases between individuals or legal bodies and one member state. As in the case between the white Zimbabwean farmers and the *Mugabe* administration the issues in the other cases were mostly about (human) rights violations and in how far they violated SADC's legal principles. In the latest case, the Zimbabwe Human Rights NGO Forum ([364]) has taken the Zimbabwean Government to the Tribunal for not honoring a Zimbabwean court order to compensate victims of torture. It will have to be seen if the new Zimbabwean Government reacts differently to a possible Tribunal verdict than the old one.

8.3.7. Challenges Ahead

The integration process has again gained momentum over the last few years due to the eventually successful implementation of the SADC reforms and, in particular, through the establishment of the SADC FTA. There are, however, still some areas which need to be taken care of in order to make the regional integration process more sustainable:

- The full Implementation of the financial reform: despite the changed formula for membership fees, not all member states pay up regularly. In particular, the funding for the construction of the new building for the Secretariat is not being contributed sufficiently.

- The alignment of national policies to regional integration goals and strategies: if the speed of Protocol ratification is anything to go by, then the commitment of most of the member states to RI is moderate but not yet very high. Translating SADC goals into national policies is still far more often the exemption than the rule.
- The full implementation of the SADC Electoral Advisory Council's SADC Principles and Guidelines Governing Democratic Elections has faced a first successful test with the Zimbabwean Elections in April

364 see: www.thezimbabwean.co.uk/index.php?option=com_content&task=view&id=20613&Itemid=109 - 30k

2008, but needs to be repeated in other potentially controversial elections as well.

- The translation of SADC Declarations, Charters and Memorandum of Understandings into regional policies has not proceeded very far. Particularly, the SADC Declaration on Macro Economic Convergence has to be turned quickly into an agreed and accepted regional policy if the Customs Union is to be achieved by 2010. The establishment of a Macroeconomic Policies and Convergence Unit at the Trade and Finance Directorate of SADC in 2006 and the subsequent studies undertaken by the Unit on the state of macro-economic convergence ([365]) are important steps but not yet sufficient.

- A convincing concept for the bi-annual Consultative Conferences has to be developed which will attract the international cooperating partners into a lasting cooperation with SADC. Currently, the unique and potentially useful tool is on the verge of collapse because the SADC Secretariat has not followed through on the ideas agreed in the JTF meetings and SADC leaders have shown little interest to attend. Instead of making the Consultative Conferences into a transparent forum for exchange the last meeting in Mauritius (2008) brought few results of substance and reinforced the uneasiness about SADC's political course vis-à-vis Zimbabwe.

- The Tribunal has to be strengthened in terms of enforcement of its rulings or unresolved disputes could lead to the implosion of the RI process. The flagrant ignoring of the Tribunal's ruling on the issue of farm seizures through the Zimbabwean Government and the unwillingness of the Summit to deal with the Tribunal's complaint about it demonstrate a low degree of political will when it comes to the implementation of decisions of supra-national decisions at national level. SADC needs to agree on a way of how to ensure that the Tribunal's rulings will have to be enacted at national level.

365 See: www.sadc.int/tifi/macroeconomic_policies_convergence/structure.php

Chapter 9: The Socio-Economic Dimension of Regional Integration in SADC

So far, we have dealt mainly with the conceptual requirements of RI, historical experiences made with it in Africa and the organisational and policy-related framework provided for RI by SADC. In this chapter, the focus will be on the (empirical) economic and later, political realities of RI in the SADC region.

One of the major economic pre-conditions for successful RI as outlined in chapter 1, is the existence or at least the potential for the development of complementary demand and supply structures. In other words, the national economies must not produce the same or a very similar set of goods and services. It was explained also in chapter 1, that another important factor for successful RI relates to the preparedness for economic policy convergence and the absence of huge differences in national incomes and employment levels between member states. Lastly, the experience from other RI attempts indicates that in the developing world, regional integration has a greater chance of being successful if the region possesses a certain degree of physical (roads, communication, electricity etc) and cultural integration (languages, religion etc). Are these economic success factors for RI evident in SADC?

9.1. The Physical Preconditions for Regional Integration

Trade integration will only succeed if the physical pre-conditions for it are in place and functioning. This has always been the conviction of the political leaders of Southern Africa and was even part of the rationale to start regional cooperation under SADCC. And today, the SADC region in comparison to other RI schemes in Africa has a comparatively well developed physical infrastructure partly as a result of colonial investments and partly because of the reinforced cooperation efforts starting during the SADCC period (see chapter 7.1.3.).

9.1.1. Integration in the Transport Sector

The road and rail systems are connecting most of the member states on the continent and especially the six landlocked member states with the main harbors of the region. Furthermore, with Johannesburg as the regional hub, the SADC region is well connected to international air traffic. As seen in chapter 8.3.4.3. railway lines link all but one country (Malawi) to the regional harbors. The regional road system has incorporated not only all countries, but has linked also remoter areas in some member state with the regional transportation system.

However, for the last decade transportation, especially road transportation has been hampered because of the decay of the Zimbabwean economy and as a consequence of its physical infrastructure. For years, it was nearly impossible to buy fuel in Zimbabwe and trucks had to use extra tanks to cross Zimbabwe. While petrol or diesel can now be found again against hard currency, the main 'highways' and several bridges in Zimbabwe are in a state of bad repair. But Zimbabwe remains the crucial link between the landlocked countries such as Zambia and Malawi to the South African and Mozambican ports. Although trade barriers have been removed with the establishment of SAFTA, the physical preconditions for facilitating more trade are not in the best shape.

In other member states the state of roads is deteriorating because increasingly transport of bulk products is transferred from rail to road; many roads are not built to a standard that they can serve continuously heavy loads. A special case is the transportation of copper rods from Zambia to the region's harbors. The trucks carrying the copper are often overloaded. On the Zimbabwean road system (from *Chirundu* via *Harare* and *Masvingo* to *Beitbridge*) they have deformed the tarmac on some stretches to such an extent that it has become dangerous for limousines to drive on it ([366]). After a brief slump in demand for copper due to the world financial crisis in 2008/9 demand has recently picked up again and the use of the already collapsing roads in Zimbabwe will also increase again. If nothing is done to reroute the copper exports either to other harbors (e.g. *Dar es Salaam*) or different means of transport (rail) Zimbabwe can soon become impassable as it lacks the resources to repair and maintain the roads.

The only country, which is merely loosely linked with the region's transportation system, is the DRC. Being the biggest geographical country in Africa, it has never fully integrated internally. Its southern part (the mineral-rich *Katanga* region) is connected to the south, but the rest of the country has either closer links to Ruanda, Burundi and Uganda or is oriented towards its own Atlantic harbor *Pointe-Noir*. To bridge this gap SADC developed a new special corridor-project, the North-South Corridor linking both the DRC and the

---

366 The author travelled the road from *Harare* to *Beitbridge* several times himself until 2005 and has seen the huge trucks carrying heavy copper loads; he witnessed the damage done to the roads.

Tanzanian port of *Dar es Salaam* to the South African harbor of *Durban* ([367]). At a special North-South Corridor Conference in Lusaka – which was convened jointly by COMESA, EAC and SADC and attracted more than 1,000 participants – in April 2009, USD 1.2 Billion was raised from donors for several projects including the upgrading of roads and railways, new bridges and border posts ([368]).

As transport investments require substantial amounts of finance, most governments in the SADC region cannot afford, they have started to involve the private sector both in the construction and management of transport systems. One preferred method are *Public Private Partnerships* (PPP), another is the outright privatization of e.g. railway companies. PPP's have been used in the transport sector first by the South African authorities, who auctioned off construction and /or rehabilitation contracts to private bidders for certain highway sections against 18-year management contracts with the right to obtain toll fees for using the roads. Other countries – e.g. Mozambique and Zambia – have either followed this example or are about to although in some countries raising the required funds poses a considerable challenge ([369]).

With regard to transport SADC has sufficient infrastructure to promote intra-regional trade and investments and thus the further integration of the region. Rail, road and also flight connections are connecting nearly all member states on the continent; only the island members (Madagascar, Mauritius, and Seychelles) are obviously not closely linked to the rest of the region. Room for improvement exists with regard to the modernization of rail and road systems and the expansion of transport corridors.

9.1.2. Integration in the Energy Sector

The Southern African Power Pool (SAPP) connects most SADC member states on the African continent with the exception of Malawi. The power shortages in South Africa in 2006, 2007 and 2008 have, however, demonstrated that the

367 See: Mahlalela, Gideon (2007): Rail Service to the Ports: presentation given at the Maputo Corridor Conference, 4.9.2007, *Maputo*.

368 See: Inter Press Service (IPS), New North-South Corridor to tackle trade bottlenecks. 9.4.2009

369 See: Mutambara, Tsitsi (2008): Regional transport challenges within SADC and their implications for economic integration and development. In: Bösl et al (eds) (2008): Monitoring Regional Integration in Southern Africa Yearbook, Vol. 8. Stellenbosch:39f

existing regional interconnections and electricity generation reserves are not yet sufficient to balance demand and supply in the region. The interconnectors between the surplus producers such as DRC, Zambia or Mozambique and deficit countries such as South Africa and Zimbabwe have proven to be too weak to bridge sudden extra demands. Only after South Africa was faced with serious power shortages, its power utility Eskom began to negotiate with the Mozambican utility *EDM (Electricidade de Moçambique*) about the construction of stronger interconnectors and delivery of more electricity from *Cahora Bassa* to South Africa ([370]).

Other countries such as Malawi are still not part of the regional network because of the neglect of previous administrations, and as such vulnerable to internal failures such as the one in 2003. Zimbabwe's power stations (in particular the *Hwange* coal-fired power station) are in such a bad state of repair that they only produce part of their installed capacity. The country has become highly dependent on electricity imports from South Africa, Mozambique and DRC, for which it, however, gradually stopped payments ([371]) due to the worsening foreign exchange shortage.

The strong economic growth in the SADC region since 2002 has increased the demand for electricity to a level higher than the existing power generation capacities in the region. This reflects both the vulnerability of the predominant mode of power generation in SADC as well as the insufficient coordination of national energy policies within the region. The electricity supply crisis which hit South Africa in 2007 and 2008 underscores this: it was a result of higher than anticipated demand growth ([372]), a mild drought (lowering the output of hydro-electrical plants), neglected maintenance of power stations, inaction with regard to modernize and expand the existing power stations as well as insufficient options to import electricity from the region.

As shown in chapter 8.3.4.4. electricity supply in the SADC region (on the continent) is potentially sufficient but is prone to interruptions and problems due to its high dependence on hydro plants. The region's dependence on hydro-

---

370 See: SADC Today Volume 10 No.6, June 2008: Energy trading gains momentum, by Richard Nyamanhindi.

371 See: http://www.africagrowth.net/index.php?option=com_content&task=view&id=90&Itemid=1; Zimbabwe was owing DRC's SNEL around USD 5 Mill. and Mozambique' HCB more than USD 26 million. The latter cut supplies with effect from 1.1.2008.

372 According to the South African media, the power cuts were also a result of bad management and political indecisiveness; http://news.bbc.co.uk/2/hi/africa/7208542.stm

power – with the exception of South Africa and to some extent Zimbabwe which both have coal-fired power stations – makes it highly vulnerable to periods of lower rainfall, which occur regularly and can affect the watersheds of the main river systems. A diversification of energy supplies is only slowly taking effect. The South African utility *Eskom*, is looking after experiencing severe supply problems in 2006-8 into the potential of renewable energies such as wind and solar, but is also contemplating the construction of another nuclear plant.

Since the ratification of the Protocol on Energy in 1998, the Governments of several SADC countries have discussed in various fora, the coordination of their energy policies. It was agreed that facilitated through SAPP the degree of energy trading should increase and balance the structural deficits in some countries. A number of plans have been developed to build better power lines and stronger interconnectors, expand existing or construct new power stations but progress has been slow. It required the sobering energy crisis of 2007 and 2008 in South Africa, Zimbabwe and Tanzania to speed up investments and energy trade agreements. In 2008, new interconnectors between Zambia and the DRC and two more between Zambia and Tanzania were completed which allow additional energy trade of up to 660 MW ([373]).

However, improvements and strengthening of the interconnecting lines to allow for an increase of regional energy trade is not sufficient to address the structural imbalances of the SADC energy market. South Africa's growing demand for electricity – and it is by far the biggest consumer and producer of electricity in the SADC region – is outstripping not only its own production capacity but also the currently installed regional capacity. Even if the interconnecting lines are expanded, the available electricity for export in the other SADC countries is not sufficient to satisfy South Africa's medium-term needs. Only when *Cabora Bassa* is fully connected to the South African grid and the hydro-power resources of the DR Congo are developed will there be sufficient energy supply to cover the needs of the regional market.

For SADC to achieve a stable and regionally balanced energy supply situation a comprehensive regional energy policy has to be developed and implemented. The attempts made so far are not addressing the core of the problem. The energy demand of the region but in particular of South Africa will rise further in future and will outstrip the supply side if necessary investments in the expansion of energy production and distribution are not made. Most countries have under-utilized potential to generate energy but require large funds for investment to achieve this. The other major challenge SADC faces is related to climate change

373 See: Volume 10 No.6, June 2008

and clean energy production. Being highly dependent on coal and controlling large coal deposits Governments in the SADC region might be tempted to continue to base their power generation on coal or even expand this. Renewable energy production – if one excludes large scale hydro-power plants – has not yet been sufficiently recognized as an alternative source of energy. The majority of people in the SADC region has so far no access to electricity and other forms of 'modern' energy and relies largely on biomass for their energy consumption thus destroying through over-utilization the increasingly precarious natural resource base in their countries. Sufficient energy supply and a sustainable use of natural resources in producing them is an important factor for RI in Southern Africa. Without adequate power industrial development will be hampered, without the application of sustainable natural resource planning the ecological base for further development will be destroyed. SADC has to acknowledge this dual challenge in its future energy planning.

9.1.3. Integration in the Communication Sector

In terms of communication, the SADC region is quite well interconnected. All countries have established at least one mobile telephone network which have eased the notorious communication bottlenecks (see table 9.1.). The number of internet users in the SADC region is also rising steadily. Of the more than 54 million internet users in Africa in 2008 ([374]), 8.7 million (16.1%) were based in the SADC region (see table 9.2.).

More than two thirds of all Internet users, however, can be found in South Africa and Zimbabwe. There are still many SADC member states with small numbers of Internet users as compared to the total population. In the DRC, Madagascar, Mozambique, Malawi and Tanzania it is 1% or less of the population which are using the Internet.

---

374 See: http://www.internetworldstats.com/stats1.htm

Table 9.1.: Telephone Users in the SADC Region 2000 and 2006 (in Number of Lines per 100 Inhabitants)

Country	Fixed Lines		Mobile users	
	2000	*2006*	*2000*	*2006*
ANGOLA	0.49	0.62	0.2	14.33
BOTSWANA	8.27	7.78	12.17	46.78
DRC	...	0.02	...	7.44
LESOTHO	1.24	2.97	1.21	19.99
MADAGASCAR	0.34	0.68	0.39	5.47
MALAWI	0.45	0.8	0.47	3.33
MAURITIUS	23.53	28.45	15.08	61.5
MOZAMBIQUE	0.5	0.33	0.3	11.6
NAMIBIA	6.19	6.84	4.61	24.37
SOUTH AFRICA	10.88	9.97	18.28	83.33
SWAZILAND	3.16	4.27	3.27	24.29
TANZANIA	0.5	0.4	0.32	14.78
ZAMBIA	0.78	0.79	0.92	14.02
ZIMBABWE	2.19	2.56	2.34	6.49

Source: OECD/AfDB (2008

Table 9.2.: Internet Users in the SADC Region

Country	Internet users		% of population	Growth (in%)
	2000	2008		
ANGOLA	30,000	498,000	4.0	+1,560
BOTSWANA	15,000	100,000	5.1	+567
DRC	500	230,000	0.3	+50,000
LESOTHO	4,000	70,000	3.3	+1,650
MADAGASCAR	30,000	110,000*	0.5	+267
MALAWI	15,000	140,000	1.0	+830
MAURITIUS	87,000	340,000	26.7	+291
MOZAMBIQUE	30,000	200,000	0.9	+567
NAMIBIA	30,000	200,000	4.8	+237
SOUTH AFRICA	2,400,000	4,590,000	9.4	+91
SWAZILAND	10,000	42,000	3.7	+320
TANZANIA	115,000	400,000	1.0	+248
ZAMBIA	20,000	500,000*	4.3	+2,400
ZIMBABWE	50,000	1,351,000	11.9	+2602
Total	**2,845,500**	**8,771,000**		

* = 2007

Source: http://www.internetworldstats.com/stats1.htm#africa

As the development of both cellular telephone networks and internet access makes rapid progress also in Southern Africa, the figures provided here might already be outdates when the thesis is submitted. Nevertheless the statistics above provide an idea about the communication bottlenecks which are still existing in Southern Africa. The capital cities and most of South Africa and Mauritius are already integrated into the global communication and information network but rural areas in most other SADC member states are without reliable communication and information access. SADC needs to put an emphasis on connecting rural areas and smaller cities to the internet and to promote the expansion of cellular phone networks by allowing private companies into this market.

9.1.4. Conclusion

The SADC region has on the African continent probably the best physical infrastructure for further regional integration. However, especially the regional energy network and policy are not yet sufficient to cater to the region's demand and to address upcoming issues such as mitigation of and adaptation to climate change. The transportation sector is hampered by the crisis in Zimbabwe but is, in most parts rather well regionally integrated. With regard to communication, SADC countries are getting better connected, better informed and also more flexible thanks to mobile phone networks and the increasing expansion of Internet connections although especially rural areas are still lagging behind.

9.2. Social and Cultural Preconditions for Regional Integration in SADC

Regional Integration does not only build on trade, production and physical integration it also requires a social basis. In functioning RI, areas such as the EU or ASEAN the political leaders put a lot of emphasis on fast social convergence. This includes adjustment of incomes and wealth, provision of at least similar chances for social and economic upward mobility and attainment of basic needs including health.

The most obvious and pressing challenge most SADC member states especially on the African continent are faced with is the HIV/AIDS pandemic. Currently, Southern Africa is the region with the highest HIV/AIDS prevalence rate and victims in the world:

"The combined population of the SADC Member States is about 4% of the world population, yet globally the region accounts for more than 37% of the people living with HIV and AIDS. It is estimated that between 11.7 and 18.8 million people of the region are currently living with HIV" ([375]).

Worldwide, South Africa is with 2.2 million the country with the highest number of people infected with HIV/AIDS. In 2008, more than 350,000 people in South Africa alone had died of the disease in that year. In the whole of SADC the figures of people dying of HIV/AIDS every year are close to 1 million over the last years. The countries with the highest HIV/AIDS prevalence rate in the world (2008 figures) are found in the SADC region as well: Botswana (23.9%), Lesotho (23.2%), Swaziland (20.1%) and South Africa (18.1%). Only the island member states of SADC have low HIV/AIDS prevalence rates (see table 9.3).

Table 9.3.: HIV/AIDS in the SADC Region (2002 to 2008)

Country	2002		2006		2008			
	Death	**Prevalence Rate (%)**	**Death**	**Prevalence Rate (%)**	**Death**	**Prevalence Rate (%)**	**AIDS Orphans**	**Life expect.**
ANG	37,000	3.1	30,000	2.5	17,000	2.1	50,000	42
BOT	21,000	27.4	9,000	25.3	11,000	23.9	95,000	50
DRC	36,000	1.5	35,000	1.5	24-34,000	1.5	270-380,000	46
LES	18,000	25.1	19,000	24.5	18,000	23.2	110,000	43
MAD	<500	0.2	1,200	0.2	<1,000	0.1	3,400	59
MAL	77,000	14.1	71,000	13.1	68,000	11.9	560,000	48
MAU	<100	0.7	<500	3.4	<500	1.7	<500	73
MOZ	81,000	12.5	100,000	14.4	81,000	12.5	400,000	42
NAM	10,000	17.6	6,100	17.7	5,100	15.3	66,000	52
RSA	300,000	20.5	400,000	21.0	350,000	18.1	1,400,000	51
SWA	11,000	27.6	12,000	27.3	56,000	20.1	56,000	41
TAN	130,000	7.2	120,000	6.6	77,000	5.4	1,200,000	52
ZAM	93,000	16.6	79,000	16.3	56,000	15.2	600,000	42
ZIM	180,000	25.9	160,000	17.9	140,000	15.3	1,000,000	43
Total	**974,600**		**942,800**		**904-14,600**		**5,810-920,900**	

Source: UNAIDS; World Bank (2009); own compilation

375 http://www.sadc.int/sadcaidsinfo/ (accessed on07.02.2010)

The AIDS pandemic not only reduced the average life expectancy in the SADC region (see table 9.3.) considerably over the last two decades – Swaziland is currently the country with the lowest life expectancy world wide (39.6 years [[376]]) – but put also a terrible strain on most of the respective societies and economies:

- HIV/AIDS has been affecting particularly the socio-economic better-off professionals and skilled workers – due to their life style ([377]) – and as such left huge gaps in administration, civil service organizations, the business sector and research. One of the coping strategies of big companies for example in South Africa has been to train at least two people for the same job in case one of them dies of HIV/AIDS, which has increased costs and undermined their productivity. In many countries crucial positions in various ministries have not been filled because of the lack of qualified personnel. That has most probably also affected the ability of countries to engage in constructive regional integration policies.
- The social fabric of societies suffering the loss of a large number of family members, friends and colleagues becomes worn out and might break. The impact for many societies in Southern Africa, which are relying on family and informal community-based social security systems, is rather devastating. The coping mechanisms developed for dealing with the impact of HIV/AIDS are often dysfunctional with regard to long-term (sustainable) development and regional integration. Often a short-term orientation – understandable against the background of the probability of dying young – in planning and implementation prevails, which expresses itself in:

  ➢ a mercantilist rather than production-oriented approach to economic development, which undermines the ability of SADC member states to integrate further (see chapter 9.3.).

---

376 According to data of www.United Nations World Population Prospects: 2006 revision (Table A.17 for 2005-2010) the life expectancy in Swaziland was even below 40 years; according to the CIA World Factbook 2008, the figures for most countries are even much lower, with Swaziland at 31.88 years; see: https://www.cia.gov/library/publications/the-world-factbook/geos/xx.html

377 With rising income levels promiscuity among men in Southern Africa tends to rise as well and with that the spread of HIV/AIDS. The author observed in several SADC countries (Zambia, Zimbabwe, Malawi, South Africa, Botswana, and Swaziland) the degree of promiscuity coupled with the preference of unprotected sex amongst his colleagues. Without making moral judgements about this behaviour or having access to detailed empirical studies on this phenomenon the author is of the opinion that this has greatly contributed to the spread of HIV/AIDS in Southern African societies amongst the better educated and affluent sections of society.

  - an increased corruption proneness because people either want to provide for their families in case of an early death or are no longer afraid of being caught.
  - a decreased ability of many countries in Southern Africa to ensure food security as crucial productive members of the family in rural areas are dead or too weak to till the land. The result is often reduced private investments in rural development and a growing reliance on Government or NGO hand-outs increasing in turn the already strong dependency syndrome.
- The increasing financial costs of dealing with the HIV/AIDS pandemic as the traditional social security systems – based on family networks – is collapsing and the costs for treatment of HIV/AIDS victims are rising. Health costs – although still comparatively low – are rising in several SADC states while the budget allocations to health are only increasing if the respective country has higher revenues ([378]).

Although the statistics (see table 9.3.) may give the picture as if the peak of the HIV/AIDS pandemic in Southern Africa might have been reached as prevalence rates and death figures are starting to decrease, the socio-economic costs will remain high for the years to come. Not only have millions of so called "AIDS-orphans" to be looked after and the anti AIDS-campaigns (including the provision of antiretroviral [ARV] drugs) to be funded ([379]) but also the losses in skilled manpower to be replaced and the provision of food in rural areas to be ensured. The impact of HIV/AIDS on RI is apart from the general social pain because of the loss of life particularly felt with regard to professional skills and critical institutional memory. Several high-ranking SADC officials as well as national officials including ministers have perished over the last two decades and left knowledge gaps which delayed the integration process. So far SADC has developed several programs how to combat HIV/AIDS, how to ease the social impact of the pandemic and how to provide ARVs but has not developed any policy of how to deal with the frequent loss of crucial SADC officials.

---

378 In Botswana, the health budget rose in absolute figures but stagnated or even shrunk in relative size even at a time when the Botswana Government realized strongly increasing income due to the mineral boom until 2008; see: Republic of Botswana, Ministry of Finance and Development Planning, (2008), The 2008 Budget Speech in brief. Gaborone. http://www.sarpn.org.za/documents/d0002982/Botswana_budget_in-brief_Feb2008.pdf . In South Africa the share of the health budget rose from 10% in 1994 to 11% in 2004 against a rapid increase of HIV/AIDS cases; see: Proceedings of the Fifth Southern African Forum on Trade (SAFT) held in Pretoria, South Africa, on 6–7 August 2008:80; mimeo

379 Much of the funding to combat HIV/AIDS comes from private foundations such as Bill & Melissa Gates Foundation (www.gatesfoundation.org) or the Clinton Foundation (www.clintonfoundation.org).

With regard to regional socio-economic inequalities SADC has so far made few attempts to address the very pronounced discrepancies in national income and employment levels. In SADC there is a converse North-South gradient: the richer countries with better employment opportunities, higher incomes and better infrastructure are located in the South, the poorer ones in the North. The Human Development Index (HDI) of UNDP underlines the discrepancies between the southern SADC member states and those to the North (see table 9.4.). While Botswana, Namibia and South Africa all have scores above 0.600 – which puts them in the category of countries which have reached a medium level of human development – the northern SADC countries are all in the category of countries with a low level of human development as they scored between 0.389 (DRC), 0.402 (Mozambique), 0.453 (Zambia), 0.493 (Malawi) and 0.530 (Tanzania) in 2007. It should be noted that the overall trend especially amongst the countries with a low development level is quite positive. With the exception of the DRC, Lesotho and Zambia as well as South Africa all other SADC member states have improved their HDI values since the year 2000.

Table 9.4.: Human Development Index (HDI) for SADC Countries 2000-2006

Country	2000	2002	2004	2005	2006	2007	Trend
Angola	0.403	0.381	0.439	0.446	0.484	0.564	+
Botswana	0.572	0.589	0.570	0.654	0.664	0.694	+
DR Congo	0.431	0.365	0.391	0.411	0.361	0.389	-
Lesotho	0.535	0.493	0.494	0.549	0.496	0.514	-
Madagascar	0.482	0.469	0.509	0.533	0.533	0.543	+
Malawi	0.400	0.388	0.400	0.437	0.457	0.493	+
Mauritius	0.772	0.785	0.800	0.804	0.807	0.804	+
Mozambique	0.322	0.354	0.390	0.384	0.366	0.402	+
Namibia	0.610	0.607	0.626	0.650	0.634	0.686	+
South Africa	0.695	0.666	0.653	0.674	0.670	0.683	-
Swaziland	0.440	0.407	0.430	0.547	0.542	0.572	+
Tanzania	0.433	0.389	0.407	0.467	0.503	0.530	+
Zambia	0.551	0.491	0.491	0.434	0.453	0.481	-
Zimbabwe	0.403	0.381	0.439	0.513	n/a	n/a	+
SADC	**0.510**	**0.491**	**0.508**	**0.536**	**0.536**	**0.566**	+

Source: UNDP, Human Development Reports, various years

As a consequence of the uneven distribution of human development in the region, the labor markets of South Africa, Botswana but also to some extent of Swaziland and Namibia have been a magnet for labor migrants from other countries within the region. This has to some extent colonial roots – the mines in

South Africa needed workers, which were recruited from countries as far as Malawi and Zambia – but has been reinforced since the end of apartheid because of the relative affluence of the economies in the south and their need for qualified labor. This had led to a constant brain drain of the northern SADC member states such as Malawi, Zambia, Mozambique and especially since the beginning of the millennium Zimbabwe.

However, the majority of immigrants in South Africa are illegal and often unqualified workers who try to escape poverty in their home countries. The crisis in Zimbabwe has swelled their numbers tremendously. In South Africa particularly, commercial farmers and plantations often employ – under horrible conditions and at very low wages – illegal Zimbabwean and Mozambican immigrants. The majority of illegal immigrants are drawn, however, to the big cities such as *Johannesburg, Cape Town, Durban and Gaborone.* This has contributed strongly to the outbursts of xenophobia in Johannesburg and other South African cities in 2008, which claimed several lives, resulted in massive expulsion of immigrants from Zimbabwe, Malawi, Mozambique and Zambia from their homes and caused substantial damage to their properties ([380]).

The northern SADC states are losing through the brain drain their most valuable and needed professionals. Although it is not just South Africa or Botswana which are luring professionals from Malawi, Zambia, Zimbabwe or Mozambique to 'greener pastures' but also Europe ([381]), the US and lately the oil-rich Gulf states, the highest number of labour migrants still heads for the south of the African continent. The impact on the economies of these countries is devastating. One indicator is the low number of doctors in countries such as Malawi, Mozambique, Zambia and Zimbabwe:

- In 2003, Malawi with a population of about 12 million people had only 252 registered doctors of which a little more than half (129) were Malawian. Of the 72 specialists only 23 were Malawian ([382]).

---

380 See e.g. the impressive documentation at http://www.boston.com/bigpicture/2008/06/xenophobia_in_south_africa.html; International Organization for Migration (IOM), Towards Tolerance, Law, and Dignity: Addressing Violence against Foreign Nationals in South Africa. See: http://www.boell.org.za/web/110-270.html Chingono/Nakana (2009):402. A study by Romi Sigsworth, Collet Ngwane and Angelica Pino (2008), The Centre for the Study of Violence and Reconciliation. The Gendered Nature of Xenophobia in South Africa. http://www.boell.org.za/web/110-378.html

381 It is widely claimed in Malawi, that there are more Malawian medical doctors in the city of Manchester in UK than in the whole of Malawi.

382 See: http://www.pubmedcentral.nih.gov/articlerender.fcgi?artid=1831970

- In 2006, Zambia had about 646 doctors ([383]) for a population of ca. 11.6 million.
- In 2007, Mozambique had ca. 650 doctors and needed some 8,000 more ([384]) to cater for its population of ca. 20.9 million.
- In 2008, the public health system in Zimbabwe had more or less collapsed as the hospitals run out of drugs, sick people had no money to travel to hospital and doctors and nurses left the country in large numbers because they were paid wages below the poverty line ([385]). In 2008, Zimbabwe's population stood at ca. 11.4 million ([386]).

Similar trends are discernible for professions such as engineers, architects, crop scientists, chemical engineers or biologists in most of the poorer SADC member states.

Both, the continuing brain drain and the xenophobic fears amongst the population of the South African townships, indicate that two central precondition for regional integration – a balanced regional labour market and tolerance for other cultures – are not yet sufficiently developed. As long as the economies of the northern SADC member states are considerably less wealthy, provide fewer chances of prosperity and are less capable of guaranteeing the provision of basic needs than those of the southern part of the region labour migration will continue and destabilize the still precarious social relations particularly in South Africa. The reluctance of SADC leaders to agree on a Protocol on the Free Movement of People is clearly related to the structural socio-economic imbalances in the region.

The progress made by different SADC countries in achieving the → ***Millennium Development Goals (MDGs)*** provides an indication on the chances to address the current socio-economic imbalances in the region. The MDGs (see TEXT BOX 9.1.) have been adopted in 2001 by the UN as a strategy to provide the poorest nations with a realistic chance for development by improving their social and economic conditions ([387]). Coordinated by UNDP, donors have been making substantial contributions towards overcoming poverty, improving health and education as well as reversing environmental degradation.

---

383 See: J. Schatz (2008),Zambia's health-worker crisis. In: *The Lancet*, Volume 371, Issue 9613, Pages 638-639

384 See: http://www.reuters.com/article/healthNews/idUSL2573526720070625

385 See: Physicians for Human Rights (PHR) (2009), Health in Ruins. A man-made disaster in Zimbabwe. Cambridge (USA). http://physiciansforhumanrights.org

386 See: http://www.indexmundi.com/zimbabwe/population.html The population figures in Zimbabwe declined from roughly 12.7 million in 2003 due to emigration.

387 See: www.un.org/millenniumgoals

According to the African Economic Outlook Report 2007/8 ([388]) which analysed the progress made in achieving selected targets from seven of the eight MDGs only Mauritius and Malawi were making good progress. They had either achieved or were at least 'on track' in achieving the nine evaluated indicators (see table 9.5.). The others – including South Africa – showed only slow or no progress (DRC, Zambia, Zimbabwe) in achieving some of the MDGs. The biggest achievements were recorded for MDG 3 referring to promoting gender equality by eliminating gender disparities in primary and secondary school enrolment. The least progress has been made for MDG 4 – reducing child mortality rates – and MDG 6 combating diseases (in this case tuberculosis). Also regarding the indicator for MDG 1 pertaining to halving the number of people who suffer from hunger, only three countries in the SADC region were on track: Angola, Mozambique and Namibia.

Table 9.5.: Progress in Achieving Selected MDG Targets in the SADC Region in 2007

Coun-try	**MDG 1**	**MDG 2**		**MDG 3**		**MDG 4**	**MDG 5**	**MDG 6**	**MDG 7**	**To-tal**
	Tar-get 2	Target 1		Target 1		Target 1	Target 1	Target 3	Target 3	
	Indi-cator	Ind .1	Ind 2	Ind 1	Ind 2	Indi-cator	Indi-cator	Indi-cator	Indi-cator	
ANG	OT							OT		**2 / 9**
BOT				OT	A		OT		OT	**4 / 9**
DRC										**0 / 9**
LES				A	A					**2 / 9**
MAD		OT		OT	OT					**3 / 9**
MAL	OT	OT		A	OT	OT			A	**6/ 9**
MAU		OT	OT	A	OT		A		A	**6 / 9**
MOZ	OT	OT					OT			**3 / 9**
NAM	OT		OT	A	A				A	**5 / 9**
RSA				OT	A				OT	**3 / 9**
SWA				OT	OT		OT			**3 / 9**
TAN		OT		OT					OT	**3 / 9**
ZAM				OT						**1 / 9**
ZIM				OT						**1 / 9**
TOTAL	**4**	**5**	**2**	**7/3**	**4/4**	**1**	**3/1**	**1**	**3/3**	**41 / 126**

Source: OECD/AfDB (2008):44f
Explanations: OT = on track A = achieved
for detailed goals and targets see Text Box 9.1.

388 See: OECD/AfDB (2008):44ff.

This indicates that overall living conditions and people's welfare are not improving much in the SADC region. Mauritius, one of the better performing countries with regard to achieving the MDGS, is hardly physically integrated into SADC as a small island state. The other better performer, Malawi, is still not making much progress with regard to the poverty related MDGs. That means that also in the near future the social and economic disparities between the SADC member states will continue and the migration pressure on the southern member states will not cease.

TEXT BOX 9.1. The Millennium Development Goals (MDGs)

The Millennium Development Goals (MDGs) are based on the eight chapters of the United Nations Millennium Declaration, signed in September 2000.

The eight goals, which are concretized by 21 targets, are:

1.Eradicate extreme poverty and hunger

Target 1: Reduce by half the proportion of people living on less than one dollar a day by 2015.
Target 2: Reduce by half the proportion of people who suffer from hunger by 2015

2.Achieve universal primary education

Target 1: Ensure that all boys and girls complete a full course of primary school by 2015

3.Promote gender equality and empower women

Target 1: Eliminate gender disparities in primary and secondary education preferably by 2005 and at all levels by 2015.

4.Reduce child mortality

Target 1: Reduce by two thirds, between 1990 and 2015, the under-five mortality rate.

5.Improve maternal health

Target 1: Reduce by three quarters, between 1990 and 2015, the maternal mortality ratio
Target 2: Achieve, by 2015, universal access to reproductive health.

6.Combat HIV/AIDS, malaria, and other diseases

Target 1: Have halted by 2015 and begun to reverse the spread of HIV/AIDS.
Target 2: Achieve, by 2010, universal access to treatment for HIV/AIDS for all those who need it.
Target 3: Halve, by 2015, the proportion of people without sustainable access to safe drinking water and basic sanitation.

7.Ensure environmental sustainability

Target 1: Integrate the principles of sustainable development into country policies and programs; reverse loss of environmental resources.

Target 2: Reduce biodiversity loss, achieving, by 2010, a significant reduction in the rate of loss.
Target 3: Halve, by 2015, the proportion of people without sustainable access to safe drinking water and basic sanitation
Target 4: By 2020, to have achieved a significant improvement in the lives of at least 100 million slum dwellers.

8.Develop a global partnership for development
Target 1: Develop further an open trading and financial system that is rule-based, predictable and non-discriminatory. Includes a commitment to good governance, development and poverty_reduction - nationally and internationally.
Target 2: Address the special needs of the least developed countries. This includes tariff and quota free access for their exports; enhanced program of debt relief for heavily indebted poor countries; and cancellation of official bilateral debt; and more generous official development assistance for countries committed to poverty reduction.
Target 3: Address the special needs of landlocked and small island developing states.
Target 4: Deal comprehensively with the debt problems of developing countries through national and international measures in order to make debt sustainable in the long term.
Target 5: In cooperation with pharmaceutical companies, provide access to affordable essential drugs in developing countries.
Target 6: In cooperation with the private sector, make available the benefits of new technologies, especially information and communications.

Source: http://www.un.org/millenniumgoals/

On the cultural side, SADC is rather homogenous with English as the dominant (business) language and a predominantly Christian religious environment ([389]). The majority of the SADC member states are former British colonies or protectorates and have as such, a similar administrative culture and system. The two former Portuguese colonies, Angola and Mozambique used to stand out to some extent within SADC because of language but also administrative system. However, over the last decade, the proficiency of English has increased in both countries out of economic necessity and because of the increased influx of English-speaking business people particularly from South Africa.

The expansion of SADC towards the north (DRC) and East (Madagascar and Seychelles) has added French as a third official language and another bureaucratic culture. It needs to be seen if SADC can deal with all three working languages, incorporate different administrative systems and develop its own distinct regional culture. At the moment, it is just costly and cumbersome to have three official working languages as additional translation services are

389 There are in some places strong Muslim communities in the SADC region, particularly in Tanzania (Zanzibar) and also along the coast in Mozambique and in Malawi. There is also a strong Muslim minority in Mauritius. However, in total they account for less than 10% of the population of the region.

needed at SADC conferences and for all official documents. All this slows down the speed of communication and sometimes decision-making. It is not by accident that with Angola and the DRC ([390]) two countries from outside the English-dominated cultural sphere in the region have signed and ratified the least number of SADC Protocols (see table 8.3.).

In conclusion, the SADC region is characterized by pronounced socio-economic disparities between the member states, which make further integration not easy. Factors facilitating RI are the region's dominant British–influenced culture with regard to language and administrative systems and the strong prevalence of Christianity – in different denominations – as the regions main religion. However, this dominance is being diluted since SADC embarked on an expansionist course and other languages, administrative cultures and religious beliefs are becoming part of the region.

9.3. Production Structures and Potential for Trade Integration

SADC chose very early a "trade-integration" approach for regional integration as evidenced by the SADC Treaty and the Trade Protocol (signed in 1996). ECA defines trade integration to be achieved when;

> *"...product flows between countries are on the same terms and conditions as within countries. In an integrated market, prices of identical products are the same across countries/geographical jurisdictions ..."* ([391])

For this to happen, goods and services must be produced and traded within the RI area. If only imported goods are traded from one country to another, their prices should be rather similar, at least from the stage of customs union and onwards ([392]); however, the additional socio-economic benefits for the member states would in such a case be doubtful as the regional external tariff might be higher than previously at country level. Functional trade integration should thus be based on complementary production structures which allow for → ***trade creation***.

390 Madagascar is not yet a member long enough to be judged about Protocol ratification.

391 AU/ECA (2008), ARIA III:31

392 As from this integration stage onwards, a common external tariff level exists.

9.3.1. Production Structures in the SADC Region

In the case of SADC the complementarity of economic structures is limited. Most member states – with the notably exception of South Africa – are producers of minerals and agricultural raw materials and importers of capital and intermediary goods. The production side is reflected in the composition of the GDP, which in most SADC countries is dominated by the tertiary (services) sector.

Officially, the 'primary sector' comprises of all agricultural activities and mining, the 'secondary sector' includes manufacturing, construction and the production and distribution of electricity, gas and water while the 'tertiary sector' consists of all service related activities such as trade, transportation, communication, banking, insurance, real estate and business services as well as restaurants and hotels. However, some countries attribute economic activities differently and this is why for example Angola or Botswana appear to have a strong secondary sector, while in reality the economic activities listed in this sector are mostly related to mining and should have been recorded in the primary sector ([393]). The incorrect sectoral attribution is also be the explanation for the surprisingly strong secondary sectors in countries like Swaziland or Madagascar ([394]).

Table 9.6 shows the development of the economic strength and composition of the GDP of SADC member states in detail from 2000 until 2006. Remarkable is the fivefold increase of the GDP in Angola, which is predominantly owed to the end of the devastating civil war and to the increase in oil production and oil prices.

Particularly the secondary sector is important for RI as it includes the manufacturing industry, which is supposed to be the engine of trade-based RI. Agricultural products and minerals or electricity and water are only of relevance for intra-regional trade if there are member states which need these products as inputs for their manufacturing or mining industries and can afford to import them from other member states.

---

393 For the real contribution of the sub-sectors towards the generation of GDP see also table 9.7.

394 The high percentage of economic activities in the secondary sector in Lesotho is a reflection of the country's increase in power and water production for the South African market; see below.

Table 9.6.: GDP (in USD bill. current) and GDP Composition (in %) in SADC Member States

Country	2000				2004				2006			
	GDP	Prim	Sec	Ter	GDP	Prim	Sec	Ter	GDP	Prim	Sec	Ter
ANG	*9.1*	6	72	22	*19.8*	9	66	25	*45.2*	9	70	21
BOT	*6.2*	2	59	39	*9.8*	2	53	45	*11.0*	2	55	43
DRC	*4.3*	50	20	30	*6.6*	47	24	29	*8.5*	46	28	26
LES	*0.9*	18	41	41	*1.3*	17	40	43	*1.5*	16	43	41
MAD	*3.9*	29	14	57	*4.4*	29	16	55	*5.5*	28	15	57
MAL	*1.7*	40	18	42	*2.6*	37	19	44	*3.2*	34	20	46
MAU	*4.5*	6	31	63	*6.1*	6	30	64	*6.4*	6	26	68
MOZ	*4.3*	23	23	54	*5.7*	27	27	46	*6.8*	28	26	46
NAM	*3.4*	11	28	61	*5.6*	10	30	60	*6.6*	11	31	58
SA	*132.9*	3	32	65	*216.4*	3	31	66	*254.9*	3	31	66
SWA	*1.4*	15	45	40	*2.4*	9	47	44	*2.8*	8	46	46
TAN	*9.1*	45	16	39	*11.4*	46	17	37	*14.2*	45	17	38
ZAM	*3.2*	22	25	53	*5.5*	23	28	49	*10.9*	21	33	46
ZIM	*7.4*	18	25	57	*4.7*	17	21	62	*3.4**	19*	24*	57*
TOTAL	***192.3***	**9**	**21**	**70**	**302.3**	**8**	**33**	**59**	**380.9**	**8**	**35**	**57**

* = 2005

Sources: World Bank 2008, IMF, various country reports 2005-2008; SADC 2008;

Table 9.7. compares the relative strength of the manufacturing, mining and agricultural sectors in ten SADC member states.

Table 9.7.: Manufacturing, Mining and Agriculture as % of GDP in 2006 in Selected SADC Member States

Country	Manufacturing Sector	Mining Sector	Agricultural Sector
ANG	5	59	8
BOT	4	41	2
DRC	5	9	48
MAL	17	2	33
MAU	19	0	5
MOZ	15	1	28
NAM	13	13	11
RSA	18	8	3
TAN	8	3	27
ZAM	11	5	21

Source: OECD/AfDB 2008

In SADC, only South Africa has a manufacturing sector worth talking about. In South Africa, the share of the secondary sector in the GDP stood at 31 % in 2006, that of the manufacturing industry alone at 18%. In comparison with EU countries or Japan, this still is not a very high percentage but in terms of value produced, the South African manufacturing sector is with ca. USD 48 billion (2006), the biggest in sub-Saharan Africa.

The relatively high percentage figures for the secondary sector as shown in table 9.6. for Lesotho (40-43%), Swaziland (45-47%), Botswana (53-59%) and Angola (66-72%) are owed to particular economic settings. In the case of Lesotho, the production of water and energy for South Africa; in the case of Swaziland, the sugar refining process of the country's vast sugarcane production which contribute to a large extent towards the relatively strong standing of the secondary sector; in the case of Botswana, diamond production is the reason for the high share of secondary sector in GDP generation. The extremely high percentage of the secondary sector for Angola is nearly all owed to the production of oil and its rapid price increase until 2008 ([395]). Other countries also with mining resources such as the DRC, Zambia and Namibia show a relatively strong secondary sector – but in all those countries, the manufacturing sector is rather weak (see table 9.7.).

The figures drawn from the African Economic Outlook 2007/8 of the OECD and the AfDB show that the actual share of the manufacturing industry in relation to the GDP (in 2006), is apart from South Africa, above 10% only in Mauritius, Malawi, Mozambique and Zambia ([396]). These economies are all relatively small; their sizes ranging from USD 2.2 billion (Malawi) to Mozambique with a GDP of USD 7.5 billion in 2007. Apart from South Africa, only Mauritius has a manufacturing industry which produces consumer goods in larger quantities (textiles and processed food). It is currently the second most industrialized country in SADC. Starting as a sugar-producing mono culture, it successfully diversified since the 1970s into tourism, textile production and food processing, but is currently also hard hit by the world economic crisis.

According to the IMF, Lesotho also has a relatively high share of manufacturing activities (16% of GDP) ([397]). This was due to a strong influx of Chinese companies into textile and apparel manufacturing over the last years, which not only wanted to take advantage of Lesotho being a member of SACU, but also

---

395 In Botswana and Angola mining and oil production are grouped under the secondary sector and not under ‚primary sector'.

396 The report does not provide country profile for Lesotho, Swaziland and Zimbabwe and has no specific figures regarding the composition of GDP for Madagascar.

397 See IMF (2008a), Namibia. Country Report 08/82.

being entitled to duty-free exports to the USA under the 'African Growth and Opportunities Act' (AGOA). Of the remaining member states, Zimbabwe used to have a rather large and also growing manufacturing industry during the 1990s, but the crisis since 2000 has more or less destroyed the Zimbabwean manufacturing industry.

However, the majority of SADC member states are producers of mineral or agricultural raw materials. Southern Africa is one of the most mineral-rich regions in the world; the Congo-Basin being another one. The SADC region has substantial reserves of gold, copper, cobalt, coal, diamonds, oil (Angola), nickel, uranium, zinc, manganese, tungsten, gas, asbestos, gemstones and *coltan*. At the same time, it is also a major producer of agricultural raw materials such as sugar, coffee, tobacco, tea, cotton, maize, beef, pulp, cashew nuts and lately biofuels. As few SADC member states have the industrial processing facilities for the raw materials they produce – which is at least partly an inheritance of the exploitative structures established by the colonial regimes – they are only left with the option of exporting them unrefined and without much value added. Due to inherited production and trading structures (railways, roads, harbors and electricity) later reinforced by the independent governments, Southern Africa has thus always been – although unevenly – integrated into the world market, delivering raw materials and importing capital and consumer goods as well as fuel.

Globalization enhanced this even further especially when the prices for raw materials surged, and as a result, provided countries such as Angola, Zambia, Namibia or Botswana with sudden windfall profits. Despite positive fiscal balances and increasing foreign exchange reserves due to growing incomes from high commodity prices the domestic investment rations are still comparatively low, which indicates that not much effort is undertaken to invest into the processing of raw materials within the SADC region. The current world economic crisis, however, has reduced Government revenue and may lead in some countries to a serious economic 'hangover'. In Zambia, revenue from export taxes fell sharply ([398]):

- The mining company tax fell from USD 44 million in the second quarter of 2008 to USD 7.5 million in the fourth quarter of 2008.
- The mineral royalty tax fell from USD 24.4 million in the second quarter of 2008 to USD 16.9 million in the fourth quarter of 2008.
- The windfall tax fell from USD 33.7 million in the third quarter to USD 2.2 million in the fourth quarter of 2008.

398 See: SADC (2009c):6f

9.3.2. Intra-SADC Trade Development

Due to the production structure and the uneven integration into the world market, the exports of SADC member states are dominated by mineral and agricultural raw materials while on the import side capital, intermediate and consumer goods prevail (see table 9.8.). Only Lesotho and Madagascar list at least one category of manufactured goods (textiles) amongst their main exports. The structure of the main imports (according to available figures for the period between 2002 and 2006) is for most of the SADC member states biased towards manufactured goods and machines and transport equipment (mostly vehicles) which account for between 46% and 67% of all imports; fuel imports had a share around 12% in most SADC countries.

The import structure changed dramatically in 2007 and 2008 when international oil prices more than doubled and also prices for food items and chemicals rose sharply. However, there are no comparable figures for these years available yet. The overall picture remained the same: SADC member states export raw materials and import capital and consumer goods as well as fuels; value adding in the SADC region is limited.

As a result of the concentration of production in minerals and agricultural raw materials and the rather weak manufacturing base the scope for intra-regional trade within the SADC region appears limited. While the end of apartheid in South Africa in 1994 and its subsequent accession to SADC gave the intra-regional trade (exports) a boost (see table 9.9.) it was a rather lopsided one as the trade between other members of SADC for a long time grew only marginally. According to the ECA's Economic Report on Africa 2008 ([399]), intra-regional trade in SADC averaged at 10.13% of total trade for the period between 1995 and 2005. Intra-regional exports during this period grew by 7% as compared to 9% for the total exports of the SADC region. For the period between 2000 and 2005, intra-regional exports averaged 19.9% and imports even 33.1% in SADC ([400]). But given the production structure within SADC these figures may in fact already be close to the current maximum potential for intra-SADC trade.

---

399 ECA (2008b). Economic Report on Africa 2008. Africa and the Monterrey Consensus. Addis Ababa 2008:85.

400 See: ECA/AU (2008a):35

Table 9.8. The Main Export Goods of SADC Countries

Country	Main export goods (in % of total exports) 2006	Main imports (in % of total imports) 2005
ANG	Oil (96%) Diamonds (3.6%)	Consumer goods (60%); Capital Goods (29%); Intermediate Goods (11%)+
BOT	Diamonds (78.6%); Nickel (11.4%);	Manufactured Goods (34%); Machines& Vehicles (33%); Food and Beverages (13%); Fuel (4%) ²
DRC	Diamonds (31.2%) Cobalt (18.2%); Copper (9.7%)	n/a
LES	Textiles (81%); Diamonds (10%);	Manufactured Goods (38%); Food & Beverages (22%); Machines& Vehicles (12%); Chemicals (12%); Fuel (8%) ³
MAD	Textiles	Machines& Vehicles (31%); Fuel (23%); Manufactured Goods (23%); Food & Beverages (10%)*
MAL	Tobacco (53%),	Manufactured Goods (26%); Chemicals (21%); Machines& Vehicles (22%); Food and Beverages (16%); Fuel (10%)
MAU	Textiles; Sugar (15%)	Manufactured Goods (28%); Machines& Vehicles (28%); Fuel (16%); Food and Beverages (16%)
MOZ	Aluminum (73%): Seafood (6%), Minerals/Gas (4%)*	Machines& Vehicles (26%); Manufactured Goods (18%); Food and Beverages (13%); Fuel (6%)
NAM	Diamonds; Zinc	Machines& Vehicles (32%); Manufactured Goods (31%); Food and Beverages (14%); Fuel (10%) ²
SA	Platinum (9.4%), Diamonds (5.9%); Gold (5.7%);	Machines& Vehicles (36%); Fuel (14%); Manufactured Goods (22%); Chemicals (11%)
SWA	Sugar (14.3%); gas turbines (9.2%); odoriferous substances (8.6%)	Manufactured Goods (30%); Machines& Vehicles (23%); Food and Beverages (17%); Fuel (13%) ³
TAN	Tobacco (7.6%); Fish (6.9%); Cotton (6.7%)	Machines& Vehicles (33%); Manufactured Goods (30%); Chemicals (20%); Food & Beverages (10%)
ZAM	Copper (72.0%); Copper wire (4.7%)	Machines& Vehicles (31%); Manufactured Goods (30%); Chemicals (20%); Fuel (12)
ZIM	Nickel (16.8); Tobacco (10.0%); Ferro-chromium (9.1%)	Machines& Vehicles 26%); Fuel (14%) Manufactured Goods (21%); Food & Beverages (16%); Chemicals (12%) *

Source: OECD/AfDB 2008 ([401])
³ = for 2002 ² = for 2003 * = for 2004 + = for 2006

401 The tables for the main export products did not contain data on countries starting with the letters M – P; a printing error must have occurred.

Table 9.9.: The Development of Intra-SADC Exports (in% of total Exports) ([402])

Country	1984	1994	1998	2000	2006
Angola	0.2	0.3	0.1	n/a	0
Botswana	5.0	17.2	7.8	13.6	12.2
Lesotho	0	n/a	61.9	n/a	19.4
Malawi	5.8	20.1	5.3	34.0	31.3
Mauritius	n/a	0.9	0.8	6.5	7.4
Mozambique	10.4	23.7	17.9	35.8	19.1
Namibia	n/a	n/a	6.6	33.5	33.2
South Africa	n/a	22.4	18.3	19.4	9.1
Swaziland	3.0*	64.7	31.3	76.8	7.4
Tanzania	1.3	18.7	2.4	5.3	18.9
Zambia	3.9	4.8	3.0	29.1	35.4
Zimbabwe	9.8	32.8	23.8	26.9	n/a

Sources: Peters-Berries (2001e), Stahl (1999), SADC (2008b), IMF (2005) Zimbabwe country report; ECA/AU (2008a):35, Kalaba/Tsedu (2008)

The SADC countries most active in intra-regional trade are apart from the SACU members Zambia, Malawi, Zimbabwe and Tanzania ([403]). Of the original SADC members only Angola and Mauritius have no or just a weak link to the intra-regional trade network. For South Africa, particularly the intra-regional exports are of some – although varying – relevance. Most member countries have a negative trade balance with SADC. This is caused by the dominant economic position of South Africa, which provides considerable shares of their consumer and capital goods to several SADC countries (see table 9.5.). In the Zambian and Mauritian cases, the negative trade balance with other SADC member states was caused predominantly by the trade deficit with South Africa. The Zambian trade deficit with South Africa in 2005 was even higher than the overall trade deficit with the SADC region. Two thirds of intra-regional trade in SADC in 2005 was still with South Africa ([404]).

402 The figures compiled in the table are from several different statistical sources and may not always have been calculated on the same or at least comparable basis. However, they provide a good overview and appear not to be dissimilar.

403 See: tips/AusAid (2007), Intra-SADC trade performance Review 2007. tips. mimeo

404 See: Kalaba, M. and Tsedu, M. (2008b), Intra-SADC trade performance and the implementation of the Trade Protocol. tips, April 2008. http://www.tips.org.za/files/Kalaba_M._April08_Intra-SADC_Trade_Performance.pdf

Table 9.10.: Integration Into Intra-Regional Trade of Selected SADC Member States

Country	Exports			Imports		
TANZANIA	**2000 (in USD mill.)**	**2005 (in USD mill.)**	**Share (%) 2005**	**2000**	**2005**	**Share (%) 2005**
SA	11.8	289.4	18.9	162.6	400.0	12.3
SWA	-	-	-	13.0	23.6	0.7
MAU	-	-	-	2.5	4.6	0.1
ZAM	5.7	8.9	0.6	2.4	4.5	0.1
MAL	7.7	8.0	0.5	1.8	3.8	0.1
MOZ	1.5	7.2	0.5	0.1	2.0	0.1
ZIM	-	-	-	4.3.	2.0	0.1
BOT	0.1	4.2	0.3	-	-	-
Trade Balance	**2001: USD -200.6 mill. 2004: USD -213.4 mill.**					
ZAMBIA	**2000 (in USD mill.)**	**2005 (in USD mill.)**	**Share (%) 2005**	**2000**	**2005**	**Share (%) 2005**
SA	166.8	342.4	18.6	480.7	1,220.3	47.6
DRC	37.1	99.0	5.4	-	-	-
TAN	5.5	94.3	5.1	8.9	65.6	2.6
ZIM	17.1	76.2	4.1	66.7	110.4	4.3
MAL	15.6	63.4	3.4	2.4	14.4	0.6
BOT	3.1	42.1	2.3	5.6	11.5	0.4
NAM	1.9	8.8	0.5	1.5	6.3	0.2
MAU	0.4	1.5	0.1	-	-	-
Other SADC	0.8	3.0	0.2	9.2	10.3	0.4
Trade Balance	**2000: USD -346 mill. 2005: USD -736 mill.**					
MAURITIUS	**2000 (in USD mill.)**	**2005 (in USD mill.)**	**Share (%) 2005**	**2000**	**2005**	**Share (%) 2005**
MAD	76.3	116.0	5.7	33.6	15.0	0.5
SA	9.0	27.3	1.3	312.3	274.6	8.6
SEY	5.6	14.3	0.7	-	-	-
TAN	2.5	2.7	0.1	1.0	2.7	0.1
ZIM	5.8	1.8	0.1	7.1	2.9	0.1
MOZ	1.0	1.3	0.1	1.9	15.8	0.5
ZAM	-	-	-	0.2	8.7	0.3
Trade Balance	**2000: USD -309 mill. 2006: USD -166 mill.**					

Source: Tips/AusAid (2007); own compilation

These examples ([405]) are a clear indicator for the imbalanced trade structure within the SADC region. While the overall intra-regional trade figures appear to be high particularly when compared to that of other African RECs they disguise the South African economic dominance and the resulting fundamental problem for SADC: how long will the smaller economies within SADC accept or tolerate that the major beneficiary of trade integration is South Africa? So far the positive side effects of the South African trade dominance – availability of crucial capital and consumer goods; expansion of South African based supply chains (supermarkets, car dealers etc) – have prevented critical voices from questioning the wisdom of the current trade integration process. However, that can change once the South African economic presence becomes too over-bearing and the costs of the trade integration process – e.g. preventing local industries to develop; dominance of 'foreign' businesses – politically sensitive. As will be demonstrated later, the South African trade dominance is accompanied by a strong investment drive; this amplifies the visible South African economic dominance in the region further.

South Africa also disagrees with the interim EPA the other members of SACU signed with the EU in late 2007. It fears that certain regulations under the EPA such as procurement prescriptions, the liberalization of services and the elimination of export taxes could undermine basic pillars of the country's socio-economic development strategy. At a SADC ministerial meeting in early 2008 South Africa called for a renegotiation of the interim EPA and afterwards fears were voiced that South Africa could use the EPA issue to dissolve SACU, which many decision-makers in South Africa regard as an unnecessary burden([406]).

A related issue is the multiple memberships in integration schemes of several SADC member states. According to WTO rules no country is allowed to belong to more than one customs union ([407]). If SAFTA is transformed as planned into a customs union in 2010 SACU's existence – even as a special unit within SADC – might be called into question. At the same time Tanzania will have to decide if it prefers to belong to the customs union of the EAC or to that of SADC. The same applies to the SADC member states also belonging to the recently

405 Apparently the data availability in the SADC region was not sufficient to allow the consulting company Tips to analyse the regional trade integration of more countries; see: tips/AusAid (2007) Intra-SADC trade performance review 2007.

406 See: Vines, A. (2008),Regional Integration in Southern Africa: Challenges and Opportunities. Speech delivered to the *Instituto Superior de Relacoes Internacionais (ISRI),* Maputo, 26.03.2008. www.chathamhouse.org.uk

407 ibid.

launched COMESA customs union ([408]) – DRC, Madagascar, Malawi, Mauritius, Seychelles, Swaziland, Zambia, Zimbabwe – which would face the same predicament once the SADC customs union is established. This was realized by the Governments involved and might have been one of the factors kicking off discussions and negotiations about a Free Trade Area combining COMESA, EAC and SADC in October 2008 ([409]). The tripartite Summit held in *Kampala* (Uganda) *inter alia*;

> *"... approved the expeditious establishment of a Free Trade Area (FTA) encompassing the member/partner States of the 3 RECs with the ultimate goal of establishing a single Customs Union..." ([410]).*

By announcing these objectives, the member states of the three RECs – without announcing it publicly – might hope for more time under the WTO rules to harmonize their varying trade regimes.

Another issue not yet sufficiently dealt with in SADC concerns *non-tariff barriers* (NTB) which can constitute a formidable obstacle to intra-regional trade by causing (unnecessary) costs. A NTB is any measure that impedes international trade other than tariffs (see Text Box 9.2.).

SADC has been acutely aware of the danger NTBs pose for trade integration and has in the Trade Protocol explicitly agreed in Article 6 that all member states must:

> *"a. Adopt policies and implement measures to eliminate all existing forms of NTBs.*
> *b. Refrain from imposing any new NTBs" ([411]).*

Three of the five annexes of the Trade Protocol also deal in one way or another with the elimination of NTBs.

Starting with a workshop in 1997, jointly organized by the SADC Secretariat, GTZ and the *Konrad Adenauer Stiftung* in *Livingstone* (Zambia), SADC undertook a series of consultations with the business sector, customs authorities

---

408 The COMESA customs union was officially launched in August 2009 in Victoria Falls (Zimbabwe); see: http://www.comesa.int/lang-en/component/content/article/34-general-news/168-comesa-launches-its-customs-union

409 See: www.africa-eu.org/.../file/COMESA-EAC-SADC_EN_221008.pdf

410 COMESA, EAC, SADC (22.10.2008) Final Communiqué of the COMESA-EAC-SADC Tripartite Summit of Heads of State and Government. Kampala (Uganda):4. www.africa-eu.org/.../file/COMESA-EAC-SADC_EN_221008.pdf

411 See: SADC (1996), Protocol on Trade. www.sadc.int Article 6

and experts to build up an inventory of NTBs prevalent in the region. In 2004, SADC commissioned an inventory report on NTBs, which was updated in 2007 and which formed the basis for the formulation of a *SADC Action Plan for Monitoring and Eliminating NTBs* ([412]). Parallel to that, detailed research on the forms, impact and costs of NTBs on intra-SADC trade was conducted ([413]).

In the 2004 SADC inventory ([414]) three categories of NTBs relevant for the SADC region were identified:

1. Health, safety and environment NTBs such as export bans, restrictive sanitary and phytosanitary requirements or conformance requirements.
2. Trade policy NTBs, which include public export assistance, export taxes, import licenses, import quotas, production subsidies, state trading and import monopolies, tax concessions, anti-dumping measures or safeguard and countervailing measures.
3. Administrative NTBs including customs clearance delays, insufficient transparency and consistency in customs procedures, overly bureaucratic and arbitrary processing methods, documentation requirements for consignments, high freight and transport charges or unfriendly user services.

Three years later, SADC agreed in the context of the *SADC Action Plan for Monitoring and Eliminating NTBs* on a reporting mechanism – developed along the lines of one already in place in COMESA – to eliminate NTBs; intra-SADC exporters can now challenge any alleged NTBs ([415]). As a first concrete step, South Africa introduced the "*Single Administration Document*" for any cross-border trade from 01.10.2006 has probably been the closest to harmonizing border crossings as it increased the speed of customs clearance on the South African side but not yet on the Zimbabwean. After the good results of South Africa, SADC member states agreed to test the use of the single customs administrative document for commercial traffic from South Africa to Malawi via

412 See: www.sadctrade.org/files/Chapter6-2007-Non-tariff-barriers-in-SADC.pdf; and http://www.sadctrade.org/files/Chapter6-2007-Non-tariff-barriers-in-SADC.pdf

413 One study was undertaken with regard to the trade between South Africa and Botswana (Pierides, 2007), another study dealt with the special problem of the *Beitbridge* border post between South Africa and Zimbabwe (FESARTA, 2006); a third study (Mthembu-Salter; 2007) looked at northbound traffic from South Africa to Zambia and the DRC; see: SADC (2007c), Trade Performance Review. Gaborone:137ff

414 ibid:135

415 ibid:136

Zimbabwe and/or Mozambique in early 2007. The results show that transit times were reduced by up to 40% ([416]).

According to various studies and research amongst transport industry stakeholders the most severe and costly NTBs in detail, which are still hampering intra-SADC trade, are ([417]):

TEXT BOX 9.2. Nontariff Trade Barriers according to the WTO

1. Government Participation in Trade and Restrictive Practices Tolerated by Governments

(i) Government aids, including subsidies and tax benefits
(ii) Countervailing duties
(iii) Government procurement
(iv) Restrictive practices tolerated by Government
(v) State trading, government monopoly practices etc.

2. Customs and Administrative Entry Procedures

(i) Anti-dumping duties
(ii) Customs valuation
(iii) Customs classification
(iv) Consular formalities and documentation
(v) Samples
(vi) Rules of origin
(vii)Customs formalities
(viii)Import licensing
(ix) Pre-shipment inspection

3. Technical Barriers to Trade

(i) Technical regulations and standards
(ii) Testing and certification arrangements

4. Sanitary and Phytosanitary Measures

(i) SPS measures including chemical residue limits, disease freedom, specified product treatment etc.
(ii) Testing, certification and other conformity measures

5. Specific Limitations

(i) Quantitative restrictions
(ii) Embargoes and other restrictions of similar effect
(iii) Exchange controls

---

416 ibid:140

417 See: SADC/GTZ/KAF (1997), Non Tariff Trade Barriers and Regional Trade Promotion, Conference Report. Joint Conference, *Livingstone*, Zambia, 26-29.11.1997. mimeo; SADC (2007c): 137ff; SADC (2008f), SADC FTA Handbook. Gaborone:8

(iv) Discrimination resulting from bilateral agreements (v) Discriminatory sourcing (vi) Export restraints (vii)Measures to regulate domestic prices (viii)Tariff quotas (ix) Export taxes (x) Requirements concerning marking, labelling and packaging
6. Charges on Imports (i) Prior import deposits (ii) Surcharges, port taxes, statistical taxes, etc. (iii) Discriminatory film taxes, use taxes, etc. (iv) Border tax adjustments
7. Other (i) Intellectual property issues (ii) Safeguard measures, emergency actions (iii) Distribution constraints (iv) Business practices or restrictions in the market

Source: RTFB (2007)

- Cumbersome custom clearance procedures such as physical inspection requirements due to unclear specifications about norms and standards, insufficient information about forms, irregular change of forms etc. which lead to lengthy border delays. The most notorious border crossing is *Beitbridge* between South Africa and Zimbabwe.
- High road user fees and dilapidated roads.
- Transport bottlenecks at ports such as *Durban*, rail systems (including South Africa's) and numerous toll fee stations.
- High import licenses and other customs charges, which at times replace an abolished tariff with an NTB ([418]) and can be charged in foreign exchange (see table 10.5).
- Insufficient market and institutional/regulatory information.
- Special indirect taxes such as the requirement for exporters to convert major parts of their foreign exchange earnings into the local currency at the official rate ([419]).
- Inadequate communication structures.

---

418 In the Zimbabwean case, imports are regarded as services which attract a higher withholding tax (20%) than mere goods; see: SADC (2007c):141.

419 In the case of Zimbabwe, the 2007 regulation that 25-40% of export earnings had to be changed at the official rate at a time when inflation was running at several thousand percent and the official exchange rate was not at all reflecting the real value of the money anymore amounted to a tax which made virtually all legal exports unviable; see SADC (2007c):142

One way of lowering the costs for intra-SADC trade recommended by experts for more than a decade is the establishment of one-stop border posts ([420]). In December 2009 the first such border posts (at *Chirundu* between Zambia and Zimbabwe) has been opened in the SADC region – however, commissioned by COMESA ([421]). A SADC report from 2008/9 meticulously lists the number of documents needed (between five and twelve), the time required (between 16 and 73 days) and the costs to be incurred (between USD 677 and 3,999) for intra-regional trade activities (see table 9.11.). A functioning FTA looks different.

Some NTBs in SADC are the result of administrative inefficiencies others, however, must be regarded as deliberate to impede trade or ensure that a phasing out of tariffs can be compensated by new taxes and fees. A third category of NTBs are those which are applied for legitimate reasons e.g. health standards, national security reasons or to protect through rules-of-origin local industries under threat from cheap imports in case of a FTA.

Table 9.11.: SADC – Trading Across Borders 2009

Country	No. of documents to export	Time to Export (Days)	Cost to Export (USD)	No of documents to import	Time to import (days)	Costs to imports (USD)
MAU	5	17	725	6	16	677
RSA	8	30	1,445	9	35	1,721
BOT	6	31	2,508	9	42	3,064
NAM	11	29	1,686	9	24	1,813
ZAM	6	53	2,664	9	64	3,335
SEY	6	17	1,839	5	19	1,839
SWA	9	21	2,184	11	33	2,249
LES	6	44	1,549	8	49	1,715
TAN	5	24	1,262	7	31	1,475
MAL	12	45	1,671	10	54	2,550
MOZ	8	26	1,200	10	32	1,475
MAD	4	23	1,279	9	27	1,660
ZIM	7	53	2,678	9	73	3,999
ANG	12	68	2,250	9	62	3,325
DRC	8	46	2,607	9	66	2,483

Source: SADC (2008d):20.
Note: The cost to export or import is US$/container.

420 See: chapter 8.3.4.3.
421 See: Sub-Saharan Informer (*Addis Abeba*), 4.12.2009

NTBs, despite having been identified as an impediment, are even after the establishment of the SADC-FTA a serious obstacle to intra-SADC trade facilitation. They constitute for countries such as Zimbabwe a quiet opportunity to replace diminishing revenue from tariffs with new fees and taxes without blocking the liberalization of intra-regional trade in an open manner. However, if NTBs remain unchecked and countries violating the spirit of regional trade liberalization are not called to account the envisaged establishment of a SADC customs union will have difficulties to function.

The reality of intra-regional trade in the SADC-region is thus characterized by five main issues:

1. The relatively high percentage of intra-regional trade within SADC is due to the special role of South Africa as the main provider for consumer and selected capital goods.
2. All SADC member states have a negative trade balance with South Africa and are dependent on South Africa for the regular supply of crucial imports.
3. The volume of intra-regional trade excluding South Africa is still rather low despite the introduction of tariff reductions in the context of the FTA over the last decade.
4. In the context of EPAs and WTO rules South Africa's national interests might threaten the SADC trade agenda as it disagrees with the interim EPA the other SACU members have signed with the EU. SACU's continued existence might be at stake from this end and all the more as the WTO forbids that countries can belong to more than one customs union.
5. Physical and political obstacles have not been cleared by the introduction of the FTA and impede intra-regional trade further.

These trends indicate that the potential for a further increase in intra-regional trade in SADC is limited. The main underlying reasons are the low complementarity of the production structures in SADC, the unequal but hardened integration into the world market of most SADC economies, the continuing low attractiveness of Southern Africa as an investment destination with regard to manufacturing industries and the political unwillingness of the Governments of some SADC states to comply with agreed integration procedures ([422]).

422 See: Chingono and Nakana (2009):401ff

9.3.3. Intra-Regional Investment Patterns in SADC

As shown above, Southern Africa attracts predominantly FDIs in the mineral, agricultural and tourism sectors but hardly any in manufacturing. *Intra-regional investments* could bridge that gap and create some of the so far missing complementary production structures crucial for a further increase in intra-regional trade. As discussed in chapters 2 and 3, the elimination of internal tariffs in a FTA or Customs Union can stimulate intra-regional investments. The establishment of SAFTA in August 2008 is supposed to have provided such a stimulus and thus expand and diversify the regional manufacturing base. However, the sudden world economic crisis which started to affect Southern Africa in late 2008 has probably cooled down interests in this respect; empirical evidence seems to indicate so far that the new economic opportunities created by SAFTA have not been realized yet in the anticipated manner. Since 2000, when the first tariffs were abolished no significant change has occurred in the intra-regional investment pattern. Only South African companies have continued to invest in other SADC countries but predominantly into retail, banking, tourism, mining and agriculture but hardly into manufacturing.

The observed cross-border investments in SADC have not created the required up-stream linkages for production processes within SADC. The major motivation for cross-border investments has in nearly all cases been the expansion of already existing business linkages or the desire to obtain a greater share of business in local markets.

The major source of cross-border investments has been South Africa. Its private and state-owned companies have quickly conquered the regional markets once other member states liberalized their economies or expanded their investment portfolios.

Available data from 1994-2004 shows clearly that South African FDI is a major investor in the SADC region. 22% of all FDIs to the SACD region in this period were from South Africa (see table 9.12.). South African companies have substantial FDI stocks in eleven out of the 15 SADC member states (see table 9.13.) with Mauritius, Mozambique and Tanzania being the preferred investment destinations.

Table 9.12.: South Africa's FDI to SADC 1994 – 2004 (in Rand million)

Year	Total FDI to SADC	FDI to SADC from South Africa	South Africa's share of FDI to SADC
1994	60	26	43%
1996	1149	97	8%
1998	5085	1988	39%
2000	904	281	31%
2001	9808	1585	16%
2002	4600	1884	41%
2003	7443	932	13%
2004*	4976	397	12%
Total**	**39244**	**8781**	**22%**

Source: Rwelamira/Kaino (2008):79
* = only for first half of the year
** = sum of all years from 1994 to 2004

Table 9.13.: South Africa's FDI Stocks in SADC Countries 2000-2006 (in Rand million)

Country	2000	2001	2002	2003	2004	2005	2006
Botswana*	n/a	511	307	551	619	572	859
Lesotho*	n/a	188	162	204	256	227	239
Mauritius*	n/a	6,625	2,649	4,106	8,116	3,440	33,893
Mozambique*	n/a	4,117	6,896	5,071	4,396	4,584	5,331
Namibia*	n/a	1,405	1,095	1,151	840	834	872
Swaziland*	n/a	153	232	937	841	423	810
Zambia*	n/a	89	146	415	412	586	413
Zimbabwe*	n/a	587	603	2,033	645	671	1,253
Tanzania **	**348.4**	**418.9**	**550.3**	**786.7**	**1,587.6**	**1,771.5**	**n/a**
Malawi**	**75.8**	**108.1**	**100.9**	**93.4**	**101.2**	**n/a**	**n/a**
Madagascar ***	n/a	n/a	**1,200**	**400**	**2,200**	**10,408**	**5,500**

Source: Rwelamira/Kaino (2008):79
* = in *Rand* million
** = in USD million
*** = in *Ariary* million (€ 1.00 = Ar 2,924.80; Jan.2010)

Some of the major South African investors in the region are:

- *South African Breweries* (SAB), which invested in Zimbabwe, Zambia, Mozambique, Tanzania, Botswana and is trying also to get a foothold into Namibia and Malawi.

- South African banks such as *ABSA* and *Stanbic* and insurance companies such as *Old Mutual* have opened branches in most SADC member states and have invested in manufacturing, tourism and farming interests in Botswana, Swaziland, Lesotho, Namibia, Zimbabwe, Zambia and Mozambique.
- *Anglo American* and its subsidiary *de Beers* (diamonds), play a dominant role in the mining sector of many SADC countries although the company created a stir when it pulled out of an already agreed takeover of the Zambian state owned Zambian Consolidated Copper Mines (ZCCM) in 2001.
- *Southern Sun* and *Protea Hotels* have been investing in almost all lucrative tourism destinations throughout the SADC region, including: Botswana, Namibia, Swaziland, Namibia, Malawi, Mozambique, Mauritius, Tanzania, Zambia and Zimbabwe. Several smaller South African companies or private business people have invested in Zambia, Namibia and Mozambique.
- *Shoprite/Checkers* and to a lesser extent, *Woolworth* and *Game* have aggressively invested in the retail sectors in the SACU member states, Zimbabwe, Zambia, Malawi, Mozambique and Tanzania. Especially *Shoprite* did not only cover the capitals, but went out into smaller regional towns in Zambia, Zimbabwe, Malawi and Mozambique as well.
- *Eskom*, the South African power utility, has made strategic investments in Mozambique, Zambia, Zimbabwe and the SACU states. Its interest is to link the huge electricity generation potential of the DRC to South Africa, which has experienced in 2007 and 2008, a higher demand for electricity than could be satisfied by *Eskom*. To this end it had co-founded the *Westcor* consortium which in August 2009 pulled out of the multi-billion Dollar endeavor ([423]). In Zimbabwe, *Eskom* wants to acquire a stake in the *Zimbabwe Electricity Supply Authority* (ZESA) as compensation for unpaid electricity exports to the country ([424]).
- *Anglo American* and other companies are also holding large interests in the agricultural sectors of Mozambique, Zimbabwe and Zambia. Smaller private South African investors have been particularly attracted by Mozambique, which offered, – in a controversial deal – large tracts of fertile but sparsely populated land to South African farmers.

---

423 See: Pana news agency, 13.08.2009; http://www.afriquejet.com/news/africa-news/westcor-pulls-out-of-inga-iii-power-project-2009081333393.html

424 See: http://www.newzimbabwe.com/pages/fuel9.12934.html. Already in 2004, ZESA owed USD 21 mill. to Eskom.

- Investments of South African companies into biofuels production – sugarcane, palm oil, oil seeds – are the latest trend in cross-border investments. Targets are particularly Angola, Mozambique and Tanzania ([425]).

However, focusing on large-scale South African investments does not give the true picture of the South African investment drive.

> *"... according to the list compiled by South Africa Business Forum (SABF) [...], there are over 65 South African companies operating in Tanzania in various sectors, including financial services, agribusiness, mining, commerce and trade, transport and communications, management consultancy, brewing, satellite television and tourism" ([426]).*

The South African investments have been mainly directed towards the primary and tertiary sectors but few investments into manufacturing by companies from South Africa or other SADC member states took place. Neither was there much investment in upstream industries which could provide the South African manufacturing industry with raw materials or semi-processed inputs. This can be largely attributed to the structure of the South African manufacturing industry. It major products are

- consumer products such as processed foods, beverages, furniture, textiles, shoes etc.;
- simple parts for the car manufacturing industry complementing the imported majority of parts for the assembly plants of *BMW, VW, Mercedes, Toyota* and *Nissan*;
- refined fuels both from oil imports and coal conversion;
- paper products made from pulp produced both in South Africa and Swaziland,
- simple chemicals.

South Africa either has the required raw materials for its manufacturing industry itself or can source them on the world market at competitive prices. Its manufacturing industry did so far not look for inputs from SADC member states.

---

425 See Watson, Helen (2009), External Impacts of European Union (EU) Bio fuels Policies. Report prepared for Institute for European Environmental Policy (IEEP), Belgium, January 2009; OECD/AfDB (2008): 123ff

426 Rwelamira/Kaino (2008):80

Of the SADC member states most have invested in at least one other SADC country. As table 9.14 shows, Zimbabwean companies have been at least until 2006 the most active in terms of FDI apart from South Africa. Malawi and Mozambique have been the most attractive SADC member states receiving intra-regional FDIs apart from South Africa.

Table 9.14.: Intra-Regional Investment Stocks in SADC (1995-2006)

Country	Has FDIs from...	Has invested in...
Botswana	South Africa	South Africa, Malawi and Tanzania
Lesotho	South Africa	South Africa
Madagascar	South Africa and Mauritius	None
Malawi	South Africa, Botswana, Mauritius, Mozambique, Zambia and Zimbabwe	Tanzania and Mozambique
Mauritius	South Africa	Malawi, Madagascar, South Africa
Mozambique	South Africa, Malawi, Swaziland and Zimbabwe	Malawi
Namibia	South Africa	South Africa
South Africa	Botswana, Lesotho, Mauritius, Namibia, Zimbabwe	
Swaziland	South Africa	Tanzania and Mozambique
Zambia	South Africa	Malawi and Tanzania
Zimbabwe	South Africa	South Africa, Mozambique, Malawi and Tanzania

Source: Rwelamira/Kaino (2008):85ff and own compilation

Before the Zimbabwean economy started to implode from 2000 onwards ([427]) there were a number of Zimbabwean businesses which started to engage in cross-border investments. The private mobile telephone company, *Econet Wireless* of Zimbabwean business tycoon *Strive Masiyiwa*, had invested into the Botswana mobile telephone network. Zimbabwean banks such as *Standard Chartered, Barclays (Zim)* and *First Banking Corporatio*n had also ventured into Botswana, Swaziland, Tanzania, South Africa and Zambia and were planning to open branches in Mozambique and Namibia as well ([428]). Mauritian

427 See: chapter 11

428 See Muzorewa, Basil (2000), Measurement of the Deepening of Financial and Monetary Integration: The case of SADC. In: Peters-Berries/Marx (2000): 116

companies have invested into sugar plantation and hotels in Madagascar, Mozambique and, for a while, also in Zimbabwe ([429]).

One exception to the general trend of South African companies investing in the region's financial, services, agricultural, mineral extraction and trading industries but hardly ever into the manufacturing sector, however, has to be singled out: the huge *Mozal* aluminum smelter located in a special business zone close to the Mozambican capital *Maputo* – an investment worth ca. USD 2.1 billion – started production in 2000. It uses bauxite found in South Africa and converts it into aluminum, which is exported to the world market. The decision to build the smelter in Mozambique and not in South Africa (as first planned) was based on the obvious advantages Mozambique could offer: vicinity to the bauxite deposits and a harbor with additional capacity (*Maputo*) as well as the availability of sufficient and cheap electricity (from the *Cabora Bassa* dam). *Mozal* is so far, the first and only major foreign direct investment (a joint venture of Australian and South African investors) into the SADC region created because of the opportunities of regional integration. It is using the raw materials from one member state (South Africa) to be processed because of more lucrative production factors in another member state (Mozambique).

Foreign Direct Investment (FDI) from outside the region as another source of possible investments into production of processed and/or semi-processed goods has increased since 2000 as compared to the 1990s. But the bulk of FDI went into oil exploitation in Angola and mining ventures in South Africa, Zambia, Namibia and Botswana. Mozambique and Tanzania (see table 9.15.) also received substantial FDI which went to a larger part into agricultural production, tourism and mining. The available statistical sources such as the African Economic Outlook or the UNCTAD Handbook on Statistics do not differentiate according to the sector of investment but it can be safely assumed from secondary sources that most of the FDI into the SADC region has been earmarked for mineral ventures, a smaller part for agricultural and tourism projects and very little for manufacturing. In other words, the current increase in FDI is only reinforcing the structurally lopsided and unequal integration of Southern Africa into the world market but does little to promote or facilitate regional integration.

In summary, the SADC region has similar rather than complementary production structures and established trade patterns biased against intra-regional trade reinforced by current investment patterns. This means that the trading potential within SADC is limited. With the exception of oil, bauxite (see above)

429 Personal knowledge from the time when the author lived in Zimbabwe (1992-2000), such deals were at the time reported in Zimbabwean newspapers.

and perhaps pulp (for producing paper), none of the other raw materials produced by the SADC member states are of significance to the economy of other SADC members. The potential for intra-regional trade is also therefore limited. As can be seen from table 9.4., intra-SADC exports increased after South Africa joined the club in 1995 but stayed on similar levels ever since (with country variations). Cross-border investments have increased in the past decade, but have predominantly been limited to investments without regional impact.

Table 9.15.: Net Foreign Direct Investment in SADC Countries 2001-2006 (USD mill.)

Country	2001	2002	2003	2004	2005	2006	2007
ANG	2,146	1,672	3,505	1,449	-1,303	-1,140	-1,500
BOT	31	405	419	392	281	274	495
DRC	82	117	158	10	-79	180	720
LES	28	27	42	53	57	57	106
MAD	93	61	95	95	86	230	997
MAL	60	6	7	22	27	30	55
MAU	-28	32	63	14	42	105	339
MOZ	255	347	337	245	108	154	427
NAM	365	182	142	226	348	327	697
SA	6,789	757	734	799	6,251	-323	5,692
SWA	29	92	-61	70	-50	36	37
TAN	389	388	308	331	448	377	600
ZAM	72	82	172	364	380	350	984
ZIM	4	26	4	9	103	40	69
TOTAL	**10,315**	**4,194**	**5,925**	**4,079**	**6,699**	**697**	**9,718**

Source: OECD/AfDB (2008):663; ECA (2009b)

The major source of such cross-border investments has been South Africa, whose interest is the expansion of its market share in other SADC member states rather than setting up up-stream investments in other SADC countries which could provide the South African industry with raw materials or semi-processed goods.

Unless substantial investments in manufacturing industries in different SADC countries occur over the next few years, the potential for further integration through trade appears limited – even if the existing NTBs are removed – and largely dependent on the output and direction of development of the South African manufacturing sector.

9.4. Potential Areas for Further Regional Integration

As shown in previous chapters, the SADC region has a number of areas, which have the potential for further integration ranging from industrial production to energy and transportation. Additional to these crucial sectors, the region has also regional integration potential especially with regard to agricultural production and food security as well as tourism.

Apart from minerals, agricultural raw materials such as cotton, tobacco, sugar, coffee, tea, sisal or beef but also maize are the region's second most important category of export goods. Lately, biofuels have joined the list of important export products. Producers of agricultural exports are usually corporations (sugar, biofuels, tea, coffee) or large-scale commercial farmers (tobacco, maize, cotton, beef). Smallholder agriculture has only a small part in export production.

Although in some parts of the region, fertile agricultural land is becoming scarce (Malawi, Namibia, Swaziland, Zimbabwe) there are also large sections e.g. in Mozambique, Zambia, Angola and Tanzania which are sparsely populated and potentially attractive for agricultural investments. The exodus of white commercial farmers from Zimbabwe over the last decade has demonstrated in two ways the importance of an entrepreneurial class for the flourishing of agriculture. In Zimbabwe, the eviction of more than 4,000 white farmers from their farms, and the absence of equally skilled and motivated black Zimbabwean farmers, resulted in the collapse of the once highly productive commercial agriculture ([430]). But what damaged Zimbabwe's economy benefited its neighbors in SADC. Commercial agriculture in Malawi, Mozambique, Zambia and even Tanzania expanded and became more productive and market-oriented ([431]) due to the influx of the expelled white Zimbabwean farmers.

Over the past three decades, the SADC region has on the average produced sufficient food to ensure regional food security. However, increasingly volatile weather conditions with a rapid succession of droughts and floods – probably due to the impact of global warming – and the collapse of commercial agriculture in the previous regional bread-basket Zimbabwe, have eroded the region's capacity to produce sufficient staple foods. The experience of several

430 This line of argumentation is purely economic; the social and political justification of land reform in Zimbabwe is not discussed.

431 The author witnessed the impact of the migration of Zimbabwean farmers after 2000 at a number of occasions in Zambia, Malawi and Mozambique and also in Zimbabwe when in 2004 one of the last big white-owned farms close to Odzi was taken over by the Zimbabwean Government.

devastating droughts in the 1980s and 1990s and equally destructive floods especially since 2000, have taught the SADC-leaders to pay special attention to the agricultural sector. In 2004, they agreed in *Dar Es Salam* at a special Summit on the "*Dar-Es-Salam Declaration on Agriculture and Food Security*" ([432]) and a respective Plan of Action, called *inter alia* for

- an increase of budgetary allocations to agriculture to at least 10% of the budget;
- a substantial up-scaling of the use of inorganic fertilizer; and
- the introduction of a tracking system for the progress made in implementing the Plan of Action.

However, to date, only Malawi has reported an allocation of at least 10 percent of the budget to agriculture and a marked increase in the use of inorganic fertilizer ([433]). Most of the other member countries showed, for various reasons ([434]), a rather lacklustre response to the call to focus on agriculture and food security.

The region, with or without Zimbabwe, has the potential to feed itself. The concern and commitment of the SADC leaders to achieve sustainable food security against the unpredictability of the impact of weather and climate change exists. However, in order to realize this considerable integration potential, jointly agreed regional policies on food security need to be taken more seriously.

The other main and so far not fully realized regional integration potential pertains to tourism. Southern Africa has developed into a major international tourist attraction with its variety of national parks, beaches, mountains and even deserts. Table 9.16. shows that the overall number of tourist arrivals to the SADC region has significantly increased between 2000 and 2006. But it also shows that only Botswana, Madagascar, Mauritius, Namibia, South Africa and Tanzania are attracting well-paying international tourists in sizeable numbers; in these cases the income from tourism is at least USD 300 per arrival. The bulk of the visitors captured in the category "tourist" in the SADC region are in fact from within the region as the low spending levels indicate and probably just mere labour migrants and/or traders.

---

432 See: http://www.sadc.int/archives/read/news/106

433 Against the advice of the World Bank, Malawi re-introduced subsidies for fertilizer in 2005/6 and was awarded by bumper harvests in 2006/7 and 2007/8; see SADC (2008) Review 2007/8 and IPS (8.9.2008): Going against the Grain on Subsidies.

434 The impact of HIV/AIDS on the rural labour market may be one of the factors undermining the ability of some SADC member states to react positively to the „*Dar-Es-Salam*" Declaration; see chapter 9.2.

Table 9.16.: Tourist Arrivals (in '000) and Income (USD million) in the SADC Member States 2000-2006

Coun-try	2000		2004		2005		2006	
	Arrivals	Income	Arrivals	Income	Arrivals	Income	Arrivals	Income
ANG	51	34	194	82	210	103	121	91
BOT	1,306	226	1,722	582	1,885	561	n/a	n/a
DRC	103	n/a	36	n/a	61	n/a	55	n/a
LES	302	n/a	304	n/a	304	n/a	367	n/a
MAD	160	152	229	239	277	290	312	386
MAL	228	30	427	36	438	43	n/a	n/a
MAU	678	732	739	1,156	782	1,189	807	1,302
MOZ	n/a	n/a	711	96	954	138	1,095	145
NAM	759	n/a	986	426	973	363	1,032	473
RSA	6,001	3,338	6,815	7,380	7,518	8,448	8,509	8,967
SWA	281	24	459	75	839	78	873	74
TAN	501	381	583	762	613	835	644	950
ZAM	457	n/a	515	n/a	669	n/a	757	n/a
ZIM	1,967	125	1,854	194	1,559	99	2,287	328
Total	**12,794**		**15,574**		**17,082**		**16,859**	

Source: OECD/AfDB (2008)

So far, most tourist destinations in Southern Africa are developed as national destinations. The concept of cross-border products, which are combining tourist attractions from two or more countries, is still fairly underdeveloped although there is a substantial potential for it. Even when a tour operator offers a package including destinations in two countries, this is often not advertised as such. Some South African package tours for international tourists, for instance, include a trip to the *Victoria Falls* (which are on the border between Zimbabwe and Zambia) pretending they are located in South Africa ([435]).

During the 1990s, the idea of establishing cross-border National Parks in SADC emerged as a way of combining tourism and natural resource assets in various countries into one management area and a single tourism product. The biggest project in this respect has been the creation of the *Transfrontier National Park* which 'mirrors' the South African *Kruger National Park* into Mozambique. A few other projects such as the *Upper Zambezi Region Development Initiative* (UZAREDI) between Botswana, Namibia, Zambia and Zimbabwe or the initiative to jointly manage the *Kalahari Gemsbok National Park* between Botswana, Namibia and South Africa have sprung up but failed to take off. An attempt of provincial tourism authorities from South Africa, Mozambique and Swaziland to form a joint tourism promotional body (*South East African*

435 Personal observations of the author at several South African travel agencies.

Tourism Committee [SEATOC]) did in the end, not work because of divergent national interests and a lack of vision ([436]).

Thus far, these and similar projects did not take off not only because of conflicting national interests and the absence of committed 'drivers' but also because of a host of practical bottlenecks:

- borders between SADC member states are still not easy to cross and the idea of creating cross-border parks with relative open borders has been met with stiff resistance in the security establishments of several countries;
- cumbersome and expensive visa requirements for tourists who would like to visit more than one country; the idea of a SADC tourist visa has not yet been realized;
- the insufficient knowledge of tourism stakeholders both in the private sector and governmental agencies about each others tourism markets and potentials;
- the so far rather ineffective, *Regional Tourism Organization of Southern Africa* (RETOSA), which is the SADC institution tasked with promoting tourism in the region.

Tourism development in the SADC region still has tremendous potential especially if it is conceptualized as a regional and not a national development issue. The promotion of tourism as a regional product can create additional employment, generate income, and also contribute to a deepening of the regional integration process.

9.5. Approaching Macro-Economic Convergence

Following the example of the EU and responding to the macroeconomic requirements of RI, SADC has started to embark on a macroeconomic convergence program that aims at establishing the basis for the introduction of a common market and regional currency. The first official SADC document referring to macroeconomic convergence was the MoU on Macroeconomic Convergence adopted in 2001. In the RISDP of 2003, macroeconomic convergence is regarded as one of the strategic pillars to achieve the ambitious objectives of further RI ([437]).

---

436 See: Peters-Berries/Marx (2000):61f

437 See: Kalaba, M. et al (2006):22ff

TEXTBOX 9.3.: Is There Convergence in SADC?

Regional integration requires political and economic convergence to be successful and sustainable. Political convergence can be described in terms of

1. Political systems
2..Adherence to rule of law
3. Degree of political and civil liberties
4. Social equity.

Economic convergence in the case of SADC can be best analysed by looking at:

1. Budget deficits
2. Inflation rates
3. External debt levels
4. Economic growth rates
5. Aid dependency.

In SADC the discrepancies between the region's biggest economy and political heavy-weight South Africa and the other 13 members is huge. South Africa accounts for more than 75% of the regional GDP, more than 85% of intra-regional trade and for more than 90% of the intra-regional investments. Regional integration to be successful has to narrow down this gap – at least in the medium to long-run. In this respect the recent organisational and structural reforms SADC has embarked on will only have an impact if SADC will converge both politically and economically.

What are the chances that this convergence will occur? In economic terms the trends to be observed throughout most of the 1990s was quite encouraging. With the exception of a few cases such as Angola and DRC (and later Zimbabwe) budget deficits and inflation rates came down in the other countries, external debt levels stabilized and economic growth rates picked up. Only in terms of aid dependency the differences between countries such as Botswana, Mauritius, Seychelles and South Africa on the one hand and Lesotho, Malawi, Mozambique, Tanzania and Zambia on the other hand widened. With the turn of the millennium economic trends changed to the worse. Growth rates plummeted in most countries, inflation rates and budget deficits picked up and debt levels rose again despite debt reduction efforts of most donors. Today the discrepancies between South Africa and the next most diversified economy Zimbabwe are wider than 5 years ago. At the bottom end of the economic scale only Mozambique was able to continue growing but countries such as DRC, Malawi, Tanzania and Zambia and Zimbabwe fell even further behind.

Similar developments occurred in the political field. While the 1990s saw a trend towards democratic multi-party systems ('electoral democracies') with the exception of only Swaziland (monarchy) and DRC (autocracy). At the beginning of 2003 this has not changed on the outside but developments in several countries point at a steady deterioration of the rule of law (Zimbabwe, Angola, Swaziland, Malawi, DRC, Zambia);

It has to be noted that the end of the civil wars in Angola and DRC, the stabilisation of democracy in Lesotho and the prevention of an unconstitutional third presidential term in Zambia are encouraging signs as far the democratic process is concerned. In general, however, the political convergence between countries in the 'democratic consolidation zone' (Breytenbach) and the mere 'electoral democracies' and autocracies has widened over the last few years. Widening gaps in political convergence are a strong indicator for crumbling internal legitimacy and stability which in turn will impede economic recovery and further regional integration.

What does that mean for SADC and what can SADC do? On the political side:

1. ambiguities towards violations of good governance principles and/or democracy must be avoided;
2. deviant regimes (Zimbabwe) must not be supported;
3. inter-state conflicts must be settled regionally;
4. an enforceable regional democratic code of conduct should be agreed upon.

On the economic side:
1. the private sector must have bigger role to play in the formulation of sectoral policies and protocols;
2. costs and benefits of regional integration measures (protocols) must become more transparent to policy makers and civil servants;
3. South Africa must avoid dominating (if not bulldozing) the much smaller economies into submission;
4. the implementation capacity and responsibility of the Secretariat must be strengthened so that the regional integration can speed up.

Source: Peters-Berries, C. (2003):4

SADC chose four primary indicators and five secondary indicators to monitor the process and eventually the achievement of macroeconomic convergence. It also set a ten-year timeframe starting in 2008 between the first measuring - or checkpoint - and the final stage of achieving macroeconomic convergence. Of the four main indicators, the inflation target is regarded as the most important by SADC:

> *"Low inflation cannot be achieved on a consistent basis in the absence of stability-oriented macroeconomic policies, and the achievement of low inflation therefore indicates that other policies are being implemented in a manner that is supportive of macroeconomic stability."*([438])

The inflation targets on the roadmap towards macroeconomic convergence – single digit inflation in 2008, below 5% in 2012 and below 3% in 2018 – pose quite a challenge to the economic and political management of SADC member states. In times of elections Government spending usually increases and thus threatens price stability goals; the same is true for periods of socio-economic crisis either due to natural disasters (floods, droughts) or external developments

438 SADC (2009a):13

such as global economic downturn which started in late 2008 and has not yet been overcome.

To keep inflation in check Governments have to get their fiscal balance right; excessive budget deficits are the main cause of inflation. As such, the second indicator is vital for the attainment of the inflation target. However, while inflation is in general easy to measure and results are ready available fiscal data not only lacks consistency in the SADC region ([439]) but is also often provided with a considerable time lag. In other words, it may not always be possible to have sufficiently current and correct data on the fiscal balance of each SADC member state at the time when the checking of the indicators is due. If a monetary union is the objective of RI – as it is in SADC, which strives to establish a monetary union by 2016 and introduce a regional currency by 2018 ([440]) – convergence regarding the fiscal balance must be particular strict. SADC's aim to reach a situation where no member state exceeds a fiscal deficit of 3% of GDP by 2012 looked feasible during the primary commodity driven economic boom until 2007/8 but might be more difficult to achieve under conditions of a global recession.

Choosing the level of public debt as a third indicator for macroeconomic convergence is probably strongly owed to the European example but may be misleading as the underlying economic conditions in Europe and the SADC region are quite different. The reasoning for SADC to select the ratio of debt to GDP is that it *"... is an important determinant of and contributor to macroeconomic stability, fiscal stability and balance of payments stability"* ([441]). However, while public debt in Europe is *homogenous* (in local currency on commercial terms) it is generally rather *heterogeneous* with respect to SADC member states. Some of the public debt is in a foreign currency (USD or €), other in local currency; some is concessional, some commercial and it can also have strongly varying durations. The economic burden of debt (repayment and interest) is therefore different between European countries, which repay in local currency, and SADC member states, which have to service the bulk of their public debt in "hard" currency. SADC states have only achieved manageable levels of debt servicing quite recently thanks to the HIPC initiative. Another difference is the type of debt; European countries service commercial debts, which are comparatively expensive while SADC member states often have to service less costly concessional debts with a long-term repayment period. In

439 Some countries calculate the fiscal balance on the basis of an IMF manual while others are using a different method (called GFS 2001); see: SADC (2009a):15

440 See: FINMARK (2004), SADC initiative to harmonize financial regulation: Implications for the financial Sector. Pretoria. SADC (2003), RISDP

441 SADC (2009a)::17

Europe, the 60% debt to GDP ratio is probably a fair expression of the bearable economic burden, in SADC such a high level might lead to a slackening of fiscal discipline and the building up of high mortgages for the future. Thus, the uniform indicator of 60% debt to GDP for macroeconomic convergence may not be as helpful as envisaged. With the exception of the failing states of Zimbabwe and the DRC the other SADC member states should have no problem to adhere to the 60% debt limit.

The fourth and last indicator selected to monitor and measure the process of macroeconomic convergence is the state of the current account balance. The sustainability of a current account deficit depends on a number of variables related to access to and inflow of foreign exchange (FDI, ODA, exports, transfers, credit etc.), the exchange rate regime, the level of foreign exchange reserves and the use of capital imports (long-term infrastructural projects or short-term consumptive expenditure) and may thus vary from country to country. In the case of SADC, the 9% current account deficit to GDP ratio is set quite high for the first two rounds of assessment in 2008 and 2012.

In 2007, SADC produced the first report on its macroeconomic convergence program ([442]), analysing the state of macroeconomic convergence in 2005. The second report was published in April 2008 ([443]); the third report came out in May 2009 ([444]) and had been awaited with great interest as it was seen as a reality check for SADC on the question if the member states were able to achieve the quantitative targets set in the MoU on macro economic convergence for 2008. The targets set for 2008 were the first agreed benchmark on economic convergence to be met by the member states. All reports have been produced by the *Macroeconomic Policies and Convergence Section* of the TIFI Directorate in the SADC Secretariat The section had been established especially to coordinate the implementation of Annex 2 of the Protocol on Finance and Investment.

After a steady economic growth period in the first part of the new Millennium the first macroeconomic convergence report was quite upbeat about the possibility of SADC member states to be able to meet the criteria set for 2008. The second report looking at the macroeconomic performance in the region in 2007 went deeper in its evaluation and analysed the state of convergence per member country. The results were even more hopeful and summarised as follows:

---

442 See: http://www.sadc.int/tifi/macroeconomic_policies_convergence/reports.php

443 See: SADC (2008c), Review of Macroeconomic Convergence Performance. Gaborone, April 2008

444 See: SADC (2009a), Review of the SADC macroeconomic convergence programme for 2008. Gaborone May 2009.

> *"With regard to macroeconomic convergence indicators, Member States have made noticeable progress and the general picture is that the region is converging to some extent" ([445]).*

Regarding the primary indicators, (see table 10.16) eleven out of the then 14 member states met the inflation target (below 10%) in 2007. As the overall regional picture was heavily distorted by the inflation figures from Zimbabwe's collapsed economy ([446]) SADC excluded Zimbabwe when calculating the official results. Without Zimbabwe, the region just met the below-10%-target envisaged for 2008 with an average inflation rate of 9.7%. The target regarding the fiscal deficit (below 5% of GDP) was easily met in 2007 with a regional surplus of +0.6%. Twelve out of 14 countries had a fiscal deficit of below 5% of GDP; in fact, nine countries had a fiscal surplus! The result for the third indicator – a debt to GDP ratio of less than 60% - had similar good results. On average, the region had a debt/GDP ratio of 46.4%. Just two out of the twelve member states for which data was available did not reach the target. Only for the last indicator, the overall performance was slightly worse. But still the region had with -1.8% on average a much lower current account deficit (as % of GDP) than targeted for 2008 (< 9% of GDP). Four countries did not meet the target ([447]).

The third report ([448]), provided average regional figures only for the ratio between current account balance and GDP; the other three primary indicators were only given on a country basis. Overall, the emerging picture was less positive than in 2007 as the regional targets were not met in several cases. According to the report:

- Only four countries (Madagascar, Malawi, Mauritius and Tanzania) had single digit inflation rates and thus met the target set for 2008. Towards the middle of the year average inflation rates peaked at 14.0% ([449]).
- Apart from Malawi and Zimbabwe, all SADC member states met the fiscal balance target for 2008.
- All SADC countries except DRC and Zimbabwe met the public debt target for 2008.

445 SADC (2008c):4

446 See: chapter 11

447 See: SADC (2008c):4ff

448 SADC (2009a)

449 See: SADC (2009b), Update on the Impact of the Global Economic Crisis on SADC. TIFI Directorate. Gaborone, September 2009

- Nine out of fifteen SADC member states met the target set for 2008 with regard to the current account balance; on average, the region missed the target of a current account deficit of not more than 9% of the GDP by 0.9%.

The secondary indicators for macroeconomic convergence showed (see table 9.17) an even less friendly picture than the primary indicators:

- Average regional growth stagnated at 5.9% in 2008, missing the envisaged 7% by quite a margin. Only five out of the 15 SADC member states met the 7% threshold ([450]). Projections for the years to come see the regional growth rate drop to nearly zero in 2009 before picking up again to reach about 4.1% in 2010 ([451]).
- In 2007, external reserves stood at 6.4 months on average; in 2008, these fell to 5.4 months but were still well above the threshold of 3 months.
- Domestic investments rose from 21% of GDP in 2007 to 24% in 2008 but on average still missed the target of 30% by a wide margin. Only two countries (Botswana and Madagascar) had ratios above the targeted 30%. SADC projects that the domestic investment rate will remain more or less stable at around 24-25% of GDP in 2009 and 2010 ([452]).
- Domestic savings showed a similar picture with a slight rise from 18% in 2007 to 20% of GDP in 2008 against a target of 25% for 2008. However, only half of the SADC countries were able to provide current figures on savings and investments casting a doubt on the overall ability of SADC to monitor the attainment of the macroeconomic convergence indicators sufficiently close to the target years. Projections are that domestic savings will fall towards 10% of GDP in 2009 before recovering slightly in 2010 ([453]).

Compared to 2006 and 2007, SADC countries were less close to macroeconomic convergence in 2008. However, this should not be attributed to the global economic crisis which impact only started to be felt in 2009 but to the preceding overheating of the global and regional economy ([454]). In 2006 and 2007, five countries complied in full with the set of primary convergence criteria set for

---

450 See: SADC (2009a):5

451 See: SADC (2009b):8f

452 ibid:7

453 ibid:7

454 Which was largely due to speculation for example with regard to oil and commodity prices. While this benefitted some mineral-rich SADC countries such as Angola, Namibia, Botswana or Zambia others felt the downside of higher import costs for fuel, food and other vital imports.

2008: Lesotho, Namibia, South Africa, Swaziland and Zambia. It is no coincidence that four out of these five SADC member states are part of SACU.

Table 9.17.: Trends in Regional Macro-Economic Convergence in SADC in 2006-2008*

Indicator/ Year	2006 (average)	2007 (average)	2008 (average)	2008 Target	2012 Target	2018 Target
PRIMARY INDICATORS						
Inflation (%)	9.7	8.3	n/a	**<10**	<5	<3
Fiscal Balance/ GDP (%)	+2.6	+0.6	n/a	**<-5**	<3	<3
Public Debt/GDP (%)	-34.9	-46.4	n/a	**<-60**	<60	<60
Current Account Balance/GDP (%)	-0.7	-4.4	-9.9	**<-9**	<9	<3
SECONDARY INDICATORS						
GDP Growth Rate (%)	+5.9	+6.6	+5.9[2]	**>+7**	>+7	>+7
Domestic Investment/GDP (%)	20.7	21.0	24.0	**>30**	>30	>30
External Reserves (import cover, months)		6.4	5.4	**3**	6	6
Domestic Savings (% of GDP)		18.0	20.0	**25**	30	30

Source: SADC (2008c; 2009a)

Explanations:

* The fifth secondary indicator (Central bank credit to Government as % of revenue) was not covered by the SADC report.

[2] If Zimbabwe is included the regional growth rate is dropped to 4.6%

Lesotho's, Namibia's and Swaziland's currencies are pegged to the South African Rand and as such their economic policies are to a large extent determined by South Africa, which pursued under former Minister of Finance, *Trevor Manuel*, a strictly stability-oriented economic policy course. In 2008, not one SADC member state complied with all four indicators for macroeconomic convergence (see table 10.18). The failure of SADC states to meet the terms set for the course to macroeconomic convergence for 2008 is due to sharply rising inflation rates; the compliance with the set targets for the other three indicators remained quite good.

The global economic developments have a strong bearing on the economic situation in the SADC region. The vulnerability to external shocks has probably increased over the last years and is for the years to come endangering the macroeconomic convergence process of SADC. The biggest problem for SADC countries will be to control inflation rates. This is both a structural and a political problem. Many SADC countries have a history of high inflation, which was often caused by weak fiscal discipline due to political factors and a high elasticity regarding changes in prices for imports. Compared to the 1990s, the inflation rates for 2006 and 2007 in the SADC member states have been impressively low. In 1998 for example, only one country (Mozambique) had an inflation rate below 5% ([455]) while this was achieved by seven countries in 2006 and eleven in 2007. However, the impact of the overheating of the world economy in terms of fuel and food prices in 2008 exposed the fragility of price stability in most SADC countries. For 2009, lower fuel and food prices may have a dampening effect on price levels ([456]).

Another indicator that started to show signs of deterioration in 2008 was the current account situation. In 2007, eleven of the 15 member states had current account balances better than -9% of the GDP; in 2008, this figure had dropped to nine countries. According to SADC's own predictions ([457]) this will be worsening considerably in 2009 and 2010. With respect to the current account balance the low elasticity regarding imports (fuel, food, capital goods) and the high dependency from export earnings and transfer payments (e.g. from the *diaspora* and/or migrant workers) is starting to have a devastating effect. SADC member states were thus amongst the recipients of an IMF emergency rescue package for struggling economies; they received in September 2009 SDR 3.76 Billion to stabilise their currencies and allow for the importation of strategic goods. South Africa with an allocation of SDR 1.565 Billion, the DRC with SDR 0.425 Billion, Zambia with SDR 0.401 Billion and even Zimbabwe with SDR 0.328 Billion were the biggest recipients ([458]).

---

455 See: Peters-Berries/Marx (2000):48

456 See: SADC (2009b):2; inflation rates in all SADC member states showed a downward trend according to the latest available figures.

457 See: SADC (2009b):6

458 ibid:10

Table 9.18.: Attainment of Primary Macro-Economic Convergence Criteria in SADC 2006 – 2008

Country	Inflation target (single digit)			Fiscal balance target (< 5% of GDP)			Debt target (< 60% of GDP)			Current Account target (<-9% of GDP)			Score in 2008
	2006	2007	2008	2006	2007	2008	2006	2007	2008	2006	2007	2008	
ANG	12.2	11.8	*13.2*	-3.4	-0.1	*+8.9*	19.2	n/a	*33.0*	+16.4	+4.0	*+21.2*	**3 of 4**
BOT	11.6	7.1	*12.6*	+8.1	+0.6	*-0.8*	0.0	0.0	*6.0*	+20.9	+14.5	*+15.0*	**3 of 4 ↓**
DRC	18.2	9.9	*23.8*	-0.7	+2.8	*+0.7*	2.6	105	*n/a*	-7.5	-3.7	*-7.3*	**2 of 4 ↓**
LES	6.0	7.9	*10.8*	+13.3	+5.3	*-1.0*	49.9	46.6	*55.0*	+1.8	+11.9	*+12.6*	**3 of 4 ↓**
MAD	10.8	10.3	*9.4*	+37.5	-4.7	*-4.7*	29.3	35.3	*30.0*	-8.8	-19.3	*-22.8*	**3 of 4**
MAL	13.9	7.5	*8.8*	-0.7	-1.9	*-6.3*	26.3	22.6	*46.4*	-14.0	-17.2	*-6.3*	**3 of 4**
MAU	8.9	8.8	*9.7*	-4.3	+3.8	*-3.4*	62.8	63.1	*57.7*	-9.5	-5.4	*-10.5*	**3 of 4**
MOZ	13.3	8.2	*10.3*	-1.1	+1.9	*-2.8*	52.8	45.0	*40.0*	-9.3	-3.7	*-6.1*	**3 of 4 ↓**
NAM	5.1	5.7	*10.3*	+2.1	+4.8	*+4.7*	31.4	28.3	*18.7*	+18.3	+17.8	*+3.8*	**3 of 4 ↓**
RSA	4.7	6.2	*11.6*	+0.6	0.5	*-0.7*	29.3	27.4	*32.0*	-6.5	-6.7	*-7.4*	**3 of 4 ↓**
SWA	5.3	8.2	*12.6*	-2.1	+2.6	*-1.3*	17.9	14.4	*17.8*	+8.1	+3.0	*-15.4*	**2 of 4 ↓**
TAN	7.3	7.0	*10.3*	-4.8	+3.8	*-3.8*	63.5	40.4	*38.0*	-12.2	-17.1	*-12.5*	**2 of 4 ↓**
ZAM	9.1	8.9	*13.6*	-2.8	-1.2	*+1.0*	25.8	24.1	*18.1*	-1.4	-2.1	*-4.2*	**3 of 4 ↓**
ZIM	1,033	12,563	*1,594,745*	-5.5	-10.0	*+29.9**	78.3	128	*114.7*	-5.5	-0.8	*-16.6*	**1 of 4**
TOTAL			**3 of 14 ↓**			**13 of 14**			***12 of 14 ↑***			**9 of 14 ↓**	**↓**

Sources: SADC (2008c; 2009a,b,c); own compilation
Figures for 2008 are taken from SADC (2009c)
Explanations: *=The high surplus in the case of Zimbabwe is not the product of prudent economic policies but the result of the collapse of the economy: revenue collected in local currency was impossible to be spend by the Government as a result of its loss of value (SADC [2009c:10]. Under normal circumstances, Zimbabwe would have recorded a fiscal deficit.

With regard to keeping fiscal balances and the debt burden in check, SADC countries have achieved remarkable results since the beginning of the Millennium. Once a region with huge fiscal deficits and moaning under large debts, in 2008 all but one of the SADC members had their fiscal deficits under control and four (not counting Zimbabwe) showed even a fiscal surplus. Thanks to the HIPC initiative, nearly all SADC countries received substantial debt relief, which made their external debt positions manageable once again. Tanzania was the last of the eligible SADC member states to reach the completion point under the HIPC initiative giving it some debt relief in 2007. Countries such as the DRC, Madagascar, Malawi, Mozambique and Zambia had already received forgiveness of substantial parts of their bilateral debt in 2005 and 2006 under the HIPC scheme.

However, the good fortunes are beginning to change due to the contracting world economy in 2009; predictions by SADC for 2009 and 2010 are that Government revenue in most SADC countries will decrease ([459]). The worsening of the fiscal balance will be the consequence.

Taking into account the rather conducive international framework conditions (raw material boom; rising levels of ODA; Chinese investments etc.), it is not that surprising that most SADC countries were on the way of meeting the targets set for macro-economic convergence. SADC summarised the economic framework conditions, on which the region's boom has been based until 2008 as follows:

> *"These positive developments relied on strong economic policies; a favourable external environment, especially rising commodity prices; and debt relief and aid from the international community."* ([460])

The picture will change for the worse in 2009 and 2010 when the impact of the global economic crisis will eventually been felt in the SADC region. Due to the worldwide slump in production, prices and demand are falling for most of the export commodities of the SADC countries; prices for major imports (capital and consumer goods), however, are decreasing less strongly. The third macroeconomic convergence report thus expects hat

> *"... the medium-term impact of the global crisis on SADC countries will [...] be an important determinant of whether Member States will be able to meet the 2012 targets"* ([461]).

459 ibid:7
460 SADC (2009c):5
461 SADC (2009a):7

In detail, it is predicted that the SADC member states will face in the next two to three years;

- Reduced capital inflows;
- slower economic growth;
- balance of payments problems most likely leading to larger current account deficits in the short-term;
- larger fiscal deficits;
- higher public debt;
- (probably) lower inflation rates

The probability of meeting the more ambitious macroeconomic convergence targets set for 2012 and for the establishment of the Common Market in 2015 are thus slim ([462]). However, despite the current economic slump and the difficulties of SADC member states to achieve the necessary but ambitious convergence criteria the overall trend of macroeconomic development has been surprisingly positive in the SADC region as compared to a decade before. While it might not be realistic to expect that SADC as a region will be able to meet the 2012 macroeconomic convergence criteria the medium to longer terms prospects are still positive – if the world economy picks up again. For SADC this would mean to evaluate to what extent the region lags behind in reaching the targets set for 2008 and 2012 respectively and to agree on a more appropriate timetable.

9.6. The Economic Reality: Limited Scope for Regional Integration

In summarizing the analysis of the regional economic integration potential the following – sometimes sobering – realities have to be taken into account:

1. The concept of ***creating deeper RI in SADC through intensified intra-regional trade*** has limitations. For one, the production structure of the SADC member states is only to a limited extent complementary and, as such, capable of stimulating intra-regional trade. For the time, the level of

---

462 ibid:3ff. However, the rather gloomy predictions of the SADC economists might have underestimated the power of international speculation on raw materials. According to DER SPIEGEL, 48/2009:75 the prices for oil, copper and sugar haven risen between January and November 2009 by 112%, 133% and 79% respectively, thus cushioning the negative effect of the economic crisis at least for Angola (oil), Zambia (copper), Swaziland (sugar), Mauritius (sugar) and the DRC (copper) to some extent.

intra-SADC trade may have already come close to its full current potential given the existing structures of production. Unless new investments into the manufacturing sector itself or into industries producing processed and semi-processed inputs for the manufacturing industries especially in South Africa take place, neither the already existing FTA nor the planned customs union will increase intra-regional trade and thus deepen RI much further. Secondly, due to the firmly established and actively maintained production and trade structures, which force the SADC region into the role of a supplier of mineral and agricultural raw materials for the world market, the envisaged regional free trade regime may not be sufficient to encourage the much needed investments into the manufacturing sector. More active and regionally coordinated investment policies are needed to overcome the established production and trade integration patterns.

2. The SADC region shows considerable ***differences in wealth and living conditions amongst member states,*** which prevent the liberalization of the movement of people in the region. While the liberalization of goods and to some extent services is being realized through the adoption of a FTA (August 2008) and the planned establishment of a customs union (for 2010), the crucial next step of allowing for the free movement of people for an optimal allocation of production factors will not be realized soon, if ever. The socio-economic North-South gradient is so steep that removing the existing barriers would cause an avalanche of labor migrants rushing to South Africa, Botswana and Namibia. This would further unsettle the unstable labor markets in these countries and probably cause more outbreaks of xenophobia. Furthermore, it would deplete the already thin reservoir of professionals and skilled workers in the poorer countries of SADC. Both these effects would destabilize RI efforts. But without the free movement of people RI is not deepening enough to realize its full economic potential.
3. The huge ***macro economic imbalance in the region*** with South Africa completely dominating the region's economy requires not only checks and balances for its economic power, but calls also for the creation of strong instruments/mechanisms for ensuring an equal sharing of costs and benefits emanating from RI if SADC is to progress further. Currently, South Africa is accounting for roughly two thirds of the region's GDP (see table A1) ([463]), is the only country with a sizeable and privately

463 The latest available comparable GDP figures for 2007 may to some extent be distorted as the temporary boom for mineral prices and particular for oil boosted the economies of countries such as Angola, Mozambique and Tanzania much stronger than the South African. The sudden drop of prices for minerals and oil in the second half of 2008 in the context of the unfolding world recession will deflate the economies of a number of

organized manufacturing sector, the source of most of the regional cross-border investments and the location of the region's most important harbor, (Durban). As the dominant economy, South Africa has on a number of occasions ensured that its interests are enforced: in the negotiations for the region's FTA, the interests of the South African business community prevailed. It is South Africa which slows down the progress on a Protocol regarding the free movement of people; South African private and public companies dominate the decisions regarding the creation of a regional energy supply system; and it is South Africa which will eventually decide if SADC is to become a real or just a nominal building bloc of the envisaged African Economic Community (AEC). The SADC tribunal – although currently tested by Zimbabwe's intransigence and utter contempt of its decisions (see chapter 9.3.6.) – can become one of the required balancing mechanisms, but others are still needed such as a custom revenue distribution mechanism (for the envisaged customs union) or a regional competition board preventing the emergence of (South African) monopolies.

4. Most of the ***economies of the SADC countries are not fully integrated nationally*** and as such, lack a national business class, which makes it all the more difficult to facilitate their regional integration. Especially the economies of Angola, DRC, Madagascar, Malawi, Mozambique, Tanzania, Zambia and Zimbabwe and even South Africa all have strong informal sectors which exist independently from governmental controls but constitute an important survival mechanism for the poorer strata of society. In nearly all SADC member states, subsistence agriculture together with the informal sector provide for the livelihood of the majority of people. The formal parts of the economies are often strongly export-oriented (minerals and agricultural raw materials) and have only limited ties with the rest of the national economy. It is rather difficult to find common ground regarding regional integration between national small informal businesses ([464]) and export-oriented companies. A private sector driving on the basis of its own interests the regional economic integration process does not exist in many SADC states; the only exceptions are South Africa and to a lesser extent Mauritius. Consequently, when there are not sufficient private stakeholders to drive the economic integration aspect forward, it is left to the Governments.

---

mineral-depending SADC member states. As a result the South African economy will grow in its relative regional strength again.

464 The quite substantial informal cross-border trade within the region has neither national nor regional representative bodies which could voice the traders' interests. In fact, the informal cross-border trade is highly fragmented and often *ad hoc* in nature.

5. The size of the combined SADC economy is with USD 267 billion, not even as big as the economy of Denmark, one of Europe's smaller economies. South Africa's economy is comparable to that of Belgium or Norway. When compared to other RI bodies such as ASEAN or *Mercosur*, SADC appears to be on the smaller side. The SADC region is thus not yet economically strong enough to overcome poverty, initiate sustainable socio-economic growth and develop relevant regional economic actors (with the exception of South Africa). SADC has apart from South Africa no other 'emerging economy' amongst its members. As such, the SADC region is still ***heavily dependent on foreign aid*** (ODA) ([465]) and external actors to support its integration course. Until 2008, such funds were increasingly forthcoming but the current international economic crisis might reduce the flow of ODA in the coming years. This can slow down the speed of RI.
6. Regional integration in SADC threatens to erode ***government revenue*** in all SADC member states but South Africa. SACU member states receive up to 58% (Lesotho) of their revenue from trade taxes, but even countries such as Zambia collect more than 30% of the total revenue from trade taxes. Only South Africa with a share of only 3%, stands out ([466]). Despite publicly made commitments towards further trade liberalization, the immediate interest of many SADC leaders might be not to loose this crucial and easy to collect source of state revenue. In an attempt to compensate for the gradual loss of trade taxes during the implementation of the FTA, some Governments started to levy fees on intra-regional transportation, environmental conservation and even new duties ([467]).The preparedness for further trade liberalization in many of the smaller SADC states might thus depend on the development or availability of alternative sources of revenue.
7. The ***Chinese export offensive*** has undermined the potential for national and even regional industrial development in the SADC region. The infant industries in several SADC member states – in most cases producing textiles, garments and simple consumer products – have collapsed under the flood of cheap imports or even been taken over by Chinese business people in the last decade. Without such 'starter-industries' and their

---

465 See table D in the Annex. According to the African Economic Outlook 2007/8 of OECD and AfDB the countries of the SADC region received USD 9.845 billion in total ODA in 2006; in 2007 the amount increased to USD 9.8 billion; Sewadah, Mirvat (2009), The global economic crisis, trying times for the region. In: INSAT No 15 (January 2009):5.

466 See: Kalaba, Mmatlou (2009), Liberalization of SADC trade towards 2012 and beyond. In: INSAT, No 15 (January 2009):8

467 ibid.

potentially beneficial impact on the skills and attitude development of the labor force as well as technology transfer, it will be all the more difficult for many SADC member states to attract or initiate themselves the urgently needed investments into the manufacturing sector.

8. ***Macro-economic convergence***, though there have been encouraging signs, is far from being achieved in SADC. Despite the existence of a MoU regarded macro-economic convergence dating back to 2001, the development of convergence criteria in the Annex of the Protocol on Finance and Investment, and the establishment of the 'Macroeconomic Policies and Convergence Section' in the TIFI Directorate of the Secretariat, SADC member states have not agreed and embarked on a coordinated regional policy aimed at achieving economic convergence. The promising results until 2007/8 must be regarded more as a result of good economic fortunes than a coordinated policy approach; the failure in 2008 of any SADC member to meet the targets set for that year gives rise to some concerns and might lead to a discussion about an adjustment of the agreed timetable for achieving macroeconomic convergence. In view of the existing economic imbalances in the region, the insufficient internal integration of national economies and limited intra-regional trade potential, a gradual harmonization of economic policies and a convergence regarding central macro-economic indicators is of high importance. However, the impact of the global economic crisis felt in all SADC member states since the last quarter of 2008 has undermined the economic room for maneuver and exposed the vulnerability of the SADC economies in terms of growth rates, balance of payments positions, fiscal deficits and FDIs from global developments outside their control or even ability to influence. Judging from the latest figures it will take SADC longer to achieve macroeconomic convergence and thus the basis for attaining higher levels of RI than planned.

On the other hand, the SADC region possesses also a number of economic potentials and assets, which could facilitate further and deeper RI. These economic factors are:

a. The region has a ***transportation system*** that connects all countries on the continent, at least by road, most of them also by rail; some also have pipeline links with regional ports. So far, this caters mostly for the efficient transportation of raw materials to the region's harbors, the importation of capital and consumer goods as well as oil to the region's interior. However, the existence of a functioning regional transportation system can also be regarded as an incentive for investments into the *in loco* processing of minerals and agricultural raw materials. With transportation costs increasing because of the inevitable rise of fuel prices, it will be economically more proficient to lower the bulk of the transportation volume by undertaking, at least, part of the processing near the source of the raw material. This in turn would facilitate the much needed investments in processing if not manufacturing industries in the region. The latest approach by SADC to focus on "development corridors" might help to attract further investments and fill the few remaining gaps in the regional transport network.

b. The ***energy sector*** of the SADC region provides substantial potential for regional integration both through the expansion of the regional electricity grid and regional investments into the development of further power plants. Hydropower has so far, the biggest proven potential for generating energy (electricity) in the region particularly in the DRC, but also in Angola, Mozambique and Zambia. Apart from that, the potential for other renewable energies such as wind or solar energy needs to be developed as well. If the region can agree on a comprehensive and feasible plan to develop its energy resources, this may facilitate further investments into the processing of the region's raw materials.

c. The ***region's mineral wealth and agricultural potential*** while considered by some more of an impediment to the development of an industrial base, constitutes in fact also one of its major economic potentials. The availability of a working transportation system and a sufficient energy base will make it in the future increasingly attractive to invest in the processing of raw materials *in loco* instead of exporting them unfinished. The current slump in demand for and prices of many raw materials looks to improve in the coming years when the global economy gets back into gear. The earnings from a renewed raw material boom should be treated by the SADC member states one the one hand as start-up capital for industrial development and on the other hand as a security fund for the times when the raw materials are exhausted. Botswana can serve as an example in this respect.

d. Southern Africa and the three island states belonging to SADC are already a ***major tourism destination*** in the world but are far from having yet realized their full potential. If the SADC member states develop regional tourism promotion strategies and destinations instead of only pursuing national interests, the tourism sector could become one of the major vehicles for further regional integration ([468]).

e. Although the expansion of SADC to include the DRC and more recently, Madagascar and again the Seychelles has added French as a third official language, SADC is still a rather ***homogenous regional bloc*** with English

468 The 2010 Soccer World Cup in South Africa provides an opportunity for regional tourism marketing.

as the main language and a dominant British influenced bureaucratic culture. This is in contrast to e.g. ECOWAS where a continuous struggle between the French and British influenced countries is often slowing RI. Cultural homogeneity makes intra-regional interaction easier and can facilitate RI as well.

From an economic point of view, the deepening of RI in the SADC region is not a foregone and automatic conclusion. The economic realities are stacked against intensified RI in SADC. If the region is willing to be led by South Africa and South Africa is willing to take the lead, the speed of RI might quicken again. However, this will probably only be possible if sufficient compensation mechanisms for the smaller and weaker SADC economies will be introduced and (indirectly) funded (as in the case of SACU) by South Africa. So far, the economic benefits from RI are rather limited for most SADC member states while the costs are rising particularly when the income from trade related taxes are falling away. South Africa's more developed economy with a sizeable manufacturing industry and a need for some of the region's (natural) resources such as water and electricity, is benefiting most from the economic integration process so far. It needs to be seen if the South African Government is willing to share these benefits through compensation mechanisms with other member states.

Chapter 10: The Political Dimension of Regional Integration in SADC

RI in SADC has been driven so far, more from political than economic actors. The Governments of the member states pushed the integration process forward first to find common ground against an overpowering *apartheid* South Africa, later to integrate a liberated South Africa into the regional community and gain a bigger voice internationally. Political factors have been instrumental in starting and promoting RI in Southern Africa and they are an important variable for intensifying and deepening it. Without a stable political environment and calculable economic and development policies – which can only be guaranteed by democratically legitimized and transparent governments – the economic mechanisms of a RI process might not work. Therefore, it is important to ask to which extent the political structures and power arrangements and interests of individual SADC countries are supportive to further and deepen RI and which are obstructive?

10.1. Political Interests Shaping Regional Integration in SADC

The political interests of a country are usually a combination of the self-interests of ruling elites, objective general (economic and political) development and/or survival conditions. In the case of SADC, they are determined by the following factors:

- ***Social stratification:*** economic and social developments lead inevitably to a differentiation of socio-economic interests in various groups or 'classes'. During the industrial revolution in the 19th century in Europe and the USA, this resulted in the dichotomy of labor and capital, which expressed itself eventually in political parties. They still dominate the political landscapes of the industrialized world but new actors (environmental, religious and regional interests) have entered the stage as well. In Africa, the social differentiation in most countries even today is much less pronounced: the majority of the citizens are peasants, only weak labor movements and national bourgeoisies exist. Often the most influential social 'class' is composed of bureaucrats, managers of public enterprises, security personnel and religious leaders, the so called 'state class' ([469]). The major form of social stratification is along ethnic, regional and in some cases,

469 See Tetzlaff, Rainer/Jacobeit, Cord (2005), Das nachkoloniale Afrika. Wiesbaden 2005: 125ff

religious lines. With the exception of South Africa and Mauritius in the other SADC countries, only small national interest groupings exist which have a distinct position on RI. The groups most interested in intensified RI in an African country would normally ([470]) be local entrepreneurs (including private commercial banks) engaged in trade and services. For them, liberalized trade regimes would be beneficial. However, in most countries interest groups of such entrepreneurs are either not (yet) existing or if they do not powerful enough to influence political decisions on RI. As such a country's policy towards RI or more concrete SADC is due to limited social stratification predominantly shaped and determined by 'state classes' anchored in the bureaucratic apparatus of the respective country and motivated by political (stabilizing and maintaining power) rather than economic (developmental) factors.

- ***Structural economic 'interests'***: access to markets, resources and – in the case of land-locked countries – ports may also shape political decisions. Such ' structural economic interests' ([471]) are crucial for the survival of a political regime and tend to be pursued with some vigor. In the case of SADC, six countries out of the twelve continental member states are land-locked and thus dependent on other countries to facilitate their trade. This is for them a strong incentive to foster RI and promote the idea of further trade-based integration. For countries such as South Africa, previously Zimbabwe and increasingly Mauritius – where entrepreneurial classes exists –, the access to markets in the region is or has been an important reason to support the idea of RI.

- ***Natural resource scarcity:*** an insufficient natural resource base to ensure the country's existence such as water and/or fertile land as well as inadequate natural resources to provide sufficient energy are further factors determining the political interest of a country. Numerous wars have been waged and several civil wars been fought over access to, or the defense of scarce or valuable natural resources ([472]). In the SADC region, South

470 That is in absence of manufacturing interests.

471 In contrast to individual economic interests of entrepreneurs/companies and/or economic associations.

472 In the African context the Rwandan genocide was at least partly caused by increasing land scarcity; the subsequent war in the DRC in which several African countries got involved was basically a war over mineral resources. The Liberian and Sierra Leonean civil wars were equally fought over access to valuable timber and diamonds. The use of the proceeds from the sales of these resources for financing ongoing civil wars resulting in further bloodshed promulgated the formation of the international NGO '*Global Witness*', who facilitated the outlawing of at least the sale of 'blood diamonds'

Africa has a strong interest in RI because it needs on the one hand, water from Lesotho and eventually from the Zambezi Basin states (Zambia, Botswana, Zimbabwe and Mozambique) for its industries and growing urban agglomerations and on the other hand, electricity from the vast resources of the DRC to satisfy its rapidly increasing energy needs. Zimbabwe and Tanzania have similar energy deficits which they would like to address through intensified RI. Access to the water of the Okavango is at the core of a dispute between Botswana and Namibia over islands in the Okavango delta. Both countries could probably settle this conflict easier if their water and energy concerns would be addressed in the context of SADC.

- ***Legitimization of political power:*** Political power is in many African countries a strongly contested resource and not easy to hold on to as the political/ developmental performances of many political actors are not output-oriented but determined by personal interests. Legitimization of political power is thus secured through a combination of different means and mechanisms such as claims to traditional and historical rights ([473]), the aptitude to keep internal peace, the co-optation of potentially opposing elites, the ability of satisfying the immediate needs of a patronage system (through access to state resources) and the regional and international status of the respective Presidents. Being seen as an important figure in RI and accepted by other regional Heads of State (who may be popular in an entire region such as *Nelson Mandela*), can boost the acceptance and legitimacy of a political leader at home. Organizing and hosting the highly prestigious SADC Summits are a further factor strengthening internal political legitimacy of a regime or a particular leader. In this respect, most Heads of State in the SADC region appreciate the public stage RI provides to them. However, if RI leads to a decline in state revenue and thus in the resources available to the ruling class to fund the expansive patronage system – as the SADC FTA and anticipated customs union undoubtedly will result in – the interest in RI might become a negative one.

- ***Control over executive resources:*** Even in democratic states, the control over 'executive resources', i.e. the army, police and secret services, is a crucial factor for upholding the rule of law and public order. In countries with less pronounced democratic structures, this becomes even more important. The membership in SADC enhances the control over national

---

and is still fighting to ban the sale of other 'conflict resources' as well; see www.globalwitness.org

473 As in Zimbabwe, Angola or Namibia where the ruling elites base their claims to power to some part on their merits in the liberation wars.

executive resources as it makes it much more difficult for the security forces to stage a coup d'état and achieve regional recognition. In fact, coup leaders must even fear that other SADC countries would intervene militarily to restore the rightful Government. The example of the SADC intervention in Lesotho in 1995 serves as a warning. The latest example is the suspension of Madagascar from SADC over the unconstitutional removal of President *Ravalomanana* ([474]).

In general, sufficient national political interests exist to expect that also in future SADC member states will pursue and advance RI. It is at least neither against the dominant self-interests of the political elites in SADC member states to support RI, nor against the structural national interests. However, the impact of the reduction of trade tax revenue on the willingness of SADC members to pursue deeper RI has to be monitored.

10.2. Political Development Conditions for SADC

10.2.1. Historical Factors

Southern Africa ([475]) is a region with a particularly violent past. The region has been coined by British and Portuguese colonialism in general and by settler colonialism in particular. Due to the especially oppressive nature of colonialism, several bloody liberation wars (Angola, Mozambique, Namibia, South Africa and Zimbabwe) took place. The perseverance of the South African *apartheid* system until 1993/4 fuelled two civil wars, (Angola and Mozambique) and stunted development efforts in the region for at least two decades.

However, the fight against settler colonialism and *apartheid* in particular also created very early on, a common sense of belonging together as a region and forged political alliances and links ([476]). Most of the region has not only a

474 See: Mail&Guardian (South Africa) 31.03.2009; http://www.mg.co.za/article/2009-03-31-madagascars-neighbours-mull-sanctions

475 The DRC is not being considered in this reflection as it belongs neither geographically nor historically to Southern Africa. Admitting the DRC to SADC in 1997 happened predominantly for economic reasons as South African business interests were keen to secure a share in exploiting the DRC's massive mineral wealth and developing its energy and water resources.

476 See for example Nelson Mandela (1994), Der lange Weg zur Freiheit. Frankfurt am Main, in which Mandela describes the solidarity and support he and the ANC were

common history and shares similar colonial experiences and administration systems, but has also been linked by a regional transportation system for close to a hundred years. This provided – notwithstanding the suffering of the population during colonialism and liberation wars – a strong basis for regional cooperation and later integration.

The negative experience with lopsided regional integration in the Central African Federation (CAF; 1953-1963), the challenges to manage a customs union such as SACU between unequal partners and the positive experience with functional regional cooperation in SADCC (1980-1992) added valuable insights to the design of SADC.

These are the historical political factors in favor of RI in Southern Africa. However, other political developments or particularities of the region are less favorable for further integration.

10.2.2. Membership Composition

While the admission of South Africa and Mauritius in 1994 were very necessary steps to consolidate the newly established SADC, the two expansions in 1997 (DRC and Seychelles, which left SADC in 2004 but rejoined it in 2007) and 2005 (Madagascar) might have weakened the regional coherence. Neither of the newcomers has a common history with the rest of the region, nor speaks the same language. The island states but also the DRC has none or weak physical links with Southern Africa.

A further problem SADC is faced with regarding internal cohesion is the multiple memberships of several member states in other RECs. As table 10.1. shows, most member states belong to at least, one other REC, some to even more. Although SADC had passed a resolution that none of its member states should belong to a competing REC, only Tanzania, Mozambique and Angola reacted and left COMESA. Zambia, however, even houses the headquarters of COMESA and has often shown conflicting loyalties. The logic behind the multiple memberships is a nationalistic one: in order to maximize the real and imagined gains of RI governments tend to join two or more regional bodies ([477]).

getting already in the 1950s and 60s from other liberations movements and the first independent African Governments in the region in Tanzania and Zambia.

477 See: Chingono/Nakana (2009):404

Table 10.1.: Overlapping Memberships with RECs and EPAs

SADC Member State	Membership in other RECs	Membership in EPA
ANGOLA	ECCAS	SADC EPA
BOTSWANA	SACU	SADC EPA
DRC	CEEAC, ECCAS	CEMAC EPA
LESOTHO	SACU	SADC EPA
MADAGASCAR	COMESA	ESA EPA
MALAWI	COMESA	ESA EPA
MAURITIUS	COMESA	ESA EPA
MOZAMBIQUE	none	SADC EPA
NAMIBIA	SACU	SADC EPA
SEYCHELLES	COMESA	ESA EPA
SOUTH AFRICA	SACU	SADC EPA (observer status)
SWAZILAND	COMESA, SACU	SADC EPA
TANZANIA	EAC	SADC EPA
ZAMBIA	COMESA	ESA EPA
ZIMBABWE	COMESA	ESA EPA

Source: own compilation; Meyn 2006:147

Tanzania is also a member of the new EAC, and as such, confronted not only with an orientation problem regarding its infrastructural connections but also with the major dilemma of belonging to one FTA (SADC) on the verge of transforming itself into a customs union (in 2010) and newly established customs union (EAC). When the East African Customs Union starts to function, Tanzania could be an open gate for duty-free EAC exports into SADC which would violate the interests of the other SADC members and vice versa. In fact, the rules of the WTO regarding customs unions stipulate that a country can only belong to one customs union ([478]). If this rule is taken serious Tanzania must make a choice to stay in SADC and leave the EAC or vice versa. Currently, Tanzania would most probably turn towards the EAC.

A similar predicament applies to the relationship between COMESA and SADC, which have either recently established a customs union (COMESA) or is about to (SADC). The recently started talks between COMESA, EAC and SADC to go back one step and form a joint FTA ([479]), may be a way out of this predicament. However, the different depth of RI, levels of protectionism and degree of

478 See: Vines (2008):4; Elago/Kalenga (2008):129 and Jacobeit, Cord, Hartzenberg, Trudi and Charalambides, Nick (2005), Overlapping Memberships in COMESA, EAC, SACU and SADC. Trade Policy Options for the Region and for EPA Negotiations. Study for GTZ. Eschborn 2005

479 See: Daily Monitor (Addis Ababa) 29.10.2008

implementation capacity in the three RECS are forming formidable obstacles which are not easy to overcome.

As long as the overlapping membership issue is unsolved, SADC is faced with problems of divided 'loyalty' and economic orientation in at least two of its member states (Tanzania and Zambia). The planned new FTA between COMESA, EAC and SADC does not appear feasible at this moment.

Another big challenge for the further development and internal cohesion of SADC are the EPAs as SADC member states belong to three different EPA groupings unaligned to their membership in regional integration bodies (see table 10.1.). While the future of the EPAs as proposed by the EU seems to hang in the balance as only a few interim EPAs have been signed so far ([480]), the underlying problem of the non-alignment between regional groupings and the EPAs for Southern and Eastern Africa remains. If agreeable terms will be approved between the EU and the countries of Southern and Eastern Africa the contradictions of the membership in EPAs and regional bodies will surface again. Only half of the SADC members opted also to belong to the proposed SADC EPA; the other half chose membership in the ESA EPA, which is predominantly COMESA and EAC oriented; the DRC belongs to the central African CEMAC EPA.

Particularly surprising is the choice of Tanzania: as a member both of SADC and the EAC (although not of COMESA) and strong historical, economic and political links to East Africa it opted for the SADC EPA. This may be explained with Tanzania's objections against COMESA trade policies ([481]) and its self-image as one of the founders of SADC. The obvious disadvantages of the choice (geographical and political isolation, contradicting EAC's internal objectives etc.), however, might soon force Tanzania to change its decision.

The choice of Malawi, Zambia and Zimbabwe to join the ESA EPA rather than the SADC EPA also appears not entirely logical at first glance. All three countries have stronger infrastructural, economic and political connections with SADC than with Eastern Africa or COMESA. Zambia, however, has a strong

---

480 According to WTO rules, EPAs would have had to be signed between the EU and ACP countries by the end of 2007 in order "to make ACP-EU trade relations WTO compatible, i.e. trade preferences must be granted on a reciprocal basis." Under the EU proposal regarding the EPAs this would also include LDCs although they would have a rather long period of adjustment; see: Jacobeit et al (2005):2f

481 When Tanzania withdraw from COMESA in 1999 it cited COMESA's intention to reduce customs duties by 90% which was against the interests of the country; see Jacobeit et al (2005):24

national interest to promote COMESA as it houses its headquarters and might thus have a certain preference to the ESA EPA as this represents the majority of COMESA member states. As for Malawi, the choice to join the ESA EPA might have been influenced by the fact that its current President *Bingu wa Mutharika* once had been the Executive Secretary of COMESA and the country thus has a special relationship with COMESA. Zimbabwe's preference for the ESA EPA might have been influenced by *Mugabe's* precarious position in the region. By joining the ESA EPA the Zimbabwean regime probably wanted to signal to SADC that it had other options for RI and at the same time to broaden its relations with African Governments.

The issue of the EPA memberships indicates that short-term national and in some cases even personal preferences of leaders are decisive factors for shaping a country's regional policy in SADC. If such opportunistic interests take precedence over longer term national and regional interests they run contrary to the agreed principles and objectives of RI and undermine the intra-regional cohesion. In the case of SADC, the split into three EPA groups and the different reactions of SADC countries with regard to the EPAs reveals a still not sufficiently strong commitment to these regional goals and identity.

While the differentiated membership of SADC countries to three EPA groups signals a low level of regional organizational cohesion the actual test for regional integration and unity lies still ahead: what will be the effects if the EPAs are signed?

So far, the majority of ACP countries did not sign EPAs with the EU because they did not agree with conditions attached and the attitude of the EU negotiators ([482]). The initial deadline of 31.12.2007 was not met by most ACP countries and even the compromise offered by the EU – to agree on an interim EPA which would allow for more time to negotiate a final agreement and still allow the ACP states to enjoy the most preferred status in exports to the EU under WTO rules – was agreed to by barely half of the 79 ACP countries of which 18 were from Africa ([483]).

482 ACP countries did not like the clause to open their markets without restrictions – although over a long adjustment period - to EU imports. At the same time the often rather arrogant attitude and behaviour of EU officials such as the former Trade Commissioner *Peter Mandelson* was alienating several Governments especially in Africa; see: Roux, Wallie (2009), Keine Unterschrift! Warum Namibia kein Interim-EPA eingehen sollte. In: afrika süd - zeitschrift zum südlichen afrika, Nr. 4, Juli/August/September 2009 .

483 ibid.

Of the 15 SADC countries, however, nine had until September 2009 signed an interim EPA and one (South Africa) has a special Free Trade Agreement with the EU. From the countries grouped in the SADC EPA Botswana, Lesotho and Swaziland signed an Interim EPA by June 2009 and Mozambique joined two weeks later; Angola and Namibia, however, refused to comply citing the threat to regional unity and integration as a reason. South Africa was at the beginning not included in the negotiation round with the EU and not offered the same conditions as the other SADC members because of its already existing separate preferential trade agreement with the EU but later on strong pressure from particularly Namibia admitted and partially included.

Amongst the SADC member states in the ESA EPA so far Tanzania, Mauritius, Seychelles, Zimbabwe and Madagascar have signed an interim EPA ([484]), while Malawi and Zambia have not yet decided if such an agreement would be to their advantage.

If fully fledged EPAs are signed between the EU on the one side and SADC member states in three different EPA groupings the effect would be negative for the unity in SADC and undermine at the same time the ability of SADC to determine and control their own fiscal, industrial and trade policies.

> "The IEPA negotiations exposed major divisions and fractures in the SADC regional integration project. SADC split into different configurations, each with its own separate liberalisation schedule. The current situation is incompatible with a SADC CU in 2010, which requires a common external tariff (CET)" ([485]).

In the past, SADC leaders have shown at times surprising political abilities in dealing with difficult situations but usually only when action was urgently required. A last minute compromise as far as membership affiliations, trade liberalisation schedules and EPA commitments seems to be the most probable outcome of the rather complicated situation.

---

484 See: http://www.eia.org.uk/view.php?id=622 and http://zunia.org/post/agritrade-executive-brief-on-esa-epa-negotiations/

485 Southern African Forum on Trade (SAFT) (2008), Communiqué of the 5th SAFT meeting; in: FES (ed.) (2008), Proceedings of the Fifth Southern African Forum on Trade (SAFT) held in Pretoria, South Africa, on 6–7 August 2008:11

10.2.3. Autocratic Political Culture

Southern Africa has – as other parts of sub-Saharan Africa as well – a tradition of strong, often_autocratic Heads of States. This particular trait has once fittingly been described as "personal rule" ([486]) and is linked to arbitrary decision-making, abolishing systems of checks and balances, ignoring the rule of law, while fostering nepotism and corruption, a low development-orientation as well as internal oppression. Although the majority of SADC member states now observe constitutional limits for the tenure of rulers ([487]), some SADC countries are being ruled by the same Head of State for more than 20 years ([488]) or have changed their Presidents by non-constitutional means ([489]). Not only have those long-serving autocratic Presidents and Kings developed into 'personal rulers' but also several of the democratically elected SADC leaders tried to establish such a personalized system of governance under the cover of a formal democracy. Former Presidents *Frederick Chiluba* (Zambia), *Bakili Muluzi* (Malawi) or *Sam Nujoma* (Namibia) would fit the description of a 'personal ruler' as well as current leaders such as *Bingu wa Mutharika* (Malawi). Especially, the erratic political behavior of *Robert Mugabe* (e.g. with regard to the OPDS; currently as far as the ruling of the SADC tribunal is concerned) has demonstrated, that such 'personal rulers' are hardly concerned about existing agreements to facilitate regional integration when their personal political survival is at stake. They even try to use the regional integration body for their political protection and risk damaging its reputation in the course of action. Other 'personal rulers' like Angola's *Eduardo dos Santos*, neglected SADC for several years, did not attend important meetings nor sign most of the SADC agreements (see table 9.3.). Such democratically unaccounted for autocratic leaders are a heavy liability to RI as their political actions are unpredictable,

486 Jackson, Robert H. /Rosberg, Carl G. (1982): Personal Rule in Black Africa – Prince, Autocrat, Prophet, Tyrant. Berkeley/Los Angeles/London.

487 Botswana, Lesotho, Malawi, Mauritius, Mozambique, Namibia, South Africa, Tanzania and Zambia had peaceful changes of Presidents since 1990; Mauritius and Zambia had even peaceful changes of Government. Only Angola, Swaziland and Zimbabwe have no constitutional limitations for the President's (King's) office tenure.

488 Longest-serving President is *Eduardo dos Santos* in Angola (since 1979), followed by *Robert Mugabe* in Zimbabwe (since 1980) and King *Mswati* III. In Swaziland (since 1986).

489 The non-elected President of the DRC, *Laurent Kabila*, was murdered 2001 and followed by his son Joseph, who won an election in 2007. In Madagascar, the former President *Didier Ratsiraka* was forced to resign in 2002 after disputed elections because of violent mass protests against him; his successor *Marc Ravalomanana* was in turn ousted by army-supported mass action in March 2009 and replaced by *Andy Rajeolina.*

their behavior damages the reputation of the regional body and their disregard for the rule of law undermines the very foundation economic development is based on.

Autocratic and 'personalistic' leadership is an expression of an underlying autocratic political culture, which aids the rise of

- corruption, not only amongst the ruling elite, but in society as a whole;
- self-enrichment tendencies amongst the ruling elite as their major motivation for staying in power instead of development orientation;
- patronage networks undermining democratic constitutions and checks-and-balances;
- an executive dominance over legislative and judicative;
- ethnic strife because of discrimination and political maneuvering;
- oppression of a free media and civil society as potential sources of criticism of the ruling party and its leader;
- non-participatory, top-down styles of administration discouraging decentralization and devolution of power.

The autocratic leadership style and the undemocratic political culture it is based on, has not changed much in the majority of SADC member states since the region got caught in the 'second wave' of democratization which swept through Africa in the 1990s. Formally, most political systems in the SADC region changed from one-party states to electoral democracies and officially only one autocratic system (Swaziland) remained (see table 10.2.)

The persistence of autocratic leadership structures and autocratic political culture is also the main reason for the severe problems with state consolidation in a number of SADC member states. State consolidation refers to the process of a Government exerting full control over its territory including having the monopoly of force. Leaders, who are legitimizing their power through personal 'charisma' – even if they are confirming this power through elections – rather than economic or political success, tend to alienate social, ethnic or religious sections of society. In extreme cases, this can lead to the loss of territorial control in parts of the country. In the SADC region, this phenomenon can be observed in varying degrees of loss of control in Angola, the DRC, Lesotho, Madagascar, Mozambique and even Zambia and Zimbabwe. Incomplete state consolidation in these countries means a restricted ability to pursue RI effectively. Urban areas out of the direct control of the Zimbabwean Government might not really harm its ability to engage in RI. But the lack of state structures and authority in many parts of the DRC may make the development of the Inga III dam, export of electricity or construction of railway lines to mineral rich areas in central Congo difficult. The mutiny of soldiers in Lesotho in 1998 could easily have endangered the finalization of the Lesotho Highland Water Project, which is providing urgently needed water to South Africa's urban areas.

Table 10.2. Political Systems and Democratization in the SADC-Region 1980-2008

Country	EPS until	Regime change	Current regime	Multiparty Elections	Democratic Change of Head of Government	No. of parties in Parliament
ANG	2008 (1)	No	MPS	2009	None	
BOT	--	No	MPS	1984, 1989, 1994, 1999, 2004, 2009	Yes, three times	4 (+ 1 independent)
DRC	2007 (2)	Yes 1997(5)	MPS	2006	None	67 (+ 63 in-dependents)
LES	1993	Yes 1993	MPS	1993, 1998, 2002, 2007	Yes, three times	3
MAD	1992	1993	Unclear (6)	1993, 1996, 2001, 2006	Yes, three times (7)	3
MAL	1994	Yes 1994	MPS	1994, 1999, 2004, 2009	Yes, twice	6 (+32 in-dependents)
MAU	--	No	MPS	1982, 1987, 1991, 1995 2000, 2005	Yes, four times	3
MOZ	1994	No	MPS	1994, 1999, 2004, 2009	Yes, once	3
NAM	--	No	MPS	1990, 1995, 2000, 2005, 2009	Yes, once	9
RSA	--(3)	Yes 1994	MPS	1994, 1999, 2004, 2009	Yes, four times	13
SWA	n/a (4)	No	Monarc hy		None	0
TAN	1992	No	MPS	1995, 2000, 2005	Yes, three times	2
ZAM	1991	Yes 1991	MPS	1991, 1996, 2001, 2006, 2008	Yes, three times	5 (+ 2 in-dependents)
ZIM	--	No	MPS	1980, 1985, 1990, 2000, 2002, 2005, 2008 (8)	None	3 (+ 1 in-dependent)

Explanations:

(1) Angola held the first parliamentary elections since 1992 in 2008. The 1992, elections were not recognized by the losing party UNITA, which went back to civil war.
(2) The 2007 elections were the first in the DRC since the end of Mobutu's rule and were made possible only through massive support by the UN and major donors.
(3) Until 1994, South Africa did not allow for the political representation of the majority of its population.
(4) Swaziland is a non-party system, as no parties are allowed and it's powerless Parliament consists of individual local representatives.
(5) Laurent Kabila took power in 1997 after he conquered the capital Kinshasa by force.
(6) The ousting of President Ravalomananain March 2009 is considered a putsch by SADC. The newly installed President Rajoelina has not been elected and is not recognized by the international community.
(7) The change of power in 2002 from Ratsiraka to Ravalomanana was partially forced by public action against the manipulation of election results by the Ratsiraka regime.
(8) Only Parliamentary Elections.

Source: own compilation

Examples for overcoming autocratic political systems are also available in the SADC region. The best known example is South Africa overcoming *apartheid* and establishing a liberal democracy that has so far prevailed and was able to remove a President (*Thabo Mbeki*) in a democratic correct way. Botswana, Mauritius and Namibia are also regarded as stable democracies that hold regular elections, change their President's according to tenure rules and enjoy high legitimacy.

In general, democratic and autocratic developments are rather evenly balanced in the SADC region. However, the prevalence of autocratic political cultures and a tendency in most political systems to turn to autocratic solutions when under strain put the democratic credentials of SADC into questions ([490]).

10.2.4. Is South Africa Dominating SADC Politically?

While there is hardly any doubt that South Africa is the economic superpower within the SADC region – expressed through its large share of the region's GDP

490 See: Chapter 10.2.5.

or the dominating role of its public and private companies throughout the region – the country likes to downplay its political dominance to some extent.

In international institutions and for a, South Africa is regarded as one of Africa's main representatives. Its ambition to get a permanent seat on the UN's Security Council is testimony to that. However, within SADC, South Africa has exercised a certain degree of political constraint.

This became evident when South Africa agreed e.g.:

- not to insist on a seat at the SADC Tribunal,
- to a funding formula for the SADC budget that differentiates the membership fee according to economic strength of member states and accordingly asks the highest contribution from South Africa,
- to a differentiated application of the tariff reduction schedules in implementing SAFTA allowing broad duty free access of goods from other SADC countries at an early stage of trade liberalisation.

Nevertheless, South Africa has also lost some of its natural regional political dominance during the indecisive tenure of President *Thabo Mbeki*. His so-called 'quiet diplomacy' approach towards Zimbabwe did not only leave western Governments baffled, but also some of his SADC counterparts. Under his leadership, South Africa neglected the development of an energy development strategy, which had a negative impact on the energy supply in the whole of SADC, especially in 2008. His peculiar stance on HIV/AIDS and the resulting inactivity in providing drugs to infected people – although not directly affecting SADC – cost him a lot of popularity and credibility. South Africa's politically strong position in the region has suffered and needs to be rebuilt by the new President *Jacob Zuma*.

Notwithstanding the phase of current weakness, South Africa's political resources ([491]) backed by its overwhelming economic strength make it the natural leader in Southern Africa. The other SADC countries either are too small, politically to instable or not sufficiently endowed with political resources to even think about challenging South Africa. The questions evolving are, will South Africa:

- assert its regional leadership position by leading by example as far as the promotion of democracy and the rule of law, fair distribution of costs

491 These are military power, political expertise, negotiation skills, international reputation and democratic stability.

and benefits of RI and respect of national interests of other SADC member states are concerned ,or

- revert to bullying tactics against its partners in SADC in a misunderstood attempt to show 'strength'?

South Africa's political (and not only economic) behavior in the region will to a large extent determine if SADC will remain united and stable enough to further pursue RI.

10.2.5. Slow Democratic Convergence in SADC

Democratic convergence describes the collective process within a regional integration body towards the adoption and practice of higher degrees of democracy at national level. If all member countries of a regional integration scheme become increasingly more democratic, they are converging towards democracy. If only some countries are becoming more democratic while others stagnate or even regress, the process of democratic convergence is interrupted or slowed down. Reaching the same or similar high levels of democratization within a regional body is crucial for RI, because this ensures equal political and economic conditions in all member states. Less democratic or autocratic states are also less predictable in their application of the rule of law, regime stability and economic development orientation.

There are no special indicators which are expressing democratic convergence as such. It can only be measured by looking at a combination of various sectoral indicators. The most accepted and utilized indicators dealing with special aspects of democratic transition are the:

- HDI of UNDP, which measures the conditions for human development in most countries in the world. The HDI can indirectly also be interpreted as an indicator for the effectiveness of policy delivery of a Government/state and non-state actors as it consists of a summary of indicators for income, health and education development (for SADC see table 9.4.).
- CPI of Transparency International ([492]), which measures the perceptions of stakeholders and experts on the level of corruption in a country. It is not an objective indicator, but one based on subjective expert opinions (perceptions) and varying numbers of studies (see table 10.3.).

---

492 www.transparencyinternational.org

- BTI of the Bertelsmann Foundation ([493]), which measures through detailed country evaluations the level of political and economic transformation towards democracy and a market-economy and the required management capacities and performance for 128 transformation countries over a two-year period. In the context of this assessment, only the political transformation ratings ("*status index*") are being considered (see table 10.4).
- Freedom House Index ([494]), which measures the degree of 'freedom in the world' by looking at two criteria: the extent to which 'civil liberties' and 'political rights' are respected in all the countries in the world (see table 10.5.).
- Ibrahim Index of the Mo Ibrahim Foundation ([495]), which provides a ranking of African countries only according to governance quality by "*measuring the delivery of public goods and services to citizens by government and non-state actors*". The Ibrahim Index is a composition of four separate indices: "Safety and Rule of Law"; "Participation and Human Rights"; "Sustainable Economic Opportunity"; and "Human Development" (see table 10.6.).

With regard to SADC, the development of the HDI from 2000 to 2007 has been generally positive. The regional average has reached a value of 0.568 (on a scale from 0 to 1) up from 0.510 in 2000. However, human development conditions slightly worsened in four of the 14 SADC member states: the DRC, Lesotho, South Africa and Zambia. Despite a general positive trend in SADC with regard to HDI, it also has to be noted that the average level of human development in the region is still low and that SADC's biggest economy, South Africa, is showing a negative development.

The picture for corruption in the SADC region is, on the whole, negative. The perceived level of corruption in the SADC member states was in 2008 higher than in 2000 although it marginally improved as compared to 2004 and 2006. In seven out of 12 member states, corruption levels rose while they fell in five. Again, South Africa is among those countries in which perceived corruption levels have increased. On the whole, the majority of SADC member states are perceived as being corrupt (ratings of below 4 on the CPI scale) and only two (Botswana and Mauritius) show a value of above five on the overall scale of 1 (= totally corrupt) to 10 (=totally transparent).

---

493 www.bertelsmann-stiftung.de
494 www.freedomhouse.org
495 www.moibrahimfoundation.org/en/section/the-ibrahim-index

Table 10.3.: Corruption Perception Index for SADC Countries 2000-2009

	2000		2004		2006		2008		2009		Trend
	Rank	Index	Rank	Index	Rank	Index	Rank	Index	Rank	Index	
ANG	85	*1.7*	129	*2.0*	142	2.2	158	1.9	162	1.9	+
BOT	26	*6.0*	29	*6.0*	37	5.6	36	5.8	37	5.6	-
DRC	n/a	n/a	133	*2.0*	156	2.0	171	1.7	162	1.9	-
LES	n/a	n/a	n/a	n/a	n/a	n/a	92	3.2	89	3.3	+
MAD	n/a	n/a	82	*3.1*	84	3.1	85	3.4	99	3.0	+
MAL	43	*4.1*	90	*2.8*	105	2.7	115	2.8	89	3.3	-
MAU	37	*4.7*	54	*4.1*	42	5.1	41	5.5	42	5.4	+
MOZ	81	*2.2*	90	*2.8*	99	2.8	126	2.6	130	2.5	+
NAM	30	*5.4*	54	*4.1*	55	4.1	61	4.5	56	4.5	-
SA	34	*5.0*	44	*4.6*	51	4.6	54	4.9	55	4.7	-
SWA	n/a	n/a	n/a	n/a	n/a	n/a	72	3.6	79	3.6	**0**
TAN	76	*2,5*	90	*2.8*	93	2.9	102	3.0	126	2.6	+
ZAM	57	*3.4*	102	*2.6*	111	2.4	115	2.8	99	3.0	-
ZIM	65	*3.0*	114	*2.3*	130	2.4	166	1.8	146	2.2	-
Aver		**3.7**		**3.3**		**3.3**		**3.4**		**3.4**	-

Source: www.transparencyinternational.org; various years; own compilation

The BTI 2010 ([496]), portrays a divergent picture of the development of political transformation of the counties of the SADC-region. While four member states are categorized as democracies (Mauritius, Botswana, Namibia and South Africa), five as democracies with deficiencies (Madagascar, Tanzania, Zambia, Malawi and Mozambique), three are classified as outright autocracies (Angola, DRC and Zimbabwe). Only Angola, the DRC and Malawi improved their ratings between 2003-5 (BTI 2006) and 2007-9 (BTI 2010); three other member states (Lesotho, Tanzania and Zambia) maintained more or less their values while the other six countries covered by the BTI showed a deteriorating level of democratic transformation ([497]). On the whole, the SADC region shows a worsening picture as far as democratic transformation is concerned. This is influenced by the problems in Zimbabwe, the DRC and Madagascar but is also reflecting

496 Covers the period between February 2007 and January 2009.

497 See: Bertelsmann Stiftung (ed.) (2008), Bertelsmann Tranformation Index 2006; 2008; 2010. Politische Gestaltung im internationalen Vergleich. Bielefeld.

Table 10.4.: Transformation to Democracy and a Market Economy in SADC 2006- 2010

	2003-5	2005-7	2007-9	Trend
ANG	3.41	3.82	4.56	++
BOT	7.98	7.94	7.81	-
DRC	2.62	3.16	3.53	++
LES	n/a	n/a	5.35	0
MAD	6.45	6.23	5.30	--
MAL	4.89	5.35	5.56	+
MAU	8.17	8.33	7.94	-
MOZ	6.01	5.56	5.71	-
NAM	7.15	7.32	6.99	-
SA	7.98	7.98	7.16	-
TAN	5.65	5.84	5.58	0
ZAM	6.07	5.97	5.99	0
ZIM	3.38	3.39	3.01	-
Average			5.74	-

Source: www.bertelsmann-stiftung.org, different years; own compilation

The Freedom House Index on '*freedom in the world*' reports a slight improvement for the SADC region between 2000 and 2006. Seven countries improved their ratings; four countries remained at the same level and in two member states, 'freedom' became more restricted. Not surprisingly, one of them is Zimbabwe but the other is, again, South Africa the most important member state of SADC. However, six of the 13 rated SADC countries are considered as 'free' amongst them also South Africa (the others are Botswana, Lesotho, Malawi, Mauritius and Namibia), four as 'partly free' and three as 'un-free' (Zimbabwe, Angola and DRC). The overall picture provided by the Freedom House ratings, is more positive than that of the BTI but, predominantly, the countries of the SADC region have not yet reached the level of free and democratic states.

The trend of good governance depicted by the Ibrahim Index in general was that of steady improvement for most countries in the SADC region. Only two of the 14 SADC member states (without the Seychelles) had lower values for 2007 than for the year 2000: Mozambique and Zimbabwe. Some countries in the region, such as Angola, the DRC, Lesotho and Zambia showed a considerable improvement. Of the ten top performers for 2007 six were from the SADC region ([498]). With the exception of the DRC and Zimbabwe and the, however, rapidly improving Angola all the other SADC member states show results which

498 The country data and composite values of the Mo Ibrahim Index are usually two years old when published. The Ibrahim Index of 2009 will thus depict data of 2007.

are above the African average. Four top performers are sticking out: Mauritius, Botswana, South Africa and Namibia.

Table 10.5: Development of Political Freedom in SADC 2000-2007

	2000	2002	2003	2004	2005	2006	2007	Trend
ANG	6.0	5.5	5.5	5.5	5.5	5.5	5.5	+
BOT	2.0	2.0	2.0	2.0	2.0	2.0	2.0	**0**
DRC	6.5	6.0	6.0	6.0	6.0	5.5	5.5	+
LES	4.0	2.5	2.5	2.5	2,5	2,5	2.5	+
MAD	3.0	3.5	3.0	3.0	3.0	3.0	3.5	-
MAL	3.0	4.0	3.5	4.0	2.0	2.0	4.0	-
MAU	1.5	1.5	1.5	1.0	1.0	1.5	1.5	**0**
MOZ	3.5	3.5	3.5	3.5	3.5	3.5	3.0	+
NAM	2.5	2.5	2.5	2.5	2.0	2.0	2.0	+
SA	1.5	1.5	1.5	1.5	1.5	2.0	2.0	-
TAN	4.0	3.5	3.5	3.5	3.5	3.5	3.5	+
ZAM	4.5	4.0	4.0	4.0	4.0	3.5	3.5	+
ZIM	5.5	6.0	6.0	6.5	6.5	6.5	6.5	-
SADC	**3.65**	**3.54**	**3.46**	**3.50**	**3.35**	**3.35**	**3.46**	+

Source: www.Freedomhouse.org; different years; own compilation

After awarding the very lucrative ([499]) *Mo Ibrahim Prize* for "*excellence in African leadership*" to former democratically elected heads of state in the past to *Nelson Mandela*, *Joaquim Chissano* of Mozambique and *Festus Mogae* of Botswana, in 2009 no former African statesman received this award. This may be a reflection of the low number of former African heads of state and Government, who were not only democratically elected but also stepped down after their tenure was over or admitted defeat rather than of a decline in governance standards.

The emerging image – if all five indices are seen together – is that of a divergent region with three distinct groups of countries as far as democratic convergence is concerned:

499 The laureate will receive USD 5 million over a period of ten years and afterwards USD 200,000 annually for the rest of their lives. The winner of the prize is selected by an independent committee; see www.moibrahimfoundation.org/en/section/the-ibrahim-prize

Table 10.6.: Governance in the SADC Member States 2000-2007

	2000	2003	2005	2007	Trend
ANG	26.16	33.18	35.77	41.02	+++
BOT	72.10	71.35	73.55	73.59	+
DRC	25.77	25.40	30.02	33.25	++
LES	54.18	58.01	60.15	61.18	++
MAD	56.73	55.87	56.78	58.37	+
MAL	50.57	50.03	51.11	53.03	+
MAU	76.37	76.78	77.96	82.03	++
MOZ	52.95	53.79	53.83	52.38	-
NAM	67.59	67.70	68.15	68.81	+
SA	69.41	69.06	70.16	69.44	**0**
SWA	45.48	45.27	47.83	49.43	+
TAN	53.53	52.42	55.28	59.24	+
ZAM	49.77	51.08	52.98	55.30	++
ZIM	34.59	34.38	33.46	31.29	-
Average	**52.55**	**53.09**	**54.77**	**56.29**	+

Source: www.moibrahimfoundation.org; different years; own compilation

- the ‘democratic’ group of countries with Botswana, Mauritius, Namibia and South Africa;
- the group of countries which have deficient democracies including, Lesotho, Madagascar, Malawi, Mozambique, Tanzania and Zambia; and
- the ‘autocratic’ group of countries with Angola, DRC, Swaziland and Zimbabwe.

The dynamics in the ‘democratic’ group point to a gradual worsening of democratic features especially as far as South Africa is concerned. The development in the ‘intermediate’ group is towards more democracy and adherence to democratic procedures. The third group of autocratic states is rather static and has been even worsening as in the case of Zimbabwe until very recently ([500]). It must be doubted if the recent elections in Angola have put this country back on the track towards democracy given the autocratic history of the ruling party.

As a conclusion, it can be stated that SADC is faced with a rather slow process of democratic convergence. The gap between the group of countries with democratic features and those with autocratic ones is not narrowing. The only positive development can be observed amongst SADC member states which

500 It is still much too early; to tell if the Government of National Unity in Zimbabwe, which was inaugurated in February 2009, will really work or if this is not just another ‘trick’ of Robert Mugabe to prolong his devastating stay in absolute power.

have been categorized as not yet fully democratic. Some of these states, such as Malawi, Tanzania or Mozambique seem to be embracing principles that are more democratic. However, for RI to work or even gain momentum, the participating countries should be at a similar –preferably high – level of democratic development. The differences in democratic achievements in SADC are quite pronounced and the absolute degree of democratic achievement in SADC is overall, currently neither high nor improving much.

10.2.6. Conflict Areas

The previous chapters have concentrated on the political potential for RI and some of the structural factors, which determine the ability of SADC to integrate further. The next step is to look at some of the immediate political problem areas emanating from the process of RI itself. Such areas of existing or potential conflict are:

- The question of giving up areas of → ***national sovereignty*** in favor of regional supra-national authorities such as the SADC Secretariat or the SADC Tribunal is a crucial and indispensable step of achieving deeper integration. Governments without strong internal legitimacy and full authority over their territory will hesitate to relinquish areas of power to a supra-national body such as the SADC Secretariat. The establishment of SAFTA, for instance, has been slowed down because several Governments have been reluctant to dispense with parts of their revenue originating from external tariffs. When the pressure to comply with the agreed procedures of liberalizing internal trade became too strong to withstand any longer, some SADC countries introduced new fees and tariffs to compensate for the loss of revenue. This can, be regarded as a clear sign of how difficult it is for some SADC member states to adhere to even such first steps of further RI.
- Short-term 'national' interests of SADC member states may stand in the way of fulfilling regional commitments. The fact that Zambia has so far made no attempts to clear its position regarding the issue of overlapping membership (SADC and COMESA), is probably owed to Lusaka being the seat of the COMESA headquarters. While the SADC membership is politically and economically more important for Zambia than belonging to COMESA, the international prestige emanating from being the seat of the headquarters of a regional organization and the jobs generated by that are reason enough to ignore the SADC decision to abolish double memberships. A similar disparity between official commitment to

SADC and practical action applies to the choice of EPA affiliation, which split SADC into three groups of countries. The low payment morale of some SADC member states as far as membership fees are concerned is another example in this respect.

- With the establishment of the SADC Tribunal, member states have officially accepted a regional 'enforcement' body. However, the ruling of the Tribunal in favor of white Zimbabwean farmers suing the Zimbabwean Government for unlawful expropriation of land revealed how difficult it is especially for politically weak Governments to accept verdicts that are not in their favor. So far, the Tribunal has not been able to fulfill its function because its own enforcement resources are too weak – it has to rely on the good will of the Governments of the SADC member states to implement them. If – as must be expected – arbitration cases with regard to conflicts over trade issues (→ ***rule of origin***, the introduction of → ***nontariff trade barriers*** or even new tariffs) will emerge, the Tribunal needs more than the goodwill of the member states to be effective and further RI.
- Ensuring the just distribution of benefits and costs of regional integration must be based on a political consensus and needs instruments other than the SADC Tribunal. As SADC moves towards the establishment of a customs union, demands of the smaller member countries to agree on a revenue-sharing formula favorable to them (and perhaps modeled along the SACU formula) will be inevitable. If South Africa and other large importers (such as oil-rich Angola) will agree to that, has yet to be seen.
- The dominating role of Governments vis-à-vis society regarding RI excludes relevant stakeholders from shaping RI. Although SADC has accepted civil society bodies and interest groups such as, the SADC Council of NGOs or the Association of SADC Chambers of Commerce and Industry (ASCCI) and opened special channels of communication with them, the contribution of organised interest groups towards the process of RI is still very weak ([501]). Concerns that are regularly raised by local and international NGOs about the potential environmental damage of the expansion of hydropower plants and dams, the loss of cultural diversity or human rights violations in Zimbabwe are hardly noticed by the SADC institutions. In a functional RI scheme, business interests are the main drivers and shapers of economic integration. In SADC, business interests have only been invited by South Africa, Mauritius and, for a while, by Zimbabwe to participate in the negotiations regarding the establishment of the FTA. There have been

501 See: Chingono/Nakana (2009):404f

consultations between SADC and energy utilities and transportation companies on the regulations in the respective Protocols but so far, business interests have not been given appropriate space and mechanisms to express their needs and concerns. For RI to develop its own momentum, it requires interest-driven non-state actors to take an active interest and be allowed an active role in economic integration.

- The existence of arbitrary autocratic regimes in Angola, DRC, Swaziland and Zimbabwe in the confines of SADC is damaging the international reputation of SADC and raising doubts about its predictability. Member states, which are not adhering to the rule of law, where Presidential (or royal) decisions can override constitutional rights, international agreements and court orders or disrespect human rights, are a liability for a regional integration body. For SADC, the most severe damage was caused by the inability or unwillingness of the regional body to ensure the respect for the rule of law and human rights in Zimbabwe. As a result of its misdirected economic policies and donor sanctions, Zimbabwe's economy imploded (see also chapter 12) with negative consequences for the regional transportation, energy and trade relations. Regional bodies such as SADC can only attract FDI's and donor support and receive international recognition if they are adhering to a set of legal rules and are predictable. In this respect, SADC needs to develop internal political consultation mechanisms that are capable of addressing and even correcting such problems.

The previous chapters have highlighted that RI is in the political interests of most SADC countries on the one hand, but on the other hand, important political preconditions for further RI are still missing, the integration process itself has led to conflicts and disputes that need to be addressed urgently if RI is not to be slowed down or even derailed. In the next chapter, we will take a closer look at the crisis in Zimbabwe and the role SADC played in trying to end it. This chapter wants to highlight some of the structural deficits SADC is faced with when it comes to crisis management. For many external observers and commentators the treatment of the Zimbabwe crisis shows the weakness of SADC and its low commitment to democracy and the rule of law.

Chapter 11: The Zimbabwe Crisis and Regional Integration in SADC

In this chapter – which is to some extent, a case study of a country in crisis – we will look briefly at the causes of the crisis in Zimbabwe ([502]) and then focus more specifically on the crisis phenomena, the reaction of SADC and the regional and international repercussions for SADC.

11.1 Anatomy of the Crisis in Zimbabwe

The crisis in Zimbabwe has been described as politically induced, accelerated and reinforced by regional and international actors ([503]). There will be in the years to come a lot of debate about the causes and development of the crisis in Zimbabwe before a clear and objective analysis will emerge. However, even now, some factors appear to be evident:

- Growing social disparities, of which highly uneven access to fertile land was just one and the challenge of the undisputed monopoly of political power by *Mugabe* and his ZANU-PF party by a new urban-based opposition were at the root of the crisis.
- President *Mugabe* instrumentalized the land questions and militarized 'war veterans' from 1999 onwards to defeat the first serious political challenge to his hold onto power. This triggered the actual crisis ([504]).
- The deep political rift between Zimbabwe and Great Britain and their respective leaders *Mugabe* and *Blair* ([505]), translated into a conflict between the EU and Zimbabwe which reinforced the conflict as it blocked the search for possible alternative solutions.

---

502 See: Text Box 11.1.

503 See: Peters-Berries, C (2001a); Peters-Berries, C. (2002)

504 The British Economist, although not without bias against Mugabe, summarized his personal responsibility to the point: "The Mess One Man Makes"; The Economist, 20.4.2000

505 Mugabe felt personally insulted when – on a private trip to London – a gay's rights activist tried to affect a citizen's arrest on Mugabe because of his utterances against gays. The British Government regretted the incident but did not prosecute the gay activist. Mugabe retaliated by referring to the British Government as to 'Blair and his gay cabinet'; see Peters-Berries (2001a):10.

Against the background of illegal farm invasions, the total ignorance of the rule of law combined with the intimidation and eventual expulsion of the last few independent judges, the Mugabe regime won a highly disputed narrow victory in the 2000 Parliamentary Elections. In the aftermath of the elections, the terror campaign by the regime's semi-official enforcers – first the 'war veterans' and later also the 'Green Bombers' ([506]) – against the opposition party MDC, their supporters and the remaining white farming community, continued in order to destroy the opposition. In reaction to these massive violation of human rights and international agreements ([507]) the EU, the USA and other donors imposed sanctions against the regime including a travel ban for its central representatives and freezing their private assets in the EU and the USA. The impact of these sanctions was amplified by first the exclusion from preferential and later, all borrowing from international finance institutions such as the IMF, the World Bank and the AfDB ([508]).

TEXT BOX 11.1.: The Role of President Mugabe in Zimbabwe's Decline

Obwohl sich das Politbüro der ZANU-PF 1990 entscheiden hatte, auf die offizielle Einführung eines Einparteienstaats zu verzichten vermochte es *Mugabe* in der Folgezeit eine perönliche Herrschaftsform durchzusetzen, in der die Unterschiede zwischen Partei, Regierung und Staatsapparat oft bis zur Unkenntlichkeit verwischten. Mugabe gelang dies einerseits mittels strategischer Personalentscheidungen innerhalb der Partei – er besetzte nach und nach alle Schlüsselpositionen mit treuen, oft ihm persönlich verpflichteten, Anhängern – und andererseits unter Bezugnahme auf die verfassungsrechtliche Ausweitung seiner präsidentiellen Befugnisse die zwischen 1987 und 1990 durchgesetzt worden waren. Dank ihrer unangefochtenen politischen Machtposition seit 1987 besaß ZANU-PF die direkte Kontrolle über weite Teile der Verwaltungsstrukturen und des Militärs sowie Teile der Wirtschaft. Ein dichtes Patronagenetzwerk sicherte der Partei die soziale und oft auch ökonomische Kontrolle über weite Teile der Gesellschaft.

Einher mit der gesellschaftlichen Kontrolle ging die Ausweitung der präsidentiellen Machtbefugnisse: durch etliche Verfassungszusätze entwickelte sich *Mugabe* – in den Worten eines simbabwischen Kommentators – zu einem „*presidential monarch*", der unter dem

506 The 'Green Bombers' are a militant, trained and armed youth group dispatched to terrorise opposition supporters.

507 The forceful expulsion of several of the white farmers was in clear breach of bilateral investment protection agreements Zimbabwe had signed with e.g. UK, Germany and the USA.

508 Between 2000 and 2007, the AfDB loaned Zimbabwe only USD 350,000 (as a poverty alleviation measure) while it cancelled commitments worth USD 272 million; by 2007, Zimbabwe owed the AfDB more than USD 226 million; see AfDB (2008a):9ff. In February 2009, the President of the AfDB said that Zimbabwe owed the Bank USD 460 million.; see: http://allafrica.com/stories/200902270711.html

Deckmantel einer demokratischen Verfassung nahezu absolutistische Machtbefugnisse beanspruchte. Die enorme Machtfülle des *Robert Mugabe* beinhaltete (*bis 2008, CP*) vor allem folgende Elemente:

- Er ist Oberbefehlshaber der Armee.
- Er kann gegen jeglichen Gesetzentwurf sein Veto ohne Angabe von Gründen einlegen.
- Er kann das Parlament ohne Begründung jederzeit auflösen, und sich damit des einzigen Kontrollorgans entledigen, das ihn des Amtes entheben könnte (zwar kann das Parlament mit einer 2/3 Mehrheit das Veto des Präsidenten überstimmen, aber der Präsident kann das Parlament zuvor auflösen – er hat in jedem Fall das ultimative Machtmittel).
- Er kann mittels präsidentieller Verordnungen, die 181 Tage Geltung haben und beliebig wiederholbar sind, ohne Parlament regieren und Gesetze außer Kraft setzen oder überstimmen.
- Er ernennt zusätzlich zu den gewählten 120 Abgeordneten weitere 30 Parlamentarier, von denen er 12 frei bestimmen kann, 8 die Provinz-Gouverneure und 10 traditionelle Häuptlinge sind.
- Er kann per präsidentiellem Pardon alle Gerichtsurteile überstimmen – ein Recht von dem *Mugabe* immer dann Gebrauch machte, wenn einer seiner Gefolgsleute gerade rechtskräftig verurteilt worden war.

Unabhängig vom Parlament wird der Präsident alle sechs Jahre, das Parlament alle fünf Jahre direkt vom Volk gewählt (*bis 2008; CP*). Diess stärkte lange seinen Nimbus als exekutiver Präsident.

Die weitgehend unkontrollierbare Machtfülle verstärkte die bereits unzweifelhaft vorhandenen autokratischen und selbstherrlichen Tendenzen in der Persönlichkeit von *Robert Mugabe*. *Mugabe* betrachtet Simbabwe als sein persönliches Eigentum, die ihm gegebene Macht als ewigwährend und empfindet Kritik an seiner Politik und besonders an seiner Person als Majestätsbeleidigung. Das drückt sich u.a. im permanenten Gebrauch des *pluralis majestatis* aus, macht die Hartnäckigkeit erklärlich, mit der er selbst unbedeutende innenpolitische Gegner verfolgt und gibt den Hintergrund ab für seine irrationalen öffentlichen Wutausbrüche gegenüber der nach seiner Ansicht von Homosexuellen durchsetzten Regierung des britischen Premierministers *Tony Blair*. Der Persönlichkeitsstruktur des Präsidenten kommt angesichts der ihm verliehenen Machtfülle, aber auch aufgrund der starken Autoritätshörigkeit in der simbabwischen Gesellschaft, mehr Bedeutung bei der Erklärung politischer Entscheidungen zu, als dies in Europa, Amerika oder Asien normalerweise der Fall ist.

Mugabe verfeinerte während der 90er Jahre sein persönliches Herrschaftssystem in einer Weise, daß er selbst zum Garanten der Systemstabilität wurde. Am besten läßt sich *Mugabes* Herrschaftssystem wie folgt beschreiben: Toleranz und mitunter sogar Ermutigung gegenüber der ungehemmten, oft illegalen Selbstbereicherung seiner unmittelbaren Vertrauten und Minister, solange sie ihm treu ergeben und absolut loyal sind, aber sofortige Bestrafung der ‚Ungehörigen', Illoyalen und Putschgedanken-Verdächtigen durch Entzug des strafbefreienden präsidentiellen Schutzes und Überantwortung der allgemeinen Gerichtsbarkeit. Von der damit inoffiziell sanktionierten Korruption und Vetternwirtschaft wurde nahezu die gesamte politische, bürokratische und militärische sowie einige Teile der zumeist afrikanischen wirtschaftlichen Elite des Landes erfaßt.

Der zweite Pfeiler des Herrschaftssystems *Mugabes* beruht auf der geschickten Ausbalancierung ethnisch-regionaler Differenzen innerhalb der Regierungspartei ZANU-PF. Diese besitzt ihre Basis vornehmlich unter der shonasprachigen Mehrheit der Bevölkerung (ca. 75%), die sich wiederum in einige regionale Untergruppen differenziert:

- Die *Zezuru* im simbabwischen Kernland, zu denen *Mugabe* selbst und eine Reihe seiner engsten Berater zählen und die eine gewisse Hegemonie innerhalb der ZANU-PF errichtet haben.
- Die *Manyika* in der Manicaland-Provinz im Osten des Landes, die im Befreiungskrieg lange die Führungselite von ZANU-PF stellten, deren Führer aber unter z.T. mysteriösen Umständen ums Leben kamen. Der langjährige Minister *Didymus Mutasa* führt die linientreue Fraktion.
- Die *Karanga* aus der *Masvingo*-Provinz stellen die zahlenmäßig größte der Shona-Untergruppen die in zwei Fraktionen gespalten ist, von denen die eine von (*mittlerweile verstorbenen; CP*) Vize-Präsident *Simon Muzenda*, die andere vom Minister ohne Portfolio, *Eddison Zvobgo (mittlerweile ebenfalls verstorben; CP)*, geführt wird. Letzterer versuchte letztlich vergeblich, sich mit seiner Hausmacht eine unabhängige Position innerhalb der ZANU-PF zu verschaffen.
- Die *Korekore* aus der Mashonaland Zentral Provinz sind die kleinste und am wenigsten repräsentierte Untergruppe der Shona innerhalb der Machtelite von ZANU-PF.

Daneben stellen die ndebelesprachigen Gruppen aus den beiden *Matabeleland* Provinzen und Teilen der *Midlands* eine größere ethnisch-regionale Einheit, die bis zur Vereinigung von ZANU-PF und PF-ZAPU im Dezember 1987 letztere unterstützten. Präsident *Mugabe* gelang es, die Leitfiguren der verschiedenen ethnisch-regionalen Fraktionen innerhalb der ZANU-PF in einer Weise politisch einzubinden, daß sie sich gegenseitig neutralisierten und ihm und seiner Zezuru-Hausmacht großen Manövrier-Raum gaben. Provinz-interne Fraktionierungen wie in der *Manicaland*- und der *Masvingo*-Provinz mußten ihm aus machttaktischen Gründen durchaus willkommen sein, reduzierten sie doch das politische Gewicht der beiden anderen großen ethnisch-regionalen Gruppierungen.

...

Aufgrund einer weitgehenden Kontrolle über das öffentliche Leben erzielten ZANU-PF und *Mugabe* ab 1990 eine Reihe von klaren Siegen bei Parlaments- und Präsidentschaftswahlen. Die eigentliche Machtbasis für ZANU-PF lag schon immer in den ländlichen Gebieten, in denen nicht nur die Mehrzahl der Wähler (ca. 65%) lebt, sondern auch der Spielraum für Patronagepraktiken der Regierungspartei – Brunnen gegen Stimmen – weitaus höher war und ist als in den Städten. ZANU-PF und Mugabe versuchten seit jeher in der klassischen Manier von Einparteiensystemen dem Umschlagen von sozio-ökonomischem Unmut auf Wahlergebnisse entgegenzuwirken. Dazu setzten sie systematisch auf

- Einschüchterung der Wahlbevölkerung und der politischen Gegner;
- Mißbrauch staatlicher Ressourcen (Fahrzeuge, Zeitungen, Fernsehen und Radio);
- geheimdienstlich initiierte Spaltung der Opposition; und
- selektive Wahlrechtsbeugung.

...

Im Gegensatz zu vielen anderen Ländern, die sich plötzlich am politischen und wirtschaftlichen Abgrund wiederfinden, gab es in Simbabwe viele Warnzeichen, die jedoch in der politischen Führung kaum jemand wahrnehmen wollte. Das deutlichste Krisensignal erklang zur Jahresmitte 1997, als von der unabhängigen Presse ein neuer Skandal aufgedeckt wurde: die Ausplünderung eines Kompensationsfonds für Kriegsveteranen, die unter Spätfolgen des Befreiungskrieges litten, durch die politische Elite. Nahezu das gesamte Kabinett, etliche Abgeordnete, Staatssekretäre, hohe Militärs und Polizeioffiziere hatten sich in hohem Maße Kriegsversehrtheit attestieren und beträchtliche Entschädigungen ausbezahlen lassen.[509]

Die eigentlichen Adressaten des Kompensationsfonds – mittellose Kriegsveteranen – organisierten nach der Aufdeckung des Skandals Protestaktionen. Der bis dahin öffentlich kaum in Erscheinung getretene Verband der Kriegsveteranen störte die Feierlichkeiten am Heldengedenktag 1997, forderte Aufklärung und Entschädigung. Was westlichen Beobachtern als vergleichsweise harmlose Manifestation sozialen Protestes vorgekommen sein mag, wurde in Simbabwe als schwere Form der Majestätsbeleidigung und eindringliche Warnung an die Regierung aufgefaßt. *Mugabe* versprach kurz darauf, allen registrierten Kriegsveteranen (ob versehrt oder nicht) eine lebenslange monatliche Rente von ZW$ 2.000 und eine einmalige Pauschale von ZW$ 50.000[510] zu zahlen. Innerhalb weniger Wochen ließen sich fast 70.000 Simbabwer als Kriegsveteranen registrieren. Ein in Polen ausgebildeter Mediziner, *Chenjerai Hitler* (sic!) *Hunzvi*, entpuppte sich als die treibende organisatorische Kraft der Kriegsveteranen.

Mugabes Alleingang verblüffte nicht nur die Öffentlichkeit, sondern auch die politischen Beobachter. Was hatte ihn dazu bewogen, den Protesten derart widerstandslos und dazu noch so großzügig nachzugeben? Die meisten Erklärungsversuche drehten sich um die angebliche militärische Macht und den politischen Einfluß der Veteranen, die *Mugabe* persönlich bedroht haben sollen. Dies ist insofern schwer nachvollziehbar, als daß es keine direkte Verbindung zwischen den protestierenden Veteranen auf der Straße und den Veteranen in Machtpositionen gab. Die hatten sich wie viele Minister an der Ausplünderung des Fonds beteiligt. Auch ein zweiter Erklärungsversuch, der auf eine moralische Empörung bei *Mugabe* abstellt, scheint wenig glaubwürdig vor dem Hintergrund der Herrschaftspraxis von *Mugabe*. Was an Erklärungsansätzen übrig bleibt, sind einerseits eine schlichte Fehleinschätzung der machtpolitischen Situation durch *Mugabe* – er fühlte sich subjektiv bedroht und reagierte in Panik – oder andererseits das beleidigte Ego des stolzen Präsidenten, der sich solch einer demütigenden Situation wie während des Heldengedenktages nicht nochmals ausgesetzt sehen wollte. In beiden Fällen zeugt die Entscheidung, sich die Gewogenheit der Veteranen zu erkaufen, von wenig Gespür für die tatsächlichen Verhältnisse und von politischer und besonders wirtschaftspolitischer Kurzsichtigkeit.

Die unmittelbare Zeche der Kriegsveteranen-Abfindung für den simbabwischen Staat belief sich allein für 1997 auf ZW$ 3,5 Mrd. (zu diesem Zeitpunkt ca. € 280 Mio.). Die Folgekosten für die nächsten Jahre wurden mit mindestens ZW$ 1,7 Mrd. angegeben. Mugabe wies seinen Finanzminister zunächst an, die ungeplanten Ausgaben mittels einer Kriegsveteranen-Abgabe finanzieren zu lassen. Der Gewerkschaftsbund *Zimbabwe Congress of Trade Unions* (ZCTU) verhinderte im November 1997 durch einen Generalstreik und die Androhung weiterer Aktionen die Einführung dieser Abgabe, die danach aus dem laufenden Budget beglichen werden mußte. Damit befand sich die Regierung *Mugabe* in einem Dilemma: wie Weltbank und IWF zufriedenstellen, die ihre Unterstützung nur bei einer

509 Zwischen umgerechnet Euro 15 und 50.000 für Appetitmangel, Schlaflosigkeit und Fettleibigkeit als Folge von 15 bis 20 Jahre zurückliegenden Kriegserlebnissen.

510 Zu diesem Zeitpunkt waren dies etwa US$ 180 bzw. US$ 4.500.

budget-neutralen Finanzierung der Kriegsveteranenabfindung fortsetzen wollten, ohne die Versprechungen an die Kriegsveteranen zu brechen? *Mugabe* riskierte den Konflikt mit den *Bretton-Woods*-Institutionen, wohl im Kalkül, daß diese Simbabwe auf Dauer nicht aufgeben würden. Dadurch gewann er zwar kurzfristig wieder innenpolitischen Handlungsspielraum, bürdete dem Land aber enorme wirtschaftliche Kosten auf, die letztlich zur Unterminierung seiner Position beitrugen. IWF und Weltbank froren ihre Zusagen über US$ 63 Mio. umgehend ein.

Anstatt jedoch nach einer gemeinsamen Lösung mit IWF und Weltbank zu suchen, forcierte die Regierung *Mugabe* die Konfrontation mit der internationalen Gebergemeinschaft weiter. Sie hielt ihre Ankündigung aufrecht, 1.700 weiße Farmen enteignen zu wollen und einer Landreform zugänglich zu machen; die britische Regierung als ehemalige Kolonialmacht sollte die Kosten dafür aufbringen. Diese erklärte, nur eine transparente und die Armut bekämpfende Landreform unterstützen zu wollen. Eine groß angekündigte Geberkonferenz zur Landreform im Oktober 1998 hatte keine nennenswerten Fortschritte zur Folge, sondern bestärkte die Geber nur noch darin, auch weiterhin einen transparenten Reformprozeß zur Vorbedingung jeglicher Finanzierung zu machen.

Die Haltung der Regierung *Mugabe* ist oft mit internem politischen Druck erklärt worden, endlich die lang angekündigte Landreform durchführen zu müssen. Das greift jedoch zu kurz. Die politische Handlungsfreiheit der Regierung *Mugabe* hätte es durchaus zugelassen, eine regulierte und transparente Landreform durchzuführen. Die Konfrontation mit den Gebern und vor allem mit der neuen britischen Regierung, die sich stärker als ihre Vorgänger an Prinzipien wie Einhaltung der Menschenrechte, *good governance* und Transparenz orientierte, beruhte weitgehend auf den Perzeptionen von Präsident *Mugabe*, der Großbritannien als Feind ansah,[511] und der glaubte, mit Feindbildern von den eigenen Verfehlungen ablenken zu können. Wie sich nämlich 1999 herausstellte, hatte die Regierung rund 275 zum Teil sehr große Farmen aus Staatsbesitz nicht für die Landreform benutzt, sondern langfristig an einflußreiche Politiker, Funktionäre und Geschäftsleute verpachtet. Es bleibt festzuhalten, daß Präsident *Mugabe* aus kurzfristigen politischen Erwägungen und einer schon autistisch zu nennenden Wahrnehmung der internationalen Umwelt politisch törichte Entscheidungen getroffen hat.

Die „politische Unvernunft der Regierenden" (*Krippendorff* 1985) in Simbabwe trat ein weiteres Mal im August 1998 zu Tage: *Mugabe* entsandte – zusammen mit Namibia und Angola – mehrere tausend simbabwische Soldaten in die DR Kongo, um seinen von Rebellen bedrängten Kollegen *Laurent Kabila* zu unterstützen. Die Mittel für die Militärexpedition wurden zunächst dem laufenden Haushalt entnommen und später über Schattenhaushalte finanziert. Dies trieb das Budgetdefizit – eines der Hauptkriterien für IWF und Weltbank bei der Vergabe von Stabilisierungskrediten – auf Werte über 12% des BIP.

Die *Bretton-Woods*-Institutionen, die kurzfristig ihre Hilfe wieder aufgenommen hatten, brachen daraufhin erneut mit Simbabwe, was umgehend eine weitere starke Abwertung zur Folge hatte. Der Simbabwe-Dollar fiel auf eine Rate von 38:1 zum US$. Als deswegen weitere Preissteigerungen drohten, führte die Regierung Preiskontrollen für Güter des

---

511 Hier spielt auch die Kritik britischer Medien an Mugabes Haltung gegenüber Homosexuellen eine Rolle.

täglichen Bedarfs ein, um Unruhen zu vermeiden. Gleichzeitig verständigte sie sich mit den Geschäftsbanken auf einen künstlich stabilisierten Wechselkurs. Die verhinderte vorübergehend zwar soziale Unruhen, beschleunigte jedoch den Niedergang der Wirtschaft.

IWF und Weltbank versuchten im Juni 1999 nach langen Verhandlungen den wirtschaftlichen Niedergang mit einem neuen Stützungskredit aufzuhalten, nachdem ihnen die simbabwische Regierung zugesichert hatte, die Kosten für die andauernde militärische Intervention in der DR Kongo beliefen sich lediglich auf rund US$ 3 Mio. pro Monat und könnten aus dem Haushalt bestritten werden. Kaum war die erste Tranche ausgezahlt, wurde ein interner Bericht des Verteidigungsministeriums bekannt, der die Kosten für das Kongo-Abenteuer auf nahezu US$ 30 Mio. pro Monat für die erste Hälfte des Jahres 1999 bezifferte. Das Stabilisierungsprogramm wurde umgehend wieder abgebrochen. Andere Geber, wie die EU und einige nordische Staaten sowie Holland folgten nach und stellten ihre Hilfen – soweit sie keine direkten Projekthilfen waren – an Simbabwe ein.

In der zweiten Jahreshälfte 1999 wurde absehbar, daß Simbabwes Wirtschaft dicht vor dem Kollaps stand:

➢ Die internationale Wettbewerbsfähigkeit der simbabwischen Industrie erodierte aufgrund der galoppierenden Inflation. Für 2000 wird mit Exporteinbußen bei Tabak, Textilien und Gold von bis zu 40% gerechnet (hierzu trugen jedoch auch die Farmbesetzungen und andere Unsicherheitsfaktoren bei).

➢ Die Devisenreserven erschöpften sich rasch bis auf wenige Tage Exportdeckung und führten zur Entstehung eines blühenden Schwarzmarktes für Devisen, der im August 2000 eine erste Abwertung um 24% und eine kontrollierte weitere Abwertung in kleinen Schritten notwendig machte.

➢ Es häuften sich Zahlungsrückstände (u.a. bei der Weltbank; insgesamt gegenwärtig rund US$ 400 Mill.) und das Land verlor seine international Kreditwürdigkeit, was dazu führte, daß

➢ Versorgungsengpässe vor allem bei Benzin, Diesel, Paraffin und Strom stark zunehmen. Die Benzin- und Dieselversorgung brach seit Dezember 1999 immer wieder phasenweise zusammen. Im Juni 2000 drohte der südafrikanische Stromversorger ESKOM mit der Einstellung jeglicher Stromexporte nach Simbabwe, da Zahlungsrückstände von rund € 20 Mill. Aufgelaufen waren;

➢ Arbeitslosigkeit und soziales Elend nahmen zu, da die Abwertung rapide Preiserhöhungen bei Brennstoffen (Paraffin), Transport und Grundnahrungsmitteln nach sich zogen und etliche Firmen Arbeiter entlassen oder ganz schließen mußten.

Durch eine Reihe von politischen Fehlentscheidungen hatte die Regierung *Mugabe* innerhalb von zwei Jahren die auf Erholungskurs liegende simbabwische Wirtschaft aus dem Gleis geworfen. Die indirekten wirtschaftlichen und politischen Kosten der Kriegsveteranenabfindung, der angedrohten Enteignungspolitik gegenüber weißen Farmern, der Kongo-Intervention und des Konfliktes mit IWF und Weltbank lassen sich wie folgt zusammenfassen:

➢ Der Schwund der Devisenreserven ließ den Außenwert des Simbabwe-Dollars erodieren: innerhalb von drei Jahren verlor der Simbabwe-Dollar gegenüber dem US-Dollar rund 350% an Wert.

➢ Wachsende Budgetdefizite, hervorgerufen durch drastisch gestiegene Ausgaben bei

sinkenden Einnahmen, und ein sinkender Außenwert des Simbabwe-Dollars heizten die Inflation auf bis 70% an.
➢ Dadurch mit hervorgerufene Preissteigerungen für Grundnahrungsmittel (Brot und Maismehl) führten im Januar 1998 zu schweren Unruhen in urbanen Ballungsgebieten und gaben der Opposition starken politischen Auftrieb.

… Zur Torheit der Regierenden kam … die Arroganz der Macht.

Source: Peters-Berries, C. (2000):11-13;14; 21-25

Zimbabwe had already in 1998 started to have problems complying with the conditions of an IMF-stand-by program due to excessive politically motivated spending (compensation for the 'war veterans' and the intervention in the DRC). As a result, its international credit ranking dropped, the value of the Zimbabwean $ fell sharply against the US-$, and both short-term credit and long-term loans were difficult to obtain. Ordinary Zimbabweans first realized something was wrong when fuel supplies dried up in 1999; fuel shortages persisted for the next years until purchases were only possible against hard currency. The fuel shortages were only a first – although highly inconvenient – symptom of the enfolding crisis. In macro-economic and social terms, the crisis in Zimbabwe can be summarized as follows:

- A massive macro-economic contraction: between 2000 and 2007, the economy shrunk by about 34% (see table 11.1.); other sources even estimate that the contraction is close to 50% over the last decade ([512])
- A world record inflation, which spiralled totally out of control in 2008 reaching heights of 231,000,000% ([513]) and destroying eventually the local currency, which had to be replaced in January 2009 by the US-$ and the South African Rand.
- A collapse of exports: Zimbabwe's export earning fell from USD 3,281 million in 2000 to USD 941 million in 2006 ([514]).
- A serious shortage of foreign exchange: the latest available figures for 2002 show a mere USD 83 million foreign exchange reserves ([515]), which represent less than 14 days import cover. However, through remittances of the diaspora and black market trading, considerable amounts of foreign currency are available in Zimbabwe; only that nobody puts these monies into the banking system anymore. This has the effect that the official reserves are much less, than the actual amount of foreign currency floating in the (informal) economy.

512 See: Capital Newspaper (Addis Abeba) 12.10.2008
513. ibid
514 See: UNCTAD (208):103
515 Ibid:354

- A breakdown of food supply, medical drugs and chemicals which has not only increased hunger but also caused the serious cholera epidemic in 2008 which claimed more than 3,600 lives already in Zimbabwe and threatens to spill over into neighbouring countries ([516]).
- The collapse of industrial production, commercial agriculture and tourism increased unemployment rates to up to 90%. The absurdly high inflation made it unattractive to work in the formal sector for most people ([517]). The alternative for many was to engage in petty trading, smuggling or in outright emigration. Although there are no reliable figures of the number of Zimbabweans outside the country, estimates go as high as 4-5 million people, which means that about one third of the entire Zimbabwean population has left the country.

The African Economic Outlook 2007/8 of the OECD, no longer contains a country chapter on Zimbabwe as neither reliable economic data is available nor are the experts able to make any further predictions about the development of the Zimbabwean economy. It looks as if the OECD has given up on Zimbabwe economically as long as the *Mugabe* regime is in control of the Government.

The economic melt-down and the worsening of the socio-economic living conditions in Zimbabwe were accompanied by growing corruption. The *Mugabe* regime used its total control of executive resources to plunder the rich resources of the country; partly to reward its supporters, partly to enrich themselves and partly to pay for immediately necessary imports. The fertile farms taken over from the white farmers were only to some extent distributed amongst the landless poor; the best farms were grabbed by top officials, generals and well connected businessmen ([518]). Lucrative concessions for minerals (platinum, zinc, gold) were sold to Chinese investors and large tracts of land mortgaged to Libya for the delivery of oil.

---

516 See: CNN, 17.2.2009. http://www.cnn.com/2009/WORLD/africa/02/17/Zimbabwe.cholera.crisis/

517 In 2007, a teacher earned on average Z$ 3 million a month, which was then worth USD 12, while a 'war veteran' whose only task was to intimidate the opposition, received Z$ 5 million a month (=USD 20); see International Crisis Group (2007), Zimbabwe: A Regional Solution?, Africa Report No. 132, 18.09.2007.:8.

518 See the rather personal but still impressive account of the farm invasions and expulsions by Godwin, Peter (2006), When the crocodile eats the sun.

Table 11.1.:Macro-Economic and Social Indicators for Zimbabwe's Decline 2000-2007

	2000	2003	2005	2006	2007
GDP growth (%)	- 7.3	-10.4	-5.3	-4.8	-6.2
GDP at factor costs (at 2000 prices) (in USD million)	7,456	6,029	5,490	5,226	4,905
Budget Deficit (in % of GDP)	-18.6	-0.2	-6.0	-7-3	-24.6
Trade Balance (in USD mill.)	+315	-108	-392	-49	+6
Current Account Balance (in USD mill.)	+33	-308	-511	-219	-139
Agricultural Production Index (1999-2001 = 100)	106.6	78.0	73.7	73.3	n/a
Manufacturing Production Index (2000 = 100)	100	71.2	62.6	64.1	n/a
Total Debt (in USD mill.)	2,774	3,588	3,258	3,452	n/a
Inflation (%)	55.9	365.0	313.3	1016.7	6723.7
Illiteracy (in%)	11.3	9.4	8.1	7.8	7.2
Life expectancy (in years)	42.7	40.7	42.1	42.8	43.5
Daily Calorie supply	2054	2006	1978	n/a	n/a

Source: AfDB 2008 (2)

The political opposition was systematically targeted by the regime's oppressive arsenal. Opposition supporters were sent for re-education exercises into (concentration) camps, others were attacked or even killed. The leadership of the opposition was prosecuted for alleged treason (and never convicted) and on several occasions, physically attacked and mistreated by the police despite the fact that they were elected Members of Parliament. The pictures of a severely beaten MDC leader *Morgan Tsvangirai* in 2007 caused an outcry around the world and also shocked some of the African leaders out of their silent tolerance for *Mugabe*. Until then, SADC and African leaders had played down the internal oppression and *Mugabe's* contempt for human rights as an internal affair:

- The obviously rigged elections in 2002 (for Presidency) and 2005 (for Parliament) which ended in clear victories for *Mugabe* and ZANU-PF, were hardly criticized by *Mugabe's* South African protector *Thabo Mbeki* ([519]). Only the observer mission of the SADC Parliamentary

519 The South African observer team in the 2002 elections concluded that "the poll was legitimate", which was supported by the ANC, who said that "the will of the people of Zimbabwe has prevailed"; see EISA compilation of reactions to the Presidential

Forum condemned the 2005 elections; international election observers were not allowed into the country.

- A new media law made it extremely difficult for non-governmental newspapers to continue their work; either because they were refused a license ([520]) or were sued for libel.
- The right of assembly was severely limited by the authorities using an unchanged law from colonial times.
- The reckless campaign against urban squatters and the informal sector in 2005 (“*Murambatsvina”*) in the direct aftermath of the 2005 elections in an attempt to prevent a feared civil uprising in the urban areas, cost ca. 700,000 Zimbabweans their homes or livelihoods ([521]). While condemned by critics such as Archbishop *Desmond Tutu*, most SADC leaders kept quiet.
- The economically insane ‘operation *Dzikisa Mitengo*’ (“Reduce Prices”) in 2007, was an attempt to force the business sector to halve their prices regardless of their production or importation costs. This campaign, which led to the arrest of about 8,500 shop owners and business executives (including foreign managers), was mainly aimed at weakening *Mugabe's* rival, former army general, *Solomon Mujuru* ([522]).

11.2. SADC's Response

In full view of what was happening in Zimbabwe and being affected by the economic meltdown, social crisis and political turmoil, SADC leaders under the tutelage of South Africa's former President *Thabo Mbeki*, kept conspicuously mild on Mugabe and called their policy of non-interference ‘quiet diplomacy’. Under the pretext of respecting the → ***national sovereignty*** of Zimbabwe, they refused for a long time to criticize the Zimbabwean President or even consider using economic pressure to enforce reforms in Zimbabwe. As already pointed

---

elections in Zimbabwe in 2002; mimeo. Regarding the 2005 Parliamentary Elections, the South African delegation said the poll was “free, credible and reflected the will of the people of Zimbabwe”, while the SADC Observer Mission, led by the later Vice-President of South Africa and then Minister of Energy and Minerals, *Phumzile Mlambo Ngcuka*, even went so far as to say, "We are saying that this election was free”. See: Daily News (Zimbabwe), 03.03.2005.

520 The Daily News e.g. had severe problems in 2003 to get the renewal of their license to operate; see: MISA press release, 24.09.2003.

521 See: International Crisis Group (2005) Operation *Murambatsvina*. The Tipping Point. Africa Report No 97, 17.05.2005

522 See: International Crisis Group (2007):3

out above, SADC endorsed the flawed elections in 2000, 2002 and 2005; in 2005, the SADC leaders did not insist on the application of the by then already officially adopted SADC election code.

SADC either kept silent or engaged *Mugabe* in clandestine talks. South Africa, especially, was unwilling to use its economic leverage to 'convince' *Mugabe* to make political concessions ([523]). By 2005, South Africa was Zimbabwe's main provider of essential support in form of fuel, electricity and credit lines, without which the *Mugabe* regime could not have survived. The support the *Mugabe* regime received first from Libya ('farms for oil'), and later on from China and Angola, rescued Zimbabwe from being expelled from the IMF in 2006 ([524]).

It took until 2007, when international consternation and outrage over the social situation and treatment of the opposition, reached a first climax and the economic impact of the crisis on SADC countries could no longer be ignored, that SADC leaders agreed on a formal process to end the Zimbabwe crisis. In March 2007, an extra-ordinary SADC Summit in *Dar es Salaam*, SADC, called for a South African-led mediation process between *Mugabe's* ZANU-PF and the MDC, and an economic rescue package. *Thabo Mbeki* was appointed negotiator between the two parties. Although the party talks started very slowly and were interrupted before the 2008 elections, they achieved in the end one result important for the further development of the Zimbabwe crisis: the rules and procedures of the SADC Electoral Code ([525]) were to be applied in the Zimbabwe 2008 Elections. That included the regulation to immediately make public the election results at each polling station. This allowed civil society groups and opposition parties to control the official results and prevent outright manipulation as in previous elections ([526]).

The 2008 election result was a shock for Mugabe and his supporters as he not only lost the Presidential Election race against *Tsvangirai* ([527]), but his party ZANU-PF also secured just 99 against the 110 seats of the combined MDC-factions in the Parliamentary elections. However, the late announcement of the results through the Zimbabwean Electoral Commission, gave *Mugabe* time to

523 See: International Crisis Group (2007),:12

524 See: http://news.bbc.co.uk/2/hi/business/4790332.stm

525 Officially called, "Principles for Election Management, Monitoring and Observation in the SADC-region".

526 See: EISA (2008): Interim Statement. EISA Regional Election Observer Mission. The 2008 Harmonized Elections in Zimbabwe. Harare, 31.03.2008. http://aceproject.org/regions-en/eisa/ZW/reports/EISA%20EOM%20Zim%20-%20Interim%20Statement%2031%2003%202008%20(2).pdf

527 Tsvangirai won 47.9% of the vote against Mugabes 43.2%; see: International Crisis Group: http://www.crisisgroup.org/home/index.cfm?id=1233&l=1

regroup and prepare for the constitutionally demanded Presidential run-off Election ([528]). With the help of the security forces and party militias, ZANU-PF run a massive voter intimidation campaign directed against journalists, MDC-officials, polling agents, teachers, doctors and people who had voted for MDC, which cost already in the first weeks, 43 lives and displaced thousands who fled the violence ([529]).

After the election in March 2008, President *Thabo Mbeki* continued to shield *Mugabe* and refused at first to put any pressure on the Zimbabwean authorities to release the election results. He tried to talk *Mugabe* in private meetings into conducting non-violent run-off elections, but this did not bear any fruit ([530]). In the end, *Tsvangirai* pulled out of the contest saying that under these circumstances, no fair elections could take place. *Mugabe* eventually stood as the sole candidate and declared himself President after the elections on 27.06.2008 ([531]).

None of the international observer missions endorsed the elections. The SADC Observer Mission stated that:

> *"The pre-election phase was characterised by politically motivated violence, intimidation, and displacements. ... the Mission is of the view that the prevailing environment impinged on the credibility of the electoral process. The elections did not represent the will of the people of Zimbabwe." ([532])*

In the light of the obvious stark violations of the SADC Electoral Code and the violence committed, the AU adopted (immediately) a resolution calling for a Unity Government ([533]), which was followed by a similar call from SADC. At the SADC Summit in August 2008 in Johannesburg, negotiations for a Unity Government were set in motion as Mugabe finally understood that he would not be recognised even by his peers in SADC. Despite signing a power-sharing deal

---

528 The Zimbabwean Constitution calls for a run-off election within 21 days after the announcement of the initial result in case none of the Presidential candidates won an absolute majority. However, the Mugabe regime issued an emergency law giving it 90 days to organise the run-off election; see International Crisis Group (2008b), Negotiating Zimbabwe's Transition. Africa Briefing No 51, 21.05.2008:5

529 ibid:6

530 See: International Crisis Group (2008b):8f. According to the report, one of the major obstacles in the mediation and negotiation processes facilitated by *Mbeki*, was his strong dislike of *Tsvangirai*.

531 See: EISA (2008): Zimbabwe: 2008 Presidential run-off. Statement 14.07.2008

532 Quoted from EISA (2008)

533 See: http://www.newser.com/story/31392/african-union-pushes-unity-government-in-zimbabwe.html

in September 2008, negotiations about forming a Unity Government made no real progress because Mugabe did not want to relinquish his grip on the security forces and *Tsvangirai* was reluctant to become a Prime Minister without real power. ZANU-PF's internal resistance against the power-sharing deal ([534]) complicated things even further. It took two more extra-ordinary SADC Summits in November 2008 in Johannesburg, and January 2009 in Pretoria, to finally 'convince' *Mugabe* and *Tsvangirai* to form the Government of National Unity SADC and AU leaders were advocating for. Under this agreement, *Mugabe* remained President while *Tsvangirai* took the newly created position of Prime Minister. Ministerial posts went more or less in equal numbers to MDC and ZANU-PF but the latter kept control of the security apparatus. On February 10, 2009, *Mugabe* swore in *Tsvangirai* as the new Prime Minister of Zimbabwe.

It is much too early to assess the new SADC-enforced unity government approach in Zimbabwe, but some problems are already evident:

- Unclear topical responsibilities between MDC and ZANU-PF run ministries and institutions (e.g. financial reform policies or energy policy).
- Ongoing prosecutions of MDC representatives despite them being elected to Parliament or even proposed for a ministerial portfolio (e.g. *Roy Bennet*) ([535]).
- Lacking controls of ZANU-PF-led security forces and militias.
- Fresh farm invasions by ZANU-PF militants as a way to undermine the authority and credibility of the MDC ministers.

In November 2009, *Tsvangirai* and his ministers briefly boycotted cabinet meetings and threatened to let the Government collapse if *Mugabe* would not stop the prosecution of members of MDC and agree to a new arrangement regarding the authority over financial matters. In an emergency meeting of SADC in Swaziland the crisis was – for the time being – put to rest and *Tsvangirai* commenced cooperation again; it remained unclear, however, how long the new arrangement will last as *Mugabe* still tend to rule arbitrarily and make decisions on the base of short-term political interests.

It has been the pressure SADC eventually put on *Mugabe* and *Tsvangirai*, which led to the first real attempt to solve the crisis in Zimbabwe. However, it took SADC more than seven years to develop a joint constructive position, which

---

534 See: Africa Confidential N0.21 (2008), Vol. 49, 17.10.2008:4 , which reports that a strong faction of ZANU-PF was unhappy about handing over the ministries and Governorships to MDC representatives. Mugabe also tried to use this for weakening his internal rival, *Solomon Mujuru*.

535 See: Daily Monitor (Addis Abeba), 15.10.2009; 16.10.2009; 14.11.2009; 16.11.2009

was taking, at least to some degree, account of the political and economic realities in Zimbabwe. This had several reasons:

- As long as *Thabo Mbeki* was President of South Africa, *Mugabe* was shielded if not protected from open criticism and pressure. The reasons for *Mbeki's* soft stand on Zimbabwe and *Mugabe*, have been widely discussed, but have not yet been satisfactorily explained ([536]). Only when *Mbeki* was 'toppled' as ANC, and subsequently as South African President in 2008, things started to move regarding Zimbabwe. The interim South African President, *Kgalema Motlanthe* is credited with reaching the final compromise.
- Since 2004/5, a new generation of leaders emerged in Southern Africa, which were less impressed by *Mugabe's* liberation movement credentials and rhetorics than fellow liberation-fighter-Presidents (such as *Chissano, dos Santos, Nujoma, Mbeki*) or had a personal history with Mugabe (such as *Chiluba, Muluzi/wa Mutharika, Mogae, Makapa*). The late Zambian President *Levy Mwanawasa*, the new President of Botswana, *Ian Khama*, and the Tanzanian President *Kikwete* were especially more critical of *Mugabe* than the old guard and pushed apparently for a solution for the crisis in Zimbabwe.
- The socio-economic situation in Zimbabwe has completely spilled out of control since 2007, with inflation rates only comparable to those of Germany in 1923, a collapse of the healthcare system and more than 3,600 victims of a Cholera-outbreak, constant food shortages and piling un-serviced external debts. It was no longer possible for SADC leaders to ignore the humanitarian catastrophe as also the international community "re-discovered" the crisis in Zimbabwe.
- The non-stop flood of refugees from Zimbabwe caused in 2008 in South Africa, xenophobic attacks on foreigners from other African countries. This particularly damaged South Africa's international reputation, and probably reinforced the critical faction's stance in the South African leadership on how to deal with the crisis in Zimbabwe more decisively.
- The results of the 2008 elections showed that *Mugabe* and ZANU-PF no longer had a majority in Zimbabwe – not even by using intimidation tactics and the full arsenal of state resources. The terror campaign against the opposition after the 2008 elections damaged the last goodwill *Mugabe* had from other SADC leaders. It also put Zimbabwe high on the agenda of the AU.

---

536 See for example: Peters-Berries, C. (2002); International Crisis Group (2008b);

- *Mugabe's* increasingly unpredictable, arrogant and reckless behaviour against his own people cost him much of his reputation as the African leader who stood up against western Governments. He was seen more and more, as a ruthless, self-centred dictator who threw lavish birthday parties when his people were dying of hunger and diseases.

11.3. Conclusion

The Zimbabwe crisis highlighted some of the structural weaknesses of SADC:

- Its inability to react to a politically caused crisis, which threatened to take on a damaging socio-economic dimension when there was still time to salvage the situation.
- The slowness to reach a common position, which was critical, of one of its member, states, because of the absence of a suitable mechanism and insufficient resources to enforce such a position.
- The strong influence of personalities in the decision-making process in SADC which revealed the lack of democratic mechanisms and procedures to reach rational policy decisions. The positions promulgated by leaders are not rational or are based on personal feelings rather than political reasons. *Mbeki* appears to have been the main obstacle to achieve progress in dealing with Zimbabwe, because of his affinity to *Mugabe*.
- The absence of clear-cut principles on how to deal with a deviant member state such as Zimbabwe. SADC leaders never even considered economic and political sanctions against Zimbabwe, unlike e.g. ECOWAS, which suspended member states such as Mauritania and Guinea after unconstitutional changes of Government occurred ([537]).
- The apparent disrespect for civil society by political leaders, who have been socialized in an autocratic political culture enabling them to ignore the suffering of an entire nation and have sympathy with the leader responsible for the plight of his own people. If SADC would have been less dominated by authoritarian political leaders and more open to

537 It is, however, interesting to note that Madagascar was immediately suspended by SADC after the ousting of President *Ravalomanana* in March 2009.Althotugh the change of power in Madagascar was more flagrant in its violation of the constitution than the gradual erosion of the same in Zimbabwe and SADC felled compelled to react fast, it can be argued that SADC's swift reaction was influenced by its failure to address the Zimbabwean crisis in good time.

influences from organised social and economic interests, the Zimbabwe crisis might have been dealt with in a more constructive manner.

The consequences for SADC from its inapt handling of the Zimbabwe crisis pertain to:

- A severely damaged international public image particularly regarding its credibility as a regional body pursuing good governance and democracy.
- A fragmented internal cohesion, as some member states were supporting *Mugabe* (South Africa, Angola), while others became increasingly critical of him (Botswana and Zambia under *Mwanawasa).*
- A slowed-down economic integration process because of the meltdown of the Zimbabwean economy, the transportation and trade obstructions emanating from it, and the problems of the Zimbabwean administration to implement SADC Protocols on time.
- The socio-economic burden the crisis put on the shoulders of Zimbabwe's immediate neighbours. South Africa and Botswana have to look after probably as many as three million refugees from Zimbabwe; Zambia and Malawi experienced delays with regard to transit trade; South Africa, Mozambique, Zambia and the DRC are owed substantial amounts of money by Zimbabwe for electricity, food and fuel imports. The impact on investments into the transportation and energy infrastructure has not yet been assessed.
- The damage to SADC institutions and Protocols. The disregard of the verdict of the SADC Tribunal regarding the land expropriations by Zimbabwe, has given one of the most important institutions for safeguarding further regional integration process, a bad start. The implementation of any policy on the free movement of people within SADC will probably be postponed for a number of years after the traumatic experiences with the attacks on fellow Africans in South Africa in 2008.

The Zimbabwe crisis nearly became a SADC crisis. Only the change of leadership in SADC's leading power South Africa and the danger of a total humanitarian catastrophe, spurred SADC into eventually decisive action. SADC lacked, most of the time, the political will to intervene when the crisis in Zimbabwe unfolded. Perhaps the first, but then quite an important contribution of SADC towards addressing the Zimbabwe crisis, was the negotiated agreement to apply the SADC electoral code which called for a publication of election results outside each polling station and thus allowed for the electoral defeat of Mugabe and his party.

Chapter 12: SADC in Comparison

12.1. SADC Compared with Other African Attempts at Regional Integration

The timetable of the AU for the creation of an African Economic Community (AEC) foresees the creation of a continent-wide customs union by 2019, an African Common Market by 2023, and a continent-wide economic and monetary union by 2028 ([538]). At a first glance there seems to be sufficient time to achieve these objectives as most RECs are progressing on the course of establishing customs unions or even common markets. However, previous experiences with regional integration timetables, both in Africa and internationally, call for caution. How realistic these plans are, can be best assessed when looking at the main building blocs for the AEC and how far they have achieved a consolidated stage of RI.

It has been argued earlier ([539]) that of the eight RECs officially recognized by the AU, only four – namely COMESA, EAC, ECOWAS, and SADC – have made sufficiently strong progress to have a chance of complying with the AU's plans for a united African continent. Other recognized RECs such ECCAS, IGAD, AMU and CEN-SAD, are seen as lagging further behind. In the following, the more successful four RECs will thus be compared with regard to their

- structural economic potential for a deepening of a trade-led RI process;
- intra-regional trade levels;
- infrastructural base for further RI
- progress on achieving macroeconomic convergence
- progress on achieving democratic convergence.

12.1.1. Comparative Assessments of Regional Integration in Africa

As a first step, however, two attempts to assess regional integration in various RECs in Africa will be reviewed to provide a background for further appraisal.

538 See: ECA/AU (2008a):28f

539 See: Chapter 7

So far there have been two major attempts to assess the state of RI in Africa. The first one was a study by German scholars ([540]) which focused only on EAC, ECOWAS and SADC. The second assessment was conducted by the ECA ([541]) and looked at all RECs in Africa. However, both assessments are a bit outdated using figures and information from the late 1990s.

The first comparative assessment by *Mair* and *Peters-Berries* focused on the one hand on structural indicators and on the other hand on goal attainment (shaded in grey in table 12.1.). The study ranked the three RECs based on a comprehensive analysis of their development, organisational structure and policy achievements. Regarding both structural indicators and goal attainment, SADC showed on average the best results although ECOWAS had more 'top positions' than SADC (but also more 'last positions'). On average, SADC in 2000 looked the most effective of the three RECs as far as structural integration and achieving its objectives was concerned.

Table 12.1. Comparing Achievements of EAC, ECOWAS and SADC

Criteria/REC/average Score	EAC: 2.2	ECOWAS: 2.1	SADC: 1.8
Efficiency of decision-making bodies	1	3	2
Efficiency of secretariats	2	3	2
Efficiency of conflict management mechanisms	3	1	2
Participation of civil society	2	3	1
Financial independence	3	1	2
Free trade	3	1	2
Free movement of persons	2	1	3
Cross-border investments	2	3	1
Convergence of economic and fiscal policies	1	3	2
Implementation of regional norms	3	1	2
Sector cooperation	2	3	1

Source: Mair/Peters-Berries (2001): 53, 62.

Integration progress in SADC was more even than in ECOWAS and EAC. Especially regarding the structural indicators the inconsistencies in ECOWAS

540 Mair/Peters-Berries (2001)
541 ECA (2004)

and EAC were quite pronounced. While ECOWAS was e.g. rated as the best performer regarding conflict management it held last place as far as involvement of civil society was involved. EAC was regarded as having the most efficient decision-making bodies but being neither efficient in conflict management nor financially independent. It appears that at the time of the assessment both EAC and ECOWAS member states followed the principle to engage in areas of mutual interests and comparative strength; areas of disagreement and/or obvious disputes were put aside. This can in the case of EAC be explained with the relative short time that it had been in existence when the assessment was undertaken; in the case of ECOWAS the continuing disputes between the Anglophone and the Francophone member states as well as the unresolved crises in Sierra Leone and Liberia at the time of the assessment might have contributed to the concentration on issues such as conflict management rather than organizational efficiency.

The second assessment of the process of RI in Africa was conducted in 2003 by ECA and looked at the RI efforts in general. It came to rather sobering results. The report warned in general against too much optimism as far as RI in Africa is concerned as there are:

> *"... overall substantial gaps between goals and achievements of most RECs, particularly in greater internal trade, macro economic convergence, production, and physical connectivity."* ([542])...

and

> *"Regional integration efforts in Africa, though moving in the right direction and broadly based, are sorely inadequate".* ([543])

In detail, the report noted *inter alia* that ([544]):

- The political will for RI has not been adequately translated into action.
- The regional institutional architecture in general, is weak.
- The integration agenda is too wide in scope and in need of a review.
- An impact of trade and market integration has yet to be seen.
- Private sector involvement in integration is recognized, but still very limited.
- Self-financing is still a long way from being achieved, while donor dependency is on the rise.

542 ECA (2004):1

543 ibid:71

544 ibid: 57ff

- The continental as well as regional infrastructure still has missing links due to a lack of investment resources.
- Labor mobility is still limited.
- The manufacturing sector shows little signs of cooperation as the private sector lags behind.
- Crosscutting issues such as peace & security are a major concern, or as in health and gender, not fully mainstreamed.

Table 12.2.: Integration Ranking of the Eight AEC Building Blocs by Sector

REC	Intra-regional exports	Intra-regional imports	Intra-regional manufactures exports	Transport integration (*)	Cellular telephone integr. (²)	Internet integration (³)	Integra-tion Indices
AMU	5	5	3	4	3	2	8
CEN-SAD	3	3	2	n/a	5	3	4
COMESA	4	4	4	2	2	4	6
EAC	6	7	6	1	7	5	7
ECCAS	8	8	8	6	4	8	3
ECOWAS	2	2	5	5	6	6	2
IGAD	7	6	7	5	8	7	5
SADC	1	1	1	3	1	1	1
Year/ period	1994-2000			2000	2001	2001	1999

Explanations: * = percentage of missing intra-regional highway network
² = users per 100 people
³ = users per 10,000 people

Source: ECA (2004):94, 96, 135,149f, 230; own compilation

With regard to the eight RECs which are supposed to be the building blocs for the AEC the ECA assessment noted ([545]) (see also Table 12.2.):

- SADC showed the highest percentage of intra-regional exports and imports (for the period1994-99), followed by ECOWAS. EAC ranked 7th out of 13 RECs.
- SADC had by far, the highest exports of manufactured goods of all African RECs between 1994 and 1999. ECOWAS ranked 5th and EAC ranked 6th.

545 ibid: 94ff

- ECOWAS and EAC were rated best as far as tariff reductions were concerned. The SADC FTA was at the date of assessment, not yet implemented.
- ECOWAS was commended on its progress towards liberalizing the movement of people and vehicles.
- SADC and EAC were pointed out as having advanced their regional infrastructure.
- ECOWAS and SADC were commended on their contribution to achieve peace and stability in their regions.

In total, the ECA report arrives at a similar overall result as the previous study: SADC is regarded as the best performer amongst the African RECs, although it was at the time of the assessment still far from achieving all its objectives.

12.1.2. Comparing Macro-Economic Convergence in COMESA, EAC, ECOWAS and SADC

Attempting to assess how SADC has developed viz-a-viz to COMESA, ECOWAS and EAC during the first decade of the new millennium, first the basic economic indicators (see table 12.3.) of these RECs are compared. Then the changes in important structural economic pre-conditions for RI – such as the sectoral composition of the GDP (see table 12.4.), the macro-economic convergence (see table 12.5.) and development of intra-regional trade (see table 12.6.) – are compared which includes also an assessment of the availability of the physical preconditions for RI such as intra-regional transport and energy links. In a final step also the democratic convergence of the four regions are compared as far as the available data allows (see table 12.7.)

The comparison of the basic economic indicators show that although EAC is in terms of membership (five countries), population size and GDP, much smaller than the other three, it grew at similar rates, and had a comparable debt burden and inflation rates. However, when it comes to absolute figures regarding FDI and ODA, EAC countries received less than the bigger regional bodies. ECOWAS received the highest absolute amount of FDI in 2007 and the highest ODA per capita. SADC has the biggest regional economy (thanks to South Africa), the highest per capita income and on average, also the highest FDI inflows but also the highest regional debt burden and inflation rates. COMESA is the biggest REC in terms of population, shows the highest absolute amounts of ODA and has the lowest debt bruden but also the lowest economic growth rates, average FDI per country and ODA per head.

The degree of external dependency – measured in absolute and per capita aid flows – is highest in COMESA and ECOWAS, followed by EAC. The debt burden appears to be still rather high in SADC, ECOWAS and EAC; since 2006 and 2007 most African countries have received massive debt relief under the HIPC Initiative. In general terms, however, all four RECs must be regarded as externally dependent.

It has been argued before that the sectoral composition of a country's economy influences if not determines the degree of its ability to integrate regionally. The higher the share of manufacturing with regard to the GDP the higher the possible degree of complementarity of that economy in the regional context. The opposite holds true for agriculture and mineral production: the higher their shares to the GDP the lower the ability to increase intra-regional trade and investments. The same concept can be used to compare the economic integration potential of different RI organizations. RI schemes with high and growing shares of manufacturing of GDP are better positioned than those with dominant primary (agriculture and mineral production) sectors.

Table 12.3.Comparing COMESA, EAC, ECOWAS and SADC: Macro-Economics

	COMESA			EAC			ECOWAS			SADC		
	2002	**2005**	**2006**	**2002**	**2005**	**2007**	**2002**	**2005**	**2007**	**2002**	**2005**	**2007**
GDP *(USD bill.)*	188.6	238.0	347.9	27.5	36.5	41.1	85.5	98.9	108.1	162.6	234.3	267.3
GDP per capita *(USD)*	500.0	595.5	827.5	296.3	314.4	323.1	379.7	368.5	382.7	783.6	1,008.2	1,039.3
Average GDP growth rate*	1.9	4.0	5.0	4.7	6.5	6.3	3.7	4.8	4.7	4.4	4.5	7.0
Population *(in million)*	372.0	399.6	420.4	*92.8*	*116.1*	130.8	225.2	268.4	282,5	207.5	232.4	257,4
Inflation Rate (%)*	6.3**	9.3**	9.0**	0.6	5.3	7.9	7.5	8.5	6.0	27.8**	26.9**	8.3**
FDI *(USD bill.)*	0.6	2.6	2.9	0.5	1.0	1.8	2.8	4.7	15.1	3.4	7.3	9.9
Average FDI per country *(USD mill.)*	32	137	153	101	197	353	190	311	1,010	225	485	661
External Debt *(USD bill.)*	8.1	8.2	9.8	16.2	18.9	15.6	61.3	68.5	47.3	64.6	50.2	117.2
ODA *(USD bill.)*	7.7	13.0	13.9	3.2[2]	4.4[2]	6.9[2]	4.9	11.8	9,1	7.6	9.0	10.4
ODA per cap. *(USD*	20.1	32.0	33.2	24.4[2]	26.7[2]	53.0[2]	22.3	43.6	60.9	31.4	36.6	38.1

* = for 2001 [2] = including Burundi and Rwanda ** = without Zimbabwe

Source: ECA (2008a),(2009b), AfDB (2008b)

Table 12.4.: Sectoral Composition of Regional Economies

Region	Sector	2003	2004	2005	2006	2007
North Africa	Industry	32.0	33.9	35.4	34.1	33.3
	Manufacturing	*12.3*	*12.0*	*11.6*	*12.2*	*12.7*
	Agriculture	20.4	19.2	17.6	17.3	16.1
	Services	47.6	46.9	47.1	48.7	50.6
West Africa	Industry	21.6	22.0	22.8	25.6	26.2
	Manufacturing	*8.5*	*8.7*	*8.7*	*7.9*	*7.5*
	Agriculture	36.5	34.8	35.0	31.0	30.7
	Services	41.9	43.3	42.1	43.4	43.1
Central Africa	Industry	45.4	50.6	54.0	54.7	50.0
	Manufacturing	*8.8*	*8.0*	*7.8*	*8.0*	*9.2*
	Agriculture	21.7	19.4	18.1	18.0	18.7
	Services	32.8	30.0	27.9	27.3	31.3
East Africa	Industry	18.3	18.8	18.3	18.2	18.9
	Manufacturing	*8.5*	*8.6*	*8.3*	*8.0*	*8.4*
	Agriculture	31.6	31.4	31.7	30.5	27.5
	Services	50.1	49.8	49.6	50.8	53.2
Southern Africa	Industry	35.6	33.6	36.4	38.1	38.8
	Manufacturing	*16.2*	*15.8*	*15.3*	*15.8*	*15.9*
	Agriculture	14.9	14.6	14.3	13.8	13.5
	Services	49.6	49.9	49.3	48.1	47.7
Africa in total	Industry	28.1	29.2	30.1	31.8	32.0
	Manufacturing	*10.7*	*10.6*	*10.3*	*10.4*	*10.7*
	Agriculture	26.7	25.6	25.3	23.3	22.0
	Services	45.2	45.2	44.6	44.8	45.9

Explanation: using simple averages; the share of manufacturing industry is expressed in % of total value added but forms part of the contribution of industry.
Source: ECA (2008a:73)

Although table 12.4. does not show the sectoral composition of GDP as per REC but only per region it still provides an idea of which REC has the strongest manufacturing sector and is thus best placed for trade-led RI. Southern Africa, which includes most of the SADC member states has the strongest manufacturing sector followed by North Africa (AMU). Central (ECCAS), East (EAC; IGAD) and West Africa (ECOWAS) have on average just above half of the manufacturing sector than Southern Africa. COMESA, which includes countries from Southern, Eastern and Northern Africa, however cannot be aligned to one region only. However, as South Africa is not a member of COMESA and contributes strongly to the relatively high percentage of manufacturing in Southern Africa, it can be assumed that COMESA has similar ratios in this respect as the EAC.

SADC has with regard to manufacturing industries the best prerequisites for deeper RI amongst the AU-acknowledged African RECs.

Map 12.1.: Electricity Grids in Various African RECs

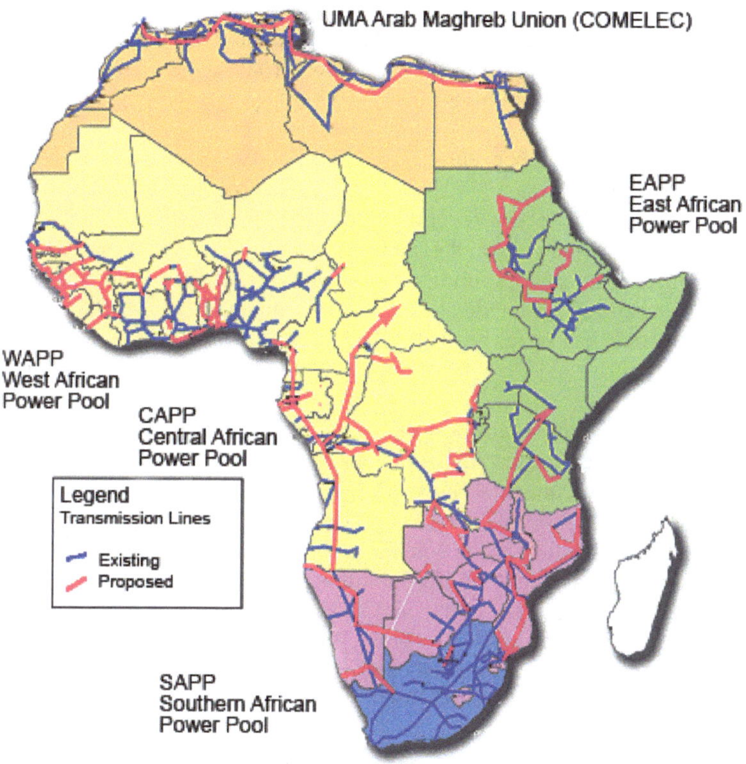

Source: D. Tenzer (2010) based on Costa, R. (2009), slide13

The energy links within the four main RECs in Africa appear to be best developed in SADC followed by the EAC (see map 12.1.). In West Africa three so far not interconnected energy supply systems exist. If the planned energy links materialize in Southern and Eastern Africa COMESA will also have some degree of interlinkage in terms of energy at least in its Southern half. But until then no interlinked network exists as there are gaps between its Southern and

East African members, as well as between the East African states and the North African section. SADC has by far the best prerequisites for deeper RI with regard to energy amongst the four assessed RECs. When the planned extensions both in energy generation and distribution are realized Southern Africa has an energy supply network that allows for investments in almost all countries irrespective of their geographic location – energy will be available. From an energy point of view SADC is already well integrated.

In the transport sector SADC is also better integrated compared to the EAC and ECOWAS. COMESA benefits from the various road and rail links SADC and its predecessor SADCC built for its southern part. The northern part of COMESA, however, starting with the Sudan is still very much disconnected from the rest of the member states. The road systems are so far developed to some extent in West Africa and in Southern Africa (see Map 12.2.). In Southern Africa the network of tarred secondary roads is quite extensive and provides additional links between most the member states while in West Africa such roads are much scarcer. The tightest bottlenecks in African road links exist in East and Central Africa, which affects predominantly COMESA. The road system in the EAC has so far not yet linked Burundi and Rwanda to their bigger neighbors.

Train links in Africa are again best developed in Southern Africa. As shown in chapter 10.2.1. all countries in SADC on the continent except Malawi and Angola are currently connected by working railway systems. The rehabilitation of rail links from Angola to Zambia and Namibia is under way. Malawi is also pushing for a reconnection to the *Nacala* harbor in Mozambique. In East Africa, the existing railway systems are not including the new ECA members Rwanda and Burundi; Tanzania is not connected to Kenya or Uganda and existing lines are working mostly rather ineffectively. In West Africa, the existing railways are mostly national systems which are not interlinked. COMESA is negatively affected by the missing north-south link in the railway system in the EAC.

SADC has by far the most extensive railway network with some 45,300 km followed by COMESA with 32,500 and ECOWAS (10,200) and EAC (7,600) ([546]).

546 See: ECA (2004):135

Map 12.2. The African Road Network

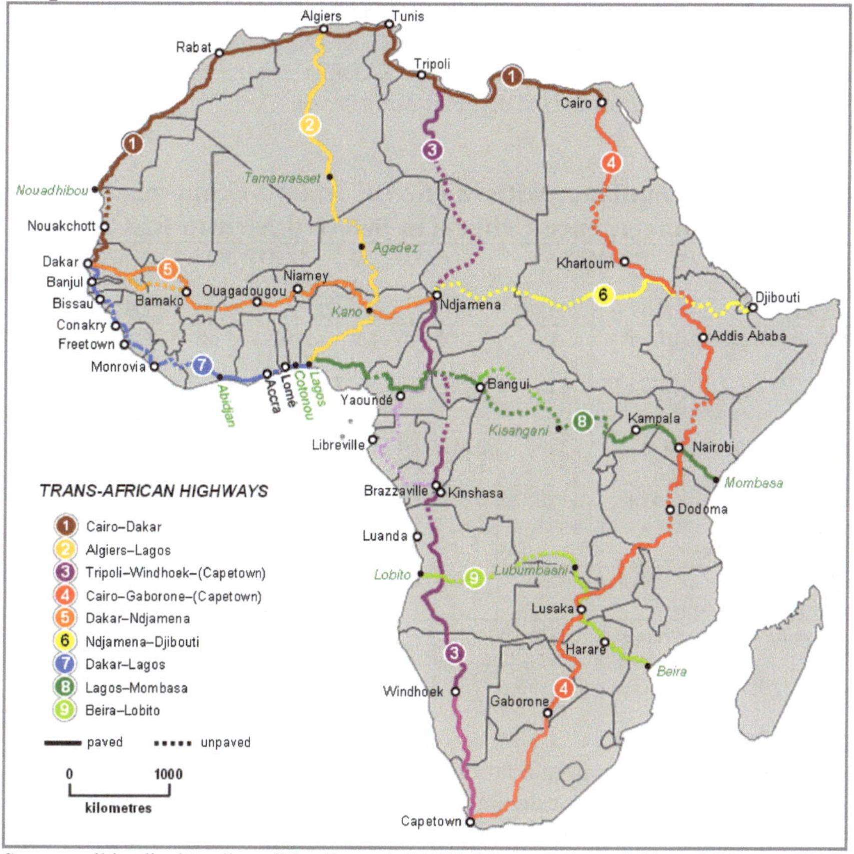

Source: wikipedia; http://en.wikipedia.org/wiki/File:Map_of_Trans-African_Highways.PNG (accessed 10.02.2010)

It can be concluded that SADC has the most regionally integrated transport system compared to COMESA, EAC and ECOWAS. The physical prerequisites for deeper regional integration are thus available in SADC while the other RECs usually lack sufficiently interconnected regional infrastructure systems.

When comparing the levels of macroeconomic convergence of the four RECs (using the criteria established by SADC [[547]]) as the next indicator for measuring the degree of preparedness for further RI, SADC is only the second best performer after the EAC (see table 12.5.). SADC's results, however, are being diluted by two bad performers (DRC and Zimbabwe).

Table 12.5: Compliance with the SADC Macro-Economic Convergence Criteria in Selected African RECs

Economic Criteria	COMESA		EAC		ECOWAS		SADC	
YEAR	2005	2007	2005	2007	2005	2007	2005	2007
Inflation Rate (< 10%)	10 of 18	13 of 18	3 of 5	5 of 5	11 of 15	14 of 15	8 of 14	11 of 14
Budget Deficit (<5 % of GDP)	12 of 18*	13 of 18	5 of 5*	5 of 5	11 of 15*	12 of 15	12 of 14	12 of 14
Debt (< 60 % of GDP)	6 of 18+	13 of 18	2 of 5+	4 of 5	4 of 15+	9 of 15	6 of 14+	13 of 14
Current Acc. Target (<-9% of GDP)	14 of 18+	11 of 18	4 of 5+	4 of 5	11 of 15+	11 of 15	11 of 14+	12 of 14
Goal Attainment (in%)	**58.6**	**69.4**	**70.0**	**90.0**	**61.6**	**76.7**	**66.1**	**85.7**

Explanations: * = average for 2000-2005
+ = average for 1997-2006
Source: AfDB (2008); own calculations

The development of intra-regional trade regarding the four RECs is difficult to compare as the data for the calculations of intra-regional trade appears not to be consistent even when the same source (ECA) is used. However, it is evident that intra-regional trade has picked up both in the EAC and in SADC while it decreased in COMESA and ECOWAS. The percentage of trade within the respective REC is not very high even for the better performers. Only the import figures for SADC for the period between 2000 and 2005 reached a level comparable to that of other successful RECs such as the EU, Mercosur or ASEAN. In general, the intra-regional trade volumes of RECs in Africa are below a level which makes trade a driving factor behind integration. SADC – due to South Africa's special role of a regional supplier of consumer and capital goods – shows overall the best trade figures of the four RECs compared although the data base is not satisfactory.

547 The SADC criteria and indicators for macroeconomic convergence are the most comprehensive of all RECs in Africa and can easily be verified through international data handbooks.

Table 12.6: The Development of Intra-Regional Trade in Selected African RECs

REC	2000-2005		1996-2006	2006	Trend
	Imports	Exports			
COMESA	11.1	8.7	9.1	4.2	-
EAC	18.7	12.6	9.1	14.3	+
ECOWAS	15.8	13.9	11.8	8.3	-
SADC	33.1	19.9	8.7	9.1	+

Source: ECA (2009a):80; ECA (2008a):35

Comparing the four RECs as far as attainment of democracy and good governance is concerned proves more difficult because there are no universally agreed indicators for democratic development as such. A pragmatic approach is to compare the achievements of the four RECs through the same indices which were used to determine the democratic convergence within SADC ([548]):

- The HDI of UNDP
- The CPI of *Transparency International*
- The BTI of the *Bertelsmann Foundation*; and
- The Freedom House Index
- The Mo Ibrahim Index

Table 12.7. indicates the latest values available for the five indices; for each index the years for which the figures are valid are shown.

Table 12.7.: The Development of Political Convergence in Selected RECs

	HDI		CPI		BTI		FH		MII		Trend
Year	2005	2007	2005	2009	2008	2010	2005	2009	2005	2007	
COMESA	0.527	0.531	2.7	2.9	0.45	0.45	4.8	4.8	47.5	49.5	+
EAC	0.472	0.469	2.6	2.5	0.53	0.52	4.3	4.3	50.3	52.6	-
ECOWAS	0.402	0.458	2.7	2.9	0.52	0.52	3.6	3.5	49.9	51.2	+
SADC	0.536 *	0.566 *	3.3	3.4	0.59	0.56	3.6	3.6	56.2	57.7	+

*Explanations:*_* without Seychelles

Sources: UNDP, Transparency International, Bertelsmann Stiftung, Freedom House, Mo Ibrahim Foundation: various years

548 See: Chapter 10.2.5.

Comparing the values of the indices measuring aspects of democracy and good governance compiled in table 12.7., SADC shows the best results of the four RECs. It not only has the highest average level of human development but is also less corrupt and at the same time has better results for good governance and transformation towards democracy. ECOWAS and EAC are more or less on an equal level of achievement while COMESA is worst performer of the four RECs on the path to more democracy and democratic convergence.

If one compares the development trends of the four RECs regarding the five indices COMESA, ECOWAS and SADC are showing a positive development with the majority of the index values improving; only the values for the EAC are deteriorating slightly.

However, none of the RECs has yet reached levels of democracy and good governance comparable to those in Europe or Latin America. In fact, the values of the indices reached by the four RECs put all of them in the category of countries in various stages of transition to democracy; none of the four RECs can be regarded as having achieved a stable and sustainable level of democracy and good governance yet. The 'lead countries' in each of the four RECs in terms of democracy and good governance are often either small and politically less important countries such as Mauritius and Botswana (SADC), Cape Verdes and Ghana (ECOWAS), and Mauritius and Seychelles (COMESA). Only in the case of EAC is the best performer also one of the lead countries in economic terms. In the other RECs such lead countries show declining levels of democracy and good governance like South Africa (SADC) or Kenya (EAC and COMESA), only Nigeria remains more or less on the same level of democratic development (not yet taking into account the developments since the last elections in 2008).

While democratic convergence is far from being achieved in SADC (see also chapter 10.2.5.) it still has achieved on average a higher degree of democratic governance than the other RECs examined. With regard to pursuing a

In conclusion, it can be stated that SADC has the best performance over the last decade with regards to achieve deeper RI. It has the potential of becoming a real building bloc for the AEC. However, taking into account the delays and deviations the SADC integration process has taken because of the Zimbabwe crisis, the expansion and difficult negotiations to balance costs and benefits of the trade integration approach, the dispute of the EPAs, it appears that RI in SADC has not achieved the depth, which could have been possible.

12.2. SADC Compared with the EU

The EU is always cited as the model when the possibilities of RI are discussed. However, it is rather daring and misleading to compare RI in SADC with that of the EU. The EU did not only have historically and structurally much better preconditions for RI, but it also gained a lot of momentum through its sheer size.

Table 12.8. Comparing the EU with SADC

REC	Regional Population (in mill.)	Regional GDP (USD billion, market prices; 2006)	Per Capita Income (PPP in USD; 2008 est.)	Literacy rates (2007; % of population)	Life expectancy (2008; in years)
EU 27 member states	497 (in 2007)	14,445	Highest Luxemb.: 85,100 Ireland: 47,800 Lowest Romania: 12,500 Bulgaria: 13,200 Average EU: 33,800	ca. 99% in central Europe; lowest Malta: 92.8%	Highest in Sweden: 80.6; lowest in Estonia: 72.3
SADC 14 member states	257.4 (in 2007)	378	Highest: Botswana: 15,800 Mauritius: 12,400 South Africa: 10,400 Lowest Zimbabwe: 200 DRC: 300 Malawi: 800	Highest Zimbabwe: 89.4. Lowest Malawi: 64.1 Angola: 67.2	Highest Mauritius: 72.9. Madagascar: 62.1 South Africa: 42.5 Lowest: Swaziland: 32.2. Angola: 37.6

Sources: own compilations from Internet research

Compared to the EU, SADC has about half the number of member states and population, but only 2.6% of its GDP. The SADC countries with the highest per capita income are on the same level as those with the lowest in the EU. In three countries with the lowest per capita income in SADC in 2008 – Zimbabwe, the DRC and Malawi –, the average per capita income per year was as high as the average per capita income per week in the EU. In addition, education and healthcare systems are considerably better in the EU than in SADC as literacy rates and life expectancy figures indicate.

These few figures illustrate the immense differences between the EU and SADC. In the EU, a huge economy with high incomes and thus, a high demand level exists which is supported by very good educational and health facilities. The overall high demand propels impressive intra-regional trade figures in the EU and contributes to the intensification of regional integration. Although EU newcomers such as Bulgaria and Romania are lagging behind in most aspects, the experience of other countries joining the EU in the last decade shows that EU membership helped their economies grow strong with a positive effect on per capita incomes.

The SADC economy is the biggest regional economy in Africa but has only one real strong economy (South Africa) which, compared to the EU economies, only of medium size (slightly bigger than that of Greece). Demand levels for industrial products in SADC are low due to low per capita income levels and thus stimulate intra-regional trade only in a limited way. While there has been a positive impact on regional growth, stability, connectivity and intra-regional trade from South Africa joining SADC in 1994, the opposite effect occurred when a second group of countries – the DRC, Seychelles and Madagascar – joined. The Seychelles drifted in and out of SADC: leaving it after only seven years and re-joining it after another three years. The DRC is not an active SADC member and has only signed few and ratified even less Protocols, is in arrears with its membership fees and only its southern part is linked by roads and rail to the SADC region. Madagascar was suspended after an unconstitutional change of political power in March 2009 after only two years of membership; as long as the country does not stabilize politically it will not be a contributing and active member of SADC.

The chances that SADC can successfully follow the example of the EU are rather slim; the structural economic differences are too big to allow for a similar socio-economic take-off. However, SADC could learn from the experiences of the EU:

- How to generate a political will for RI;
- how to allow the private sector to play a more active role, and
- which institutional architecture is required for deeper RI.

SADC has to map its own way for further and deeper RI. It should not be overawed by and fixated to the EU model, but should rationally assess which realistic potential and options it has.

Chapter 13: Outlook: Challenges and Prospects for Further Regional Integration in Africa

The analysis of RI attempts in Southern Africa has shown that SADC has made considerable strides but is also confronted by substantial impediments and challenges. SADC's achievements can be summarized as follows:

- SADC has a solid political base rooted in a common history of the main member states.
- The region is relatively well connected in terms of transportation facilities and communication systems.
- Integration progress has been made with regard to trade (establishment of SAFTA), energy connections (SAPP), transportation regulations (drivers license; border posts) and institutionally (Secretariat; Tribunal; election code).
- As compared to other African RECs, SADC is probably the most advanced regional body with the highest potential to become a real building bloc for the AEC.
- After a long political stalemate, SADC eventually broke the deadlock in Zimbabwe and facilitated a solution.

The obstacles and challenges SADC faces pertain to:

- Insufficient economic convergence as far as economic policies is concerned.
- A big regional economic imbalance with one member state (South Africa) accounting for ca. 2/3 of the region's economic strength.
- A limited intra-regional trade potential due to similar rather than complementary production structures.
- The unresolved issue of establishing a balancing mechanism for the inevitably unequal distribution of costs and benefits.
- A dominance of South African companies, products and expertise in the region which contributes to unease about South Africa's role.
- The limited role of the private business sector in promoting RI; instead of being one of the drivers, the private sector is still one of the passengers placed on the auxiliary seat when it comes to RI.
- The persistence of NTTBs, which are not phased out despite the efforts of the Secretariat.
- Insufficient institutional arrangements for fostering RI and enforcing regional decisions; the Secretariat and the Tribunal are not sufficient.

- The absence of any controlling mechanisms for RI from outside Government; civil society plays an insignificant role.
- The inadequate mechanisms to prevent member states from becoming a liability for RI, as in the case of Zimbabwe or in future, the DRC and Madagascar.
- The slowed down process of democratic convergence in SADC as few member states are transforming their autocratic systems into democratic societies.
- The persistence of an autocratic political culture allowing leaders an insufficiently checked political autonomy which impedes rational and goal-oriented decision-making.

Will SADC be able to make further integration progress despite these formidable problems and inadequacies? What is needed for SADC to realize its existing RI potential?

The establishment of SAFTA in August 2008, the breaking of the deadlock over Zimbabwe in January 2009 and the 'fresh faces' amongst the SADC-leaders (Khama, Banda, Kikwete, Tsvangirai, Zuma) might provide the regional body with the vigour and resolve it requires to address the other challenges and weather the economic storm forming at an international level. The Government of National Unity in Zimbabwe might also be the first crucial step of bringing the country back into the support structure of the international community ([549]). If the Zimbabwean economy picks up again, the majority of the refugees currently burdening the neighbouring states will probably return home, the country will once again provide transportation-related services to the region and the remnants of its manufacturing industry will increase the regionally produced industrial output.

SADC needs to take the momentum emanating from the resolution of the Zimbabwe crisis into pushing for further institutional and practical reforms:

- the strengthening of the administrative resources but eventually also executive powers of the Secretariat;
- an agreement on the development of a compensation/balancing mechanism for the countries negatively affected by the implementation of SAFTA and the envisaged customs union; especially the role of

549 By May 2009, Zimbabwe's new Government had secured more than USD 1 Billion in credit lines from SADC countries (South Africa and Botswana) and African lending institutions such as AfDB and the African Import and Export Bank at a time when western Governments are still hesitating to support Zimbabwe's reconstruction efforts; see The Daily Monitor (Addis Abeba), 14.05.2009.

South Africa in the region and in the interest of RI must be clearer defined in terms of obligations and leadership;

- the development of an implementable regional energy policy, ensuring that surplus energy can reach the deficit areas and new resources are being developed taking into account the impact of climate change particularly on the availability of water for hydropower plants;
- the drafting of a regional agenda to defend and promote democracy in order to prevent situations like the Zimbabwe crisis or the current problems in Madagascar;
- the preparation of the establishment of a customs union must be made more transparent allowing interested stakeholders such as labour unions, chambers of commerce and industrial associations to play a bigger role;
- an agreement on how to ensure that SADC decisions are being implemented by the member states and not conveniently ignored like in the case of Zimbabwe's reaction to the Tribunal's ruling; the development of a catalogue of sanctions for violations of SADC rules or rulings might be necessary.

However, the biggest challenge for the near future for SADC is how to deal with the inevitable impact of the current world economic crisis? The normal reflexes of most national governments will be to cut down on expenditure particularly on capital investments, turn to the international lending institutions in case they face a foreign reserves crisis and hope for better times. So far only South Africa seems prepared to become proactive and invest into rescue packages for its manufacturing industry.

All the indicators point to hard times for the SADC member states as their major markets are suffering from recession, global demand for minerals and agricultural raw materials is dropping sharply taking the prices for these products down with it. The major western donors will soon have to cut down on their aid budgets which will impact on the aid-dependent majority of the SADC member states negatively. Even the multilateral finance institutions such as World Bank, AfDB and IMF are already having problems to fill up their loan portfolios because their major funders – the USA, EU, Japan and the Arab countries – need funds for the rescue attempts of their economies. Additionally, the millions of emigrants from the SADC region, who work overseas will be affected from the economic crisis as well, and will send less money back to their home countries thus aggravating their foreign exchange and Balance of Payment constraints.

SADC's chances for reaching its RI objectives and the speed of RI will to a large extent depend on how fast the world economic crisis can be overcome.

However, the current world economic crisis must not obscure the view on the necessary internal reforms enabling SADC the above outlined problems and obstacles.

Currently, the outlook for RI in SADC is not as bright as it was just a year ago. But development is never linear; it is often iterative and takes a step backwards before it moves forward again!

Part 4

ANNEX

Timetable of Regional Integration in Southern Africa

1910	Establishment of the Southern African Customs Union between South Africa, Botswana, Lesotho and Swaziland
1953 - 1963	Central African Federation between Southern and Northern Rhodesia and Nyasaland, which was dominated by the settler interests of Southern Rhodesia.
1974	Formation of the Frontline States by the Presidents of Zambia, Tanzania, Botswana and the leader of FRELIMO from Mozambique. Later joined by Angola (1976) and Zimbabwe (1980).
1979	The South African *apartheid* regime announces the formation of the Constellation of Southern African States (CONSAS), which however, never progresses beyond the stage of conceptualisation
1979	*Arusha* Conference of the Frontline States which prepared the establishment of SADCC
1980	Independence of Zimbabwe with *Robert Mugabe* emerging as the victor of the first free elections.
1980	Establishment of SADCC at a special meeting in *Lusaka* (Zambia). Passing of the '*Lusaka* Declaration' in which the nine member states set both political goals (liberation of Southern Africa) and economic objectives (reduction of economic dependence).
1980	The OAU passes the '*Lagos* Plan of Action', through which the economic integration of Africa in form of an African Common Market by the year 2000 was to be achieved.
1982	Creation of the PTA as part of the strategy to realize the '*Lagos* Plan of Action'.

1984 Signing of the '*Nkomati'* Accord between South Africa and Mozambique through which the *apartheid* state wanted to break up the cohesion of SADCC and Mozambique wanted to end the civil war; both hopes were disappointed.

1990 Release of *Nelson Mandela* from prison and begin of the transition phase in South Africa that culminated in the election victory of the ANC 1994 and *Mandela* becoming President of a now democratic South Africa.

1990 Independence of Namibia with *Sam Nujoma* becoming the first President of the new state. Namibia becomes the 10th member of SADCC.

1992 Transformation of SADCC into the Southern African Development Community (SADC) at a summit in *Windhoek*, Namibia. The '*Windhoek* Declaration/SADC Treaty'

1994 Transformation of the PTA into COMESA

1994 In the ratified '*Abuja* Treaty' the OAU calls for the creation of continent-wide African Economic Community.

1996 The Organ for Politics, Defence and Security OPDS is established by the SADC Heads of State.

1997 The OPDS is temporarily suspended after serious disputes between SADC Chairperson *Nelson Mandela* and OPDS Chairperson *Robert Mugabe*

2000 South Africa and the EU sign a preferential trade agreement

2001 At a Summit in *Windhoek* the SADC Treaty is amended.

2001 The OPDS becomes functional again.

2001 The Secretariat is restructured and operates with four Directorates and a Gender Unit

2002 The AU is established

2002 Signing of new SACU-Treaty with a new formula for the distribution of customs duty revenue and the creation of SACU institutions.

2003 The RISDP is adopted at a Summit in *Dar es Salaam*.

2004 The Seychelles leave SADC.

2005 The SADC Tribunal becomes operational.

2005 Madagascar joins SADC

2007 For the first time the crisis in Zimbabwe becomes a topic at an extraordinary SADC Summit in *Dar Es Salam*.

2007 The Seychelles rejoin SADC

2008 The SADC Free Trade Area is officially established after an eight year long process of tariff reductions.

2008 An extraordinary SADC Summit fails in facilitating a power-sharing agreement in Zimbabwe.

2008 A Tripartite Summit between COMESA, EAC and SADC in *Kampala* (Uganda) resolves to establish a joint FTA

2009 A second extraordinary SADC Summit in South Africa achieves the break-through on a power-sharing agreement in Zimbabwe and the formation of a Government of National Unity.

2009 Madagascar is suspended from SADC after an unconstitutional change of power.

Socio-Economic Information on SADC

Table A (1): Basic Economic Information on SADC countries 2007

Country	Area km² ('000)	Pop. (mill.) 2007	GDP 2007² (bill. USD)	GDP per capita² 2007 (USD)	GDP growth 2007*	Current Account* 2007 (%GDP)	Trade Balance 2007 (%GDP)*
ANG	1,247	17.0	21.2	1,246	19.8	+14.9	+49.6
BOT	582	1.9	8.4	4,439	6.0	+18.1	+13.6
DRC	2,345	62.6	5.8	93	6.2	-7.9	- -0.8
LES	30	2.0	1.1	1,104	4.9	+0.7	n/a
MAD	587	19.7	4.8	246	6.3	-12.6	-11.8
MAL	118	13.9	2.2	158	6.8	-7.8	-18.0
MAU	2	1.3	5.9	4,649	5.6	-5.2	-15.9
MOZ	799	21.4	7.5	348	7.2	-7.6	-9.4
NAM	824	2.1	4.7	2,246	3.8	+13.7	-0.2
SA	1,221	48.6	177.7	3,657	4.9	-6.9	-2.7
SWA	17	1.1	1.6	1,626	2.1	+0.2	n/a
TAN	945	40.5	16.3	403	6.6	-10.7	-15.8
ZAM	753	11.9	4.6	385	5.8	-3.9	+9.5
ZIM	391	13.2	5.5	414	-6.2	-2.9	n/a
TOTAL	**9,861**	**257.2**	**267.3**				

Sources: UNDP (2008); SADC Review 2007/8; OECD (2008)

* =estimates

² = in 2000 constant prices

Table A (2): Basic Economic Information on SADC Countries 2007

Country	Debt (in USD bill.)	Debt (in % of GDP)	Debt Service (% of exp)	% of population below nat. pov. line
ANG	9.4	20.7	8.7	68.0
BOT	1.3	12.3	16.3	30.3
DRC	5.3	61.4	9.3	71.3
LES	0.6	41.9	6.1	56.6
MAD	1.8	32.2	5.3	67.5
MAL	4.5	191.0	11.3	45.0
MAU	0.9	14.3	8.4	n/a
MOZ	2.4	34.5	17.2	54.1
NAM	1.4	19.9	2.6	28.0
SA	57.1	22.2	8.4	43.2
SWA	0.4	16.5	1.2	40.0
TAN	8.6	60.3	4.9	35.7
ZAM	0.5	4.9	1.6	68.0
ZIM	5.3	95.5	10.5	34.9

Source: OECD/AfDB (2008)

Table B (1): Trade of selected SADC Countries with Africa in % of Total Trade

Country	1990		2000		2006	
	Imp	Exp	Imp	Exp	Imp	Exp
ANG	2.3	0.5	20.2	0.2	7.7	1.3
DRC	11.7	7.2	43.5	2.2	49.7	6.8
MAD	2.0	5.5	6.4	3.3	12.1	2.7
MAL	42.1	15.0	71.8	18.0	56.7	40.6
MAU	12.9	2.2	18.6	7.6	11.1	8.9
MOZ	11.1	3.1	51.8	36.0	39.5	20.2
RSA	0.4	1.7	2.1	13.2	5.0	14.9
TAN	3.6	8.2	20.6	19.1	25.4	18.3
ZAM	31.5	7.8	69.1	41.8	59.9	36.3
ZIM	32.9	39.4	49.8	17.9	78.1	67.0

Source: UNCTAD 2008

Table B (2): Value of Total Exports (USD mill.) of SADC Member States 2000-2007

Country	2000	2004	2005	2006	2007
ANG	267	323	177	1,484	n/a
BOT	325	780	854	771	963
DRC	n/a	n/a	n/a	n/a	n/a
LES	43	64	56	60	57
MAD	364	425	498	698	n/a
MAL	34	41	54	52	n/a
MAU	1,070	1,456	1,618	1,671	2,162
MOZ	325	256	342	389	628
NAM	222	475	414	529	n/a
SA	5,046	9,682	11,157	12,014	13,518
SWA	273	250	284	283	n/a
TAN	627	1,134	1,269	1,483	1,571
ZAM	115	232	272	305	n/a
ZIM	331	317	298	292	277
TOTAL	**9,114**	**15,605**	**17,637**	**20,418**	**22,455**

Source: UNCTAD 2008

Explanation: the discrepancies between the SADC Total and the sum of exports of the individual countries can be explained by the missing data for the DRC and the other countries for 2007. However, the figures were taken from two different tables of the UNCTAD Handbook of Statistics 2008 and might thus be compiled differently.

Table B (3): Development of the Terms of Trade (ToT) for SADC (Year 2000=100)

Country	2002	2004	2005	2006
ANG	89	128	173	198
BOT	97	98	92	96
DRC	97	99	114	128
LES	100	90	86	83
MAD	85	82	77	77
MAL	92	84	82	85
MAU	99	90	87	90
MOZ	91	98	111	131
NAM	99	101	104	127
SA	103	110	115	126
SWA	98	93	93	95
TAN	101	108	102	117
ZAM	91	110	122	190
ZIM	98	104	95	94

Source: UNCTAD 2008

Table C: Total ODA to SADC Member States 2001-2006 (in USD mill.; all Donors)

Country	2001	2002	2003	2004	2005	2006
ANG	283	414	493	1,145	437	171
BOT	29	37	28	47	48	65
DRC	243	1,175	5,416	1,824	1,827	2,056
LES	56	76	79	96	69	72
MAD	374	369	539	1,248	914	754
MAL	401	376	513	501	578	669
MAU	21	24	-15	32	34	19
MOZ	931	2,201	1,037	1,235	1,277	1,611
NAM	109	134	146	173	115	145
SA	428	505	641	628	680	718
SWA	29	22	34	22	46	35
TAN	1,264	1,236	1,704	1,751	1,481	1,825
ZAM	349	639	589	1,125	935	1,425
ZIM	162	199	186	186	376	280
TOTAL	**4,679**	**7,409**	**11,390**	**10,013**	**8,817**	**9,845**

Source: OECD/AfDB (2008): 664f

Bibliography

Adedeji, Adebayo (2002), History and Prospects for Regional Integration in Africa. Paper presented at the Third Meeting of the African Development Forum, Addis Abeba, 5.3.2002.

Adelmann, Martin (2003): Regionale Kooperation im südlichen Afrika, Freiburg.

Adelmann, Martin (2008): Fundraising or common foreign policy? 30 Years of SADC Consultative Conference. In: Bösl, T. et al (eds.) (2008), Monitoring Regional Integration in Southern Africa Yearbook. Volume 8. Stellenbosch:356-377

AFREXIMBANK (2008), African Trade Report 2007. Riding the Commodity Boom amid Global Financial Turmoil. Cairo.

AFREXIMBANK (2009), African Trade Report 2008. Riding out the Storm. Cairo.

African Development Bank (AfDB) (1993), Economic Integration in Southern Africa, Abidjan.

African Development Bank (AfDB) (2008a), Compendium of Statistics on Bank Group Operations. 2008 Vol. XXXI. Tunis

African Development Bank (AfDB) (2008b), Selected Statistics on African Countries. 2008. Vol. XXVII. Tunis

African Union (AU) (2002) Constitutive Act of the African Union. http://www.au2002.gov.za/docs/key_oau/au_act.htm

African Union (AU) (2008), Assessment of Progress on Regional Integration in Africa. First Joint Annual Meetings of the AU Conference of Ministers of Economy and Finance and ECA Conference of African Ministers of Finance, Planning and Economic Development.Addis Ababa, Ethiopia. 29 February 2008.

Alden, Chris (2007), China in Africa. London. New York. Cape Town

Anadi, S.K.McDonald (2005), Regional Integration in Africa. The case of ECOWAS. PhD Thesis presented to the Faculty of Arts of the University of Zurich

Arnold, Guy (2005): Africa. A Modern History. London

Awoumou, C. D. G. (2008): ECCAS or CEMAC? Which regional economic community for Central Africa? In: Ayangafac, C. (ed), Political economy of regionalisation in Central Africa. Tshwane (2008): 109-149

Ayangafac, C. (ed), Political economy of regionalisation in Central Africa. Tshwane (2008). ISS Monograph No 155

Balassa, Bela (1961), The Theory of Economic Integration. London.

Bechler, Ekkehard (1976): International Arbeitsteilung und Dritte Welt – Handelsbeziehungen auf Kosten oder im Dienste der Entwicklungsländer? Köln.

Bösl, A., Breytenbach, W., Hartzenberg, T., McCarthy,C. & Schade, K. (eds). (2006), Monitoring the Process of Regional Integration in Southern Africa in 2006. Vol 6. Stellenbosch 2006

Bösl, A., Breytenbach, W., Hartzenberg, T., McCarthy,C. & Schade, K. (eds). (2007), Monitoring the Process of Regional Integration in Southern Africa in 2007. Vol. 7. Stellenbosch 2007

Bösl, A., Breytenbach, W., Hartzenberg, T., McCarthy,C. & Schade, K. (eds). (2008), Monitoring the Process of Regional Integration in Southern Africa in 2008. Vol 8. Stellenbosch 2008

Brandt, H., Gsänger, H. et al (2000), Ansatzpunkte zur Förderung der Regionalintegration in der Southern African Development Community (SADC). Bonn

Bratton, Michael & van der Walle, Nicolas (1997), Democratic Experiments in Africa. Regime Transitions in Comparative Perspective. Cambridge.

Breytenbach, Willie (2000): Security in the SADC Region: What a Performance Index of the Organ tells about Co-operation and Integration. In: Peters-Berries, Christian and Marx, Michael T (2000), Monitoring the Process of Regional Integration in SADC, Harare 2000:93-104

Breytenbach, Willie (2002), The African Renaissance, NEPAD and the African Union: The Prospects for Co-operation and Integration in Africa. In: Hansohm, Peters-Berries, Breytenbach, Hartzenberg, Maier, Meyns, Monitoring Regional Integration in Southern Africa, Volume 2 – 2002. Windhoek 2002: 169-183

Cernicky, J. (2007): Was nützt ECOWAS? In: KAS Auslandsinformationen 8/2007:78-111

Chauvin, Sophie & Gaulier, Guillaume (2002): Regional Trade Integration in Southern Africa. CEPII Working Paper 12/2002. Paris

Chingono, M. and Nakana, S. (2009), The challenges of regional integration in Southern Africa. In: African Journal of Political Science and International Relations. Vol. 3 (10):396-408, October 2009

Clapham, C. (2001): The Changing World of Regional Integration in Africa. In: South African Institute of International Affairs (SAIIA) (2001), Regional Integration Southern Africa: Comparative International Perspectives. Johannesburg:56-59

Costa, Rui (2009), The Africa-EU Energy Partnership. Presentation made in Brussels on 29.01.2009 for a briefing at Heinrich Böll Foundation Offices. mimeo

Deutsches Institut für Entwicklungspolitik (DIE), 1/2009: Demokratieförderung: Kein Ende der Geschichte. Analysen und Stellungnahmen. Bonn 2009

Disenyana, Tsidiso (2009), Towards an EAC, COMESA and SADC Free Trade Area. Issues and challenges. AfDB Working Paper, October 2009.http://www.afdb.org/fileadmin/uploads/afdb/documents/Knowledge/2009%20AEC-%20Towards%20an%20EAC %20COMESA%20and%20SADC%20Free%20Trade%20Area% 20Issues%20and%20Challenges.pdf

Dlamini-Zuma, Nkosazana (2009), Talking Notes for post council media briefing by Dlamini Zuma, Chairperson of the SADC Council of Ministers. Cape Town, 27.2.2009. www.sadc.int

Economic Commission for Africa (ECA) (2004), Assessing Regional Integration in Africa (ARIA I). Addis Abeba.

Economic Commission for Africa (ECA) (2006), Assessing Regional Integration in Africa. Rationalizing Regional Economic Communities (ARIA II). Addis Abeba.

Economic Commission for Africa (ECA) (2007), Macroeconomic Policy and Institutional Convergence in Member States of Southern African Development Community. Addis Abeba.

Economic Commission for Africa (ECA) (2008a), Assessing Regional Integration in Africa (ARIA III). Towards Monetary and Financial Integration in Africa. Addis Abeba.

Economic Commission for Africa (ECA) (2008b), Economic Report on Africa 2008. Africa and the Monterrey Consensus. Addis Abeba

Economic Commission for Africa (ECA) (2009a), Economic Report on Africa 2009. Developing African Agriculture through Regional Value Chains. Addis Abeba

Economic Commission for Africa (ECA) (2009b) African Economic Outlook 2009, Addis Abeba 2009

Elago, Paulina and Kalenga, Paul (2007), Wither the SADC Customs Union? In: Bösl et al. (eds), Monitoring Regional Integration Yearbook 2007. Stellenbosch 2007:118-130

European Commission (2007): How the European Union Works. Your guide to the EU Institutions. Brussels.

Fandrych, Sabine (2008), Die Afrikanische Union – auf dem Weg zu den United States of Africa? In: Friedrich Ebert Stiftung, Hintergrund-informationen aus der internationalen Entwicklungszusammen-arbeit. November 2008

Fontaine, Pascal (2006), Europe in 12 Lessons. Brussels

Friedrich Ebert Stiftung (FES) (ed.) (2008), Proceedings of the Fifth Southern African Forum on Trade (SAFT) held in Pretoria, South Africa, on 6–7 August 2008:11

Gibb, R. (2001), The State of Regional Integration: The Intra- and Inter – regional Dimensions. In: South African Institute of International Affairs (SAIIA) (2001), Regional Integration Southern Africa: Comparative International Perspectives. Johannesburg:71-85.

Gieler, Wolfgang (Hg.), International Wirtschaftsorganisationen. Entstehung – Struktur – Perspektiven. Münster 2005

Giuffrida, L. and Müller-Glodde, H. (2008):Strengthening the SADC institutional structures – capacity development is the key to the SADC Secretariat's effectiveness. In: Bösl, T. et al (eds.) (2008), Monitoring Regional Integration in Southern Africa Yearbook. Volume 8. Stellenbosch:120-142

Green, R.H. and Seidman, A. (1968), Unity or Poverty? The Economics of Pan-Africanism. Harmondsworth.

Godwin, Peter (2006), When a Crocodile Eats the Sun. London.

Hammerstad, A. (2003), A long road to SADC security integration: Is the OPDS heading in the right direction? In: Hansohm, Dirk; Breytenbach, Willie; Hartzenberg, Trudi (eds.) (2003): Monitoring Regional Integration in Southern Africa. Yearbook, Vol. 3- 2003. Windhoek: 140-153

Hanlon, Joseph (1986), Beggar Your Neighbours. Apartheid Power in Southern Africa. London

Hansohm, Dirk; Peters-Berries, Christian; Breytenbach, Willie; Meyns, Peters (eds.) (2002): Monitoring Regional Integration in Southern Africa. Yearbook, Vol. 1- 2001. Windhoek

Hansohm, Dirk; Peters-Berries, Christian; Breytenbach, Willie; Hartzenberg, Trudi, Maier, Wolfgang, Meyns, Peters (eds.) (2002): Monitoring Regional Integration in Southern Africa. Yearbook, Vol. 2- 2002. Windhoek

Hansohm, Dirk; Breytenbach, Willie; Hartzenberg, Trudi (eds.) (2003): Monitoring Regional Integration in Southern Africa. Yearbook, Vol. 3- 2003. Windhoek

Hartzenberg, Trudy (2003): The new SADC agreement: Implications for regional inte-gration in Southern Africa. In: Hansohm et al. (eds), Monitoring Regional Integration in Southern Africa Vol 3; Windhoek 2003:173-186

Haunit, Tibor (2005), AMU in: Gieler, W. (Hg.), International Wirtschafts-organisationen. Entstehung – Struktur – Perspektiven. Münster 2005: 11-20

Hazlewood, A. (1967): The economics of federation and dissolution in central Africa. In: Hazlewood, A. (ed): African integration and disintegration. Case studies in economic and political union. London/New York 1967: 184-250.

Hofmeier, Rolf (2004), Regionale Kooperation und Integration. In: Ferdowsi, Mir (ed), Afrika – ein verlorener Kontinent?, Muenchen. 189-224

International Organization for Migration (IOM), Towards Tolerance, Law, and Dignity: Addressing Violence against Foreign Nationals in South Africa. See: http://www.boell.org.za/web/110-270.html

Jackson, Robert H./Rosberg, Carl G. (1982): Personal Rule in Black Africa – Prince, Autocrat, Prophet, Tyrant. Berkeley/Los Angeles/ London

Jacobeit, Cord, Hartzenberg, Trudi and Charalambides, Nick (2005), Overlapping Memberships in COMESA, EAC, SACU and SADC. Trade Policy Options for the Region and for EPA Nego-tiations. Study for GTZ. Eschborn 2005

Johnson, Phyllis & Martin, David (1989). Apartheid Terrorism. The Destabilisation Report. London

Kalaba, Mmatlou (2009), Liberalization of SADC trade towards 2012 and beyond. In: INSAT, No 15 (January 2009)

Kalaba, M. and Tsedu, M. (2008a), Regional Trade Agreements, Effects and Opportunities. Southern African Development Research Net-work, April 2008.

Kalaba, M. and Tsedu, M. (2008b), Intra-SADC trade performance and the implementation of the Trade Protocol. tips, April 2008. http://www.tips.org.za/files/Kalaba_M._April08_Intra-SADC_Trade_Performance.pdf

Kalaba, M., Wilcox, O., Fundira, T., Wiliams, B., Alves, P. (2006), Deepening Integration in SADC. South Africa – SADC's Economic Engine. A Study conducted for the Friederich Ebert Foundation. Gaborone.

Karekezi, S., Kimani, J., Onguru, O., and Kithyoma, W. (2009): Large Hydropower, Renewable Energy and Adaptation to Climate Change. Climate Change and Energy Security in East and Horn of Africa. Nairobi. AFREPREN/FWD Occasional Paper No.33

Kersting, Norbert (2007), SADC and good governance: regional integration and electoral reform. In: Bösl, Anton; Breytenbach, Willie; Hartzenberg, Trudi; McCarthy, Colin; Schade, Klaus (eds), Monitoring Regional Integration in Southern Africa Yearbook. Volume 7 (2007)

Ki Zerbo, Joseph (1981): Die Geschichte Schwarzafrikas. Frankfurt/M.

Kritzinger-van Niekerk, L. (2005), Regional Integration: Concepts, Advantages, Disadvantages and Lessons of Experience. World Bank; mimeo.

Krippendorff, Ekkehart (1985), Staat und Krieg. Die historische Logik politischer Unvernunft. Frankfurt/M. 1985

Kühne, Winrich (1985), Südafrika und seine Nachbarn: Durchbruch zum Frieden? Zur Bedeutung der Vereinabrungen mit Mozambique und Angola im Frühjahr 1984. Baden-Baden.

Mair, Stefan & Peters-Berries, Christian (2001), Regionale Integration und Kooperation in Afrika südlich der Sahara. EAC, ECOWAS und SADC im Vergleich. München, Bonn, London.

Nelson Mandela (1994), Der lange Weg zur Freiheit. Frankfurt am Main

Martin, David & Johnson, Phyllis (1986): Zimbabwe: Apartheid's Dilemma. in Johnson/ Martin (eds.), Destructive Engagement. Southern Africa at War. Harare 1986:43-72

Maruping, Mothae (2005), Challenges for Regional Integration in Sub-Saharan Africa: Macroeconomic Convergence and Monetary Coordination. In: Teunissen, J.J. and Akkerman, A. (editors), Africa in the World Economy - The National, Regional and International Challenges. The Hague, December 2005, www.fondad.org

Mathews, A. (2003): Regional Integration and Food Security in Developing Countries. Prepared for theAgricultural Policy Support Service Policy Assistance Division. Training Materials For Agricultural Planning 45. FAO/Rome

McCarthy, C. (2007): Is African Integration in need of a paradigm change? Thinking out of the box of African integration. In: Bösl, Breytenbach, Hartzenberg, McCarthy & Schade (eds). Monitoring the Process of Regional Integration in southern Africa in 2007:6-43

Meade, James (1955), The Theory of Customs Union. Amsterdam

Meyn, Mareike (2007), Regional Integration and EPA configurations in southern and eastern Africa – what are the feasible alternatives? In: Bösl, Breytenbach, Hartzenberg, McCarthy & Schade (eds). Monitoring the Process of Regional Integration in southern Africa in 2006: 140-166

Meyns, Peter (2000), Konflikt und Entwicklung im südlichen Afrika. Opladen

Meyns, Peter (2002): The Ongoing Search for a Security Structure in the SADC Region: The Re-establisment of the SADC Organ on Politics, Defence and Security (OPDS). In: Hansohm et al (eds.) (2002):141-168.

Mushauri, Joshua (1997): Opportunities and Problems of Regional Road Freight Transport. KAF Occasional Paper, Harare

Musonda, Mwansa James (2009), The COMESA Customs Union: Challenges and Opportunities. In: INSAT No 15, January 2009:10-11.

Mutambara, Tsitsi (2008): Regional transport challenges within SADC and their implications for economic integration and development. In: Bösl et al (eds) (2008): Monitoring Regional Integration in Southern Africa Yearbook, Vol. 8. Stellenbosch:34-54

Muzorewa, Basil (2000), Measurement of the Deepening of Financial and Monetary Integration: The case of SADC. In: Peters-Berries/Marx (2000):105-142

Nathan Associates Inc. (2004), Finance and Investment Protocol SADC. Assessment of Impact on Mozambique and Mozambican Private Sector. www.nathaninc.com

Ngwenya, S. (2008): Regional Integration in COMESA. Paper prepared for the 13th COMESA Summit of Heads of States and Government in Victoria Falls (Zimbabwe), on 7-8 December 2008. mimeo

Nzongola-Ntalaja, G. (2002), Good Governance and Conflict Management – Will the African Union make a Difference? Paper presented at the Evening Forum, Norwegian Peacebuilding Empowerment Programme, Oslo, 4th September 2002.

OAU (1999) Sirte Declaration, Fourth Extraordinary Session of the Assembly of Heads of State and Government, Sirte, Libya 8.-9.9.1999

OECD/AfDB (2008): African Economic Outlook 2007/8. Paris

Oosthuizen, Gabriel H. (2006): The Southern African Development Community. The Organization, its Policies and Prospects, Midrand.

Oyejide, Ademola T. (2000): Policies for Regional Integration in Africa. Economic Research Papers No. 62, AfDB, Abidjan

Peters, Wolff-Christian (1987), Regionale Kooperation und der Konflikt im südlichen Afrika. Hamburg

Peters, Wolff-Christian (1988), Die SADCC-Konferenz in Arusha: *Development of Infra-structure and Enterprise.* in: Afrika Spectrum 23(1988)1:105-110

Peters-Berries, Christian (1995): Sambia – Von Demokraten, Drogenschiebern und Wendehälsen. Unpublished manuscript. mimeo

Peters-Berries, Christian (2000): Politische und wirtschaftliche Integration im suedlichen Afrika. KAS Auslandsinformationen 3/2000:55-79

Peters-Berries, Christian (2001a): Zwischen Abstiegsangst und Aufbruchskrise. Die Wahlen in Zimbabwe 2000. SWP-Working Paper. Berlin

Peters-Berries, Christian (2001b): Trade Relations and Politics in Southern Africa. African Perspectives Yearbook 2000. Bremen

Peters-Berries, Christian (2001c): Macht die SADC integrative Fortschritte? Unpublished paper. Harare. mimeo

Peters-Berries, Christian (2002): The Zimbabwe crisis and SADC: how to deal with a deviant member state? In: Hansohm et al (eds): Monitoring Regional Integration in Southern Africa. Yearbook, Vol. 2- 2002. Windhoek: 185-201.

Peters-Berries, Christian (2005), Is there Convergence in SADC? Essay for the SADC-Barometer. mimeo

Peters-Berries, Christian & Marx, Michael T. (1997): Regionale Kooperation und Integration im südlichen Afrika. In: KAS Auslandsinformationen 11/97:64-100.

Peters-Berries, Christian & Marx, Michael T. (1999): Regionale Integration im südlichen Afrika. Die SADC im Jahre 1998. KAS-Auslandsinformationen 5/1999: 50-69

Peters-Berries, Christian and Marx, Michael T. (2000), Monitoring the Process of Regional Integration in SADC, Harare.

Peters-Berries, Christian (2002), Is there Convergence in SADC? In: SADC Barometer /2002

Peters-Berries, Christian & Naidu, Rama (2003): Macro-Political Developments in the SADC Region April 2002 – March 2003. in: Hansohm, Dirk; Breytenbach, Willie; Hartzenberg, Trudi (eds.) (2003): Monitoring Regional Integration in Southern Africa. Yearbook, Vol. 3- 2003. Windhoek:110-127

Peters-Berries, C. (2009a): Country Report Ethiopia. Bertelsmann Transformation Index 2010. In preparation to be published online under: www.bertelsmann-stiftung.de

Peters-Berries, C. (2009b), Partnerschaft oder Auftakt zur Konfrontation? Das Treffen des „*African Partnership Forum*" zum Klimawandel. Interner Bericht, Heinrich Böll Stiftung, Sept. 2009; mimeo.

Regional Trade Facilitation Program (RTFP) (2007), Annex A, Survey of Non-tariff-barriers experienced in the SADC, COMESA and EAC. Pretoria

Rochas (2008), Regional Infrastructure Gains Ground in SADC. http://www.rtfp.org/news.php?id=77

Roussouw, J. (2006), South Africa's role in macroeconomic convergence in SADC, mimeo

Roux, Wallie (2009), Keine Unterschrift! Warum Namibia kein Interim-EPA eingehen sollte. In: afrika süd - zeitschrift zum südlichen afrika, Nr. 4, Juli/August/September 2009

Ruppel, Oliver C. and Bangamwabo, F.X. (2008): The SADC Tribunal: a legal analysis of ist mandate and role in regional integration. In: Bösl et al (eds) (2008): Monitoring Regional Integration in Southern Africa Yearbook, Vol. 8. Stellenbosch:179-221

Ruppel, Oliver C. (2009), Das SADC Tribunal – Eine Zwischenbilanz. In: Windhoeker Allgemeine Zeitung vom 5.2.2009

SADC (1993), Declaration, Treaty and Protocol of SADC. Gaborone

SADC (1996a), Communiqué of the Summit, Gaborone, 28 June 1996

SADC (1996b), The Protocol on Transport, Communication and Meteorology

SADC (2001a), Communiqué of the Extraordinary Summit, Windhoek, 9 March 2001

SADC (2001b), The Amended Treaty. Gaborone

SADC (2001c), Report on the Review of Operations of SADC institutions. Gaborone

SADC (2002a), The Protocol on Politics, Defence and Security. Gaborone.

SADC (2006a), Talking notes for Pre-Summit Media Briefing by Executive Secretary T.A. Salomao. 8.8.2006. Gaborone.

SADC (2007), Action on Infrastructure. Strategic Intervention on Accelerating. Provision of Priority Regional Infrastructure. Gaborone

SADC (2007b), Memorandum of Understanding amongst the member states of SADC on the new headquarters of SADC. Gaborone. www.sadc.int

SADC (2007c), Trade Performance Review. Gaborone

SADC (2008a). The SADC Review 2007/8. Gaborone

SADC (2008b), SADC FTA. Growth, Development and Wealth Creation. Gaborone.

SADC (2008c), Review of Macroeconomic Convergence Performance. Gaborone, April 2008

SADC (2008d), Business and Investment Outlook for 2008. TIFI Directorate. Gaborone. November 2008.

SADC (2008e), The SADC Macroeconomic Convergence Programme: Progress to Date. TIFI Directorate. Gaborone

SADC (2008f), SADC FTA Handbook. Gaborone

SADC (2009a), Review of the SADC macroeconomic convergence programme for 2008. Gaborone May 2009.

SADC (2009b), Update on the Impact of the Global Economic Crisis on SADC. TIFI Directorate. Gaborone, September 2009

SADC (2009c), Update on the Impact of the Global Economic Crisis on the SADC Region. TIFI Directorate. Gaborone, June 2009.

SADC/GTZ/KAF (1997), Non Tariff Trade Barriers and Regional Trade Promotion, Conference Report. Joint Conference, Livingstone, Zambia, 26-29.11.1997. mimeo

Sandrey, R. (2007), Living in the shadow of the mountain. In: Bösl et al (eds.) (2007): 250-270

SAPP (no year), Westcor Power Inter-Connect, mimeo

Sewadah, Mirvat (2009), The global economic crisis, trying times for the region. In: INSAT No 15 (January 2009)

Sigsworth, Romi; Ngwane, Collet and Pino, Angelica (2008), The Centre for the Study of Violence and Reconciliation. The Gendered Nature of Xenophobia in South Africa. http://www.boell.org.za/web/110-378.html

Stahl, H.-Michael (1999), The Southern African Development Community's (SADC) Regional Trade Integration Strategy – Overview and Assessment. Paper prepared for the Seminar on 'Benefiting from Regional Integration and Globalisation – Opportunities and Challenges for Malawi. 10-12.11.1999, Lilongwe, Malawi.

Sturman, Kathryn (2007), New growth on deep roots. Prospects for an African Unity Government. ISS Paper No. 146, Pretoria.

Tetzlaff, Rainer & Jacobeit, Cord (2005), Das nachkoloniale Afrika. Wiesbaden

Thompson, Carol B. (1985), Challenge to Imperialism. The Frontline States in the Libe-ralization of Zimbabwe. Harare

tips/AusAid (2007), Intra-SADC trade performance Review 2007. tips. mimeo

UNCTAD (2008) UNCTAD Handbook of Statistics 2008, Geneva and New York.

Vogt, Jörgen 2007: Die regionale Integration des südlichen Afrikas unter besonderer Betrachtung der Southern African Development Community (SADC), Baden-Baden.

Viner, Jacob (1950), The Customs Union Issue. New York

Vines, Alex (2008), Regional Integration in Southern Africa: Challenges and Opportunities. Speech delivered to the *Instituto Superior de Relacoes Internacionais (ISRI),* Maputo, 26.03.2008. www.chathamhouse.org.uk

Watson, Helen (2009), External Impacts of European Union (EU) Biofuels Policies. Report prepared for Institute for the European Environmental Policy (IEEP), Belgium, January 2009

Weeks, John (2008), Macroeconomic Convergence in East, Central and Southern Africa, 1980-2007. Paper presented at the Workshop on Macroeconomic Policy Convergence in Southern Africa. Pretoria, 23-26.09.2008.

Wegener, A (1979): Integration als entwicklungspolitisches Konzept. Bochum

World Bank (2009), 2008. The little data book on Africa. Washington 2009

World Trade Organisation (WTO) (2009), Trade Policy Review: Southern African Customs Union (SACU). Document WT/TPR/S/222. http://www.wto.org/english/tratop_e/tpr_e/tp322_e.htm

Periodicals, Newspapers and Newsletters consulted

The Sub-Saharan Informer (Addis Abeba), weekly newspaper

INSAT, Inside Southern African Trade, Gaborone (USAID, Southern African Global Competitiveness Hub)

ECAPAPA electronic newsletter (Entebbe)

Economist Intelligence Unit (EIU), London

NEPRU Policy Brief (Windhoek)

Windhoeker Allgemeine Zeitung (Windhoek)

Afika Süd, bi-monthly magazine (Bonn)

Africa Confidential (London)

Glossary

- ***African Peer Review Mechanism (APRM):*** A voluntary comprehensive socio-economic and political evaluation of a country in a two-step process in the framework of NEPAD. The first step involves a self-assessment according to generally agreed parameters; the second step is an intensive external evaluation by a group of eminent African experts. The results of the APRM are presented to and need approval from an AU Summit before they are publicized.

- ***BLS-states:*** Botswana, Lesotho and Swaziland

- ***cif:*** means 'cost, insurance, freight' and refers to the costs added to the costs of imports delivered to a country.

- ***Comparative (cost) advantage:*** refers in economic theory to the ability of a person or a country to produce a particular good at a lower opportunity cost than another person or country.

- ***Democratic convergence:*** refers to the diminishing differences in democratic governance and practices amongst member states of a regional body.

- ***Destabilisation policies:*** refers to the policies of the South African Government under apartheid against its neighbours. They were aimed to weaken and destabilize their Governments in order to prevent them from providing effective support to South African the liberation movements ANC and PAC.

- ***Economic 'balkanization':*** refers to the fragmentation of geographical regions and is derived from the political landscape of the Balkans after the First World War, which saw the emergence of several economic not viable states.

- ***Economic Partnership Agreements:*** also known as EPAs are the instrument the EU is proposing and to some extent already using to transform the trade preferences of the Cotonou Agreement between the EU and the ACP states into a format compatible with WTO rules.

- ***Economies of scale:*** refer in economic theory to the cost advantages that a business obtains due to expansion. They are factors that cause a producer's average cost per unit to fall as output rises.

- ***Economic transaction costs*** refer in economic theory to the costs – besides the prize of the good or service traded – incurred when making an economic exchange. The broker fee due for buying or selling a stock, is an economic transaction cost.

- ***European Economic Community:*** was one of the predecessors of the EU. It was The European Economic Community was an international organisation created in 1957 to bring about economic integration between Belgium, France, Germany, Italy, Luxembourg and the Netherlands. When the European Union (EU) was created in 1993, the EEC was transformed into the European Community, one of the EU's three pillars, with EEC institutions continuing as those of the EU.

- ***Frontline States (FLS):*** established in 1974 by Zambia, Tanzania, Botswana and Mozambique (FRELIMO) and later joined by Angola, Zimbabwe, Namibia and South Africa, whose liberation movements were participating from the beginning at FLS meetings. The FLS had no permanent structures and derived its political influence and acceptance from the international reputation of the Presidents of its member states. Being involved in the liberalization processes in Southern Africa put the FLS often in precarious situations as they became the target of South Africa's military and economic destabilisation. The FLS contributed on the political level to the development of a regional consciousness. Being a club of mostly small states the FLS were only marginally involved in the negotiations over the end of *apartheid* in South Africa. After South Africa's 'liberalization' in 1994 the FLS gradually dissolved only to be re-emerging in form of the Organ for Politics, Defence and Security (OPDS) in the context of SADC in 1996.
- ***Maastricht Criteria:*** refers to the criteria set by the EU for joining the "EURO-Zone" and based on the "Treaty of Maastricht" from 1992 in which the then member states of the EEC agreed to form the European Union. They include four macro-economic convergence criteria to be fulfilled by member states interested to join the EURO-Zone. These are:
  - Inflation rate: No more than 1.5 percentage points higher than the three lowest inflation member states of the EU.

- Annual government deficit: The ratio of the annual government deficit to gross domestic product (GDP) must not exceed 3% at the end of the preceding fiscal year.
- Government debt: The ratio of gross government debt to GDP must not exceed 60% at the end of the preceding fiscal year.
- Long-term interest rates: Long-term interest rate may not vary by more than two percentage points in relation to the average interest rates of the three member states with the lowest interest rates.

- ***Millennium Development Goals (MDGs):*** are the eight international development goals that 192 United Nations member states have agreed to achieve by the year 2015. They include reducing extreme poverty, achieve universal primary education, promote gender equality and empower women, reducing child mortality, improve maternal health, combat HIV/AIDS, malaria, and other diseases, ensure environmental sustainability and develop a global partnership for development.

- ***New Partnership for African Development (NEPAD):*** is an African initiative borne out of two attempts to develop a strategy for Africa's socio-economic recovery and development. It was adopted in 2001 at a Summit of the AU in Lusaka. NEPAD aims to provide an overarching vision and policy framework for accelerating economic co-operation and integration among African countries. NEPAD is the combination of two plans for the economic regeneration of Africa: the Millennium Partnership for the African Recovery Program of President Thabo Mbeki of South Africa and former Nigerian President Olusegun Obasanjo and Algerian President Abdelaziz Bouteflika, and the OMEGA Plan for Africa developed by President Abdoulaye Wade of Senegal.

- ***National sovereignty:*** refers to the independence of a country and its supreme right to define and defend its integrity and right to self-determine its destiny.

- ***Non tariff trade barriers (NTTB):*** any barriers to trade other than import or export duties.

- ***Purchasing Power Parity (PPP):*** refers in economics to a way to calculate currency exchange rates to prices paid for goods and services in any two countries. The World Bank defines the PPP conversion factor as the number of units of a country's currency required to buy the same amount of goods and services in the domestic market as 1 USD would buy in the USA.

- ***Production factors:*** are in economic theory referring to resources employed to produce goods and services: land, labor, and capital.

- ***Rand Monetary Union:*** Established in 1966 by South Africa against the background of the already existing SACU. It made the South African Rand the lead currency in SACU. The national currencies of Botswana, Lesotho and Swaziland (and later Namibia) were artificially made on par with the Rand; the Rand became the accepted currency for payment in the whole Union while the other currencies had only limited convertibility. Botswana left the Monetary Union in 1976. Today the Botswana Pula is substantially stronger than the Rand.

- ***Rules-of-origin:*** describe in economic (trade) policy the approach of deter-mining the country of origin of a product for purposes of international trade. This is a crucial tool for preventing especially in a FTA cheap goods from entering the FTA from a third country and threatening the viability of industries in the FTA.

- ***Subsidiarity:*** refers to an organizing principle that says that matters ought to be handled by the smallest, lowest or least centralized competent authority.

- ***Technology transfer:*** refers to the process of sharing skills, knowledge, technologies, methods of manufacturing, etc. among governments and other institutions to ensure that scientific and technological developments are accessible to a wider range of users who can further develop and exploit the technology for new products, processes, applications, materials or services.

- ***Trade creation:*** refers in international economics to trade which is additio-nally created by the formation of a trade-based regional integration scheme. As a result, more and more intensive trading ties between the member states are established after protectionist barriers such as tariffs, quotas, and non-tariff barriers are eliminated. The result is an increase in trade among the member states in goods and services.

- ***Trade diversion***: refers in international economics to a situation in which trade is diverted from a more efficient exporter towards a less efficient one by the formation of a free trade agreement. When a country applies the same tariff to all nations, it will always import at the lowest price. With the establishment of a regional free trade agreement, that may no longer be the case if the agreement is signed with less-efficient and thus more expensively producing states. Due to the level of external tariffs it may well be that products from within the free trade area become cheaper than those from the more-efficient external state. Consequently, after the conclusion of the free trade agreement, the importing country would acquire products from a higher-cost producer inside the free trade area, instead of the low-cost producer from outside from which it was importing until then. This is called a trade diversion.

- ***Variable geometry:*** refers in political integration policy to a situation in a regional community where not every country need take part in every policy of the regional community but some can cooperate more closely. In other words, it refers to different speeds of integration amongst the member states. An example is the EU where some countries have so far stayed out of the Euro and the Schengen passport union.

Sources: Various online encyclopaedias and own definitions

FSC
www.fsc.org
MIX
Papier | Fördert
gute Waldnutzung
FSC® C083411

Kolibri 360 GmbH
Ferdinand-Jühlke-Straße 7
99095 Erfurt, Deutschland
produktsicherheit@kolibri360.de